Charles Egbert Craddock

In the Clouds

Charles Egbert Craddock

In the Clouds

ISBN/EAN: 9783337337308

Printed in Europe, USA, Canada, Australia, Japan

Cover: Foto ©Thomas Meinert / pixelio.de

More available books at **www.hansebooks.com**

BY

CHARLES EGBERT CRADDOCK,
AUTHOR OF "IN THE TENNESSEE MOUNTAINS," "DOWN THE RAVINE,"
"THE PROPHET OF THE GREAT SMOKY MOUNTAINS," ETC.

BOSTON AND NEW YORK
HOUGHTON, MIFFLIN AND COMPANY
The Riverside Press, Cambridge
1887

IN THE CLOUDS.

I.

IN the semblance of the cumulus-cloud from which it takes its name, charged with the portent of the storm, the massive peak of Thunderhead towers preëminent among the summits of the Great Smoky Mountains, unique, impressive, most subtly significant.

What strange attraction of the earth laid hold on this vagrant cloud-form? What unexplained permanence of destiny solidified it and fixed it forever in the foundations of the range?

Kindred thunderheads of the air lift above the horizon, lure, loiter, lean on its shoulder with similitudes and contrasts. Then with all the buoyant liberties of cloudage they rise, — rise!

Alas! the earth clasps its knees; the mountains twine their arms about it; hoarded ores of specious values weigh it down. It cannot soar! Only the cumbrous image of an ethereal thing! Only the ineffective wish vainly fashioned like the winged aspiration!

It may have said naught of this to Ben Doaks, but it exerted strenuous fascinations on the sense alert to them. Always he turned his eyes toward Thunderhead, as he came and went among his cattle on the neighboring heights of Piomingo Bald, a few miles distant to the northeast. Often he left the herder's cabin in the woods below, and sat for hours on a rock on the summit, smoking his pipe and idly watching the varying aspects of the great peak. Sometimes it was purple against the azure heavens; or gray and sharp of outline on faint green spaces of the sky; or misty, immaterial, beset with clouds, as if the clans had gathered to claim the changeling.

"'Pears-like ter me ez I could n't herd cattle along of a mo' low-sperited, say-nuthin' critter 'n ye be, Ben," his partner remarked one day, sauntering up the slope and joining him on the summit. "Ye jes' set up hyar on the bald an' gape at Thunderhead like ez ef ye war bereft. Now, down in the cove ye always air toler'ble good company, — nimble-tongued ez ennybody."

He thrust his cob-pipe into his mouth and pulled away silently at it, gazing at the smoke as it curled up with delicate sinuosity and transparently blue.

Ben Doaks did not reply at once. There was no need of haste on Piomingo Bald.

"Waal, I dunno but it air a sorter lonesome place, an' a-body don't feel much like talkin' no-ways," he drawled at last. "But ye'll git used ter it, Mink," he added, in leisurely encouragement. "Ye'll git used ter it, arter a while."

Mink looked down disconsolately at the vast array of mountains below him on every side. The nearest were all tinged with a dusky purple, except for the occasional bare, garnet-colored stretches of the "fire-scalds," relics of the desolation when the woods were burned; the varying tints were sublimated to blue in the distance; then through every charmed gradation of ethereal azure the ranges faded into the invisible spaces that we wot not of. There was something strangely overwhelming in the stupendous expanse of the landscape. It abashed the widest liberties of fancy. Somehow it disconcerted all past experience, all previous prejudice, all credence in other conditions of life. The fact was visibly presented to the eye that the world is made of mountains.

That finite quality of the mind, aptly expressing itself in mensuration, might find a certain relief in taking note of the curious "bald" itself, — seeming some three or four hundred bare acres on the summit. Wild grass grows upon its gradual slope; clumps of huckleberry bushes appear here and there; occasional ledges of rock crop out. A hardy flower will turn a smiling face responsive to the measured patronage of the chilly sunshine in this rare air. The solemnity of the silence is broken only by the occasional tinkling of cow-bells from the herds of cattle among the woods lower down on the mountain side.

"I never kin git used ter it," said Mink, desperately. "I never kin git used ter hevin' sech dumbness about me, an' seein' the time go so slow. 'Pears ter me some fower or five hunderd year sence we eat brekfus',— an' I ain't hongry, nuther."

He was a tall, singularly lithe man of twenty-four or five, clad in a suit of brown jeans. He wore his coat closely buttoned over his blue-checked cotton shirt, for the August days are chilly on Piomingo Bald. His broad-brimmed white wool hat was thrust back on his head, showing his tousled auburn hair that hung down upon his collar, curling like a cavalier's. He had a keen, clear profile, a quickly glancing, dark eye, and his complexion was tanned to a rich tint that comported well with the out-door suggestions of his powder-horn and belt and shot-pouch, which he wore, although his rifle was at the cabin. He maintained the stolid gravity characteristic of the mountaineer, but there was a covert alertness about him, a certain sharpness of attention almost inimical, and slow and dawdling as he was he gave the impression of being endowed with many an agile unclassified mental faculty.

His eyes followed the flight of a bird soaring in great circles high above the "bald," sometimes balanced motionless in mid-air, — a pose of ineffable strength and buoyancy, — then majestically circling as before.

"That thar buzzard 'pears ter be a-loungin' around in the sky, a-waitin' fur we-uns ter die," he said, lugubriously.

Doaks broke with an effort from his reverie, and turned his languid gaze on the malcontent herder.

"In the name o' heaven, Mink Lorey," he said solemnly, "what is it ye *do* like ter do?"

Despite the spark of irritation in his eye, he seemed colorless, especially as contrasted with his comrade. He had a shock of fair hair and a light brown beard; the complexion which is the complement of this type had freckled in its exposure to the sun instead of tanning, and added its original pallor to the negative effect. He had good features, but insignificant in their lack of any marked peculiarity except for the honest, candid look in the serious gray eye. He too wore a broad white wool hat and a suit of brown jeans.

Mink gazed at his companion with an expression of brightening interest. He found himself and his own idiosyncrasies, even when berated, more agreeable to contemplate than the mountains. He did not reply, perhaps appreciating that no answer was expected.

"Ye don't like ter herd up hyar, an' the Lord knows I ain't keerin' ter hev ye. Ye hev gin me ez much trouble ez all the cattle an' thar owners besides. When ye wanted ter kem so bad, an' sorter go partners with me, I 'lowed ye 'd be lively, an' a toler'ble good critter ter hev along. An' ye hev been ez lonesome an' ez onconsiderate an' ez ill-convenient ez a weanin' baby," he declared, rising to hyberbole. "What *do* ye like ter do?"

Once more Mink refrained from reply. He looked absently at an isolated drift of mist, gigantic of outline, reaching from the zenith to the depths of Piomingo Cove, and slowly passing down the valley between the Great Smoky and the sunflooded Chilhowee Mountain, obscuring for the moment the red clay banks of the Scolacutta River, whose current seemed a mere silver thread twining in and out of the landscape.

"Look a-hyar at the way ye go on," said Doaks, warning to the subject, for there are few exercises so entertaining as to preach with no sense of participation in sin. "Ye went ter work at that thar silver mine in North Car'liny, an' thar ye stayed sorter stiddy an' peaceful till ye seen yer chance. An' Pete Rood, he kem an' stayed too, an' he war sorter skeered o' the ways, — not bein' used ter minin'. An' then yer minkish tricks began. Fust, when that thar feller war let down inter the shaft an' ye hed a-holt o' the windlass, ye drapped a few clods o' clay in on him, an' then a leetle gravel, an' then mo' clay. Then he bellered that the shaft war cavin' in on him, an' plead an' prayed with ye ter wind him up quick. An' ye wouldn't pull. An' when the t'other fellers run thar an' drawed that man out he war weak enough ter drap."

"I 'member!" cried Mink, with a burst of unregenerate laughter. "He said, 'Lemme git out'n this spindlin' hell o' a well!'"

He sprang up, grotesquely imitating the gesture of exhaustion with which the man had stepped out of the bucket to firm ground.

"Waal, it mought hev turned out a heap wus," said Doaks, "'kase they 'lowed down yander 'bout Big Injun Mounting, whar Rood hails from, ez he hev got some sort'n heart-disease. An' a suddint skeer mought hev killed him."

"Shucks!" said Mink, incredulously. He looked disconcerted, however, and then sat down on the rock as before. Ben Doaks went on: —

"An' that war n't enough fur ye. When they hed Rood thar a-pumpin' out water, all by himself all night, nuthin' would do ye but ye must hide up thar in the Lost-Time mine in the dark o' the midnight an' the rain, an' explode a lot o' gunpowder, an' kem a-bustin' out at him from the mouth o' the tunnel, wropped in a sheet an' howlin' like a catamount. He run mighty nigh a mile."

"Waal," said Mink, in sturdy argument, "I ain't 'sponsible 'kase Peter Rood air toler'ble easy skeered."

"They never hired ye ter work thar no mo', bein' ez that war 'bout all the use ye put yerse'f ter in the silver mine in North Car'liny."

Despite the reproof, Doaks was looking kindly at him, for the wayward Mink had evidently endeared himself in some sort to the elder herder, who was weakly conscious of not regarding his enormities with the aversion they merited.

The young man's countenance fell. His mischief differed from that of his namesake in all the sequelæ of an accusing conscience. But stay! What do we know of the mink's midday meditations, his sober, *ex post facto* regrets?

"An' what do ye do then, — 'kase they turned ye off? Ye go thar of a night, when nobody 's at the windlass, an' ye busts it down an' flings the bucket an' rope an' all down the shaft."

Mink was embarrassed. "How d' ye know?" he retorted, with acrid futility. "How d' ye know 't war me?"

"'Kase it air fairly kin ter yer actions, — know it by the family favor," said Doaks. "Ax ennybody ennywhar round the Big Smoky who did sech an' sech, an' they 'd all say, Mink. Ye know the word they hev gin ye, 'Mink by name an' Mink by natur.'"

Lorey made no further feint of denial. He seemed a trifle out of countenance. He glanced over his shoulder at the rugged horizontal summit line of Chilhowee, rising high above the intervenient mountains, and sharply imposed upon the mosaic of delicate tints known as the valley of East Tennessee, which stretches so far that, despite its sharp inequalities, it seems to have the level monotony of the sea till Walden's Ridge, the great outpost of the Cumberland Mountains, meets the concave sky.

Then, as his wandering attention returned to those sterner heights close at hand, their inexpressible gravity, their significant solemnity, which he could not apprehend, which baffled every instinct of his limited nature, smote upon him.

He broke out irritably : —

"What do ye jes' set thar a-jowin' at me fur, Ben, like a long-tongued woman, 'bout what I done an' what I hain't done, in this hyar lonesome place whar I hev been tolled ter by you-uns? I never begged ter be 'lowed ter herd along of ye, nohow. When I kem an' axed ye 'bout'n it, ye 'lowed ye 'd be powerful glad. An' ye said ez so many o' the farmers in the flat woods hed promised ter bunch thar cattle an' send 'em up ter ye fur the summer season, that ye war plumb skeered 'bout thar bein' too many fur one man ter keer fur, an' ye did n't see how ye 'd git along 'thout a partner. An' ye 'lowed ye 'd already rented Piomingo Bald right reasonable, an' the owners o' the cattle would pay from seventy-five cents to a dollar a head; an' ye 'd gin me a sheer ef I 'd kem along an' holp ye, — an' all sech ez that. An' I kem up in the spring, an' I hev been on this hyar durned pinnacle o' perdition ever sence. It 'minds me all the time o' that thar high mounting in the Bible whar the Tempter showed off all the kingdoms o' the yearth. What ails ye ter git arter me? I hain't tried no minkish tricks on you-uns."

"Ye hev, Mink. Yes, ye hev."

Mink looked bewildered for a moment. Then a shade of consciousness settled on his face. He lifted one foot over his knee, and affected to examine the sole of his boot. The light zephyr was tossing his long, tangled locks, the sun shone through their filaments. No vanity was expressed in wearing them thus, — only some vague preference, some prosaic prejudice against shears. Their fineness and lustre did nothing to commend them, and they had been contemptuously called a "sandy breshheap." His bright eyes had a fringe of the same unique tint that softened their expression. He dropped his boot presently, and fixed his gaze upon a flitting yellow butterfly, lured by some unexplained fascination of fragrance to these skyey heights.

"Ye can't make out ez I stand in *yer* way, enny," he said at last, enigmatically.

Doaks's face flushed suddenly. "Naw, I ain't claimin' ez I hev enny chance. Ef I hed, an' ye *war* in my way," he continued, abruptly, with a sudden flare of spirit, "I 'd choke the life out'n ye, an' fling yer wu'thless carcass ter the wolves. I 'd crush yer skull with the heel o' my boot!"

He stood up for a moment; then turned suddenly, and sat down again. Mink looked at him curiously, with narrowing lids.

Doaks's hands were trembling. His eyes were alert, alight. The blood was pulsing fast through his veins. So revivified was he by the bare contemplation of the contingency that he seemed hardly recognizable as the honest, patient, taciturn comrade of Piomingo Bald.

"Waal," Mink said presently, "that war one reason I wanted ter herd along o' you-uns this year. I 'lowed 1 'd make right smart money through the summer season, an' then me an' Lethe would git married nex' fall, mebbe. My folks air so pore an' shiftless, — an' I 'd ez lief live along of a catamount ez Lethe's step-mother, — an' so I 'lowed we 'd try ter git a leetle ahead an' set up for ourselves."

Doaks trembled with half-repressed excitement.

"Ye tole me ez ye an' she hed quar'led," he said. "Ye never dreampt o' sech a thing ez savin' fur a house an' sech till this minit. Ye ain't been ter see her sence ye hev been on the Big Smoky till ye fund out ez I went down thar wunst in a while, an' the old folks favored me."

"Waal," retorted Mink, hardily, "I know she 'd make it up with me enny minit I axed her."

Doaks said nothing for a time. Then suddenly, "Waal, then, ef ye air layin' off ter marry Lethe Sayles, why n't ye quit hangin' round Elviry Crosby, an' terrifyin' Peter Rood out 'n his boots? They 'd hev been married afore now, ef ye hed lef' 'em be."

"Why n't she quit hangin' round me, ye 'd better say!" exclaimed Mink, with the flattered laugh of the lady-killer. "Laws-a-massy, I don't want ter interfere with nobody. Let the gals go 'long an' marry who they please,— an' leave me alone!"

His manner implied, *if they can!* And he laughed once more.

Doaks glanced at him impatiently, and then turned his eyes away upon the landscape. Fascinations invisible to the casual gaze revealed themselves to him day by day. He had made discoveries. In some seeming indefiniteness of the horizon he had found the added beauty of distant heights, as if, while he looked, the softened outline of blue peaks, given to the sight of no other creature, were sketched into the picture. Once a sudden elusive silver glinting, imperceptible to eyes less trained to the minutiæ of these long distances, told him the secret source of some stream, unexplored to its head-waters in a dark and bosky ravine. Sometimes he distinguished a stump which he had never seen before in a collection of dead trees, girdled long ago, and standing among the corn upon so high and steep a slope that the slant justified the descriptive gibe of the region, "fields hung up to dry." The sky too was his familiar; he noted the vague, silent shapes of the mist that came and went their unimagined ways. He watched the Olympian games of the clouds and the wind. He marked the lithe lengths of a meteor glance across the August heavens, like the elastic springing of a shining sword from its sheath. The moon looked to meet him, waiting at his tryst on the bald.

He had become peculiarly sensitive to the electric conditions of the atmosphere, and was forewarned of the terrible storms that are wont to break on the crest of the great mountain.

Often Mink appealed to him as he did now, imputing a certain responsibility.

"Enny thunder in that thar cloud?" he demanded, with the surly distrust which accompanies the query, "Does your dog bite?"

"Naw; no thunder, nor rain nuther."

"I 'm powerful glad ter hear it, 'kase I don't 'sociate with this hyar bald when thar 's enny lightning around."

He had heard the many legends of "lightning balls" that are represented as ploughing the ground on Piomingo, and he spoke his fears with the frankness of one possessed of unimpeachable courage.

"That 's what makes me *despise* this hyar spot," he said, irritably. "Things 'pear so cur'ous. I feel like I hev accidentally stepped off 'n the face o' the yearth. An' I hev ter go mighty nigh spang down ter the foot o' the mounting 'fore I feel like folks agin."

He glanced downward toward the nearest trees that
asserted the right of growth about this strange and barren place. "Ye can't git used ter nothin', nuther.
Them cur'ous leetle woods air enough ter make a man
'low he hev got the jim-jams ez a constancy. I dunno
what's in 'em! My flesh creeps whenever I go through
'em. I always feel like ef I look *right quick* I'll see
suthin' awful, — witches, or harnts, or — I dunno!"

He looked down at them again, quickly; but he was
sure not quickly enough.

And the woods were of a strange aspect, chiefly of oaks
with gnarled limbs, full-leaved, bulky of bole, but all uni-
formly stunted, not one reaching a height greater than
fifteen feet. This characteristic gave a weird, unnatural
effect to the long avenues beneath their low-spreading
boughs. The dwarfed forest encircled Piomingo Bald,
and stretched along the summit of the range, unbroken
save where other domes — Silar's Bald, Gregory's Bald,
and Parsons' Bald — rose bare and gaunt against the
sky.

"Ez ter witches an' harnts an' them, I ain't never
seen none hyar on Piomingo Bald," said Doaks. "It
ain't never hed the name o' sech, like Thunderhead."

Mink placed his elbows on his knees, and held his chin
in his hand. His roving dark eyes were meditative now;
some spell of imagination lay bright in their depths.

"Hev *he* been viewed lately?" he asked.

"Who?" demanded Doaks, rousing himself.

"That thar Herder on Thunderhead," said Mink,
lowering his voice. The fibrous mist, hovering about the
summit of Thunderhead and stretching its long lines
almost over to Piomingo Bald, might in some mysterious
telegraphy of the air transmit the matter.

"Not ez I knows on," said Doaks. "He ain't been
viewed lately. But Joe Boyd, he's a-herdin' over thar
now: I kem acrost him one day las' week, an' he 'lowed
ez his cattle hed been actin' powerful strange. I 'lowed
the cattle mus' hev viewed the harnt, an' mebbe he war
tryin' ter 'tice 'em off."

IN THE CLOUDS. 11

"Ef ye 'll b'lieve me," said Mink ruminatively, after a pause, "I never hearn none o' them boys tell a word about that thar harnt of a herder on Thunderhead."

"Them t'other herders on Thunderhead don't hanker ter talk 'bout him, noways," said Doaks. "It's powerful hard ter git a word out'n 'em 'bout it; they're mighty apt ter laff, an' 'low it mus' be somebody ridin' roun' from 'cross the line. But it'll make enny of 'em bleach ef ye ax 'em suddint ef all o' Joshua Nixon's bones war buried tergether."

The mists had spanned the abyss of the valley in a sheer, gossamer-like network, holding the sunbeams in a glittering entanglement. They elusively caressed the mountain summit, and hung about the two lounging figures of the herders, — a sort of ethereal eavesdropping of uncomfortable suggestions, — and slipped into the dwarfed woods, where they lurked spectrally.

"Waal, ef ye ax 'em ef Joshua Nixon's bones war all buried tergether they'll bleach," Doaks repeated. "See that thar sort'n gap yander?" he continued, pointing at a notch on the slope of Thunderhead. "They fund his bones thar under a tree streck by lightning. They 'lowed that war the way he died. But the wolves an' the buzzards hed n't lef' enough ter make sure. They hed scattered his bones all up an' down the slope. He hed herded over thar a good many year, an' some o' the t'other boys keered fur the cattle till the owners kem in the fall."

He recounted slowly. Time was no object on Piomingo Bald.

"Waal, nobody hearn nuthin' mo' 'bout'n it fur a few years, till one day when I war herdin' thar the cattle war all fund, runned mighty nigh ter death, an' a-bellerin' an' a-cavortin' ez ef they war 'witched. An' one o' the herders, Ike Stern, kem in thar ter the cabin an' 'lowed he hed seen a lot o' strange cattle 'mongst our'n, an' a herder ridin' 'mongst 'em. 'T war misty, bein' a rainy spell, an' he lost the herder in the fog. Waal, we jes' 'lowed 't war somebody from Piomingo Bald huntin' fur strays, or somebody from 'cross the line. So we jes' went on fryin' the meat, an' bakin' the hoe-cake, an' settin' roun' the fire; but this hyar man kept on complainin' he could n't holp seein' that thar herder. An' wunst in a while he 'd hold his hand afore his eyes. An' one o' the old herders, — Rob Carrick 't war, — he jes' axed him what that herder looked like. An' Ike jes' sot out ter tell. An' the coffee war a-bilin', an' the meat a-sizzlin', an' Carrick war a-squattin' afore the fire a-listenin' an' a-turnin' the meat, till all of a suddint he lept up an' drapped his knife, yellin', 'My God! ye lyin' buzzard, don't ye set thar a-tellin' me ez Josh Nixon hev kem all the way from hell ter herd on Thunderhead! Don't ye do it! Don't ye do it!' An' Ike Stern, — he looked like he seen Death that minit; his eyes war like coals o' fire, an' he trembled all over, — he jes' said, 'I see I hev been visited by the devil, fur I hev been gin ter view a dead man, apin' the motions o' life.'"

Doaks pulled at his pipe for a few moments, his eyes still absently fixed on the purple peak shimmering in the gauzy white mists and the yellow sunshine.

"I never shell furgit that night. Thar war three men thar: one hed herded along o' Josh on Thunderhead, but Ike Stern had never seen him in life, an' me not at all. Waal, sir! the rain kem down on the roof, an' the wind war like the tromplin' o' a million o' herds o' wild cattle. We 'lowed we hed never hearn sech a plungin' o' the yellemints. The night war ez dark ez a wolf's mouth, 'cept when it lightened, an' then we could see we war wropped in the clouds. An' through all them crackin' peals them men talked 'bout that thar harnt o' a Herder on Thunderhead. Waal, nex' mornin' Stern jes' gin up his job, an' went down the mounting ter Piomingo Cove. An' he stayed thar, too. They 'lowed he done no work fur a year an' a day. His time war withered an' his mind seemed darkened."

"He 'pears ter hev toler'ble good sense now," said Mink, striving against credulity.

"Yes, he hev spryed up powerful."

"Waal," said Mink, constrained by the fascination of the supernatural, "I hev hearn ez Carrick seen the Herder, too."

"He did," replied Doaks. " Arter a while — a week, mebbe — Rob kem up ter me an' axed, ' Whar 's them cattle a-bellerin'? ' I listened, but I never hearn nuthin'. We hed missed some steers arter Ike hed seen the Herder, an' Rob war sorter 'feard they 'd run down inter the cove. He jumped on a half-bruk clay-bank colt an' rid off, thinkin' the bellerin' mought be them. Waal, time passed. I hed nuthin' in partic'lar ter do : cattle war salted the day before. Time passed. I jes' sot thar. I 'lowed I 'd wait till Rob kem back, then I 'd go a-huntin'. Time passed. I 'lowed I 'd furgit how ter talk ef I war n't herdin' along o' sech a sociable critter ez Rob, an' I wondered ef I war by myself up on Thunderhead ef I 'd hev ter talk ter myse'f a little. An' ez I sot thar in the fog — 't war September then, an' we war clouded ez a constancy — I said, jes' like a fool, out loud, suddint, ' Howdy, sir ! ' Waal, I never *did* know what I seen ez I looked up ; mought hev been the mist, mought hev been the devil. I *'lowed* I seen a man on a horse gallopin' off in the fog. Then I hearn a power o' jouncin' hoofs, an' hyar kem Rob's colt a-rearin' an' a-pawin', skeered ter death mighty nigh, with all the hide scraped off'n his knees, an' his shins barked bad. I seen he hed hed a fall; so I jumped up an' run down a leetle piece along the trail, an' thar war Rob lyin' on the groun', flunged over the colt's head ez neat an' nip ! I run up ter him. I 'lowed he war hurt. He never answered a word I axed him. His eyes war stretched open bigger 'n enny eye I ever seen, an' he said, ' Ye hev viewed him too, Ben, I know it, fur ye 've got the " harnt bleach." I know the reason now,' says Rob, ' ez he herds on Thunderhead, — 'kase his bones war n't all buried tergether, though we sarched nigh an' we sarched fur.' "

" Did the Herder tell him that? " asked Mink, with a sudden accession of credulity.

"Naw, ye durned fool!" exclaimed Doaks, scandalized at the idea of this breach of spectral etiquette. "The Herder jes' passed him like the wind, an' the colt jes' reared and flung Rob over his head."

"Waal," said Mink sturdily, "I b'lieve 't war nuthin' but somebody from the Car'liny side, ridin' roun' an' tollin' off cattle."

"Mebbe," said Doaks, non-committally. "Ye can't prove nuthin' by me. All I know is, Carrick seen his face, an' he jes' fell in a sorter stupor for a year an' a day. I hev hearn o' sech sperits ez can't kill ye, but jes' wither yer time, an' mebbe this hyar Herder on Thunderhead be one o' them."

Neither spoke for some moments. Both sat gazing fixedly at the massive mountain in the likeness of a cloud lowering aggressively over the mean altitudes of the range. What wrath of elements did it hold enchained? What bolts of heaven unhurled? What strange phenomena of being might lurk in those mystic vapors metamorphosed into the solidities of earth — this apostate cloud that asserted itself a mountain? The sky was clear about it now; the mists had all drifted over to Piomingo Bald, veiling the dwarfed forests.

Suddenly there was a vague shiver among them. Into the silence was projected the report of a rifle. The two men sprang to their feet, and looked at each other.

"Somebody a-huntin', I reckon," said Mink. He was beginning to laugh, a little shamefacedly.

"Listen!" said Doaks. "What's that?"

The cattle were bellowing with affright in the stunted woods. The earth shook under their hoofs. A young bull came plunging out of the mists. He paused as he reached the bare slope, lifted his head, and looked back over his shoulder with great dilated eyes.

"What ails the cattle?" exclaimed Doaks, running down the slope. Mink hesitated for a moment, then followed.

The boles of the dwarfed trees stood shadowy here and there, growing still more indistinct further, and fading into the white opaque blankness of the vapor. So low were their summits that one could see the topmost boughs, despite the encompassing mist.

All the cattle were in the wildest excitement, snorting and bellowing, and, with lowered horns, and tails in the air, they were making at full speed for the upper regions of the bald. Each, bursting out of the densities of the fog, separated from the others, seemed to give some individual expression of bovine rage. There might be heard, but not seen, an infuriated animal hard by, tearing up the ground.

"Waal, I never 'sperienced the like in my life off 'n Thunderhead!" exclaimed Doaks.

Mink said nothing; he sprang aside to avoid the headlong rush of a brute that shot out of the mist and into it again with the swift unreality of an apparition.

Then he spoke suddenly. "Ye never said he rid with a rifle."

"Who?" asked Doaks, bewildered. He was in advance. He looked back over his shoulder. "Who?" he repeated.

"That thar Herder from Thunderhead," said Mink.

"Ye dough-faced idjit, — what d' ye mean?"

Mink pointed silently.

A few yards distant there was a rude barricade of felled trees, laid together after the zigzag manner of a rail fence. It was intended to prevent the cattle from running down a precipitous ravine which it overlooked. Close to it in the mist a cow was lying. There was no mistaking the attitude. The animal was dead. A carefully aimed rifle-ball had penetrated the eye, and buried itself in the brain.

II.

THERE was blood upon the ground. An awkward attempt had been made to cut the brute's throat, and, this failing, the rifle had been called into use. Doaks walked up to the animal, and turned her head to look for the brass tag about her horns which would bear her owner's mark. She wore no tag, and her hide had never known the branding-iron. His eye fell on a peculiar perforation in her ear.

"Mink," he exclaimed, with a note of anguish, "this hyar critter's *my cow!*"

Mink came up, his countenance adjusted to sympathy. He had little of the instinct of acquisition. He was almost incapable of any sentiment of that marvelous range of emotions which vibrate with such fineness of susceptibility to the alternations of gain and loss. He looked like an intelligent animal as he helped make sure of the herder's mark.

"Ye hed sech a few head o' stock o' yer own, ennyways," he observed, with a dolorous lack of tact.

"Oh, Lord A'mighty, none sca'cely," exclaimed Doaks, feeling very poor. "I dunno how in this worl' this hyar cow happened ter be singled out."

"Mebbe he hed a gredge agin ye, too, 'bout them bones, bein' ez ye herded on Thunderhead wunst," suggested Mink.

"What bones?" demanded Doaks, amazed.

"Why, his'n," said Mink, in a lowered voice.

"In the name o' reason, Mink, what air ye a-drivin' at?" cried Doaks, flustered and aghast.

"Why, the Herder, o' course. Him ez skeered the cattle on Thunderhead. I 'lowed mebbe he hed a gredge agin you-uns, too."

"How 'd he kem over hyar?" demanded Doaks, with scorn, as if the harnt of a Herder were limited to the locality of Thunderhead. "It's a deal mo' likely ter be some livin' man ez hev got a gredge agin ye fur yer minkish ways, an' seein' the critter hed no tag on, an' war n't branded nuther, killed her fur ye."

Mink drew a long breath. "Waal, I hope so, the Lord knows. I'd settle him." An essentially mundane courage was his, but a sturdy endowment as far as it went.

His imagination was of the pursuant order; it struck out no new trail, but, given a lead, it could follow with many an active expression of power. He accepted at once this suggestion, with a confidence as complete as if he had never credited the grudge of a ghostly herder.

"An' I'll be bound I kin tell ye jes' who 't war," he said, stoutly, producing a corollary to the proposition he had adopted as his own. "'T war that thar pop-eyed fool Peter Rood. I reckon ye hev noticed, ef one o' them black-eyed, thick-set, big-headed men git made game of 'bout ennything, he'll pay ye back some mean way. Stiddier skeerin' me fur skeerin' him, he kems hyar an' shoots that cow."

He thrust one hand in his leather belt, and turned his bold bright glance on his partner. As he stood at his full height, vigorous, erect, a touch of freakishness in his eyes, decision expressed in his clear-cut features, a certain activity suggested even in his motionless pose, it might have seemed that the revenge of shooting the cow was the more hopeful project.

Doaks, a philosopher in some sort, and reflective, could discriminate as to motives.

"Rood never done it fur that by itself. I don't b'lieve he would hev done it *jes'* fur that. But the way ez ye hev been performin' sence 'bout Elviry Crosby air powerful aggervatin'. I hearn tell ez she hev turned Rood off, an' won't speak ter him, though the weddin' day hed been set! I reckon he felt like payin' ye back ennyhow it kem handy."

Doaks drew a plug of tobacco from his pocket, wrenched off a fragment with his strong teeth, and, talking indistinctly as he chewed, continued, the anxiety of forecast blunting the actual pain of experience.

"Ef he keeps this hyar up,' Mink, — ef it's him, an' he kems roun' shootin' at cattle agin, — he mought git some o' the owners' stock nex' time, an' they mought hold me 'sponsible. I dunno whether they could or no. I 'low he war 'quainted with this cow, an' knowed her ter be yourn, an' never drempt ez ye hed swopped her off ter me. I wisht ter Gawd the critter knew ye hed no cattle on the mounting, an' ain't 'sponsible ter the owners, ez ye never traded with them, but arter my contract war made ye jes' went shares with me."

He seated himself on the rude fence in an awkward attitude, his long legs dangling, and drew out a red cotton handkerchief with which he rubbed his corrugated brow as vigorously as if he could thus smooth out the pucker in his brain.

"Waal, waal! this mortal life!" he exclaimed, presently. "Satan won't leave ye in peace. Ye may go an' set yerse'f up on the bald of a mounting, herdin' 'mongst the dumb ones, an' the worl' an' the things o' this life will kem a-cropin' up on ye with a rifle, an' ye be 'bleeged ter turn 'roun' an' cornsider how ye kin keep what ye hev got an' how ye kin git mo'. I useter 'low ef I war a perfessin' member, *this* worl' would n't stick so in my craw; so I tuk cornsider'ble pains ter git religion, an' mighty nigh wore out the mourners' bench settin' on it so constant, till I war actually feared the Lord would be pervoked ter see me in the front row o' them convicted o' sin at *every* revival, and visit wrath on me. An' I never got religion at last; though I feel nigher ter it on Piomingo Bald than ennywhar else, till Rood, or somebody, starts up like they hed a contract with Satan to be-devil me."

Mink listened with a sort of affectionate ruefulness. Then he broke forth, suddenly, "Mebbe I mought see Rood ef I war ter go down ter Piomingo Cove, whar the boys be goin' ter shoot fur beef this evenin'. An' I kin let him know I don't own no cattle up hyar, an' hain't got no trade with the owners, an' ain't 'sponsible ter nobody."

There was a sudden expression of alarm in Doaks's face. "Don't ye let Rood know we suspicioned him, 'kase he *mought* hev hed nuthin' ter do with it."

"Naw," said Mink, with a diplomatic nod, "I'll jes' tell that whilst I'm a-spreadin' the tale 'bout the cow."

There was a short silence. Doaks still sat, with a pondering aspect, on the fence.

"Rood mought take his gredge out on you-uns some other way, Mink," he suggested presently. He felt bound in conscience to present the contingency.

"I'm ekal ter him," said Mink hardily.

In fact, Mink bore the most lightsome spirit down the mountain, scarcely to be expected in a man who goes to invite a more personal direction of the machinations of a feud. He would have dared far more to secure a respite from the loneliness of Piomingo Bald, to say nothing of the opportunity of mingling in the festivity of shooting for beef. He had not even a qualm of regret for the solitary herder whom he left standing at the fence, gazing down at him a trifle wistfully. He was out of sight presently, but Doaks heard the mare's hoofs long after he had disappeared, — the more distinctly, because of the animal's habit of striking her hind feet together.

The mists had lifted. It was a positive happiness to Mink to watch the forests expand, as he went down and down the rugged ways of the herders' trail. There were taller trees on every hand; great beds of ferns, their fronds matted together, began to appear; impenetrable jungles of the laurel stretched all along the deep ravines. Now and then a flash of crimson rejoiced the sight; from far gleamed the red cones of the cucumber tree; the trumpet-flower blossomed in the darkling places; he marked the lustre of the partridge-berry by the wayside.

The earth was moist from the recent rains, as the narrow, slippery path, curving between a sheer declivity on one side and an almost perpendicular ascent on the other, might testify. His mare traveled it in a devil-may-care fashion, snatching as she went at leaves on the slope above, regardless that a false step would precipitate both herself and her rider into eternity. Noticing this breach of manners, Mink now and then gave a reckless jerk at the bit.

"Dad-burn ye! ye buzzard! A greedy body would 'low ye hed never hearn tell o' nuthin' ter eat afore in this worl'!"

Here it was only, above these depths, that he might see the sky, — afar off, as was meet that it should be: he, the earthling, had no kinship with its austere infinities. The growths of the forest were now of incredible magnitude and magnificence. Up and up towered the massive boles, with a canopy of leaves so dense that all the firmament was effaced, and the sunshine trickling through had a white, tempered glister like the moonbeams. What infinite stretches of solitudes! What measureless mountain wilds! In these solemn spaces Silence herself walked unshod.

Yet stay! A crystalline vibration, a tinkling tremor, a voice smiting the air, so delicately attuned to all sylvan rhythms, with an accent so fine, so faint, — surely, some oread a-singing!

Nay — only the mountain torrent, dashing its fantastic cascades down its rocky channel, with a louder burst of minstrelsy and a flash of foam as its glittering swirl of translucent water revealed itself, the laurel and ferns crowding upon its banks and a cardinal flower reflected multiform in a deep and shadowy pool. A mossy log spanned it as foot-bridge, and then it slipped away into the forest, to spring out suddenly and cross the road again and again before it reached the base of the mountain. Mink reckoned the distance by its reappearances, in default of other means.

"Ye be a-travelin' toler'ble smart this evenin'," he observed to the mare. "Ye be mighty nigh ez glad ter git off'n that thar buzzard's roost up yander ez I be, though I don't crack my heels tergether 'bout it like you-uns do yourn."

He did not follow the road into Eskaqua Cove when he reached the level ground. He struck off through one of the ridges that lie like a moulding about the base of the mountains, crossed another nameless barrier, then descended into Piomingo Cove. Sequestered, encompassed by the mountains, rugged of surface, veined with rock, its agricultural interest is hardly served by the conditions which enhance its picturesque aspect. The roofs of a few log cabins at long intervals peer out from among scanty orchards and fields. Tobacco flourishes down the sides of steep funnel-shaped depressions worked exclusively with the hoe, and suggesting acrobatic capacity as a co-requisite with industry to cultivate it. The woods make heavily into the cove, screening it from familiar knowledge of its hills and dales.

Mink, trotting along the red clay road, came suddenly upon the banks of the Scolacutta River, riotous with the late floods, fringed with the papaw and the ivy bush. Beyond its steely glint he could see the sun-flooded summit of Chilhowee, a bronze green, above the intermediate ranges: behind him was the Great Smoky, all unfamiliar viewed from an unaccustomed standpoint, massive, solemn, of dusky hue; white and amber clouds were slowly settling on the bald. There had been a shower among the mountains, and a great rainbow, showing now only green and rose and yellow, threw a splendid slant of translucent color on the purple slope. In such environment the little rickety wooden mill — with its dilapidated leaking race, with its motionless wheel moss-grown, with its tottering supports throbbing in the rush of the water which rose around them, with a loitering dozen or more mountaineers about the door — might seem a feeble expression of humanity. To Mink the scene was the acme of excitement and interest. His blood was quickening as he galloped up, his hair tossing under the wide brim of his hat, his stirrup-leathers adjusted to the full length of his leg according to the custom of the country, his rifle laid across the pommel of his saddle.

"Enny chance lef' fur me?" he asked, as he reined in among the loungers.

This observation was received in some sort as a salutation.

"Hy're, Mink," said several voices at once. Other men merely glanced up, their eyes expressing languid interest.

"*Ye* don't want ter shoot, Mink," said one, with a jocose manner. "Ye knowed all the chances would be sold by now. Ye hev jes' kem 'kase ye hearn old Tobias Winkeye air out agin."

Mink's dark eyes seemed afire with some restless leaping light. His infectious laughter rang out. "Never s'picioned it, — so holp me Jiminy! *When?*"

"Ter-night. Ye keep powerful low," with a cautionary wink.

"I reckon so," promised Mink cordially.

A sullen remonstrance broke into these amenities.

"Waal, Jer'miah Price, I dunno ez ye hev enny call ter let all that out ter Mink Lorey."

Pete Rood, who delivered this reproof, was not an ill-looking fellow naturally, but his black eyes wore a lowering, disaffected expression. His swarthy square-jawed face indicated a temperament which might be difficult to excite to any keen emotion, and was incapable of nice discrimination; but which promised, when once aroused, great tenacity of purpose. He wore a suit of gray jeans, loosely fitting, giving his heavy figure additional breadth. He carried his hands in his pockets, and lounged about, throwing an occasional word over his shoulder with a jerky incidental manner.

"Why not tell Mink?" exclaimed Jerry Price. a long, lank fellow, far too tall and slim for symmetry, and whose knees had a sort of premonitory crook in them, as if he were about to shut up, after the manner of a clasp-knife, into comfortable and convenient portability. His head was frankly red. His freckles stood out plainly for all they were worth; and, regarded as freckles, they were of striking value. A ragged red beard hung down on his unbleached cotton shirt. Physically, he had not a trait to commend him; but a certain subtle magnetism, that inborn fitness as a leader of men, hung upon his gestures, vibrated in his words, constrained acquiescence in his rude logic. "Ain't Mink always been along of we-uns?" he added.

Mink dismounted slowly and hitched his mare to the limb of a dogwood tree hard by. Then, leaning upon his rifle, he drawled, "'Pears like everybody's gittin' sot agin me these days. I dunno who 't war, but this very mornin' somebody kem up on Piomingo Bald an' shot a cow ez used ter b'long ter me."

He raised his eyes suddenly. Rood had lounged off a few steps with an idle gait, swaying from side to side, his hands still in his pockets. But there was tenseness in the pose of his half-turned head. He was listening.

"Hed ye done traded her off?" asked Price, interested. "Gimme a chaw o' terbacco."

"Ain't got none. Pete, can't ye gin this hyar destitute cuss a chaw o' terbacco?"

Rood could not choose but turn his face, while he held out his plug. The crafty Mink scanned it, as he leaned his own sun-burned cheek upon the muzzle of the long rifle on which he lazily supported his weight.

"Naw, Jerry, 't war n't my cow. I can't keep nuthin' long enough ter lose it; I hed traded her off to Ben Doaks."

There was no mistaking the patent disappointment on Rood's face. One with far less sharp intelligence than Mink possessed might have descried that hot look in his eyes, as if they burned, — that vacillating glance which could fix on naught about him. The surprise of the moment deterred him from observing Mink, whose air of unconsciousness afterward afforded no ground for suspicion or fear.

Rood pocketed his plug, and presently slouched off toward the tree where the marksmen were preparing for the shooting-match.

Now and then there flitted to the door of the mill the figure of a stripling, all dusted with flour and meal, and with a torn white hat on his head. He wore ragged jeans trousers of an indeterminate hue, and an unbleached cotton shirt. When the men were strolling about, he slunk into the duskiness within. But when they were all intent upon the projected trial of skill, he crept shyly to the door, and looked out with a singularly blank, inexpressive gaze.

"Hy're ye, Tad!" called out Mink gayly.

The young fellow stood for an instant staring; then, with a wide, foolish grin of recognition, disappeared among the shadows within.

"Let the idjit be, Mink," said old Griff, the miller, querulously, — "let him be."

He was a man of sixty years, perhaps, and bending beneath their weight. His white beard was like a patriarch's, and his long hair hung down to meet it. He had a parchment-like skin, corrugated, and seeming darker for the contrast with his hair and beard. Beneath his bushy white eyebrows, restless, irritable eyes peered out. He was barefooted, as was the boy, and his poverty showed further in the patches on his brown jeans clothes.

"Naw, I won't," said Mink irreverently. "I want ter see what Tad does when he skeets off an' hides that-a-way."

He pressed into the mill, and the old man looked after him and cursed him in his beard. He swore with every breath he drew.

"Go on, ye dad-burned fool — go on ter damnation! Ever sence that thar sneakin' Mink hev been roun' hyar," he continued, addressing Price, "Tad 'pears weaker 'n ever. I can't 'bide ter keep Tad in the house. He gits into one o' his r-uproarious takin's, an' it looks like hell could n't hold him, — skeers the chill'n mighty nigh ter death. Yes, sir! my gran'chil'n. Daddy war shot by the revenuers, mammy died o' the lung complaint, an' the old man's got 'em all ter take keer of — ten o' 'em. An' my nevy Tad, too, ez war born lackin'. An' ev'y one of 'em's got a stommick like a rat-hole — ye can't fill it up. Yes, sir! The Lord somehows hev got his hand out in takin' keer o' me an' mine, an' he can't git it in agin."

"Waal, they holps ye mightily, plowin' an' sech, don't they, — the biggest ones; an' one o' the gals kin cook, that thar spry one, 'bout fifteen year old; I'm a-goin' ter wait fur her, — beats all the grown ones in the cove fur looks," said the specious Jerry Price. " An' they air all mighty good chill'n, ain't they? Oughter be. Good stock."

"Naw, sir; naw, sir!" the old man replied, so precipitately that his iterative mutter had the effect of interruption. "Durnes' meanes' chill'n I ever see. Ripenin' fur hell! Scandalous mean chill'n."

"I reckon so," said Rood suddenly. "Thar goes one o' 'em now." He pointed to a scapegrace ten years of age, perhaps, clad in a suit of light blue checked cotton. His trousers reached to his shoulder blades, and were sustained by a single suspender. A ragged old black hat was perched on the back of his tow head. He had the clothes-line tied to the hind leg of a pig which he was driving. He seemed to be in high feather, and apparently felt scant lack of a more spirited steed. In fact, the pig gave ample occupation to his skill, coming to a halt sometimes and rooting about in an insouciant manner, reckless of control. When he was pushed and thumped and forced to take up the line of march, he would squeal dolorously and set out at a rate of speed hardly predicable of the porcine tribe. "Look how he's a-actin' to that thar pore peeg," added Rood.

Old Gus Griff fixed his dark eye upon him.

"Enny friend o' yourn?" he asked.

"Who?" demanded Rood, amazed.

"That thar peeg."

"Naw, o' course not."

"Then keep yer jaw off'n him. Who set ye up ter jedge o' the actions o' my gran'chile. That thar boy's name air 'Gustus Thomas Griff — fur *me!* An' I got nine mo' gran'chil'n jes' like him. An' ye lay yer rough tongue ter a word agin one o' 'em, an' old ez I be I'll stretch ye out flat on that thar groun' they air a-medjurin' ter shoot on. Ye greasy scandal-bit scamp yerse'f!"

Rood was fain to step back hastily, for the miller came blustering up with an evident bellicose intention. "Lord A'mighty, old man!" he exclaimed, "I never said nuthin' agin 'em, 'cept what ye say yerse'f. I would n't revile the orphan!"

"Jes' stop a-pityin' 'em, then, durn ye!" exclaimed the exacting old man. "They ain't no orphans sca'cely nohows, with thar grandad an' sech alive."

"That's what I knowed, Mr. Griff," said the bland Price, standing between them. "Pete's jes' 'bidin' the time o' the fool-killer. Must be a powerful rank crap fur him somewhar, bein' ez Pete's spared this long. That's what I knowed an' always say 'bout them chill'n."

The old man, mollified for the instant, paused, his gnarled knotted hands shaking nervously, the tremor in his unseen lips sending a vague shiver down all the length of his silver beard. The excitement, painful to witness, was dying out of his eager eyes, when a mad peal of laughter rang out from the recesses of the old mill.

"What be that thar blamed idjit a-doin' of now! him an' that thar minkish Mink!"

He turned and went hastily into the shadowy place. Bags of grain were scattered about. The hopper took up much room in the limited space; behind it the miller's nephew and Mink were sitting on the step of a rude platform. They had a half-bushel measure inverted between them, and on it was drawn a geometric figure upon which were ranged grains of corn.

There was a pondering intentness on the idiot's wide face very nearly approaching a gleam of intelligence. Mink, incongruously patient and silent, awaited Tad's play; both were unaware of the old man, among the dusky shadows, peering at them from over the hopper.

At last, Tad, with an appealing glance at Mink, and an uncertain hand, adjusted a grain of corn. He leaned forward eagerly, as Mink promptly played in turn. Then, fixing all the faculties of his beclouded mind upon the board, he finally perceived that the game had ended, and that his opponent was victor. Once more his harsh laughter echoed from the rafters. "Ye won it, Mink. Ye won the coon."

"I don't want yer coon," said Mink, good-naturedly. "Ye kin keep yer coon ter bet nex' time."

"Naw, ye kin hev the coon, Mink!" He caught at a string dangling from a beam. "Kem down hyar, ye idjit!" he cried, with a strange, thick-tongued enunciation. "Kem down hyar, ye damned fool!"

The old man suddenly made his way around the hopper and stood before them. Tad rose, with a startled face. Mink looked up composedly.

"Do ye know what ye air a-doin' of, Mink Lorey?" asked the old man, sternly.

"L'arnin' Tad ter play 'five corn,'" said Mink, innocently. "He kin play right sorter peart fur a lackin' one. I dunno ez I b'lieve Tad's so powerful fursaken noways, ef ennybody would take the pains ter l'arn him. I b'lieves he 'd show a right mind arter a while."

"An' thar ye sit, ez complacent ez a bull-frog — ye that the Lord hev favored with senses," cried the old man, "sech ez they be," he stipulated, making not too much of Mink's endowments, "a-usin' of 'em ter ruin a pore idjit boy," — Mink's eyes flashed surprise, — "a-l'arnin' him ter play a gamblin' game."

"Shucks! *five corn!*" cried Mink, accustomed to the iniquity of "playin' kyerds," and scorning to rate the puerile beguilements of "five corn" among the "gambling games" which he had mastered, — "what's *five corn!* Enny child kin play it — that thar coon could l'arn it ef he hed a mind ter do it. I don't want the critter, Tad; I don't want it."

The old man's tongue had found its ready oaths. "A-fixin' on the idjit boy fur the prey o' Satan. A-l'arnin' him ter play a gamblin' game ter damn his soul. An' a-trickin' him out'n his coon."

"I never!" cried Mink, in hasty extenuation. "I jes' put up my rifle agin his coon ter make him think he war playin' sure enough! But I ain't a-goin' ter keep his coon, an' I don't want it, nuther!"

"I kin read the future," cried out the old man, suddenly, flinging up his hand and shading his peering eyes with it. "I kin view the scenes o' hell. I see ye, Mink Lorey, a-writhin' in the pits o' torment, with the flames a-wroppin' round ye, an' a-swallerin' melted iron an' a-smellin' sulphur an' brimstone. I see ye! Bless the Lord, — I see ye thar!"

"Naw, *ye don't!*" interpolated Mink, angrily.

The idiot had slunk to one side, and was gazing at the two with a white, startled face, still mechanically jerking the string, at the end of which the reluctant coon tugged among the beams above.

"I see ye thar, — damned yerse'f fur tryin' ter damn the idjit's soul!"

"Ye 'd better look arter yer own soul!" cried Mink, "an' quit l'arnin' the idjit ter cuss. He do it percisely like he gits the word from ye, an' ye air a perfessin' member, what shouts at the camp-meetin', an' prays with 'the Power,' an' laffs with the 'holy laff'! Shucks! I hev hearn ye exhortin' them on the mourners' bench."

Once more the old man broke out angrily.

Mink interrupted. "Quit cussin' me! Quit it!" he cried. He wore a more harried look than one would have believed possible, as the miller, with his hoary head and tremulous beard, pressed close upon him in the dark, narrow apartment, the idiot's white face — a sort of affrighted glare upon it — dimly visible beside him. "Quit it! I ain't a-goin' ter take nare nuther word off 'n ye!"

"How ye goin' ter holp it? Goin' ter hit a old man, — old enough ter be yer grandad, eh?" suggested the wary old creature, making capital of his infirmities.

"I 'll bust yer mill down, ef ye don't lemme out'n it.

Lemme out!" cried Mink, tumultuously, striving to push past.

Jerry Price's long, lank figure appeared in the doorway. It was not policy which animated him, for he had nothing at stake. With an inherent knowledge of human nature, some untutored instinctive capacity for manipulating its idiosyncrasies, he half consciously found a certain satisfaction in exercising his keen acumen on the men about him. It might have been employed more profitably in the field of local politics, had the gift been adequately realized and valued. He was of an amiable, even of an admirable, temperament, and he devised the adjustment of many complications, in which open interference would avail naught, by subtly appealing to some predominant motive or sentiment with the accuracy with which a surgeon can touch a nerve.

"Look-a-hyar, Mink," he said, apparently unobservant of any signs of a quarrel, "ain't you-uns a-goin' ter shoot?"

Mink's angry aspect dropped like a husk.

"Waal, I can't, ye know," he said, in a voice eager with interest. "They 'lowed ter me ez they hed done made up the money an' bought the beef, an' all the chances are gone,—six fur a dollar, shillin' apiece."

"Waal, I bought eight chances. I'll let ye hev two of 'em, ef two 'll do ye."

"Jiminy Crack-corn an' I don't keer!" exclaimed Mink, doubling himself partly in a gesture of ecstasy, and partly to reach a silver coin that led a lonesome life in the depths of his long pocket. He handed it over, and slapped his leg with a sounding thwack. "I could shoot ye all off 'n the ground, an' I kin git the fust an' second ch'ice in two cracks."

Rood, in the doorway behind Price, regarded the transaction with disapproval.

"I don't b'lieve it's 'cordin' ter rules, Jerry," he expostulated, "ter go roun' an' swap off yer chances arter ye paid fur 'em. I never seen it done afore, noways."

"Ye hold yer jaw!" said Price, imperious, though

good-natured. "I hev shot fur beef 'fore ye war born!" — a diminutive marksman, were this statement to receive full credit, since he was but a year or two older than Rood.

Irregular though it may have been, there was no appeal from the self-arrogated authority of Price, and his oft-reiterated formula as to his experience before his interlocutor's birth had all the enlightened functions of precedent.

Rood said no more, appreciating the futility of remonstrance. He stood, surly enough, in the doorway, listening absently to the garrulous clamor of the old miller, who was telling again and again of Mink's iniquity in teaching Tad "five corn," and of his threats against the mill.

"I dare ye ter lay a finger on the mill!" he cried. "I'll put ye in that thar hopper an' grind every ounce o' yer carcass ter minch meat."

Mink gave him no heed. He had joined the group of marksmen near the tree on which the targets were to be fixed. He was loading his gun, holding the ball in the palm of his hand, and pouring enough powder over it to barely cover it in a conical heap. He dexterously adjusted the "patching," and as he rammed down the charge he paused suddenly. From a little log cabin on a rise hard by, a delicate spiral wreath of smoke curled up over the orchard, and airily defined itself against the mountain. Beside the rail fence a girl of fifteen was standing; sunny-haired, blue-eyed, barefooted, and slatternly. The peaches were ripe in the weighted trees above her head; he heard the chanting bees among them. The pig was grunting luxuriously among their roots and the fallen over-ripe fruit; for his driver, 'Gustus Tom, and the elder boy, Joseph, had gone down to the mill for a closer view of the shooting; the small girls who had mounted the fence being deterred from accompanying them by feminine decorum. The dogs appertaining to the place had also gone down to the mill, and were conferring with the followers of the contestants in the match. One, however, a gaunt and gray old hound, that had half climbed the fence, hesitated, his fore-paws resting on the topmost rail, a lean, eager curiosity on his grave, serious countenance, his neck stretched, his head close to the pretty head of the golden-haired maiden.

"Howdy, sis!" called out the bold Mink, the ramrod arrested half-way in the barrel, his face shadowed by his broad-brimmed hat, his hair flaunting in the wind.

She gave a flattered smile, full of precocious coquetry.

"Sick him, Bose!" she exclaimed to the faithful dog. "Sick him!"

Bose fastened his glare on Mink, raised his bristles, and growled obediently.

The young man with a gay laugh drove the charge home, and rattled the ramrod sharply into its place.

Already the first report of the rifle had pealed into the quietude of the cove; the rocks clamored as with the musketry of a battle. Far, far and faint the sound clanged back from the ranges between Chilhowee and the river, from all the spurs and ravines of the Big Smoky. The sunshine had the burnished fullness of post-meridian lustre, mellow, and all unlike the keen, matutinal glitter of earlier day; but purple shadows encircled the cove, and ever and anon a shining curve was described on the mountain side as the wings of a homeward-bound bird caught the light. Sometimes the low of cattle rose on the air. The beef, as the young ox was prematurely called, lifted his head, listening. He stood, the rope about his neck, secured to a hitching-post near the mill, looking calmly upon the ceremonies that sealed his destiny. It is to be hoped, in view of the pangs of prescience, that the animal's deductive capacities and prophetic instincts are not underrated, or the poor beef's presence at the shooting-match might express the acme of anguished despair. He was an amiable brute, and lent himself passively to the curiosity of 'Gustus Tom, who came up more than once, gazed fixedly at him, and examined his horns and hoofs, his eyes and nozzle, doubtless verifying some preconceptions as to facts in natural history.

The young mountaineers seemed to shoot with startling rapidity. Only one green hand labored under the delusion that a long aim can do aught but " wobble the eyes." As each flung himself prostrate, with a grave intentness of expression and a certain precipitancy of gesture, it might have seemed some strange act of worship, but for the gun resting upon a log placed for the purpose, sixty yards from the mark, — the customary distance in shooting-matches with the old-fashioned rifle, — and the sudden sharp crack of the report. Their marksmanship was so nearly equal that it became readily apparent that the office of the anxious-eyed judges was not an enviable honor. Occasionally disputes arose, and the antagonists gathered around the tree, examining the targets with vociferous gesticulation which often promised to end in cuffs. Once the two judges disagreed, when it became necessary to call in an impartial " thirdsman " and submit the question. The old miller, placid once more, accepted the trust, decided judiciously, and the match proceeded.

Mink's turn came presently.

As he ran deftly in and out among the heavy young mountaineers, he seemed more than ever like some graceful wild animal, with such elastic lightness, such reserve of strength, such keen endowment of instinct. He arranged in its place his board, previously blackened with moistened powder, and marked with a cross drawn on it with a knife-blade ; each contestant had brought a precisely similar target. Then, to distinguish the centre at sixty yards he carefully affixed a triangular piece of white paper, so that it touched the cross at the intersection of the lines. As he ran lightly back to the log and flung himself upon the ground, his swift movement and his lithe posture struck the attention of one of the men.

" Now, ain't ye the livin' image o' a mink ! Ye 've got nuthin' ter do but ter crope under that thar log, like thar war a hen hidin' thar, an' ye war tryin' ter git it by the throat."

Mink cast his bright eyes upward. " Ye shet up ! " he

exclaimed. Then he placed his rifle on the log and aimed in a twinkling, — his finger was on the trigger.

At this moment 'Gustus Tom, in his overwhelming curiosity, contrived to get his small anatomy between the marksman and the tree. The jet of red light leaped out, the funnel-shaped smoke diffused itself in a formless cloud, and the ball whizzed close by the boy's head.

There ensued a chorus of exclamation. The old man quavered out piteously. Mink, dropping the rifle to the ground, leaped up, seized the small boy by the nape of the neck, and deposited him with a shake in the bosom of his aged relative.

" Ye limb o' Satan, 'Gustus Tom ! " cried out the old man. " Ain't ye got no better sense 'n ter go out fur a evenin' walk 'twixt that thar tree an' these hyar boys, ez could n't begin ter shoot agin me an' my mates when I shot for beef whenst I war young? A-many-a-time I hev fired the five bes' shots myself, an' won all the five ch'ices o' the beef, an' jes' druv the critter home, — won it all! But these hyar fool boys jes' ez soon bang yer head off ez hit the mark. Ye g' long 'fore I skeer the life out'n ye ! "

And 'Gustus Tom, in the unbridled pride of favoritism and with the fear of no man before his eyes, went along as far as the front rank of the crowd, continuing a fervid spectator of the sport.

The agitation of the moment had impaired to a slight degree Mink's aim. The shot was, however, one of the best yet made, and there was a clamor of negation when he insisted that he ought to have it over. The judges ruled against him and the sport proceeded.

As Rood made his last shot, his strongly marked dark face was lighted with a keen elation. Although, according to strictest construction, the ball had not penetrated the centre, it was within a hair's breadth of it, and it was so unlikely that it would be surpassed that he tasted all the assured triumphs of victory before the battle was won.

With Mink's second shot arose the great dispute of

the day. Like Rood's, it was not fairly in the bull's-eye, if the point of intersection might be so called, but it too lacked only a hair's breadth. Mink was willing enough for a new trial, but Rood, protesting, stood upon his rights. The judges consulted together apart, reëxamined the boards, finally announced their incapacity to decide, and called in the "thirdsman."

Mink made no objection when the miller, as referee, came to look at the board. He, too, examined it closely, holding his big hat in his hand that it might cast no shadow. There was no perceptible difference in the value of the two shots. Mink hardly believed he had heard aright when the "thirdsman," with scarcely a moment's hesitation, declared there was no doubt about the matter. Rood's shot was the fairer. "I could draw a line 'twixt Mink's and the centre."

There was a yell of derision from the young fellows. Rood wore a provoking sneer. Mink stood staring.

"Look-a-hyar," he said roughly, "ye haffen-blind old ow*el!* Ye can't tell the differ 'twixt them shots. It 's a tie."

"Rood's air the closest, an' he gits the fust ch'ice o' beef!" said the old man, his white beard and mustache yawning with his toothless laugh. "Ai-yi! Mink, ye ain't so powerful minkish yit ez ter git the fust ch'ice o' beef."

"Ye 'll hev the second ch'ice, Mink," said Price consolingly. He himself, the fourth best shot, had the fourth choice.

"I won't hev the second ch'ice!" exclaimed Mink. "It 's nobody but that thar weezened old critter ez 'lows I oughter. Fust he sent his gran'son, that thar slack-twisted 'Gustus Tom, ter git in my aim, — wisht I hed shot him! An' then, when I lets him be thurdsman, he air jes' so durned m'licious he don't even stop an' take a minit ter decide." Mink's heart was hot. He had been wounded in his most vulnerable susceptibility, his pride in his marksmanship.

"Look-a-hyar, Mink!" remonstrated Price, "ye ain't

a-goin' off 'fore the beef's been butchered an' ye git the second ch'ice. Stop! Hold on!"

For Mink was about to mount.

"I don't want no beef," he said. "I hev been cheated 'mongst ye. I won the fust ch'ice, an' I won't put up with the second."

Price was nonplused for a moment; then he evolved a solution. "I'll sell it, Mink," he cried, "an' bring ye the money! An' don't ye furgit old Tobias Winkeye," he added beguilingly.

"Who's old Tobias Winkeye?" asked the miller tartly.

Price laughed, sticking his hands in the pockets of his jeans trousers, and looked around, winking at the others with a jocosity enfeebled somewhat by his light sparse lashes. "Jes' a man ez hev got a job fur Mink," he said, enigmatically.

The old miller, baffled, and apprehending the mockery, laughed loud and aggressively, his white beard shaking, his bushy eyebrows overhanging his twinkling eyes.

"Hedn't ye better bust the mill down, Mink?" he said floutingly.

"I will, — see ef I don't!" Mink retorted, as he wheeled his mare.

Only idle wrath, an idle threat, void of even the vaguest intention. They all knew that at the time. But the significance of the scene was altered in the light of after events.

Mink's fate had mounted with him, and the mare carried double as he rode out of Piomingo Cove.

III.

THE iterative echoes of the shooting-match, sharply jarring from mountain to mountain, from crag to crag, evoked a faint reverberation even in the distant recesses of Wild-Cat Hollow. Alethea Sayles, sitting at her loom on the porch of the little log cabin, paused, the shuttle motionless in her deft hand, to listen.

All aloof from the world was Wild-Cat Hollow, a limited depression, high up on the vast slope of the Great Smoky. It might have seemed some secret nook, some guarded fastness, so closely did the primeval wilderness encompass it, so jealously did the ridgy steeps rise about it on every hand. It was invisible from the valley below, perhaps too from the heights above. And only a glimpse was vouchsafed to it of the world from which it was sequestered: beyond a field, in a gap of the minor ridges superimposed upon the mountain, where the dead and girdled trees stood in spectral ranks among the waving corn, might be seen a strip of woods in the cove below, a glint of water, a stately file of lofty peaks vanishing along the narrow skyey vista. Sunrise and sunset, — the Hollow knew them not: a distant mountain might flare with a fantasy of color, a star of abnormal glister might palpitate with some fine supernal thrill of dawn; but for all else, it only knew that the night came early and the day broke late, and in many ways it had meagre part in the common lot.

The little log cabin, set among its scanty fields, its weed-grown "gyarden spot," and its few fruit-trees, was poor of its kind. The clapboards of its roof were held in place by poles laid athwart them, with large stones piled between to weight them down. The chimney was of clay and sticks, and leaned away from the wall. In a corner of the rickety rail fence a gaunt, razor-backed hog lay grunting drowsily. Upon a rude scaffold tobacco leaves were suspended to dry. Even the martin-house was humble and primitive: merely a post with a cross-bar, from which hung a few large gourds with a cavity in each, whence the birds were continually fluttering. Behind it all, the woods of the steep ascent seemed to touch the sky. The place might give a new meaning to exile, a new sentiment to loneliness.

Seldom it heard from the world, — so seldom that when the faint rifle-shots sounded in the distance a voice from within demanded eagerly, "What on yearth be that, Lethe?"

"Shootin' fur beef, down in the cove, I reckon, from thar firin' so constant," drawled Alethea.

"Ye dunno," said the unseen, unexpectedly, derisive of this conjecture. "They mought be a-firin' thar bullets inter each other. Nobody kin count on a man by hisself, but a man in company with a rifle air jes' a outdacious, jubious critter."

Alethea looked speculatively down at the limited section of the cove visible from the Hollow above. Her hazel eyes were bright, but singularly grave. The soft sheen of her yellow hair served to definitely outline the shape of her head against the brown logs of the wall. The locks lay not in ripples, but in massive undulations, densely growing above her forehead, and drawn in heavy folds into a knot at the back of her head. She had the delicate complexion and the straight, refined lineaments so incongruous with the poverty-stricken mountaineer, so commonly seen among the class. Her homespun dress was of a dull brown. About her throat, of exquisite whiteness, was knotted a kerchief of the deepest saffron tint. Her hands and arms — for her sleeves were rolled back — were shapely, but rough and sun-embrowned. She had a deliberate, serious manner that very nearly approached dignity.

"I hopes they ain't," she said, still listening. "I hopes they ain't a-shootin' of one another."

"Waal, I'm a-thinkin' the lead would n't be wasted on some of 'em," said the acrid voice. "Piomingo Cove could make out mighty well 'thout some o' them boys ez rip an' rear aroun' down thar ez a constancy. I dunno ez I'd feel called on ter mourn fur Mink Lorey enny. An' I reckon the cove could spare him."

Looking through the window close by the bench of the loom, Alethea could see the interior of the room, rudely furnished and with the perennial fire of the wide chimney-place slowly smouldering in a bed of ashes. A half-grown Shanghai pullet was pecking about the big flat stones of the hearth in a premature and unprescient proximity to the pot. There were two bedsteads of a lofty build, the thick feather beds draped with quilts of such astounding variety of color as might have abashed the designers of Joseph's coat. The scrupulous cleanliness and orderliness of the place were as marked a characteristic as its poverty.

A sharp-featured woman of fifty sat in a low chair by the fire, wearing a blue-checked homespun dress, a pink calico sun-bonnet, and a cob-pipe, — the last was so constantly sported that it might be reckoned an article of attire. She was not so old as she seemed, but the loss of her teeth and her habit of crouching over the fire gave her a cronish aspect.

Alethea hesitated. Then, with a deprecatory manner, she said in her soft contralto drawl, "He ain't down 'mongst the boys in Piomingo Cove none."

Mrs. Sayles sneered. "Ye b'lieve that?"

"He be a-herdin' cattle along o' Ben Doaks on Piomingo Bald."

Mrs. Sayles looked at her step-daughter and puffed a copious wreath of smoke for reply.

"Reuben tole me that hisself, — an' so did Ben Doaks," persisted Alethea.

"*Mink*, I calls him, an' nuthin' shorter," said Mrs. Sayles, obdurately, — as if anything could be shorter. "But ef Ben Doaks gin the same word, it mus' be a true one."

Alethea flushed. "I know ye air sot agin Reuben, but I 'd believe his word agin enny other critter's in the mountings."

"Set a heap o' store on him, don't ye?" said Mrs. Sayles, sarcastically. "An' when he kem a-courtin' ye, an' 'peared crazy 'bout'n ye, an' ye an' him war promised ter marry, ye could n't quit jowin' at him fur one minit. Ye plumb beset him ter do like *ye* thought war right, — ez ef *he* hed no mo' conscience o' his own 'n that pullet thar, an' hed n't never hearn on salvation. An' ye 'd beg an' beg him ter quit consortin' with the moonshiners; an' a-drinkin' o' apple-jack an' sech; an' a-rollickin' round the kentry; an' layin' folkses fences down on the groun'; an' liftin' thar gates off 'n the hinges; an' ketchin' thar geese, an' pickin' 'em, an' scatterin' thar feathers in the wind, an' sendin' 'em squawkin' home; an' a-playin' kyerds; an' a-whoopin', an' ridin', an' racin'. An' ye war always a-preachin' at him, an' tryin' ter straighten him out, an' make him suthin' he war never born ter be."

Her pipe was smoked out. She drew from her pocket a fragment of tobacco leaf, which was apparently not sufficiently cured for satisfactory smoking, for she laid it on the hot ashes on the hearth and watched it as it dried, her meditative eyes shaded by her pink calico sun-bonnet.

"Naw, sir!" she continued, as she crumpled the bit of leaf with her fingers and crowded it into the bowl of her pipe, "I hev never liked Mink. I ain't denyin' it, nuther. I ain't gamesome enough ter git tuk up with sech ways ez his'n. Mighty few folks air! But I could see reason in the critter when he 'lowed one day, right hyar by this very chimbly-place, — he sez, sez he, 'Lethe, ye don't like nuthin' I do or say, an' I 'm durned ef I kin see how ye like *me!*'"

Alethea's serious, lustrous eyes, looking in at the window, saw not the uncouth interior of her home, — no! As in a vision, irradiated by some enchantment, she beheld the glamours of the idyllic past, fluctuating, waning.

Even to herself it sometimes seemed that she might have been content more lightly. Her imbuement with those practical ideas of right and wrong, the religion of deeds rather than the futilely pious fervors of the ignorant mountaineers in which creed and act were often widely at variance, was as mysterious an endowment as the polarity of the loadstone. She was not introspective, however; she never even wondered that she should speak openly, without fear or favor, as she felt impelled. Had she lived in an age when every inward monition was esteemed the voice of the Lord, she might have fancied that she was called to warn the world of the errors of its ways. Her sedulous conscience, the austere gravity of her spirit, her courage, her steadfastness, her fine intelligence, even her obdurate self-will, might all have had assertive values in those long bygone days. As an historic woman, she might have founded an order, or juggled with state-craft, or perished a martyr, or rode, enthusiast, in the ranks of battle. By centuries belated in Wild-Cat Hollow, she was known as a "perverted, cross-grained gal" and "a meddlin' body," and the "widder Jessup" had much sympathy for having in a misguided moment married Alethea's father. Sometimes the Hollow, distorted though its conscience was, experienced a sort of affright to recognize its misdeeds in her curt phrase. It could only ask in retort who set her up to judge of her elders, and regain its wonted self-complacency as best it might. Even her own ascetic rectitude lacked some quality to commend it.

"I can't find no reg'lar fault with Lethe," her stepmother was wont to say, "'ceptin' she's jes'—Lethe."

Mrs. Sayles's voice, pursuing the subject, recalled the girl's attention:—

"An' ye tired his patience out,—the critter hed mo' 'n I gin him credit fur,—an' druv him off at last through wantin' him ter be otherwise. An' now folks 'low ez him an' Elviry Crosby air a-goin' ter marry. I 'll be bound she don't harry him none 'bout'n his ways, 'kase her mother tole me ez she air mighty nigh a idjit 'bout'n him, an' hev turned off Peter Rood, who she hed promised ter marry, though the weddin' day hed been set, an' Pete air wuth forty sech ez Mink."

Alethea turned away abruptly to her work, and as she lightly tossed the shuttle to and fro she heard, amidst the creaking of the treadle and the thumping of the batten, her step-mother's persistent voice droning on: —

"An' so ye hed yer say, an' done yer preachin', an' he profited by it. I reckon he 'lowed ef ye jawed that-a-way afore ye war married, thar war no yearthly tellin' what ye *could* say arterward. An' now," rising to the dramatic, "hyar kems along Ben Doaks, powerful peart an' good enough ter sati'fy ennybody; perlite, an' saaft-spoken, an' good-lookin', an' respected by all, an' ready ter marry ye ter-morrer, ef ye 'll say the word. He owns cattle-critters" —

"An' sheep," put in an unexpected voice. A dawdling young woman, with a shallow blue eye and a pretty, inane soft face, had stepped into the back door, and heard the last words of the monologue which apparently had been often enough repeated to admit of no doubt as to its tenor. She had a slatternly, ill-adjusted look, and a snuff-brush in the corner of her mouth.

"An' herds cattle in the summer season," said Mrs. Sayles.

"He hev a good name 'mongst the cattle-owners," observed the young woman, her daughter-in-law.

"An' hev bought him right smart land," added Mrs. Sayles.

"Down in Piomingo Cove! not h'isted up on the side o' the mounting, like we-uns!" exclaimed the young woman, with more enthusiasm than one would have believed possible from the flaccid indifference of her manner.

"An' he put in all the fair weather las' winter a-raisin' him a house," Mrs. Sayles pursued.

"An' he 'lowed ter me ez every log war hefted, an' every pat o' clay war daubed on the chinkin', with the thought o' Lethe!" cried the other.

"He hev been plantin' round thar some, a'ready," said the old woman.

"Corn, pumpkins, wheat, an' terbacco," supplemented the daughter-in-law.

"An' he hev got him some bee-gums, — I never hearn how many bees," said Mrs. Sayles.

"Down in Piomingo Cove!" the climax of worldly prosperity.

"Laws-a-massy!" exclaimed Mrs. Sayles, with a freshened realization of despair. "Lethe ain't never goin' ter live in that house! I dunno what ails the gal! She takes a notion ez she likes a man with sech ways ez she can't abide, an' she quar'ls with him mornin' an' evenin'. An' then when a feller kems along, with all sort'n good ways ez she likes, she don't like *him!* Gals never acted similar whenst I war young. I 'low it mus' be the wiles o' Satan on the onruly generation."

"Lethe 'pears ter think the Lord hev app'inted the rocky way," said the other. "She be always a-doin' of what 's the hardest. An' she can't quit nowhar this side o' nuthin'! Ef ever she 's condemned ter Torment she 'll kerry a leetle kindlin' along, fur fear the fire won't be het up hot enough ter burn her fur her sins."

She was silent during a momentary activity of the snuff-brush.

"But ef *I* war you-uns, Lethe, an' hed the chance o' livin' in my own house all ter myself" — she began anew.

"Plenty o' elbow-room," interrupted Mrs. Sayles; "not all jammed tergether, like we-uns hyar."

Alethea, aware of her lack of logic, made an effort to effect a diversion.

"I never hearn o' folks a-grudgin' a gal house-room, an' wantin' her ter go off an' marry fur a place ter bide," she said, pausing in her weaving.

Mrs. Sayles, who piqued herself, not without some reason, on her kindness to her step-daughter, having her prosaic welfare, at least, at heart, retorted in righteous wrath. "An' nobody ain't never said no sech word," she declared, with amplest negation. "Grudgin' ye house-room, — shucks!"

"One less would n't be no improve*mint* ter we-uns, Lethe," said the daughter-in-law. "We air jes' like a hen settin' on forty aigs: she kin kiver 'em ez well ez thirty-nine."

"But I ain't got no medjure o' patience with this latter-day foolishness!" said Mrs. Sayles, tartly. "Whenst I war young, gals married thar fust chance, — mought hev been afeard they 'd never git another," she added, impersonally, that others might profit by this contingency. "An' I don't keer much nohow fur these hyar lonesome single wimmen. Ye never kin git folks ter b'lieve ez they ever *hed* enny chance."

"Laws-a-massy, Lethe," the daughter-in-law reassured her, still vaguely serene, "I ain't wantin' ter git shet o' ye, nohow. Ye hev tuk mo' keer o' my chill'n than I hev, an' holped me powerful. It's well ye done it, too, fur Jacob Jessup ain't sech ez kin content me with Wild-Cat Hollow. I war raised in the cove!"

"Thar's L'onidas now, axin' fur suthin' ter eat," said the uncompromising Alethea, whose voice was the slogan of duty.

The loom occupied a full third of the space on the little porch; two or three rickety chairs stood there, besides; a yoke hung against the wall; the spinning-wheel was shadowed by the jack-bean vines, whose delicate lilac blooms embellished the little cabin, clambering to its roof; on the floor were several splint baskets. A man was languidly filling them with peaches, which he brought in a wheel-barrow from the trees farther down on the slope. He was tall and stalwart, but his beard was gray, and he had assumed the manner and all the exemptions of extreme age; occasionally he did a little job like this with an air of laborious precision. He was accompanied both in going and coming by his step-son's daughter, a tow-headed, six-year-old girl, and a gaunt yellow dog. The little girl's voice, dictatorial and shrill, was on the air continuously, broken only by the low, acquiescent refrain of the old man's replies, carefully adjusted to meet her propositions. The dog paced silently and discreetly along, his appreciation of the placid pleasure of the occasion plainly manifested in his quiet demeanor and his slightly wagging tail. His decorum suffered a lapse when, as they came close to the porch, he observed Leonidas issue from the door, — a small boy of four, a plump little caricature of a man, in blue cotton trousers, an unbleached cotton shirt, and a laughably small pair of knitted suspenders. He held in his hand a piece of fat meat several inches square, considered in the mountains peculiarly wholesome for small boys, and a reliable assistant in " gittin' yer growth."

Tige paused not for reflection. He sprang upon the porch, capering gleefully about, and uttering shrill yelps of discovery with much his triumphant manner in treeing a coon. Leonidas shared the common human weakness of overestimating one's own size. He thought to hold the booty out of Tige's reach, and extended his arm at full length, whereupon the dog, with an elastic bound and extreme nicety of aim, caught it and swallowed it at a single gulp. Leonidas winked very fast; then, realizing his bereavement, burst into noisy tears. Tige's facetiousness had a discordantly sudden contrast in the serious howl he emitted as he was kicked off the porch by the child's father. This was an unkempt young fellow just emerging from the shed-room. He had a red face and swollen eyes, and there were various drowsy intimations in his manner that he was just roused from sleep. No natural slumber, one might have judged; the odor of whiskey still hung about him, and he walked with an unsteady gait to the end of the porch and sat down on the edge of the floor, his feet dangling over the ground. Tige, who had sought refuge beneath the house, and was giving vent to sundry sobbing wheezes, thrust his head out to lick his master's boots. Upon this mollifying demonstration, the man looked down with the lenient expression of one who loves dogs. "What ails ye, then," he reasoned, "ter be sech a fool as ter 'low ye kin be let ter rob a child the size o' L'onidas thar?"

And forthwith the mercurial Tige came out, cheerful as before.

In the limited interval when Leonidas — who had been supplied with another piece of meat, but still wept aloud with callow persistence because of the affronts offered by Tige — was fain to pause for breath, and between the alternate creaking of the treadle of the loom and the thumping of the batten, the man's ear caught that unwonted stir in the air, the sound of consecutive rifle-shots.

"Look-a-hyar," he cried, springing to his feet, "what's that a-goin' on down in the cove? Lethe, stop trompin' on that thar n'isy treadle, so ez I kin listen! Quit yellin', ye catamount!" with a vengeful glance at the small boy.

But the grief of Leonidas was imperative, and he abated nothing.

Jacob Jessup stood for an instant baffled. Then suddenly he put both hands to his mouth, and roused all the echoes of Wild-Cat Hollow with a ringing halloo.

"Who be ye a-hollerin' at?" asked his mother from her nook in the chimney corner.

"I 'lowed I viewed a man up yander 'mongst them woods, — mought be one o' the herders."

Alethea's foot paused on the treadle. Her uplifted hand stayed the batten, the other held the shuttle motionless. She turned her head and with a sudden rich flush on her cheek and a deep light in her lifted eyes looked up toward the forests that rose in vast array upon the steep slopes of the ridge until they touched the sky. Accustomed to the dusky shadows of their long avenues, she discerned a mounted figure in their midst. There was a tense moment of suspense. The man had wheeled his horse on hearing the halloo. He seemed to hesitate; then in lieu of response he took his way down the hill toward the cabin. The trees were fewer on the edge of the clearing. Before he drew rein by the rail fence she had turned back to the loom, and once more the shuttle winged its short, clumsy flights, like a fledgeling bird, from one side to the other, and the treadle creaked, and the batten thumped, and she spared not an instant from her work.

For it was only Ben Doaks dismounting, glad of a pretext, throwing the reins over a projecting rail of the fence, and tramping up to the house.

"Howdy," he observed comprehensively. And the family, meditatively eying him, responded, "Howdy."

"Keep yer health, Ben?" the old woman demanded. She had come to the door, and took a gourd of water from a pail which was on a shelf without. She drank leisurely, and tossed the surplus water from the gourd across the porch, where it spattered the half-grown pullet, which shunted off suddenly with a loud, shocked exclamation, as if it sported half a score of ruffled petticoats.

"Yes 'm," drawled Ben, seating himself on the edge of the porch, near Jacob, "I keeps toler'ble well."

"I dunno how ye do it, — livin' off'n what ye cooks yerse'f." She manifested a truly mundane interest in the eligible young man. She did not return to her chair by the fireside, but sat down on the doorstep. "I'd look ter be p'isoned ef I hed ter live on yer cookin'."

"Waal, I reckon *ye* could n't put up with it right handy, seein' the sorter table ye set out hyar."

Was the old woman more than human, to be untouched by this sincere tribute?

"Ye oughter kem down hyar oftener ye do, Ben, an' bide ter meals," she said, her spectacles turned upon him with a certain grave luminosity. "We'll make ye powerful welcome ter sech vittles ez we hev got. Ye ain't been hyar fur a right smart time."

"I know that, but somehows I never kin feel right welcome comin' so often," said Ben. He had leaned back against the post of the porch. He could look, without moving, into Alethea's grave, absorbed face as she worked.

"'Count o' Lethe? Shucks! thar ain't but one fool hyar. Mought kem ter see the rest o' we-uns."

Alethea's face flushed. Ben Doaks, dismayed to be the indirect occasion of her anger, and secretly affronted by the breach of decorum which he considered involved in this open mention of his bootless suit, hastened to change the subject. "Did ye hev a word ter say ter me, Jacob?" he asked. "Ye 'lowed, day 'fore yestiddy, ye wanted ter sell yer steer."

There was now no sound from the cove. The burnished glisters of the sunshine hung above it, holding in suspension a gauzy haze, through which the purple mountains were glamourous and darkly vague. Jacob, his senses yet in thrall, could hardly recall the question he had desired to ask concerning the rifle-shots that had trivially jarred its perfect serenity.

"Yes, yes," he said hastily. "Buck, ye know," with the manner of introduction. "Yander he be." He pointed to a gaunt dun-colored ox with long horns and a joyless mien, standing within a few feet of a rude trough which the spring branch kept supplied.

"Jacob," said Alethea, turning her head with a knitted brow, "ef ye sell Buck, how air we goin' ter plough our craps? How air we goin' ter live along?"

"Laws-a-massy!" exclaimed Mrs. Sayles. "I ain't s'prised none ef the man ez marries Lethe at last will find out he hev got a turrible meddler. She jes' ups an' puts inter her elders' affairs ez brash ez ef hern war the only brains in the fambly. Jacob's a-savin' ter buy a horse, child. Yer dad 'lowed Jacob mought use his jedgmint 'bout all the crappin', bein' ez yer dad 's old an' ain't long fur this worl'. So Jacob hev determinated ter buy a horse. Who wants ter work a steer when they ken hev a horse?"

Doaks looked intently at Alethea, loyally eager to range himself on her side. She was oblivious of his presence now; every faculty was on the alert in her single-handed contest against the family.

"Whar 's the money he hev saved?" she demanded.

Her step-brother seemed frowzier than ever, as he lifted his eyebrows in vain cogitation for an answer.

"Ye shet up," he said, in triumphant substitution; "ye ain't no kin ter me."

Alethea, all lacking in the bland and mollifying feminine influences that subtly work their ends in seeming submission, bluntly spoke her inmost thought:

"Ez long ez thar 's a moonshine still a-runnin' somewhar round Piomingo Cove, Jacob ain't goin' ter save no money."

"Thar ain't no still round hyar ez I knows on," said Doaks, in surprise. "Over yander in Eskaqua Cove thar air a bonded still, I know."

"That bonded still hev ter sell wholesale, hevin' no license otherwise," she retorted, "an' Jacob hain't saved enough yit ter buy by the five gallon. An' though he may 'pear sober ter you-uns, he don't ter me."

Jacob bore her scathing glance with an admirable equanimity.

"Ye shet up, Lethe; ye dunno nuthin' 'bout stills, bonded or no. Look-a-hyar, Ben, don't ye want ter buy Buck? See him thar?"

"I don't want him," said Ben.

Jacob turned fiercely on Alethea. "Why n't ye hold yer jaw, ef ye know how; ye have done spiled my trade. Look-a-hyar, Ben," he said alluringly, "it 's this hyar steer," — there was but one, — "this hyar steer; he 's wuth money. I tell ye," he vociferated, with a drunken wag of his head, "Buck 's a good steer. I dunno ef I kin git my cornsent ter trade Buck off, no-ways. Buck 's plumb like a member o' the fambly. I tell ye we-uns fairly dote on Buck."

"Waal, I don't want him. Older 'n enny of ye, ain't he?" drawled Ben. He was not a dull fellow, and he had taken his cue. He would decry the ox and forego his bargain, a consciously hopeless sacrifice to his affection.

Jacob straightened himself with an effort, and stared at his interlocutor.

"Who? Buck? Why, Buck ain't much older than L'onidas thar." He waved his hand toward the boy, who had perched on the bench of the loom beside Alethea. Now and then she patted his shoulder, which effort at consolation he received with a distinct crescendo; he had begun to relish the sound of his vocal performance, evidently attempting new and bizarre effects.

"L'onidas air about four year old, ain't he, Mis' Jessup?" Doaks asked of the young matron, who seemed placidly regardless how the negotiation should terminate.

"I b'lieve he's 'bout four," she said, without animation.

"Waal, he be toler'ble bouncin' fur that," said Doaks, looking with the eye of speculation at the boy, as if he were about to offer a bid for Leonidas, "but I kin see a heap o' diff'unce 'twixt his size an' Buck's."

The drunken man turned and stared at the diminutive person on the bench. "Waal," he said in a low-spirited way, as if he must yield the point, "I never knowed ye wanted a steer o' that size. Would n't be much use ter ye. Our'n ain't."

"He 'pears sorter jubious in his temper. Does he hook?"

"Who? Buck?" — with an air of infinite amazement. "Why, Buck's ez saaft ez L'onidas thar."

As Leonidas was just now extremely loud, the comparison was hardly felicitous.

"I don't want no work-ox, nohow," said Doaks. "I want cattle ter fatten."

"Jes' try Buck. He'll lay on fat fur ev'y ear o' corn fedded him. Ye dunno Buck. He hain't laid on much yit, 'kase, ye see," — Jessup's voice took a confidential intonation, although it was not lowered because of the roaring Leonidas, — "we-uns ain't hed much corn ter feed ter Buck, bein' back'ard las' year. The drought cotched our late corn, an' so Buck, though he worked it, he never got none sca'cely. An' that's why he ain't no fatter 'n he be."

Logical of Buck, but it availed him as little as the logic of misfortunes profits the rest of the world.

Alethea had risen and turned half round, leaning against the great clumsy frame of the loom. Her posture displayed her fine height; her supple figure was slight, as became her age, but with a suggestion of latent strength in every curve. There was something strangely inconsistent in the searching, serious expression of her grave brown eyes and the lavish endowment of her beauty, which seemed as a thing apart from her. Perhaps only Ben Doaks noted, or rather felt in a vague, unconscious way, the fascination of its detail: the lustre of her dense yellow hair showing against the brown wall, where a string of red peppers hung, heightening the effect; the glimpse of her white throat under the saffron kerchief; the lithe grace of her figure, about which her sober-hued dress fell in straight folds. To the homefolks she gave other subjects to contemplate.

"Naw," she drawled, in her soft, low voice, whose intonation only suggested sarcasm, "we did n't plant much o' nuthin' las' year, — hed no seed sca'cely, an' nuthin' ter trade fur 'em. The plenties' o' ennythin' roun' hyarabouts war bresh whiskey, an' ez Buck don't drink it he ain't no fatter 'n he be."

"Waal," said Doaks, feeling all the discomforts incident to witnessing a family row, incompetent to participate by reason of non-membership, "I 'lowed the mountings hed in an' about done with moonshinin', cornsiderin' the way the raiders kep' up with the distillers. It 's agin the law, ye know."

"I ain't a-keerin' fur the law," said Alethea loftily. "The law air jes' the men's foolishness, an' they air a-changin' of it forever till 't ain't got no constancy. Ef I war minded ter break it I 'd feel no hendrance in the sperit."

Her eyes met his. He looked vaguely away. Certainly there was no reasoning on this basis.

"'T ain't right," she said suddenly. "Jacob sleeps an' drinks his time away, an' don't do his sheer o' the work. I done *all* the ploughin' this year, — me an' Buck, — an' I ain't one o' the kind ez puts up with sech. I ain't a Injun woman, like them at Quallatown. Pete Rood, — he hev been over thar, — he 'lows the wimmen do *all* the crappin' while the men go huntin'. I 'll kerry my e-end o' the log, but when the t'other e-end draps 'pears ter me I oughter drap mine."

"What ye goin' ter do, Lethe?" said the old woman. "Goin' ter take ter idlin' an' drinkin' bresh whiskey, too?"

She laughed, but she sneered as well.

Alethea, all unmoved by her ridicule, drawled calmly on: "I dunno nuthin' 'bout bresh whiskey, an' I ain't idled none, ez the rest o' you-uns kin see; but ef Jacob don't do his stent nex' year, thar 'll be less corn hyar than this."

It was hard for Doaks to refrain from telling her that there was a home ready for her, and one to share it who would work for both. Only futility restrained him. He flushed to the roots of his light brown hair, and as a resource he drew out a clasp-knife and absently whittled a chip as he listened.

"Waal, wimmen hev ter holp men along with thar work wunst in a while," said Mrs. Sayles patronizingly. "Ye 'll find that out, child, whenst ye git married."

"Ef I war married," said Alethea, severely contemplating the possibility, — and Doaks felt a vague thrill of jealousy, — "I 'd do his work ef he war ailin' ennywise, but not ter leave him in the enjyement o' bresh whiskey."

"Ye shet up, Lethe," said Jacob, nettled. "Ye ain't no kin ter me, — jes' a step-sister, — an' ye ain't got no right ter jow at me. Ye dunno nuthin' 'bout bresh whiskey. Ye dunno whar it 's made nor who makes it."

"Ef I did" — she began abruptly.

He looked up at her with a sober dismay on his face.

"Don't go ter 'lowin' ye 'd gin the word ter the revenuers?" he said.

Mrs. Sayles dropped her knitting in her lap.

"Look-a-hyar, Lethe," she exclaimed, "it 's ez much ez yer life 's wuth ter say them words!"

"I ain't said 'em," declared Alethea. She looked vaguely away with absent eyes, disregarding Jacob's growling defense of himself, which consisted in good measure of animadversions on people who faulted their elders and gals who could n't hold their tongues. Suddenly she stepped from the porch.

"Whar be ye goin', Lethe?" demanded Mrs. Sayles, ruthlessly interrupting Jacob's monologue.

"Ter hunt up that thar lam'," replied Alethea calmly, as if nothing else had been under discussion. "I ain't seen nuthin' of it ter-day, an' some o' the chill'n — I b'lieve 't war Joe — 'lowed its dam war down yander nigh Boke's spring yestiddy, actin' sorter cur'ous, an' I reckon suthin' 's happened ter it."

Doaks looked after her as she went, tempted to follow. She took her way down the path beside the zigzag rail-fence. All the corners were rank with wild flowers, vines and bushes, among which her golden head showed from time to time as in a wreath. She was soon without the limits of Wild-Cat Hollow. More than once she paused as she went, holding her hands above her eyes, and looking at the vast array of mountains on every side. A foreign land to her, removed even from vague speculation; she only saw how those august summits lifted themselves into the sky, how the clouds, weary-winged, were fain to rest upon them. There was a vague blurring at the horizon-line, for a shower was succeeded by mist. The woods intervened presently; the long stretches of the majestic avenues lay before her, all singularly open, cleared of undergrowth by the fiery besom of the annual conflagration. It was very silent; once only she heard the shrill trilling of a tree-frog; and once the insistent clamor of a locust broke out close at hand, vibrating louder and louder and dying away, to be caught up antiphonally in the distance. Often she noted the lightning-scathed trees, the fated of the forest, writhen and blanched and spectral among their flourishing kindred. There were presently visible at the end of the long leafy vista other dead trees: their blight was more prosaic;

they stood girdled and white in an abandoned field that lay below the slope on which she had paused, and near the base of the mountain. A broken rotting rail-fence still encircled it. Blackberry bushes, broom-sedge, a tangle of weeds, were a travesty of its crops. A fox, a swift-scudding tawny streak, sped across it as she looked. Hard by there was a deserted hut: the doors were open, showing the dark voids within; the batten shutters flapped with every changing whim of the winds. Fine sport they had often had, these riotous mountain sprites, shrieking down the chimney to affright the loneliness; then falling to sobs and sighs to mock the voices of those who had known sorrow here and perhaps shed tears; sometimes wrapping themselves in snow as in a garment, and reeling in fantastic whirls through the forlorn and empty place; sometimes twitting the gaunt timbers with their infirmities, and one wild night wrenching off half a dozen clapboards from the roof and scattering them about the door. Thus the moon might look in, seeing no more those whose eyes had once met its beam, and even the sunlight had melancholy intimations when it shone on the forsaken hearth-stone. A screech-owl had found refuge among the rafters, and Alethea heard its quavering scream ending in a low, sinister chuckle. There was a barn near at hand, — a structure of undaubed, unhewn logs, with a wide open pass-way below the loft to shelter wagons and farm implements; it seemed in better repair than the house. The amber sky above the dark woods had deepened to orange, to crimson; the waning light suffused the waters of the spring branch which flowed close by the barn, the willows leaning to it, the ferns laving in it. The place was incredibly solitary and mournful with the persistent spectacle of the deserted home, suggestive of collapsed energies, of the defeated scheme of some simple humanity.

   A faint bleat rose suddenly. Alethea turned quickly. Amongst a patch of briers she caught a glimpse of something white; another glance, — it was the ewe, quietly nibbling the grass.

   Alethea had no intention of moving softly, but her

skirts brushing through the weeds made hardly a sound. Her light, sure step scarcely stirred a leaf. The ewe saw her presently, and paused in feeding. She had been making the best of her woes, remaining near her lamb, which had fallen into a sink-hole, sustained by the earth, gravel and banks of leaves held in the mouth of the cavity. Its leg was broken, and thus, although the sheep could venture to it, the lamb could not follow to the vantage-ground above. Seeing that succor was at hand, the sheep lost all patience and calmness, and ran about Alethea in a distracting fashion, bleating, till the lamb, roused to a renewed sense of its calamities, bleated piteously too. As it lay down in the cavity upon the dead leaves, it had a strangely important look upon its face, appreciating how much stir it was making in the world for one of its size. Alethea noticed this, albeit she was too self-absorbed at the moment. These treacherous hopper-shaped sink-holes are of indefinite depth, and are often the mouths of caves. To reach the lamb she must needs venture half across the cavity. She stepped cautiously down the débris, holding fast the while to the branches of an elder-bush growing on its verge. She felt the earth sinking beneath her feet. The sheep, which had jumped in too, sprang hastily out. Alethea had a dizzying realization of insecurity. She caught the lamb up in one arm, then stepped upon the sinking mass and struggled up the side of the aperture, as with a great gulp the leaves and earth were swallowed into the cavity. She looked down with that sickening sense of a sheer escape, still holding the lamb in one arm; the other hand readjusted the heavy masses of her golden hair, and the saffron kerchief about the neck of her brown dress. The sheep, one anxiety removed, was the prey of another, and pressed close to Alethea, with outstretched head and all the fears of kidnapping in her pleading eyes.

Alethea waited for a moment to rest. Then as she glanced over her shoulder her heart seemed to stand still, her brain reeled, and but for her acute consciousness she would have thought she must be dreaming.

The clearing lay there all as it was a moment before: the deserted buildings, the weed-grown fields, the rotting rail fence; the woods dark about it, the sky red above it. Around and around the old barn, in a silent circuit, three men were solemnly tramping in single file. She stood staring at them with dilated eyes, all the mystic traditions of supernatural manifestations uppermost in her mind. Once more the owl's scream rent the brooding stillness. How far that low, derisive chuckle echoed! A star, melancholy, solitary, was in the pensive sky. The men's faces were grave, — once, twice, thrice, they made the round. Then they stood together in the open space beneath the loft, and consulted in whispers.

One suddenly spoke aloud.

"Oh, Tobe!" he called.

"*Tobe!*" called the echoes.

There was no answer. All three looked up wistfully. Then they again conferred together in a low tone.

"Oh, Tobias!" cried the spokesman in a voice of entreaty.

"*Tobias!*" pleaded the plaintive echoes.

Still there was no answer. The owl screamed suddenly in its weird, shrill tones. It had flown out from among the rafters and perched on the smokeless chimney of the hut. Then its uncanny laughter filled the interval.

Once more the men whispered anxiously to each other. One of them, a tall, ungainly, red-haired fellow, seemed to have evolved a solution of the problem which had baffled them.

"Mister Winkeye!" he exclaimed, with vociferous confidence.

The echoes were forestalled. A sneeze rang out abruptly from the loft of the deserted old barn, — a sneeze resonant, artificial, grotesque enough to set the blades below to roaring with delighted laughter.

"He mus' hev his joke. *Mister Winkeye* air a mighty jokified old man," declared the red-haired fellow.

They made no effort to hold further communication with the sneezer in the loft. They hastily placed a burly jug in the centre of the space below, and laid a silver half-dollar upon the cob that served as stopper. The coin looked extremely small in this juxtaposition. There may be people elsewhere who would be glad of a silver coin of that size capable of filling so disproportionately large a jug. Then they ran off fleetly out of the clearing and into the woods, and Alethea could hear the brush crackling as they dashed through it on the slopes below.

She was still pale and tremulous, but no longer doubts beset her. She understood the wiles of the illicit distiller, pursued so closely by the artifices of the raiders that he was prone to distrust the very consumers of his brush whiskey. They never saw his face, they knew not even his name. They had no faint suspicion where his still was hidden. They were not even dangerous as unwilling witnesses, should they be caught with the illicit liquor in their hands. The story that they had left a jug and a half-dollar in a deserted barn, and found the jug filled and the coin vanished, would inculpate no one. From the loft the distiller or his emissary could see and recognize them as they came. Alethea, having crept down the slope amongst the briers in search of the lamb, had been concealed from him. She was seized instantly by the desire to get away before he should appear. She coveted the knowledge of no such dangerous secret. She walked boldly out from the leafy covert, that he might see her in the clearing and delay till she was gone.

The lamb was bleating faintly in her arms; the sheep pressed close to her side, nudging her elbow with an insistent nozzle. The last flush of the day was on her shining hair and her grave, earnest face. The path led her near the barn. She hesitated, stopped, and drew back hastily. A man was swinging himself alertly down from the loft. He caught up the coin, slipped it into his pocket, and lifted the jug with the other hand. The next moment he dropped it suddenly, with a startled exclamation. His eyes had met her eyes. There was a moment of suspense charged with mutual recognition. Then she ran hastily by, never pausing till she was far away in the deep obscurity of the woods.

IV.

THE night came on. The dark summits of the great mountains were heavily defined against the sky. Here and there along those steep slanting lines that mark the ravines a mist hung, vaguely perceived. A point of red light might gleam in the dusky depths of Piomingo Cove where the flare of a hearth-stone flickered out. All the drowsy nocturnal voices joined in iterative unison, broken only when the marauding wolf of the Great Smoky howled upon the bald. The herders ruefully thought of the roaming yearlings, and presaged calamity. All the world was sunk in gloom, till gradually a rayonnant heralding halo, of a pallid and lustrous green, appeared above the deeply purple summits; in its midst the yellow moon slowly revealed itself, and with a visible tremulousness rose solemnly into the ascendency of the night.

It was high in the sky when Mink Lorey rode along the wild mountain ways. More than once he looked up earnestly at it, not under the spell of lunar splendors, but with a prosaic calculation of the hour. Suddenly he drew up the mare. He lifted his head, listening. Voices sounded in the depths of the woods, — faint, far, hilarious voices; then absolute silence. He struck the mare with his heels. The animal pushed on unwillingly, breaking through the brush, stumbling over the stones, scrambling up and down steep slopes. All at once, with a burst of laughter, there was disclosed an opening in the forest. A glory of pale moonlight suffused the mountains in the distance and the shimmering mists in the valley. In the flecking shadow of the great trees were half a dozen figures, with hairy moonlit faces and shining eyes, seated on logs or rocks, or lying upon the ground.

Not fauns nor satyrs; not Bacchus come again with all his giddy rout. Only the malcontents because of the bonded still.

"Hy 're, Mink!" exclaimed Jerry Price. "We fund the jug hyar 'cordin' ter promise, hid in a hollow tree."

"I hope," said Mink with sudden apprehension, as he dismounted, "thar be some lef' fur me."

"A leetle, I reckon. Hyar, Mink, wet yer whistle."

Mink sat down on the roots of a tree draped from its summit to its lowest bough with the rank luxuriance of a wild grapevine. The pendent ends swayed in the wind. The dew was upon the bunches of green fruit and the delicate tendrils, and the moonlight slanted on them with a glistening sheen.

Mink took the jug, which gurgled alluringly. He removed the cob that served as stopper, and smelled it with the circumspect air of those who drink from jugs. Then he turned it up to his mouth. A long bubbling sound, and he put it down with a sigh of satisfaction.

"Ye don't 'pear ez riled ez ye did when ye rid out'n Piomingo Cove," suggested Pete Rood.

He had a swaggering, triumphant manner, although he was lying on the ground.

Mink, leaning back against the bole of the tree, the moonlight full on his wild dark eyes, his clear-cut face, and tousled hair, gave no sign of anger or even of attention.

"Whar hev ye been all this time?" asked Jerry Price.

"Waal," said Mink leisurely, "ye know that thar coon ez Tad gin me, — I won it at 'five corn:' arter I hed rid out'n Piomingo Cove an' hed started up the mounting, I hearn suthin' yappin' arter me, an' thar war Tad a-fetchin' his coon. That thar idjit hed run mighty nigh three miles ter fetch me his coon! Waal, I hed n't no 'casion fur a cap, an' the coon war a powerful peart leetle consarn, — smiled mighty nigh ekal ter a possum, — an' I 'lowed Elviry Crosby mought set store by sech fur a pet, an' so I rid over thar an' gin the coon ter her. She war mos' pleased ter death ter git the critter."

"Ye ain't been thar ever sence!" exclaimed Jerry.

"Yes," said Mink demurely. "I bided ter supper along of 'em, — the old folks bein' powerful perlite an' gin me an invite."

Jerry poked him in the ribs. "Ye air a comical cuss! Ye hev got all the gals in the mountings crazy 'bout'n ye."

Mink laughed lightly, and stayed the fleet jug, which was agile considering its bulk, and once more drank deeply. If he had needed zest for his draught, he might have found it in the expression of Pete Rood's face. He had already revenged himself, but he must needs push the matter further. He smiled with reminiscent relish, as he leaned against the tree.

"Elviry axed mighty p'inted ef I war a-goin' right straight up ter the herders' cabin ter-night, an' I tole her ez I hed a job on hand with a man named Tobias Winkeye ez I hed ter look arter fust. But she suspicioned suthin', 'count o' the name, I reckon, though she never drempt 't war jes' whiskey. She 'lowed she hed never hearn o' nobody named sech. An' I tole her she hed: her dad used ter like old Winkeye mightily, though *she* did n't know him ez well ez some. She 'lowed I war a-goin' off a-courtin' some other gal. It war toler'ble hard ter pacify her," with a covert glance at Rood. "I hed ter talk sixteen ter the dozen."

"Waal, we hed better look out how our tongues wag so slack with that thar name," said Price. "I lef' old man Griff settin' outside the mill door a-waitin' fur old Winkeye ter ride by, — bein' ez I hed gin the word he lives in Eskaqua Cove, — 'kase he wanted ter warn him not ter let no job o' work go ter Mink Lorey. He 'lowed he war goin' ter gin Mink a bad name."

Mink's blood, fired by the liquor, burned at fever heat. His roving eyes were distended and unnaturally bright as the moonlight flashed into them. His cheek was deeply flushed. Despite the rare chill air of the heights, he was hot; often he took off his hat to let the wind play in his long tangled hair that hung down to his shoulders, and lay in heavy moist rings on his forehead. Every fibre was strained to the keenest tension of excitement. He was equally susceptible to any current of emotion, to anger or mirth. He broke out indignantly: —

"Old man Griff hed better quit tryin' ter spite me. I 'll fix him fur it. I 'm goin' by thar this very night an' lift the mill gate an' set the wheel a-runnin'. It 'll be ez good ez a coon-fight ter see him kem out'n his house an' cuss!"

He burst into sudden laughter.

"Oh, ah! Oh, ah!" he sang, —

> "The wind blows brief, the moon hangs high;
> Oh, listen, folks! — the dead leaves fly.
> The witch air out with a broom o' saidge,
> Ter sweep 'em up an' over the aidge
> O' the new-made grave, ' ter hide,' she said,
> ' The prints o' my fingers buryin' the dead;
> Fur how he died — oh, ah! oh, ah!
> I 'd tell ef 't warn't fur the mornin' star.'"

His mellow, rich baritone voice, hilarious and loud, echoed far and wide, and incongruously filled the solemn solitudes.

"Who air a-goin' ter hear?" he demanded, when caution was suggested. "The herders on the mounting? Too fur off! Too high up! Asleep, besides."

"They 'd think 't war a wolf," said Peter Rood, still lying at length on the ground.

Mink had his sensibilities. On these harmonious numbers he piqued himself. He felt affronted.

"A leetle mo', an' I 'll break this jug over yer head. Nobody ain't a-goin' ter think ez my singin' air a wolf."

"Ye hand it hyar," said Pete; "nobody gits a fair show at that jug but you-uns." As he rose to his knees one foot caught in a grapevine, in his haste.

"Wait till it be empty," said Mink, making a feint of lifting it to his mouth. Then turning suddenly, he faced Pete Rood as he staggered to his feet, and dealt a blow which sent that worthy once more prone upon the ground.

There was a jumble of excited protest from the others, each vociferously trying to quiet his companions. Mink was squaring off with clenched fists.

"Kem on," he observed, "thar's ground enough hyar fur ez many ez kin kiver it."

"Look-a-hyar," exclaimed Jerry Price, whose grief that the placidities of the festivity should be frustrated very nearly resembled a regard for law and order, "ye two boys hev jes' got ter quit fightin' an' sech, an' spilin' the enjyement o' the rest o' we-uns. Quit foolin', Mink. Ye ain't hurt no-ways, air ye, Pete?"

"Laws-a-massy, naw," said Pete unexpectedly. "Mink never knocked me down nohow. I jes' cotched my foot in a grapevine. That's all."

But he lifted himself heavily, and he limped as he walked to a rock at a little distance and sat down.

Mink with his sudden change of temper let the encounter pass as a bit of fun. He referred to the jug frequently afterward, and again burst into song: —

> "Oh, ah! Oh, ah!
> The weevil's in the wheat, the worm's in the corn,
> The moon's got a twist in the eend o' her horn;
> Fur the witch, she grinned and batted her eye,
> An' gin 'em an ail ez she went by
> Ter fresk in the frost, 'an' show,' she said,
> 'I kin dance on my ankle-j'ints an' swaller my head,
> An' how I do it, oh, ah! oh, ah!
> I'd tell ef 't warn't fur the mornin' star.'"

The others joined tumultuously in the chorus. One sprang up, dancing a clumsy measure and striking his feet together with an uncouth deftness worthy of all praise in the estimation of his comrades. They broke into ecstatic guffaws, in the midst of which Mink's "Oh, ah! Oh, ah!" heralding the next verse, seemed a voice a long way off. Down the ravine was visible a collection of great white trees, girdled and dead long ago, standing in some field, all so tiny in the distance that it was as if the fingers of a ghostly hand had pointed upward at the group of revelers on the ridge.

The shadows had shifted, slanted. The moon was westering fast. Every gauzy effect of vapor had its fascination in the embellishing beam, and shone vaguely iridescent. All were drifting down the valley toward Chilhowee. Above them rose that enchanted mountain's summit, with its long irregular horizontal line, purple and romantic, suggestive of its crags, its caves, its forests, and its wild unwritten poetry. A star was close upon it. Peace brooded on its heights.

The prophecy of dawn was momently reiterated with fuller phrase, with plainer significance. Even Mink, reluctant to recognize it, yielded at last to Jerry Price's insistence. And indeed the jug was empty.

"Put the jug in the hollow tree, then, like we promised, an' let 's go," said Mink. "Mos' day, ennyhow. 'Oh, ah! Oh, ah! The daylight's apt ter break,' said the witch."

The jug was thrust in the hollow of the tree, and the drunken fellows, in the securities of their fancied quiet, went whooping through the woods. The owl's hoot ceased as their meaningless clamor rose from under the boughs. Now and then that crisp, matutinal sound, the vibrant chirp of half-awakened nestlings, jarred the air.

The group presently began to separate, some going down to Eskaqua Cove, where they would find their several homes if they could, but would at all hazards lay down their neighbors' fences. Rood lingered for a time with Mink and one or two others who cherished the design of seeing old man Griff's mill started before day. He turned off, however, when they had reached the open spaces of Piomingo Cove. It lay quiet, pastoral, encircled by the solemn mountains, with the long slant of the moonbeams upon it and the glister of the dew. The fields had all a pearly, luminous effect, marked off by the zigzag lines of the rail fences and the dark bushes that stood in corners. The houses, indicated by clumps of trees among which they nestled, were dark and silent. Not even a dog barked. When a cock crew the sudden note seemed clear and resonant as a bugle. "Crowin' fur fower o'clock," said Mink.

The road ran among woods much of the distance; through the trees could be caught occasional glimpses of the illuminated world without. But presently they gave way. A wide, deep notch in the summit of a mountain revealed the western sky. The translucent amber moon swung above these purple steeps, all suffused with its glamourous irradiation. Below, the shining breadth of the Scolacutta River swept down from the vague darkness. It was still night, yet one could see how the pawpaw and the laurel crowded the banks. The oblique line of the roof of the mill was drawn against the purple sky; its windows were black; its supports were reflected in the stream with a distinct reduplication; the water trickled down from crevices in the race with a lace-like effect, seeming never to fall, but to hang as if it were some gauzy fragment of a fabric. Beneath the great wheel, motionless, circular, shadowy, was a shoaling yellow light, pellucid and splendid, — the moon among the shallows.. The natural dam, a glassy cataract, bursting into foam and spray, was whitely visible, with surging rapids below. The sound seemed louder than usual; it deadened the snap when Mink cut a pole from a pawpaw tree and hastily trimmed the leaves. He climbed gingerly upon the timbers of the race, then paused, looked back, and hesitated.

The others had reined in their horses, and stood, ill-defined equestrian shadows, on the bank watching him.

He placed the pole beneath the lever by which the gate was raised, its other end being within the building. There was no sound but the monotone of the river. Then with a great creak the gate was lifted. The imprisoned water came through with a tumultuous rush. Mink felt the stir beneath as the wheel began to revolve. There was a sudden jar, a jerk, the structure swayed beneath him, a crash among the timbers, a harsh, wrenching sound as they tore apart. He saw the faint stars reel as in some distraught vision. He heard the wild exclamations of the men on the bank. He could not distinguish what they said, but with an instinct rather than any appreciation of cause and effect he tried to draw away the pole to let the gate down.

Too late. Through the sunken wreck of the race the water still poured over the madly plunging wheel. Mink sprang upon the bank, fell upon his hands and knees, and as he struggled to his feet he saw beneath the race the grotesque distortions of the simple machinery. Some villain's hand had adroitly contrived a series of clogs, each of insufficient weight to stop the wheel with the water still pouring over it, but as it crushed them — first an empty barrel, then a pole, then a fence-rail — giving it a succession of shocks that were fast breaking it in pieces. Thus what was designed for jest should result in destruction. The mill itself was a rotten old structure at best. Jarring with every convulsive wrench and jerk of the bewitched wheel, its supports tottered feebly in the water, and when all at once the race came down, and the wheel and the heavy beams were driven against its walls, for an instant it quivered, then careened, crashed. There was a great cloud of dust rising from the tumbled wreck on the bank. In the water, floating away on the swollen floods, were timbers, and barrels, and boards, and parts of the clapboard roof.

And then, from their midst, as if the old building had an appreciated agony in its dissolution, a great cry of pain went up. Mink turned with a white face, as he put his foot in the stirrup, to stare over his shoulder. Surely he was drunk, very drunk. Had the others heard? A twinkling light sprang up beyond the orchard boughs. The house had taken the alarm. His companions were getting away in haste. Sober enough for flight and flapping their elbows, they crowed in mockery. Mink leaped into his saddle to ride as ride he must, still looking with a lingering fear over his shoulder, remembering that quavering cry.

Was he drunk, or did he hear? Could any creature have been in the mill, undisturbed, — for they were so craftily quiet, — asleep till awakened by those death throes of the little building? Could it have been a pet fawn bleating with almost a human intonation in that common anguish of all life, the fear of death, — a pet cub? What! his heart ached for it, — he, the hardy hunter? Oh, was his conscience endowed with some subtle discernment more acute than his senses? It seemed a surly fate that had crept up on the unwitting creature in the dark, in the humble peace of its slumbers. And he was sorry, too, for the old man's mill; and then a vague terror possessed him when he thought of the trickery with the wheel. Surely the hand of another had compassed its destruction, yet when or why he could not understand, could not guess; or was he himself the miscreant? He could not remember what he had done; he had been so very drunk.

Ah, should he ever again see Chilhowee thus receive the slant of the sunrise, and stand revealed in definite purple heights against the pale blue of the far west? Should he ever again mark that joyous matutinal impulse of nature as the dawn expanded into day? The note of a bird, sweet, thrilling with gladness, came from the woods, so charged with the spirit of the morning that it might have been the voice of the light. And the dew was rich with the fragrance of flowers, and as he galloped along the bridle-path they stretched their rank growth across his way, sometimes smiting him lightly in the face, like a challenge to mirth. When he climbed the steep ridge from which were visible the domes of the Great Smoky, all massive and splendid against the dispersing roseate tints in the sky, the sunlight gushing down in a crimson flood while the dazzling focus rose higher than the highest bald, he cared less to look above than into the shadowed depths of Piomingo Cove. Did he fancy, or could he see a stir there? An atom slowly moved down the lane, and across the red clay slope of a hill, — another, and yet one more. Was the settlement already roused with the news of the disaster to the mill? He turned and pressed his mare along the rocky road, up slopes and down again, still ascending and descending the minor ridges that lie about the base of the Smoky. Sometimes he wondered at himself with a harsh, impersonal reprehension, as if his deed were another's. "How's the old man goin' ter make out ter barely live 'thout his mill?" he demanded of himself; "an' them gran'chil'n ter keer fur, an' Tad, an' all."

Then would come again the recollection of that strange muffled scream, and though the sun was warm he shivered.

Often he drew up the mare and listened with a vague sense of pursuit. Stillness could hardly be more profound. Not the stir of a leaf, never a stealthy tread. Then as he started again down the rocky way, some vagrant echo, or a stone rolling under his mare's hoof, would bring to him again that sudden affright, and he would swiftly turn to see who dogged him.

There were many curves in the path, and once in its opening vista he saw before him a girl with yellow hair outlined against the green and gold foliage of the sunlit woods, clad in brown homespun, partly leading and partly driving a dun-colored ox, with a rope knotted about his long horns.

She paused, swaying hard on it to check the animal, when she beheld the horseman, and her brown eyes were full of surprised recognition.

Mink gravely nodded in response to her grave salutation. He seemed at first about to pass without stopping, but when it was evident that she intended to let the ox trudge on he drew up the mare.

"Howdy, Lethe," he said.

"Howdy," returned Alethea.

"Enny news?"

She shook her head without speaking.

"Whar be ye a-goin' with Buck?" he asked.

"Arter the warpin' ars. They war loaned ter aunt Dely, an' she hain't got but one steer ter haul 'em home. So Buck hed ter go."

The ox had reached up his dun-colored head for the leaves, all green and flecked with golden light. She had loosed her hold upon the rope, and seriously gazed at Mink.

"I war down ter Crosby's yestiddy evenin'," he observed, watching her.

"I hopes ye enjyed yerse'f," she said, with tart self-betrayal.

He laughed a little, and turned the reins in his hands. He relished infinitely the sight of the red and angry spot on either cheek, the spark in her eye.

"I did," he said jauntily, noting the effect of his words. "I seen Elviry."

She made an effort at self-control.

"Waal," she returned, calmly, although her voice trembled a little, "I hope ye kin agree with her better 'n ye ever done with me. We war n't made fur one another, I reckon, no-ways."

"Oh, I hain't never axed Elviry; 't ain't never gone ez fur ez that. I 'lowed ez mebbe ye an' me mought make it up some day."

He was only trying her, but the vaunted feminine intuition did not detect this. Her cheek crimsoned. Her eyes were full of liquid lights. She laughed, a low gurgling laugh of happiness, that, nevertheless, broke into a sob.

"I dunno 'bout that," she said, evasively, belying the rapture in her face.

She was very beautiful at the moment. A cultivated man, versed in the harmonies of line and color, tutored to discriminate expressions and gauge feelings and recognize types, might have perceived something innately noble in her, foolish though the affection was which embellished her.

Even he was impressed by it. "I hev never axed nobody but ye," he said. "Not even arter we quar'led."

He was not bound by this, which he knew full well, and it promised nothing. But it held her love and loyalty for him, if ever he should want them.

Nevertheless, while he piqued himself on his domination, he was under her influence at the fleeting moment when he was with her. Perhaps her presence induced some tender affinity for the better things. He said with a sigh, "I hev done gone an' got in a awful scrape, Lethe. I reckon nobody never hed sech a pack o' troubles in this worl'."

With a sort of pitying deprecation of the wiles of old Tobias Winkeye she gravely listened. Once she unconsciously put up her hand and stroked his mare. He was petulant, like a spoiled child, when he told how he only meant a jest and such woful destruction had ensued. "An' me so boozy I dunno *what* I done. An' that thar pore old man! An' his mill plumb ruined! An' all his gran'chillen an' Tad ter keer fur!"

Her face had become very pale. Her voice trembled as she said, —

"Ain't sech agin the law, Reuben?"

She always called him by his name, rather than the sobriquet his pranks had earned. He was unfamiliar with himself thus dignified, and it gave him an added sense of importance.

"Yes, but 't ain't nuthin' but ten dollar fine, mebbe, an' a few days in jail,"— she gasped, — "*ef* they ketches me."

He looked at her with a swift, crafty brightness that was wonderfully like the little creature whose name he bore.

"I would n't keer fur that, though," he added after a pause. "Bein' in jail fur rollickin' roun' the kentry jes' fur fun ain't a disgrace, like fur stealin' an' sech. What pesters me so is studyin' 'bout the old man and his mill, plumb ruined. Lord! Lord! I 'd gin my mare an' hogs an' gun ef it hed never happened!"

She stood meditative and motionless against the leafy background, all dark and restful verdure close at hand, opening into a vista of luminous emerald lightened in the distance to a gilded green where the sunshine struck aslant with a climax of gold.

"I reckon ye think so, Reuben, but ye would n't," she said at last, with her fatal candor.

He winced. He was both hurt and angry as he rejoined, "An' why would n't I?"

"Why, ye be 'bleeged ter know ef ye war ter gin the old man yer mare an' gun an' hogs, he 'd be more 'n willin' ter gin it up agin ye. The mill stones air thar yit under the water, an' he could sell that truck o' yourn an' build ez good a shanty ez he hed afore, — better, 'kase 't would be new."

He looked down at her, tapping his heavy boot with the hickory switch in his hand.

"Ye ain't changed none, since we war promised to marry," he said slowly. "Then ye war forever a-jawin' an' a-preachin' at me 'bout what I done an' what I oughter do, same ez the rider. Ye talk 'bout jewty ez brash ez ef *ye* never hed none, same ez he does 'bout religion. He ain't hurt with *that*, ef ye watch him fresk 'round when they air pourin' him out a dram or settin' out the table. That 's sech grace ez he hev got, but he kin talk powerful sober ter other folks; jes' like you-uns. I 'm sorry I ever tole ye about it, ennyways. I 'm sorry I met up with ye this mornin' " —

The girl's face was as visibly pained as if he had cruelly struck her. He went on tumultuously, aggregating wrath and a sense of injury and a desire of reprisal with every word.

"I 'm sorry I ever seen ye! Ye 'mind me o' that thar harnt o' a Herder on Thunderhead the folks tells about. Ef ye happen ter kem upon him suddint, an' don't turn back but ketch his eye, that year air withered. Nuthin' ye plant will grow, an' ef the craps air laid by they won't ripen. He can't kill ye; he jes' spiles yer chance. An' ye 'minds me o' him."

"Oh, Reuben!" the girl cried, in deprecation.

"Ye do, — ye do! I tole ye, 'kase I 'lowed mebbe ye mought holp me, — more fool me! — leastways ye mought be sorry. Shucks! And now I 'm sorry I tole ye."

He struck the mare suddenly and slowly rode past. He glanced back once. If Alethea had been looking wistfully after him he might have paused. He expected it; he had even listened for her to call. The light fell with a rich tinge on her golden hair and her delicate profile as she reached up to adjust the rope on the long horns of the dun-colored ox. The vacillating color of the leaves shoaling in the wind and the sunshine seemed the more fantastic for the sober hue of her brown gown and the crude red clay path. Even when the ox resumed his journey she did not once look back, and presently the fluctuating leaves hid her from sight.

Mink's gust of temper had served to divert him for the moment from the contemplation of his perplexities. Now they reasserted themselves. Before, however, he had seen no hope of extrication. But Alethea's words had given him something. He began to appreciate the necessity of a definite plan of action. If he should go up to Piomingo Bald he would be taken at the herders' cabin by the officers of the law. His home could be no refuge. He felt a respite essential. He craved the time to think of Alethea's suggestion, to canvass the ground, to judge what was possible. At last he dismounted and turned his mare out; even here he could hear the occasional jangling bells of the herds, and the animal would soon follow the familiar sound. He took his way on foot down the mountain and through Eskaqua Cove. "The news 'll travel slower 'n me," he said.

He hardly felt hunger; he did not realize his fatigue. The red clay roads were vacant, the few daily passers were not yet astir. He avoided, as far as he might, the possibility of meeting them by taking short cuts over the mountains and through valleys. His instinct was to remove himself from his accustomed haunts. Nevertheless, he had no definite intention of hiding, for after traversing Hazel Valley, he struck boldly into the county road that leads up the eastern slope of Big Injun Mountain. He had no thought of resisting arrest. He walked along meditatively, hardly conscious even of the company of his shadow climbing the mountain with him, until he suddenly found that it had skulked away and he was bereft of this vague similitude of a comrade. For the sun was already west of Big Injun. A pensive shade lay far down the slope, but below there was again the interfulgent play of sunshine itinerant with the wind among the leaves.

Once he sat down on a rock close by the road, with his head in his hands and his elbows on his knees, and sought again to adjust his course to the best interests of conscience and policy. A woman with a bag of fruit on her back passed him presently. He replied to her "howdy;" then after a time rose and trudged up and up the road. He had known repentance before, for he was plastic morally. But in his experience there had been no perplexity. It seemed to him, with the urgency of decision and the turmoil of doubt pressing upon him, that it was happier to be resolutely reckless. The harassments of uncertainty had affected his nerves, and he gave a quick start when the abrupt jangle of a bell smote the air. On the opposite side of the road, among the great craggy steeps, there was a wide, low niche in the face of the cliff, with a beetling roof and a confusion of rocks and bushes below. Sheep had climbed into it; some were standing looking down at him, now and then stirring and setting the bell to clanking fitfully; others lay motionless in the shadowy nook. He was about to go on; suddenly he turned and began to scale the huge fragments of rock to the niche in the cliff.

"Ye clar out," he said to the sheep as they scuttled away at his approach; "ye hev got the very spot I want."

They huddled together as he crept in; two or three hastily ran out upon the rocks, — only a little frightened, for they began presently to nibble the grass growing in the rifts. He lay down, pillowing his head upon his arm, and turning his eyes on the scene without. He could see far below into the depths of Hazel Valley, with hill and dale in undulatory succession. The light glanced here and there on the minute lines of a zigzag fence; on a field in which the stark and girdled trees stood in every gaunt attitude of despair; on a patch striped with green where tobacco grew in orderly ranks, — all amongst the dense forests, upon which these tiny suggestions of civilization seemed only some ephemeral incident, ineffective, capable of slightest significance. Beyond, the wooded mountains rose in the densities of unbroken primeval wilderness, with irregular summit-lines, with graduating tones from bronze-green to blue-gray, with a solemnity that even the sunshine did not abate. Still further, the Great Smoky, veiled with mist and vague with distance, stood high against the sky, — so high that but for the familiar changeless outline it must have seemed the fiction of the clouds.

The sheep came back and crowded about him, — he lay so still. Once he was conscious of their motion; he intended to rouse himself in a moment and drive them off. And once afterward he was vaguely aware of the tinkle of the bell. Then he heard no more.

The afternoon wore on. The sunlight deepened to orange and burned to red. The mountains were all garbed in purple. The sky above that splendid summit-line of the Great Smoky caught the reflection from the west and was delicately roseate. Cow-bells were clanking in Hazel Valley, faintly, faintly. A star, most serene, was at the zenith.

The sheep in the dark niche of the crags stirred, and huddled together again, and were quiet. The moon came and looked coyly in, as if she sought Endymion. The face of the mountaineer, its reckless spirit all spent, was gentle and young in the soft, shy light.

All at once he was awake. The sheep were crowding timorously about him. A voice broke with sudden discord into the harmonies of the night.

"Nuthin' but sheep, I reckon."

There was a great scuffling among the rocks and bushes, and Mink ventured to lift his head.

He saw the mist-filled valley below; the glister of the moon in the skies above; the infinite expanse of mountain forms all along the background; and in the stony road on the verge of the precipice an equestrian group standing motionless in shadow and sheen.

He recognized the sheriff of the county among them, and the constable from Piomingo Cove was in the act of clambering up the rocks.

V.

The officer laid his hand on the jagged lower ledge of the niche. His hat and its shadow, like some double-headed monster, slowly appeared above the verge as he climbed the crag. The sheep shrank back precipitately into the cavernous place, their hoofs crowding over the young mountaineer. He lay at full length in motionless suspense.

There was a moment's pause. A cloud crossed the moon. Its shadow fell in Hazel Valley. A gust of wind stole along the mountain slopes, sighing as it went, as if its errand were of sorrow. Then, silence. The brilliant lustre burst forth again, suffusing the heights above and the depths so far below. In the midst of the craggy steeps the huddled sheep looked mildly down, with bright, apprehensive eyes, at the constable.

"Nuthin' but sheep," he said, scanning the interior of the niche.

It seemed to Mink, hidden by his fleecy comrades, that the stone walls of his refuge resounded with the loud throbbing of his heart, which must betray him.

"D' ye reckon," said the sheriff below, "ez that woman could hev made a mistake 'bout hevin' seen him on this road?"

"Mrs. Beale knows Mink Lorey ez well ez I do," declared the constable.

"Mought hev been foolin' us some," suggested the sheriff, suspiciously.

"She hain't got no call," the constable reasoned. As he partly stood on a sharp projection, and partly hung by one arm to the ledges of the niche, he took a plug of tobacco from his pocket and perilously gnawed at it.

"Waal, I reckon he ain't round hyar-abouts," said the sheriff, with an intonation of disappointment. "We hed better push on."

The double-headed monster, chewing as he went, the action reproduced in frightful pantomime on the floor of the cavern, slowly withdrew. There was heavy breathing; the sound of falling clods and fragments of rock, and of straining bushes and roots as the descending officer clutched them. A sudden final thud announced that he had sprung upon his feet on level ground.

A momentary interval, a clatter of hoofs, and the file of horsemen, with their mounted shadows erect upon the vertical cliffs of the rock-bound road, passed slowly along the wild, narrow way. Long after they had disappeared the sound of the hoof-beats intruded upon the stillness, and died away, and again smote the air with dull iteration, reverberating from distant crags of the winding road.

When all was still, Mink's mind turned again to his perplexities with a sharpened sense of the necessity of decision. The project which Alethea had suggested began to shape itself in his mind in full detail, as he lay there and thought it over. The alternative of skulking about to avoid arrest was too doubtful and limited to be contemplated.

"The sheriff air a-ridin' now," he said, "an' the constable too — an' what made 'em fetch along fower other men ez a posse?" he broke off suddenly, recognizing the incongruity.

His lip curled with satisfaction. "They mus' hev been powerful 'feared o' me," he said, his heart swelling with self-importance, "ter think 't would take six men ter arrest me fur a leetle job like that."

He appreciated, however, that the midnight caper at the mill had shaken all the securities of the mountain community, and it was to the immediate personal interest of every man within twenty miles that he should be dealt with as harshly as the law would allow. But if, he argued, without waiting for arrest, he should go down to-morrow, — not to old Griff (bold as he was, he hardly dared encounter the miller's rage), but to some man of influence, some mediator, old Squire White, perhaps, — and tell what he had done, and offer in reparation to give the miller all he possessed, his mare, his gun, his hogs, might he not thus avert the more serious phases of a prosecution, or perhaps escape altogether?

Turn as he might, he could see only the sacrifice of his little all as the price of his orgy.

"I'd hev ter pay it ter the lawyer ter defend me; or mebbe old Griff could git it out'n me ez damages ennyhow. I can't holp losing it. I'll gin it up, an' begin over, an' make it up with Lethe, — I don't keer a straw fur all the t'others, — an' git married an' be stiddy. I never war so wild nohow when me an' her war promised. Mebbe bein' jawed at, an' sech, air good fur folks, an' holped ter keep me quiet in them days, — leastwise ez quiet ez I war able ter be," he qualified, the recollection of sundry active vagaries constraining him.

Although doubts and fears still lurked in his mind, he found himself waiting for dawn, not with hope or impatience, but with the dull resolution of reluctant decision. He could hardly have said why, but he experienced a disappointment as he noted the weather signs. The mists thickened and pervaded the moonbeams in gigantic wavering spectral effects. Over toward the Great Smoky they slowly tended, those veiled mystic figures, with diaphanous trailing garments, and with sometimes a lifted hand as if to swear by the heaven it almost touched. He watched the throngs grow denser, lose the similitude of individuality, take on the aspect of lowering clouds. The moonbeams glittered faintly and failed. When the day broke at last, the light expressed itself only in the dull visibility of the enveloping vapors. Not the depths of Hazel Valley, not the slopes of Big Injun Mounting, could be seen as he clambered out of the niche and down upon the road. Even the log at its verge serving as a curb seemed a sort of defense against the usurping immateriality which had engulfed the rest of the world. He heard the moisture dripping from the summit of the craggy heights; sometimes, too, the quick, tumultuous patter of a shower in Hazel Valley, as if a cloud had lost its balance on the brink of the mountain and had fallen into the depths beneath.

He trudged along, seeing nothing but the blank inexpressiveness of the encompassing fog, with only the vaguest divination of the locality and the distance.

"I would n't feel so weighted ef the weather would clear," he said.

Once he paused, suddenly recollecting that the county court was in session, and that Squire White was doubtless at Shaftesville. When he thought of the unaccustomed scenes of the town, the people, their questions and comments, he wavered again. Then he remembered Alethea. "She 'lowed 't would be jestice an' the bes' ez I could do ennyhows, an' somehows the critter 'pears ter be right in her jedgmints. So I reckon I 'll jes' 'bide by Lethe's word."

Presently the mists began to lift. He could see along the green aisles of the forest how they wavered and shifted in the tops of the trees. Everywhere the flowers were blooming, — the trumpet blossom and the jewel-weed, the delicate lilac "Christmas flower," the "mountain snow," the red cardinal blossoms, and, splendid illumination of the woods, the Chilhowee lily. All along the wayside, silvery cascades tumbled over the rocks amongst fantasies of ferns, and the laurel and the ivy crowded the banks of the torrent. When he was fairly in the valley, fences bordered the road, with poke-berries darkly glittering in corners crowded with weeds. He was nearing Shaftesville now. A little house appeared here and there, a stretch of open land, stacks of fodder, an occasional passer.

High up in the air were suggestions of sunshine, yellow, diffusive, but not penetrating the vapors below. All at once the beams burst through. The mists dallied for a moment longer; then with a suggestion of spreading wings they rose in slow, shining, ethereal flights. Among them, as he skirted the crest of a hill, appeared the roofs of the little town, the tower of the court-house, the church steeple, all dissolving into invisibility like some vain vagary of the mist, as he descended into the intervenient dale.

The grass-grown streets were astir with jeans-clad countrymen already in with wagons drawn by oxen, or with a flock of bleating sheep running helter-skelter, and demonstrating their bucolic proclivities by a startling lack of adaptation to the thoroughfares of Shaftesville ; a few loungers were sitting on the barrels and boxes in front of the doors of the stores; Mink met no one he knew as he went. One man on the rickety steps of the courthouse knew him, perhaps, for he looked hard at him as he passed; then turned and stared after him with an expression which Mink could hardly analyze. He scowled fiercely in return, and took his way into the room in which several of the justices sat, amicably chatting together, for the day's proceedings had not yet been inaugurated. With a sudden irritation and bewilderment Mink beheld upon each countenance, the moment they caught sight of him, the same amazed intentness which had characterized the look of the man on the steps. He felt a sort of dull ache in his heart, a turbulence in his blood pulsing fast, a heavy, dazed consciousness which gave the scene the dim unreality of a dream: the sunshine, pale and flickering, outlining the panes of the windows on the dirty floor ; the stove, that stood in its place winter and summer; the circle of bearded, jeans-clad justices, all their faces turned toward him, seeming not unlike, with the same expression upon each.

Mink began abruptly, but with an effort, addressing the chairman. " I kem over hyar, Squair," he said, "'kase I wanter leave ter men what I done. I ain't goin' ter hide nuthin' nor run away from nuthin'. I ain't sayin' what I done war right, but I'm willin' ter abide by my deed ez fur ez leavin' it ter men, an' furder."

He was fluent now. There was an exhilaration in this

close attention from these men whom he esteemed mighty in the law, in this pose of importance before them, in the generosity of the offer he was about to make. He spoke responsive to the respectful surprise with which his fancy had endowed them.

"I war drunk, Squair. I ain't denyin' it none. Naw, sir, I ain't."

He nodded his head, and pushed his broad hat further back on his long, auburn locks.

"I 'll jes' tell ye how it war, Squair." He shifted his weight upon one stalwart leg, and bent over a little, and looked down meditatively at his boots as he arranged his ideas in his mind. "I war drunk, Squair," he reiterated, as he rose once more to the perpendicular. "How I kem so, it don't consarn me to say. But me an' old man Griff, we hed hed words 'bout my l'arnin' Tad ter play 'five corn'; he 'lowed 't war a gamblin' game, — mighty old-fashioned game, ye know yerself, Squair, — an' ez I kem along back that night I 'lowed I 'd start the mill an' see him run out skeered. An' I dunno what I done ter the wheel, but it jes' seemed ter be plumb 'witched when I lifted the gate. It jes' performed an' cavorted round like it hed the jim-jams; — ye never seen nuthin' act like it done sence ye war born, Squair. An' I tried ter let the gate down, but war plumb shuck off'n the race. An' the mill begun ter shake, Squair, an' fust I knowed down it went inter the ruver. An' ez I seen a light in the old man's house I 'lowed he war a-comin' fur me." He laughed a little. "Old Griff be a powerful survigrous old man when his dander hev riz, so I jes' rid off ez fas' ez I could."

There was no responsive smile upon the stony, staring faces turned toward him. But he was quite at ease now. He hardly cared to notice that a man went hurriedly out of the room and came back. "I 'm mighty sorry fur the old man, Squair," he resumed, "surely I am. An' ter prove it, me an' the gal I 'm a-goin' ter marry, we-uns 'greed tergether ez I 'd gin him my mare, an' my hogs, an' a gun, an' fower sheep, an' 't would build him another mill better 'n the one he hed, ef he could git the mill-stones hefted. I 'd go holp myself."

Still not a word from the justices. Other men had begun to come in. They, too, stood silently listening. Mink was all debonair and cheery again, so fairly had he exploited his mission. As to the man who had gone out and returned, Mink stared hard at him, for he was not an acquaintance, yet he approached and held out his hand. Mink slowly extended his own. A sudden grip of iron encircled the unsuspecting member; the other hand was caught in a rude grasp. A harsh, grating sound, the handcuffs were locked upon his wrists, and the deputy sheriff lifted a countenance scarlet with repressed excitement. He passed his hands quickly all along the prisoner's side to make sure that he carried no concealed weapons, then ejaculated, "Now ye 're all right!"

The young mountaineer's head was in a whirl. His heart beat tumultuously. His voice sounded to him far away. His volition seemed to rebel. Surely he did not utter the stammering, incoherent, foaming curses that he heard. They terrified him. He strove with futile strength to tear off these fetters, every muscle strained. For the first time in his life, he, the wild, free creature of the woods, felt the bonds of constraint, the irking touch of a man he could not strike. Old Squire White, who had moved out of the way with an agility wonderful in a man of his years, exhorted the deputy to his duty.

"Ye mus' gin him the reason fur his arrest, ez he hev axed fur it, Mr. Skeggs, sech bein' the law o' Tennessee. Ye 'd better tell him, sence the sher'ff hev kerried off the warrant, that he air arrested fur the drownding o' Tad Simpkins."

Mink hardly heard. He did not heed. He only tore desperately at the handcuffs, every cord standing out, every vein swelled to bursting; stamping wildly about while the scuttling, excited crowd nimbly kept out of his way. He turned the glare of reddened eyes upon the deputy, who mechanically repeated the justice's words, still following the prisoner with soothing insistence. Suddenly Mink made a burst toward the door; he was seized by a dozen willing hands, thrown down and pinioned. He fainted, perhaps, for it was only the free outer air that roused him to the knowledge that he was borne through the streets, followed by a gaping, hooting crowd, black and white. Then ensued another interval of unconsciousness. When he came to himself he stared blankly at his unfamiliar surroundings.

He was alone. He felt weak, sore. He turned his bewildered eyes toward the light. The window was barred. He sprang up from the bed on which he lay, and tried the door. He beat upon it and shouted in baffled rage. Stealthy footsteps sounded outside from time to time, excited whispers, and once a low titter.

Somehow, ridicule conquered him as force could not. He slunk back to the bed, and there he lay quiet, that no stir might come to the mocker without. Sometimes he would lift his head and listen with a sort of terror for the step, for the suppressed breathing, for the low laugh. Often his eyes would rest, dilated, fascinated, on the door. Then he would fall back, reviewing futilely the scenes through which he had passed. What was that strange thing they had said? It was indistinct for a time; he could not constrain his reluctant credulity. But those terrible words, the drowning of Tad Simpkins, beset his memory, and came back to him again and again. And then he recalled that weird cry from out the crash of the falling timbers of the mill. Could the ill-treated little drudge have slept there? He had a vague idea that he had once heard that when the old man was angry he would swear that he would not give Tad house-room, and would cast him out into the night, or shut him into the mill and lock the door upon him. And remembering that cry of despair, so anguished an echo rose to Mink's lips that he turned and buried his head in the pillow because of the scoffer in the hall without.

The room darkened gradually; shadows were glooming about him. The moon rose after a time. The beams in radiant guise came slanting in, and despite the bars stood upon the floor, a lustrous presence, and leaned against the wall. It reminded him of the angel of the Lord, — tall, ethereal, fair, and crowned with an amaranthine wreath, — who burst the bars and appeared to the disciple in prison. With that arrogation of all spiritual bounties, so pathetically human, he perceived no incongruity that such a similitude should appear to him. In some sort it comforted him. It moved from time to time, and slowly crossed, pace by pace, the floor of the cell.

VI.

THAT terrible isolation of identity, the burden of individuality which every man must bear alone, is never so poignantly appreciated as when some anguish falls on the solitary soul, while those who would wish to share it are unconscious and others uncaring.

News, the worldling, was never a pioneer, and hangs aloof from the long stretches of the wildernesses of the Great Smoky Mountains. It seemed afterward to Alethea that she had lacked some normal faculty, to have been so tranquilly uncognizant, so heedlessly placid, in the days that ensued. The glimpse of the world vouchsafed to Wild-Cat Hollow was silent, peaceful, steeped in the full, languorous sheen of the midsummer sun. To look down upon the cove, with its wooded levels, its verdure, its silver glint of waters, and its sheltering mountains, it might have seemed only the scene of some serenest eclogue — especially one afternoon when the red west flung roseate tints upon the strata clouds and the delicate intervenient spaces of the pale blue heavens, and suffused the solemn ranges and the quiet valley with a tender glamour. The voices projected upon this mute placidity had a strident emphasis. There was the occasional clamor of guinea-fowls about the barn, and some turkeys were flying up to roost on the naked boughs of a dead tree, drawn in high relief and sharp detail against the sky; they fluttered down often, with heavy wings, and ungainly flappings, and discordant cries, in their vain efforts to settle the question of precedence that harassed them. The lowing of the homeward-bound cows had fugue-like communings with their echoes. Alethea, going out to meet them, doubted within herself at times whether they had crossed the mountain stream that coursed through Wild-Cat Hollow. The blackberry brambles swayed full fruited above it; in the lucid, golden-brown, gravelly depths a swift shadow darted, turned, cleft the surface with a fin, and was gone. A great skeleton tree, broken half-way, hollow long ago, stood on the bank, rotted by the winter's floods that ceaselessly washed it when the stream was high, and bleached by the summer's suns to a bone-like whiteness. A great ball of foam, mysterious sport of the waters, caught in an eddy, was whirling giddily. One could fancy a figure of some fine ethereal essence might just have been veiled within it. The woods, dense, tangled with vines, sombre with shadows, bore already the downcast look of night. Alethea eyed them languidly as she came down to the lower fence, her piggin on her head, one hand staying it, while the other gave surreptitious aid to the efforts of L'onidas and Lucindy to take down the bars, as they piqued themselves upon rendering her this stalwart service. Tige had come too, and now and then he pawed and pranced about the calves, that were also expectantly waiting at the opening of the inclosure. One of them who had known him of yore only lifted his ears and fixed a remonstrant stare upon him. But the other, young and of an infantile expression, ran nimbly from him, and bleated plaintively, and pressed in between Alethea and the children, in imminent danger of having his brains knocked out in the wild handling of the bars.

"That's enough," she drawled presently, moderating their energies; "the calf 'll git out ef ye take down enny mo'. The cow kin step over sech ez be left."

The faint clanging of cow-bells stirred the air. The little house on the rise at one side was darkly brown against the irradiated mountains seen in the narrow vista of the gap. The martins fluttered from the pendulous gourds and circled about the chimneys, and were gone again. The sky cast its bright gold about the Hollow, on the tow heads of the barefoot children, and multiplied the shimmers in the swirls of the stream.

Alethea looked once more toward it, hearing again the far-off lowing. A sudden movement attracted her eye. Against the great hollow whitened tree a man was leaning, whittling a stick with a clasp-knife, and now and then furtively eying her.

For a moment she did not move a muscle. The color surged into her face, and receded, leaving it paler than before. A belated humming-bird, its breast a glistening green, beat the air with its multiplied suggestions of gauzy wings close to her golden head, and was gone like a flash. The children babbled on. Tige was afraid of a stick which L'onidas had brought to keep off the calf while the cow was milked, and he yelped before he was struck, without prejudice to yelping afterward.

The man presently drew himself erect, closed his knife with a snap, and walked up slowly toward the fence.

"Howdy?" he said, as he came.

She leaned one elbow on the rails, and with the other hand she held the empty piggin. She only nodded in return.

He had an embarrassed, deprecatory manner. He was tall and lank, and clumsy of gait. He had an indifferent, good-natured expression, incongruous with the gleam of anxiety in his eye. His face was almost covered by a long, straggling brown beard.

"What made ye run off so t' other night down yander ter Boke's Spring? I hed a word ter say ter ye."

"I war sorry I seen ye."

He fixed a keen look upon her.

"What fur?"

"I did n't want ter know who 't war a-moonshinin'," she said.

"Waal, ye air the only one," he declared.

He looked about him dubiously.

"I ain't keerin' none," he added. "Me an' yer mother war kin somehow; I disremember how, edzac'ly — through the Scruggses, I reckon. Ef she war alive she 'd gin ye the word ez she air kin ter Sam Marvin, sure. Nobody ain't 'spicioned nuthin' 'bout moonshinin' but you-uns, 'cept them ez be in it."

He put his hands in his pockets and leaned against the fence. The clanking of the cow-bell was nearer. The little calf bleated, and thrust its soft head over the bars.

"I wanted ter say a word ter ye," he continued, still more ill at ease because of her silence. "I seen ye comin' along o' all them chill'n," nodding at Leonidas and Lucinda, who seemed to deserve being accounted more numerous than they were, having engaged in a wordy altercation over the bars; the little fellow dragging them off to some special spot which he had chosen, of occult advantage, while the girl, older and wiser, insisted that they should lie handy where they were. Only Tige listened to the conversation, slowly wagging his tail. "I 'lowed I could n't talk ter ye 'thout bein' hendered, but I reckon I 'll try. I 'm kin ter ye, — that be a true word. An' I 'm moonshinin'. Ye ain't tole nobody 'bout seein' me an' the jug thar in Boke's barn?"

He fixed his eyes, eager with the query, upon her face.

She slowly shook her head in negation.

"An' ye won't, eh?"

He smiled beguilingly, showing his long, tobacco-stained teeth.

"Ef nobody axes me."

His countenance fell suddenly.

"Look-a-hyar, Lethe Sayles, don't ye fool with me, a-doublin' on yer words like a fox on his tracks," he said roughly. Then, more temperately, "I 'm afeard o' that very thing, — ef somebody axes ye."

"'T ain't likely," said Alethea.

"I dunno," he insisted, wagging his big head in doubtful pantomime. "I want ye ter 'low ye won't tell."

"I don't b'lieve in sech ez moonshinin' an' drinkin' liquor."

"What fur?" he demanded, with an air of being ready for argument.

"'T ain't religion."

"Shucks!" exclaimed Sam Marvin contemptuously. "D' ye reckon ef 't war n't religion I 'd plant corn an' raise my own damnation, an' sit an' bile wrath, an' still fury, an' yearn Torment, by sech? Naw, sir! Ye oughter go hear the rider read the Bible: every one o' them disciples drunk low wines in them days, an' hed it at weddin's an' sech; the low wines is on every page."

Alethea was for a moment overborne by this argument.

Then, "'T ain't right," persisted the zealot of Wild-Cat Hollow.

"Will ye listen at the gal!" he exclaimed, in angry apostrophe. But controlling himself, he added quietly, "Ye let older heads 'n yourn jedge, Lethe. Yer brains ain't ripened yit, an' livin' off in Wild-Cat Hollow ye ain't hed much chance ter see an' l'arn. Yer elders knows bes'. That's what the Bible says."

Down the shadowy vista of the path on the opposite side of the stream the long horns and slowly nodding heads of the cows appeared. The little calf frisked with nimble joy on legs that seemed hardly bovine in their agility. Lucinda ran to bring the pail of bran, and Leonidas produced a handful of salt in a small gourd. The moonshiner saw that his time was short.

"What ails ye, ter think 't ain't right, Lethe?" he asked.

"Look how good-fur-nuthin' it makes Jacob Jessup, an'—an' Mink Lorey, an' all them boys in Piomingo Cove."

"It's thar own fault, not the good liquor's. Look at me. I ain't good-fur-nuthin'. Ever see me drunk? How be I a-goin' ter keer fur sech a houseful ez we-uns hev got 'thout stillin' the corn? Can't sell the corn 'n the apples nuther, an' can't raise nuthin' else on the side o' the mounting, an' I 'm too pore ter own lan' in the cove."

The cows were fording the stream. The water foamed about their flanks. Their breath was sweet with the mountain grasses.

He looked at Alethea, suspiciously.

"Ye ain't goin' ter promise me ye won't tell ef ye be axed?" he said, with an air of finality.

In her heart the compact of secrecy was already secure. Somehow she withheld the assurance. It was all wrong, she felt. And if in fear he should desist, so much the safer for him, so much the better would the community fare.

"I ain't a-goin' ter promise nuthin'," she said, slowly, her lustrous eyes full upon his face. "I ain't goin' ter do nuthin' ter holp along what ain't right."

"Waal, then, Lethe Sayles, ye jes' 'member ez ye war warned," he said, in a low, vehement voice, between his set teeth, and coming up close to her. "An' ef ever we-uns air fund out an' raided, we-uns will keep in mind ez nobody knowed but you-uns; an' whether we be dragged off ter jail an' our still cut up an' sech or no, ye won't git off scot-free. Ye mark my words. Ye air warned."

She had shrunk from his glittering eyes and angry gestures. Nevertheless, she struck back with ready sarcasm.

"Then, mebbe I won't tell," she said, in her soft drawl, "fur I be toler'ble easy skeered."

He stared at her in the gathering dusk; then turned, and took his way across the mossy log that bridged the stream and down the path through the woods.

For a moment she had an overwhelming impulse to call him back. Long afterward she had cause to remember its urgency. Now she only leaned upon the rail fence, even her golden hair dim in the closing shadows, and gazed with uncomprehended wistfulness after him as he disappeared down the path, and reappeared in a rift of the foliage, and once more disappeared finally.

And here the cow's great head was thrust over the

bars, and L'onidas was on hand in full force to engage in combat with the little calf, and Lucindy was alert with the bucket of bran. All through the milking Alethea was sensible of a yearning regret in her heart. And although she had the testimony of good conscience and could say in full faith, " 'T ain't right," she was not consoled.

She lifted the pail of milk to her head, and as they went back to the log cabin the moon projected their grotesque shadows as a vanguard, and for all Leonidas ran he could not overtake the quaint little man that led the way.

Stars were in the sky, aloof from the moon. A mocking-bird sang on an elder-bush among the blossoms, fragrant and white; and from time to time, as he joyously lifted his scintillating wings, the boughs seemed enriched with some more radiant bloom. The rails of the fence had a subdued glimmer, — the moonlight on the dew.

Her heart, with its regretful disquiet, was out of harmony with the nocturnal peace of the scene; she had somehow an intimation of an impending sorrow before she heard the sound of sobbing from the porch.

The vines that clambered about it were drawn upon the floor with every leaf and tendril distinct. The log cabin was idealized in some sort with the silver lustre of the moon, the glister of the dew, the song of the bird, and the splendid suggestions of the benighted landscape; yet there was the homely loom, the spinning-wheel and its shadow, the cat in the doorway, with the dull illumination of the smouldering fire behind her, eying a swift, volant shadow that slipped in and out noiselessly, and perhaps was a bat. A group of figures stood in the tense attitudes of listening surprise. But a girl had flung herself upon the bench of the loom, now leaning against the frame and weeping aloud, and now sitting erect and talking with broken volubility.

"Hyar be Elviry Crosby," Mrs. Sayles said, as Alethea stepped upon the porch and set the piggin on the shelf.

The visitor looked up, with her dark eyes glistening

with tears. Her face was pale in the moonbeams. She had short dark hair, thin and fine, showing the shape of her delicate head, and lying in great soft rings about her brow and neck. As she spoke, her quivering red lips exhibited the small, regular white teeth. She was slight and about the medium height, and habited in a yellowish dress, from which the moonlight did not annul the idea of color.

"I ain't got no gredge agin Lethe," she said, gazing at her with a certain intentness, "but I hev got my feelin's, an' I hev got my pride, an' I ain't goin' ter hev no jail-bird a-settin' up ter me! I'm sorry I ever seen him!" she declared, with a fresh burst of tears, throwing herself back against the loom. "But ez Lethe never hed nobody else, *she* mought put up with the raccoon ez he fetched me, — fur I won't gin the critter house-room, now."

As Alethea gazed at her, amazed and uncomprehending, a sudden movement on the loom caught her attention. About the clumsy beams a raccoon was climbing nimbly, turning his eyes upon her, full of the peculiar brightness of the night-roaming beast. She noticed his grin as he hung above the group, as if he perceived in the situation humor of special zest.

"I ain't a-goin' ter keep it!" cried Elvira. "All the kentry will be tellin', ennyhow, ez I hev kep' company with a murderer." A low, muffled cry escaped from Alethea's lips. "He kem a-makin' up ter me till I went an' turned off Pete Rood, ez war mad ez hops. I can't hender 'em from knowin' it. But I ain't a-goin' ter hev that thar spiteful leetle beast a-grinnin' at me 'bout'n it, like he war makin' game o' me fur bein' sech a fool. I'd hev killed it, 'ceptin' I 'lowed thar hed been enough onnecessary killin' along o' Mink Lorey."

"Elviry!" exclaimed Alethea, her voice so tense, so vibrant, so charged with anguish, that, low as it was, it thrilled the stillness as a shriek might hardly do, "what hev Reuben done?"

"Oh, 'Reuben,' ez ye calls him," cried the other, sitting upright on the bench of the loom, her dark eyes flashing and dry, — "yer fine Reuben tore down old Griff's mill, an' drownded his nevy, Tad, an' war put in jail, an' air goin' ter be tried, an' hung, I reckon. That's what 'Reuben' done! He's Mink by name an' Mink by natur' — an' oh! I wish I hed never seen him."

She once more leaned on the loom behind her, and bowed her head on her hands.

"No! — no!" cried Alethea. She caught her breath in quick gasps; for one moment she seemed losing consciousness. The mountains in the background, the faint stars in the sky, the shadowy roof, the swaying vines, the raccoon in their midst with his grotesque grin, were before her suddenly as if she had just awakened. She had sunk into a chair.

"Ye kin call me a liar! So do!" cried Elvira, lifting her head defiantly. "But he went hisself down ter the court-house an' told it hisself, an' wanted ter gin his gun an' mare ef they'd let him off." She laughed — a dainty little laugh of scorn. "That's what he 'lowed the idjit war wuth. But my dad 'lows ez the law sets store on the idjit's life same ez folks ginerally."

Alethea felt as if she were turning to stone. Was it her advice that had led him into danger? Was it her fatal insistence that he should see the right as it was revealed to her?

She sprang to her feet, the eager questions crowding to her lips.

"Ye shet up, Lethe!" said her step-mother, entertained by the unwonted spectacle of Elvira's dramatic grief, and not caring to hear again the news of the tragedy already recited. As to Mink, he had only been overtaken by the disasters which must have fallen upon him sooner or later, and he was in many ways a good riddance. This phase was uppermost in her mind when she said, "Ye see now what gals git fur goin' agin thar elders' word. I'll be bound, Elviry, 't war n't yer mother's ch'ice fur ye ter take Mink an' gin Pete Rood the go-by."

"That it war n't!" cried the repentant Elvira, with a gush of tears. "I wish I hed bided by her word! I reckon I war born lackin'! I hev been sech a fool!"

Mrs. Sayles turned to look at Alethea and nod her head in triumphant confirmation. Then she remarked consolingly, "Waal, waal, I reckon ye kin toll Pete Rood back."

"I dunno," sobbed Elvira. "I met him yestiddy at the cross-roads in Piomingo Cove, an' he jes' turned his head aside an' walked by 'thout nare word. I wish — oh, I wish I hed never seen that thar minkish Mink."

"Waal," said Mrs. Sayles, who was very human, and who, despite her sympathy for Elvira, had a rankling recollection of her taunt for Alethea's paucity of the material for "keeping company," "I hopes Lethe 'll take warnin', an' not fling away her good chance, fur the sake o' the wuthless, like Mink an' sech."

"Who be her good chance?" exclaimed Elvira, the jealousy nourished on general principles checking her grief.

"Shucks, child! ye purtendin' not ter know ez Ben Doaks hev mighty nigh wore out his knee-pans a-beggin' an' a-prayin' Lethe ter listen ter him!"

Elvira was meeker after this, and presently rose to go.

"I hed ter kem arter dark, else I could n't hev hed Sam an' the mare, bein' ez she hev been workin' in the field ter-day," she remarked.

There was the mare dozing at the gate, and Sam, a boy with singularly long legs and arms, looking something like an insect of the genus *Tipula*, was waiting too. She mounted behind him, and together they rode off in the moonlight, taking their way over the nearest ridge, and so out of sight.

"Waal, waal, sir!" exclaimed Mrs. Sayles, as she reseated herself on the porch, with her knitting in her hand, "that thar Mink Lorey never hed no jedgmint noways. He could n't hev tuk ch'ice of a wuss time ter git fetched up afore a court 'n jes' now. Squair White tole me ez our Jedge Averill hev agreed ter exchange with Jedge Gwinnan from over yander in Kildeer County nex' term, ez he can't try his cases, bein' kin ter them ez air lawing. So Gwinnan will hold court in Shaftesville nex' term. I 'd hate mightily fur sech a onsartin, onexpected critter ez him ter hev enny say-so 'bout me or mine. But shucks! Men folks ennyhow," she continued, discursively, her needles swiftly moving, as if they were endowed with independent volition, and needed no supervision, " air freakish, an' fractious, an' sot in thar way, an' gin ter cur'ous cavortin'. It never s'prised me none ez arter the Lord made man he turned in an' made woman, the fust job bein' sech a failure."

There was a pause. The regular metre of the katydid's song pulsed in the interval. The dewdrops glimmered on the chickweed by the porch. The fragrance of mint and ferns was on the air, and the smell of the dark orchard. Now and then an abrupt thud told that a great Indian peach had reached the measure of ripeness and had fallen. Through the open window and door the moonlight lay in glittering rhomboids on the puncheon floor. All the interior was illuminated, and the grotesque figure of the pet cub was distinctly visible to Jacob Jessup, who was lounging on the porch without, as the creature stole across the floor, and rose upon his hind legs to reach the pine table. As he thrust his scooping claw into the bread trough, — the long, shallow, wooden bowl in which batter for corn-dodgers was mixed, — he turned his cautious head to make sure he was unobserved, and his cunning, twinkling eyes met Jessup's. Somehow the sudden consciousness of the creature, his nervous haste to be off, appealed to Jessup's lenient mood. He listened to the scuttling claws on the puncheon floor as the beast hurried out of the back door, and while he debated whether or not he should play informer, his wife, sitting on the doorstep with the baby in her arms, asked suddenly, —

"'Pears like ye air sorter sot agin this Jedge Gwinnan, mother. I never hearn afore ez ye knowed him whenst ye lived in Kildeer County. What sorter man be he?"

Mrs. Sayles wagged her head inside her sun-bonnet to intimate contempt.

"A young rooster, 'bout fryin' size," she said, laughing sneeringly, the scorn accented by her depopulated gums. It seemed very forlorn to be laughed at like that.

"Waal, a man can't be 'lected jedge till he's thirty," said Jessup, consciously imparting information. "He's been on the bench right smart time, too."

Mrs. Sayles looked at him over her spectacles, still knitting, as if her industry were a disconnected function.

"What air thirty?"

"Waal" — began Jessup, argumentatively, puffing at his cob pipe. Thirty seemed to him a mature age. And the constitution of the State evidently presumes folly to be permanent if it is not in some sort exorcised before reaching that stage of manhood. He did not continue, however, seeing that thirty was held to be very young by Mrs. Sayles, who, to judge from her wrinkles, might be some four or five hundred.

"I ain't 'quainted with the man myself," she went on presently, "an' what's more I ain't wantin' ter be. But," impressively, "I know a woman ez knowed that man's mother whenst he war a baby. She 'lowed he war a powerful cantankerous infant, ailin' an' hollerin' all night an' mighty nigh all day; could n't make up his mind ter die, an' yit war n't willin' ter take the trouble ter live."

Jessup felt it a certain injustice that the nocturnal rampages of infancy should be as rancorously animadverted upon as the late hours of a larger growth.

"Waal, Jedge Gwinnan is powerful pop'lar now'-days," he urged. "He made a mighty fine race when he war 'lected."

"Shucks! ye can't tell me nuthin'!" said his mother, self-sufficiently. "I know all 'bout him, an' Jedge Burns too, ez war on the bench afore Jeemes Gwinnan. Whenst

I war a widder-woman an' lived in Kildeer County we-uns useter hev Jedge Burns on the circuit. He war a settled, middle-aged man 'bout fifty, an' the law war upheld, an' things went easy, an' he war 'lected time arter time, till one year they all turned crazy 'bout this hyar feller, ez war run by his party through fools bein' sca'ce, I s'pose. Jeemes war 'lected. I tell ye I know all 'bout him. He war born right yander nigh Colbury, an' I know a woman ez useter be mighty friendly with his mother."

"What fambly in Colbury did he marry inter?" asked her daughter-in-law, more interested in items of personal history than in his judicial record.

"Bless yer soul, he air a single man. His heart air set on hisself. He would n't marry no gal 'thout she hed some sorter office she could 'lect him ter, ez be higher 'n jedge. He be plumb eat up with scufflin' an' tryin' ter git up in the world higher 'n the Lord hev set him, an' 't ain't religion; that 't ain't. He minds me o' Lucifer. He 'll fall some day. Not out o' heaven, mebbe, 'kase he ain't never goin' ter git thar, but leastwise out'n his circuit. Somebody 'll top him off, an' mebbe I 'll live ter see the day. I dunno, though, I — Laws-a-massy!" she exclaimed, so suddenly that both her listeners started, "look-a-yander at that thar perverted tur-r-key hen an' her delikit deedies, ez air too leetle ter roost! She's a-hoverin' of 'em in that thar tall grass, wet with the dew, an' it 'll be the death o' 'em! Why n't Lethe tend ter 'em when she kem up from milkin'? Lethe! Lethe! Whar 's that gal disappeared ter?"

With the vagrant instinct of the wild fowl still strong in the domesticated turkey, she had distrusted the hen-house, and because of her brood she was prevented from roosting high up in the old dead tree.

There was no answer to Mrs. Sayles's call. The daughter-in-law made a feint of busily rocking the baby, and after a doubtful glance at her Mrs. Sayles got up briskly, putting her knitting-needles into her ball of yarn, and thrusting them both into her deep pocket. She clutched her bonnet further forward on her head, took up a splint basket, and presently there arose a piping sound among the weeds, as she darted this way and that in the moonlight with uncanny agility, catching the deedies one by one and transferring them to her basket. The turkey hen, her long neck stretched, her wings outspread, ran wildly about, now and then turning and showing irresolute, futile fight for a moment, and again striving to elude the whole misfortune with her long, ungainly strides. When Mrs. Sayles in triumph unbent her back for the last time and started toward the house, the fluttered mother following, clamoring hysterically, she exclaimed:

"Whar *be* that thar triflin' Lethe?"

"'Pears like ter me ez I hearn Lethe go up the ladder ter the roof-room a consider'ble while ago," said the old man slowly, speaking for the first time during the evening.

Once more Mrs. Sayles paused irresolute.

"Laws-a-massy, then, ef the gal's asleep I reckon I mought ez well put the tur-r-key an' deedies inter the hen-house myse'f; but 'pears ter me the young folks does nuthin' nowadays but doze."

She took a step further, then suddenly bethought herself. "Hyar, Jacob," she said to her son, handing him the basket, "make yerse'f nimble. I reckon ye hev got sense enough ter shet that thar tur-r-key an' deedies up in the hen-house. Leastwise I'll resk it."

Sleep was far from Alethea that night. For hours she sat at the roof-room window, looking out with wide, unseeing eyes at the splendid night. And so she had given her counsel freely in the full consciousness of right, and the man she loved had done her bidding. What misery she had wrought! She winced to know how his thoughts must upbraid her. She remembered his petulant taunts, his likening her to the Herder on Thunderhead, whose glance blights those on whom he looks; and she wondered vaguely if the harnt knew the woe it was his fate to wreak, and if it were grief to him as he rode in the clouds on the great cloud-mountain.

"I reckon I know how he feels," she said.

An isolated star blazing in the vast solitudes of the sky above the peak of Thunderhead burst suddenly into a dazzling constellation before her eyes, for she felt the hot tears dropping down one by one on her hand.

Alas, Alethea! one needs to be strong to attain martyrdom for the sacred sake of the right.

Her tears wore out the night, but when the sun rose she was fain to dry them.

VII.

THE site of the old mill continued the scene of many curious groups long after all efforts for the recovery of the body had ceased. The river was dragged no more, and hope was relinquished. There had never been any strong expectation of success. The stream was abnormally high considering the season of the year, and running with great impetuosity. Though with the aggregations of its tributaries swollen by the late rains it had the volume of a river, it retained all the capricious traits of the mountain torrent which it had been. It was full of swirling rapids, of whirlpools, of sudden cataracts. Its bed was treacherous with quicksands and rugged with bowlders. Hitched to the miller's orchard fence were rows of horses, dozing under their old Mexican saddles or the lighter weight of a ragged blanket or a folded quilt; teams of oxen stood yoked under the trees of the open space beyond; children and dogs sat on the roots or lay in the grass, while the heavy, jeans-clad figures of the mountaineers explored the banks as they chewed their quids with renewed vigor, and droned the gossip in drawling voices.

The same faces were seen day after day, — often enough to excite no particular remark that, whoever came or was absent, Peter Rood was here with the dawn, and night found him still strolling along the banks, looking upon the swollen floods with gloomy, insistent dark eyes, as if he were seeking to read in the writhing lines of the current the inscrutable secret of the Scolacutta River. Sometimes, with his hands in his pockets, his lowering face shadowed by his broad hat, he would silently listen to the speculations of those who found solace for the futility of the undertaking in the enlarged conjectural field which failure afforded, discussing the relative probabilities whether the body had floated down to the Tennessee River, or whether it had been engulfed by the quicksands and buried forever, or caught among the rocks of the jagged bank and wedged in, to be found some day — a ghastly skeleton — by a terrified boy, fishing or wading at low water.

It was only when these bootless surmises had palled at last, through many repetitions and lack of further developments, that the ruins of the old mill asserted an interest. There seemed a strange hush on the landscape, here where the wheel would whir no more. A few timbers scattered about, a rotten old stump that had served as part of the foundation, the hopper washed up by the waters, several of the posts which had upheld the race, were all that was left of the old mill, so long the salient feature of the place that more than one mountaineer was beset with bewilderment at the sight, — the recollection of the oblique line of the roof against the mountain, the open door, the reflections in the water, having more reality than the bereft bank of the river.

And now the old miller — seeming older than before — was wont to come tottering out with his stick, the gay sunshine on his long, white hair, and sit on the broken timbers, forlorn amidst the ruins of his poverty. At first his appearance created renewed excitement, and his old customers and friends pressed up to speak to him and hear what he would say, feeling a certain desire to mark the moral phenomena of loss and the fine processes of grief. But he held his clasped hands upon the stick, and silently shook his bowed gray head in his ragged old hat.

"I reckon ye 'd better leave him alone," his pretty granddaughter said; for she always accompanied him, and stood, as radiant as youth may ever be, twirling the end of her tattered apron between her fingers, her tangled yellow hair, like skeins of sunshine, hanging down on her shoulders, and her blue, undismayed eyes looking with a shallow indifference upon the scene. It was replete with interest and curiosity, not to say awe, to the little four-year-old sister who hung upon her skirts, or thrust a tow head from behind her grandfather. Sometimes her lips were wreathed with a smile as she saw some child in the crowd, but if the demonstration were returned she straightway hid her head in the old man's sleeve and for a while looked out no more.

Once old Griff spoke suddenly. "'Gustus Tom," for his favorite kept beside him, "ye would n't treat nobody mean, would ye?"

"Would ef they treated me mean," said 'Gustus Tom, with an unequivocal nod, which intimated that his code of ethics recognized retribution. "'Thout," he qualified, "'t war sister Eudory thar," — he glanced at the little girl, — "I'd gin 'em ez good ez they sent."

"'T ain't religion, 'Gustus Tom, — 't ain't religion," said the old man brokenly. 'Gustus Tom, with his fragment of hat on the side of his tow head, hardly looked as if he cared.

A grizzled old mountaineer in jeans, with a stern, square face and a deep-set eye, that was lighted suddenly, spoke abruptly in a sepulchral voice.

"Ye oughter go ter camp, Brother Griff," he said in a religious twang, — "ye oughter go ter camp, an' tell yer 'speriunce! Ye hev lived long. Ye hev wrastled with the devil. Ye hev seen joy, ye hev knowed sorrow, ye hev fund grace. Yes, sir! Yes, sir! Ye air full o' 'speriunce, brother, an' ye oughter go ter camp an' comfort yerse'f, an' sing, an' pray."

"I pray no mo'," said the old man, lifting his aged, piteous face. "I 'm 'feared the Lord mought hear me an' answer my prayer." He smote his breast. "I ain't keerin' fur the mill. I ain't keerin' for the chill'n, — they 'll make out somehows. But ef my prayers could take back every word o' wrath I ever spoke ter the idjit, every lick I struck him, I 'd weary the very throne o' grace. Ef I could git him back an' begin over — but I can't! An' I won't pray fur myself, fur the Lord mought hear me. An' I want ter remember every one o' them words an' every lick, an' pay back fur 'em, wropped in the flames o' Torment."

He got up and tottered away toward the house, followed by his grandchildren, leaving the bystanders staring after him, strangely thrilled.

"Waal, I hopes they won't hear at the camp-meetin' o' his talkin' sech ez that," remarked the elderly adviser in dismay. "They hev been a-sermonizin' a good deal 'bout Tad's early death an' Mink Lorey's awful crime, an' sech, ter them young sinners over yander ter camp, an' it 'peared ter be a-sorter skeerin' of 'em, a-sorter a-shooin' of 'em inter the arms o' grace. An' I hopes none o' 'em will hear 'bout the old man a-repentin' an' wantin' ter burn, an' sech, fur the boy's hevin' been c'rected by his elders; they air perverted enough now agin them ez hev authority over 'em."

"Old Griff would change his mind 'bout burnin' ef he seen the fire one time," said another, winking seriously, as if he spoke from pyrotechnic experience. Then with a sudden change of tone, "What ails Pete Rood?"

For Rood was leaning against a tree, his swarthy face overspread with a sallow paleness, his lips blue, his eyes half closed, his hand clutching at his heart.

He said it was nothing much; he had been "tuk" this way often before; he would be better presently. Indeed, he was shortly able to walk down to the bank of the river, and sit and listen to the surmises of a half dozen idle fellows, lying in the grass, as to the drowning of Tad and the fate of Mink, and the terrible illustrations that both had furnished in the sermons at the camp-meeting in Eskaqua Cove.

And when he left them at last it was to the camp-meeting he went.

The afternoon brought a change in the weather. Rood noted it as he rode his raw-boned horse over the ranges and down the red clay roads into Eskaqua Cove. Clouds had gathered, obscuring the sun. There were no shadows, no gradations of light, no point of brilliant climax.

The foliage was heavy masses of solid color. Only in certain plumy silver-green boughs lurked a subdued glister, some luculent enchantment; for if ever the moonlight were enmeshed by a tree it is in the branches of the white pine.

Silence had fallen, as if the source of light were also source of sound. There was wind in the upper atmosphere, but no breath stirred the leaves. Twilight had sunk upon the cove before he turned off into a road leading up a wooded hill. In the dusk, sundry equine figures loomed up. The head of a horse was clearly defined against a patch of the pale sky, and a shrill neigh jarred the quiet. There were wagons, too, under the trees, empty, the teams unharnessed, and the poles lying on the ground. A dim light, deeply yellow, shone among the boles of the trees further on, a little misty, because already large drops were falling. All unmindful of the rain, a row of young men and half-grown boys perched on a rail fence in crouching attitudes, not unlike gigantic roosting fowls. Now and then a subdued, drawling voice sounded from among them, and a smothered laugh was attestation of callow humanity. They were not devoid of interest in the proceedings of the camp-meeting, but it was in the impersonal quality of spectator, and they held aloof from the tabernacle as if they had no souls to be saved. They turned to look down at Rood as he dismounted and hitched his horse, and he heard his own name passed along the row, it being a self-constituted register of all who came and went. The little gate dragged and creaked on its hinges, and resisted as if it grudged the spiritual opportunities to which it gave access, and desired to point the fact that salvation was not easy to come by. As it yielded and Rood entered the inclosure there were more yellow lights showing with misty halos in the olive-green dusk. They came from the doors of a row of shanties, floorless and windowless, which served as quarters for the crowd at night. There was a great flaring flame in the rear of each cabin, with leaping red tongues, surrounded by busy, hovering figures that cast huge distorted shadows against the encompassing foliage, as if some uncanny phenomenal beings were stalking a solemn round among the trees. These fires had uncomfortable spiritual suggestions. But they issued merely from the kitchens, the most cheerful things at camp, and here saint and sinner were equally heartily represented. Supper was over, however. The hymn rising even now from the tabernacle was far from cheerful: one of the long-drawn, melancholy songs, with wild, thrilling swells and sudden falls and monotonous recitative passages, sometimes breaking into a strange, ecstatic chant. The serried vertical lines of rain seemed to vibrate with it like the strings of a harp. Far away the thunder rolled in its pauses. More than once the sudden lightning illumined the grounds with a ghastly gleam, and the rhythmic solemn song went on like a part of the storm. It was a grave assemblage under the great roof of the rude structure, shown in the dim light of six or eight kerosene lamps fixed against the posts. At one end was a platform with a bench, on which sat some five or six of the preachers participating in the exercises. Brother Jethro Sims, a hoary-headed patriarch, was walking slowly up and down the main aisle, clapping his hands and singing with a look of ecstasy in his upturned eyes which a sophisticated religionist might vainly wonder at, finding that his superior attainments and advanced theories had bereft him of the power to even comprehend such faith, such piously prescient joys. The ground was covered with a deep layer of straw, deadening the stir among the rows of benches. Many of these, having no backs, served to acquaint their occupants with martyrdom and to offer a premium to the naturally upright. There were numbers of little children present, for as yet the lenient rule of the mountain churches tolerates their babble and even their crying in reason. Here and there one of the humbly clad young women, with her sleeping infant in her arms, the yellow light falling upon its head and on her solemn, listening, almost holy face, might remind one of another peasant mother whose Child is the hope of the world. The extreme seriousness, the devout aspiration, the sublimity of the unquestioning faith, that animated the meeting, could annul ignorance, poverty, uncouthness.

There were many canine figures on the outskirts of the crowd, now and then peering with wolfish green eyes and weird effect from the darkness among the laurel, which was beginning to sway and sound with the wind. Those in the full light, standing even beneath the roof and, with lolling tongue and wagging tail, looking upon the proceedings, seemed peculiarly idle here and to incur the imputation of loafers, despite that they are never very busy elsewhere. Others were more selfishly employed, creeping about under the benches and among the feet of the congregation, searching in the straw for the bits of bread and meat thrown aside by the frequenters of the meeting who did not camp on the grounds, but brought their lunch for the midday, and went home at night. One little dapper yellow dog had bounded on the end of the mourners' bench, and sat there, gravely gazing about him with small, affable eyes, all unnoticed by the elders, but threatening the gravity of an urchin, who grinned and coughed to hide the grin, breaking out with a wild, uncontrollable vocalization, relic of the whooping-cough, not long over-past. He was finally motioned out of the tabernacle, and scudded across in the rain to the shanty, while the little dog sat demure and unmolested on the mourners' bench.

Larger sinners were gathering there presently, albeit slowly.

"Come! come!" cried the old man sonorously over the singing. "Delay not! My brethren, I hev never seen a meetin' whar the devil held sech a strong hold! Come! Hell yawns fur ye! Come! Yer time is short! Grace beckons! Come! The fires o' perdition air kindled! The flames air red!"

And as his voice broke forth once more in the chanting, the thunder rolled as a repetition of his summons, the lightning glared, all the mountains became visible over the woods of the abrupt declivity toward the east; and higher still above the summits was revealed a vast cloud-vista in the midst of the black night, vividly white, full of silent surging motion, with strange suggestions of bending forms, of an awful glister at the vanishing point, — darkness enveloped it, and once more the thunder pealed.

As the gathering storm burst, the monotonously chanting voices seemed keyed to an awed undertone, lisping with this mighty psalm of nature, — the thunder and its echo in the mountains, the tumultuous cry of the wind, and the persistent iteration of the rain. In the intervals of its splendid periods, one might feel it a relief to hear the water timidly splashing in the little ditches that served to drain the ground on either side of the tabernacle, and the continual whisper in the pines above the primitive structure. Here and there two or three boughs hung down further than the rest, fringing the eaves. Ben Doaks noted, when the lightning flared again, that just between them the distant peak of Thunderhead loomed dimly visible, — or was it a cloud? Strain his eyes as he might, he could hardly say.

For Ben Doaks was there, the first to respond to the earnest exhortations to the sinners to come forward. He had a shamefaced look as he shambled up and took his seat on the mourners' bench, while the little dog sat unnoticed at the other end. Doaks was quick, however, to observe that one of the preachers eyed him sharply, and spoke to another, who shook his head with a gesture indeed of negation, but an expression of reluctant affirmation, and he felt sure that they recognized how often he had sat there, and that they were saying to each other that it was of no use, — he was evidently rejected by grace.

Now and then low voices sounded in the midst of the singing, — the Christians urging those convicted of sin to go up and be prayed for. Others came forward. There was more stir than before; a vivid curiosity was on many faces turning about to see who was going up, who was resisting entreaty, who ought to be convicted of sin, being admirably supplied with obliquity of which to repent.

Pete Rood sat, his black eyes on the ground, intent, brooding, deeply grave. Elvira Crosby thought at first that he affected to overlook her. Then, with a sinking of the heart, she realized that indeed he did not see her. The tears welled up to her eyes. The past was not to be recalled. When was he ever before unaware of her presence? He had been so eager, so devoted, so unlike the capricious lover for whom she had lightly flung him away. It was all over, though. She looked about her to divert her mind, to preserve her composure. She noted Mrs. Sayles in the congregation, identifying her by her limp sun-bonnet. Mrs. Sayles had long been saying that she intended to put splints in it some day when time favored her; but it still hung over her eyes, obscuring her visage, except her mouth, as she sang, and she was an edifying spectacle of a disregard of earthly pomps and a lack of vain interest in baubles and bonnets. Alethea's face, like some fair flower half enfolded in its sheath, was visible in the funnel-shaped depths of her own brown bonnet, with a glistening suggestion of her gold hair on her forehead, and one escaped tress hanging down beneath the curtain on her dark brown homespun dress. She did not sing, and she looked downcast.

In the aisle between the two benches reserved for the mourners the brethren were crowding, talking individually to the contrite sinners, sometimes with such effect that sobs and tears broke forth; and then the hymn was renewed, with the rhythmic sound of the clapping of hands, while the thunder crashed and the forked lightnings darted through the sky. The lurid scenic effects added their impressiveness to the terrible word-painting of another preacher, who was less interesting though not less efficient than that gentle old man, Brother Jethro Sims. He described hell with an accurate knowledge of its topography, its *personnel*, and its customs, which was a triumph of imagination, and made one feel that he had surely been there. A young woman suddenly broke into wild screams, shouting that she had found her salvation, and clapping her hands, and crying, "Glory!" finally fainting, and being borne out into the rain.

In the aisles they all often knelt, praying aloud in turns: sometimes, the voice of one failing in a whispered Amen! another would cry out insistently, "Let us continue the supplication!" And once more the prayer would go up.

There were no more conversions. Over and again the brethren announced in pious dudgeon that it was a stubborn meeting, and hell gaped for the sinner. It was evidence of the sincerity of the mourners, and their anxiety not to deceive themselves and others, that they could thus resist the urgency of the impassioned appeals, that with quivering nerves they could still withhold all demonstrations of yielding until the spirit should descend upon them.

Presently persons who desired the prayers of the congregation were requested to rise and make known their wish. It might be feared that some of the compliances did not tend to preserve domestic harmony. One woman asked prayers for her husband, whose heart, she stated, was not in his religion, and the defiant contradiction expressed in the face of a man seated beside her suggested that she had thus publicly made reprisal for sundry conjugal differences. Nevertheless, old Brother Sims said, "Amen!" Mrs. Sayles rose and begged prayers for the "headin' young folks o' the kentry, that they'd be guided by thar elders, an' not trest thar own green jedgmints, an' finally be led ter grace." And all the old people said, heartily, "Amen!" Many turned to look at Alethea, whose face had become a delicate pink.

And suddenly Peter Rood rose. "I want the prayers o' the godly," he said, now and then casting a hasty glance at Brother Sims, who stood listening intently, his chin in the air, his hands arrested in the gesture of clapping, "fur light ter my steps. I reckon I'm a backslider, fur I git no light when I pray. It's all dark,—

mighty dark!" His voice trembled. He was beginning to lose his self-control. "My actions tarrify me! I 'lowed wunst I hed fund grace, but in trouble I hev no helper."

The lightnings flashed once more. The swift illumination seemed to blanch his swarthy face, and lighted his uplifted black eyes with a transient gleam. "I'm in sin an' great mis'ry. I hev done wrong." He was about to sit down.

"Make reparation, brother, an' free yer soul in prayer," said the old man.

"I can't!" he cried, shrilly. "I'm 'feard! I'm 'feard o' my life. I wouldn't hev done sech 'ceptin' I war drunk, — drunk with liquor an' drunk with spite."

He felt that he was saying too much. He sat down, biting his lip till the blood started. Then he rose and faltered, "I want yer prayers fur light."

"Amen!" said Brother Sims.

Rood had recovered himself abruptly. He was looking about with furtive sharpness through the congregation, seeking to gauge the effect of what he had said when under the strong spell of religious excitement that had swayed the crowd. Fearful as he was, he detected only curiosity, interest, nothing more marked; for in the rhetoric of frenzied repentance these good men often apply to themselves language that seriously entertained could only grace an indictment.

The rain had ceased; the quiet without seemed to conduce to a calmer spirit within. The fervor of the meeting had spent itself. Only a few of the brethren were "workin'" with Ben Doaks; his face was troubled and perplexed, his anxious eyes turned from one to another.

"Can't ye feel ye air jes' a wuthless worm a-crawlin' round the throne o' grace? Can't ye feel that only mercy kin save ye? — fur ye richly desarve damnation."

"Laws-a-massy, naw," said poor, candid Ben, greatly harried. "I think mighty well o' myself!"

And so they left him in his sins. The crowd was

breaking up, chiefly seeking their several camps, as the shanties were called. But a few had come merely to participate in the exercises of the evening, and these were busy in harnessing their horses or yoking their oxen into their wagons on the hillside without the inclosure. The declivity was veined with rivulets, into which the heavy feet of the men and beasts splashed; the leaves continuously dripped; frogs were croaking near at hand in the sombre woods, — not so dark now, for the melancholy waning moon shone among the breaking clouds. The rumble of wheels presently intruded upon the low-toned conversation, the burden of which was the meeting and reminiscent comparison with other meetings. Several of the boys, not burdened with immortality, took leave less decorously, whooping loudly at each other as they galloped past the vehicles, and were soon out of sight and hearing.

The red clay road was presently lonely enough as Alethea trudged along it. There was no room for her in the little wagon which Buck drew in single harness, as might be called the ropes by which the ox, fastened between the shafts, was made to dispense with a yoke-fellow. A rope tied to his horn was intended to guide him along any intricacies of the road with which he might not be acquainted. Mrs. Sayles, her daughter-in-law, and several of the children were seated in the wagon, and sometimes Alethea walked in advance, and sometimes fell into the rear. It was no great distance that they were to travel, — their destination being her aunt's house in Eskaqua Cove, where they were to spend the night before wagoning up the Great Smoky.

Alethea was beset with her own unquiet thoughts; the remorse that would not loose its hold; the strange wrong which the right had wrought. Her conscience, forever on the alert — serving, if need were, as proxy — could find no flaw in what she had counseled; and thus perverse fate, in the radiant guise of rectitude, had led Reuben Lorey to despair, and delivered her to grief.

She hardly noted the incidents of the wayside, — the

foot-bridge over the creek; the stars amongst the ripples; the sound of the insects; the zigzag fences on either hand; the mists that lurked among the trees, that paced the turn-rows of the corn-fields, that caught the moonbeams, and glittered against the dark mountain side. It was another gleam that struck her attention; she looked again,— the slant of the rays against the windows of a little school-house. There was a deep impression of silence upon it, vacant in the night, dark but for the moonbeams. The pines that overhung it were sombre and still. The vapors shifted about it, fringing even the rotten palings that inclosed it. Her feet had followed her gaze. She was near the edge of the narrow road, as she paused to wait for Buck and the wagon to come up. She heard nothing as she listened. She said to herself that she must be a long way ahead. She was sensible of fatigue presently; the excitements of the evening were superimposed on the work of the day. She leaned against the tottering fence. Her bonnet had fallen back on her shoulders; she rested her head on her hand, her elbows on the low palings. She might have dreamed for a moment. Suddenly something touched her. She turned her head quickly; her shriek seemed to pierce the sky, for there in the inclosure, — did she see aright? — the idiot's face! white with a responsive terror upon it, vanishing in the mist. Or was it the mist? Did she hear the quick thud of retreating footsteps, or was it the throbs of her own plunging heart? As she turned, wildly throwing up both arms, she beheld Buck and the wagon on the crest of the hill, with the worshipers from the camp-meeting, and the sight restored to her more mundane considerations.

VIII.

In those long days while Mink languished in jail, he wondered how the world could wag on without him. He hungered with acute pangs for the mountains; he pined for the sun and the wind. Sometimes he stood for hours at the window, straining for a breath of air. Then the barred aspect of the narrow scene outside of the grating maddened him, and he would fling himself upon his bed; and it would seem to him that he could never rise again.

He speculated upon Alethea with a virulence of rage which almost frightened him, — whether she had heard of his arrest, how she had received the news.

"Mighty pious, I reckon," he sneered. "I know ez well ez ef I hed seen her ez she be a-goin' 'round the kentry a-tellin' 'bout my wickedness, an' how she worried an' worked with me, an' could n't git me shet o' my evil ways."

He thought of Elvira, too, with a certain melancholy relish of her fancied grief. His heart had softened toward her as his grudge against Alethea waxed hot. "*She* tuk it powerful hard, I know. I 'll be bound it mighty nigh killed her, — she set so much store by me. But I reckon her folks air glad, bein' ez they never favored me."

It seemed to him, as he reflected on the probable sentiment of his friends and neighbors, that he had lived in a wolfish community, ready with cowardly cruelty to attack and mangle him since fortune had brought him down.

"I 'm carrion now; I 'll hev ter expec' the wolves an' buzzards," he said bitterly to his lawyer, as they canvassed together what witnesses they had best summon to prove his general good character, and whom they should challenge on the jury list. There was hardly a man of the number on whom Mink had not played some grievous prank calculated to produce a rankling grudge and foster prejudice. He recited these with a lugubrious gravity incongruous enough with the subject matter, that often elicited bursts of unwilling laughter from the perplexed counsel.

This was a bluff, florid man of forty, with a hearty, resonant voice, a light blue eye, thick, yellow hair, which he wore cut straight across beneath his ears, showing its density, and thrown back without parting from his forehead. When the locks fell forward, as they often did, he tossed them back with an impatient gesture. He had a long mustache and beard. His lips were peculiarly red. Altogether he was a high-colored, noisy, confident, blustering fellow, and he inspired Mink with great faith.

"I done a better thing 'n I knowed of whenst I voted an' electioneered so brash fur you-uns ez floater in tho legislatur'," said Mink one day, in a burst of hopefulness. When he had sent for the lawyer to defend him, he had based his appeal for aid partly on his political services, and relied on them to atone for any deficiency of fees.

"Do it again, Mink, early and often!" And the floater's jolly laughter rang out, jarring against the walls of the bare room, which was, however, far more cheerful for the sound.

Mink had found in the requirements of the approaching trial, urged upon his attention by the lawyer, a certain respite from his mental anguish. But in the midst of the night, griefs would beset him. In his dreams the humble, foolish individuality of the idiot boy was invested with awe, with a deep pathos, with a terrible dignity. It seemed often that he was awakened by the clutch of a hand to an imperative consciousness of the crime of which he was accused, to a torturing uncertainty of his guilt or innocence. His conscience strove in vain to reckon with him.

"Mebbe, though, the jury kin tell?" he said one morning, piteously, to his counsel, who had come cheerily in, to find him wild-eyed and haggard.

"A jury," said the lawyer sententiously, "is the cussedness of one man multiplied by twelve."

He had flung his somewhat portly bulk into a chair which creaked beneath his weight, and he was looking at his client with calculating keenness. He had supplemented a fair knowledge of the law with a theory of human motives, deduced from his experience among men both as a politician and before the courts. In their less complex expressions he was quick to detect them. But he was devoid of intuition, of divination. His instincts were blunt. His moral perceptions were good, but elementary. His apprehension of crime was set forth in its entirety and in due detail by the code of Tennessee with the consequent penalty prescribed by the statute. He recognized no wrong unpunishable by law. The exquisite anguish of a moral doubt, the deep, helpless, hopeless affliction of remorse, the keen, unassuaged pangs of irreparability,— he had no spiritual sense to take cognizance of these immaterial issues. If Mink, escaping by his counsel's clever use of a technicality, should ever again think of the miller, dream of the boy weltering in the river, wake with the sound of that weird scream in his ears, Mr. Harshaw would wonder at him as a fool. As to the bar of conscience, how could that vague essence assume all the functions of a court under the constitution?

And still conning his simple alphabet of the intricate language of emotions, he interpreted the prisoner's wan cheek and restless eyes as the expression of fear. This induced a secret irritation and an anxiety as to how he had best conduct the case, in view of his professional reputation. He had besought Mink in his own interests to be frank, and now he was perplexed by doubts of his client's candor.

It required only a few moments' reflection to assure

himself that he had best assume, for the purposes of defense, the guilt of the prisoner until proved innocent. As he placed both hands on his knees he pursed up his lips confidentially, and with a quick sidelong glance he said, —

"We 've got some time, though, before we have to face 'em, Mink. We 're entitled to one continuance, on account of the inflamed state of public sentiment."

The brooding, abstracted look passed suddenly from Mink's face, leaving it more recognizable with its wonted bright intentness.

"Air ye 'lowin' ye 'd put off the trial furder 'n the day be set fur, Mr. Harshaw?" he asked, with the accents of dismay. "Fur Gawd's sake, don't let 'em do that. I would n't bide hyar, all shet up"— his eyes turned from wall to wall with the baffled eagerness of a caged beast — "I would n't bide hyar a day longer 'n I 'm 'bleeged ter, not ter git shet o' damnation. Lord A'mighty, don't go a-shovin' the day off; hurry it up, ef ye kin. I want ter kem ter trial an' git back ter the mountings. I feel ez ef I be bound ter go."

The lawyer still looked at him with his keen sidelong glances.

"The jury stands 'twixt you and the mountains, Mink. Might n't get out, after all 's said and done."

Mink looked at him with a sudden alarm in his dilated eyes, as if the contingency had been all undreamed of.

"They 'll be bound ter let me out," he declared. "I ain't feared o' the jury."

"If you don't know what you did yourself, you can't expect them to be much smarter in finding it out," reasoned the lawyer.

"I ain't done nuthin' ter keep me jailed this hyar way," said Mink, hardily. "I feel it in my bones I 'll git out. I never try them bars," nodding at the window, "but what I looks fur 'em ter break in my hand."

"See here," said the lawyer, sternly, "you let 'them bars' alone; you ain't going ter do yourself any good breaking jail."

He looked down meditatively at his feet, and stamped one of them that his trousers might slip further down over his boot-leg, which deported itself assertively and obtrusively, as if it were in the habit of being worn on the outside.

"I don't know," he said reflectively, "if you want to be tried speedily, but what it's best, anyhow. We won't have Averill to preside; he's incompetent in a number of civil cases, and Jim Gwinnan will hold court. He's a " — he pursed up his red lips again, and looked about with an air intimating a high degree of contempt; Mink hung upon his words with an oppressive sense of helplessness and eagerness, that now and then found vent in an unconscious long-drawn sigh — "well, he's a selfish, ambitious sort of fellow, and he's found out it's mighty popular to make a blow about cleaning up the docket, and avoiding the law's delays, and trotting the lawyers right through. He'll hold court till twelve o'clock at night, and he just opposes, tooth and nail, every motion for delay. I reckon he'd make it look as if we were afraid to come to trial, if we wanted a continuance; so it's just as well, if you feel ready, for we mightn't get it, after all."

Mink experienced a new fear. "Ain't he a mighty bad kind of a jedge ter hev?" he faltered, quaking before the mental vision of the man who held his fate in the hollow of his hand.

"No," said Harshaw musingly, "he ain't a bad judge for us for this reason, — though he's mighty apt to lean to public opinion, he's a sound lawyer, and he's mighty careful about his rulings. He don't get reversed by the S'preme Court. That's what he sits on the bench for: not to administer justice, — he don't think about justice once a week, — but to be affirmed by the S'preme Court. He's more particular than Averill in little things, and he won't let the attorney-general walk over him, like Averill does, — sorter spunky."

"I hev seen the 'torney-gineral, — hearn him speak wunst. They 'lowed he war a fine speaker," submitted

Mink, anxious concerning the untried, unmeasured forces about to be arrayed against him.

"Mighty fine," said Harshaw, derisively. "Got a beautiful voice — for calling hogs!"

He laughed and rose. "Oh, bless my soul, I plumb forgot!" he exclaimed. "There's a girl out here wanting to see you. Don't know but what she may be your sweetheart;" he winked jocosely. "Perkins said she might come in if you want to see her. Looks like she's walked about forty mile, — plumb beat out."

Mink was flattered. Instantly he thought of Elvira, and he remembered the journey with his offering of the raccoon that fateful night.

"She hev got dark hair an' eyes, an' air toler'ble leetle ter be growed up?" he asked. The remark was in the form of a question, but it was uttered with the conviction of certainty.

"Lord, no! Sandy hair, big brown eyes, and tall, and " —

He paused, for Mink had risen suddenly.

"Ye go tell her," he said, passionately, pointing at the door, — "go straight an' tell her ter keep in mind what I said bout'n the harnt on Thunderhead, an' how I 'lowed she favored him; ef she can't kill, she sp'iles yer chance."

"Why, look here, Mink," remonstrated the lawyer.

"Go 'long an' tell her!" cried Mink, imperatively. "Tell her I want her ter cl'ar out from hyar. Tell her I can't breathe ef she's nigh." He clutched at his throat, tearing open his collar with both hands. "'T war her ez brung me hyar. 'T war her ez got me locked an' barred up. An' now I don't want ter see her no mo' ez long ez I live. Gin her that word from me, — an' the Herder on Thunderhead what she favors."

The lawyer, with a gesture of expostulation, left the cell, appreciating that it was an unpleasant job to tell the travel-stained apparition at the door that her journey was in vain.

She was sitting upon the doorstep, in the sunshine, her

brown bonnet hanging half off her golden head; her homespun dress seemed dark upon the rough gray stone. She watched absently, with her serious brown eyes, the gauzy wings of a blue-bottle that droned slumberously by. She held with idle hands the yellow blossoms of the golden-rod that she had plucked by the way. There was no passing in the street, hardly a sound; so still she sat that a lizard, basking in the sun, did not scruple to run across her motionless feet. She had taken off her coarse shoes to ease them after her long walk, for they were swollen and bruised.

She looked up with a start when the lawyer stood in the door. "No, sis," he said in a debonair fashion, glancing about the street. "Mink ain't in a good humor to-day, and you can't see him."

She cast up to him her haggard eyes, full of appeal, of fear, of woe. He had no intention of stabbing her with the cruel words of the message. "You can't see him to-day; some other day." He waved his hand with a promissory gesture, and was turning away.

She sprang up with a cry. "They hendered him! They would n't let him!" she said, with quivering lips.

"Yes, yes. They hindered him," he kindly prevaricated.

Her eyes were suddenly all on fire. As he caught their gleam he hesitated, looking at her. Her cheeks were flushed. Her teeth were set. She raised her clenched hand.

"He lied ter me, that thar jailer. He 'lowed I mought see Reuben. He lied! he lied! I 'll — I 'll" — She dropped her threatening hand. "Lord! Lord! what kin I do!"

"Look here, girl," said the lawyer, alarmed at the idea of an indignant demonstration on the part of any of his client's friends. "'T ain't the jailer's fault. Mink said he would n't see you."

She stood as if stunned for a moment. Then, her confidence in Mink rebounding, "I don't b'lieve ye!" she said, bluntly.

"Well, then, maybe you will when I tell you that he told me to ask you to clear out, and to remind you of the 'harnt' on Thunderhead that he said you favored."

She shrank back as if he had struck her. He eyed her indignantly. "I reckon you'll believe me now. Well, begone. We've had enough of you."

He turned and walked off briskly. He heard the court-house bell jangling out its summons, for the chancery court was in session, and he quickened his pace. He gave a start of irritation when he became aware that she was following him. He turned and faced her.

"What do you want?" he said, abruptly.

"I want ter tell ye su'thin'," she gasped. She leaned forward as if to touch his arm. He moved suddenly back, and she almost fell. She showed no anger, but came a faltering pace nearer, with the same imploring gesture. "I mus' tell ye suthin' 'bout Reuben, soon ez I git my breath, — suthin' ye'd never b'lieve."

Perhaps it was an unreasoning anger which possessed him, but he was late, and she had cast the lie in his teeth, and somehow her presence irked him, and he vaguely sought to forecast what she had to say.

"No, you won't, for I ain't going to listen. You just take yourself off, and stay at home if you know how, and satisfy yourself with the harm you have done already. You'd better put out, and so I tell you."

He turned once more and strode away rapidly. He heard a faint cry behind him, and, for a time, pursuing steps. He quickened his own. In fact, he presently ran lightly, — marvelously lightly for a man of his bulk, — laughing within himself the while at the absurdity and incongruity of the episode, should it be noticed by any one in the sleepy streets. After a little he looked over his shoulder, half in relenting, half in curiosity.

She was not following him. She was limping back toward her shoes, that lay on the steps of the jail.

IX.

It was close upon nightfall when Alethea, on her homeward journey, reached the banks of the Scolacutta River. It still had a melancholy version of the sunset imprinted upon its surface. It was full of dreamy crimson tints, and olive-green shadows, and gentle pensive effects of undistinguishable lustres. Its ceaseless monotone was on the air; its breath was of freshness and fragrance; the bluffs that towered above it gave the austerity of rugged rocks and the dignity of great heights to the incidents of its margin. Stunted trees clung to the niches of these splintered cliffs; everywhere along the banks the leaves of the sourwood were red and gay as a banner, the tassels all gleaming and white; the dogwood showed a flaunting ochreous tint, but the sweet-gum was as yet only a dull purple, and the sumach had merely hung out its garnet tufts. An amethystine haze rested on the nearest mountains, softening the polychromatic richness that glimmered all along the great slopes; further away they wore the softened blue of autumn. The scene was familiar to her, for she had already passed through the gap of the mountain down into Eskaqua Cove, and her aunt Dely's house lay among the tawny cornfields on the other side. Very lonely this habitation was among the great company of the mountains; they rose about the cove on every side with a visible immensity of wilderness which belittled the slight hold of humanity expressed in the house, the fields, the road that seemed itself a vagrant, for there was no bourne in sight of the wide landscape to which it might be supposed to tend.

The log cabin had heard the river sing for nearly a century. It appeared for many years the ready prey of decay: the chimney leaned from the wall, the daubing was falling from the chinking, there were holes in the floor and the roof. Suddenly a great change came over it. The frivolity of glass enlivened the windows where batten shutters had formerly sufficed; a rickety little porch was added; a tiny room was partitioned off from this, and Mrs. Purvine rejoiced in the distinction of possessing a company bedroom, which was far from being a haven of comfort to the occasional occupant of those close quarters. She had always been known to harbor certain ambitions. Her husband's death, some two or three years before, had given her liberty to express her tastes more fully than when hampered by his cautious conservatism. And now, although the fields might be overrun with weeds, and the sheep have the rot, and the poultry the cholera, and the cow go dry, and the "gyarden truck" defer to the crab-grass, and the bees, clever insects, prepare only sufficient honey for their own use, Mrs. Purvine preserved the appearance of having made a great rise in life, and was considered by the casual observer a "mighty spry widder woman." Such a one as Mrs. Sayles shook her head and spared not the vocabulary. "Dely," she would observe, " air my husband's sister, an' I ain't goin' ter make no words about her. Ef she war ennybody else's sister, I'd up an' down declar' ez she hev been snared in the devices o' the devil, fur sech pride ez hern ain't godly,— naw sir! nur religion nuther. Glass in the winder! Shucks! she 'd better be thinkin' 'bout gittin' light on salvation, — that she hed! Folks ez knowed Dely whenst she war a gal knowed she war headin' an' sot agin her elders, an' run away from home ter git married, an' this is what kem of sech onregenerate ways. *Glass* in the winder! I 'll, be bound the devil looks through that winder every day at yer aunt Dely whenst she sets thar an' spins. He gits a glimge o' her when she ain't a-lookin'. The pride o' the yearth is mighty strong in her. Ye oughter sati'fy yerse'f with 'sociatin' with her in this life, fur ye ain't a-goin' ter meet up with her in heaven. Naw, sir, yer aunt Dely 'll remember that winder in the darkness o' Torment, an' ef she war ennybody else's sister than my own husband's *I 'd say so.*"

Mrs. Purvine was standing on the porch, so fine a manifestation of her pride, and gazing with unrecognizing curiosity at Alethea as the girl came up the stony hillside.

Mrs. Purvine hardly looked the woman of a vaulting worldly ambition. She had a broad, moon-like face and blue eyes with much of the whites showing, the more as she had a trick of peering over her spectacles. She had no teeth; despite her social culture she had never heard of a false set, or her mouth would have been a glittering illustration of the dentist's art. She held in her hand a short clay pipe, from which the smoke slowly curled. She wore a blue-checked homespun apron, but a calico gown, being, according to report, "too triflin'" to do very much weaving at home, and the cross-roads store was only ten miles from her house, on the road to Shaftesville. She had journeyed even to the town, twice or thrice in her life, mounted on a gray mare with a colt at her heels, and had looked from beneath her sun-bonnet at the metropolitan splendors and habits with a starveling's delight in such of the meagre conventional graces of life as the little village possessed, and as were vouchsafed to her comprehension. Nobody knew whence she derived her "vagrantin' ways;" for these excursions earned for her the reputation of an insatiate traveler, and her frivolous disposition and pride were the occasion of much reprehension and comment. They could hardly take the form of remonstrance, however, without open rupture; for Mrs. Purvine, right well aware of them, with an acumen and diplomacy grafted like some strange exotic upon her simple character, was always bewailing the frivolous tendency of the times, the pride of "some folks," the worthless nature of women nowadays, and foisting herself upon her interlocutor as an example of all homely and primitive tastes and virtues.

Her moon face suddenly assumed an expression of recognition and of stern reprobation as she came solemnly down from the door, a feat which it was difficult to perform with stateliness or even safety; for the two or three plank steps were only set against the wall, and although far more imposing than the hewn logs or rough stones customary elsewhere, they were extremely insecure. Often when a foot was placed upon the lowest of the number they careened forward with the weight.

Mrs. Purvine accomplished the descent with dignity, and as she held the gate open she addressed her niece, looking full in her tear-stained face: —

"I knowed it would kem ter this, — I knowed it, sooner or later. What's that thar step-mother o' yourn been doin' ter ye?"

Albeit Mrs. Sayles had few equals as a censor, Mrs. Purvine, with a secret intuition of her animadversions, returned them as best she might, and Mrs. Sayles's difficult position as a step-mother rendered her as a shorn lamb to the blast.

"Nuthin'," sobbed Alethea, — "nuthin' ez I knows on." She started up the steps, which bounded forward with a precipitancy that had a startling effect as if the house had jumped at her. Alethea stumbled, and Mrs. Purvine commented upon her awkwardness: —

"Look at the gal, — usin' her feet with no mo' nimbleness 'n a cow. Laws-a-massy, young folks ain't what they war in my day. Whenst I war a gal, 'fore I jined the church an' tuk ter consortin' with the saints, ye oughter hev seen me dance! Could shake my foot along with the nimblest! But I ain't crackin' up bran dances, nuther. I'm a perfessin' member, — bless the Lord! Satan hides in a fiddle. Ye always remember yer aunt Dely tole ye that word. An' ef ever ye air condemned ter Torment, don't ye up an' 'low ez ye hed no l'arnin'; don't ye do it." Then looking over her spectacles, "What ails ye, ef 't ain't that step-mother?"

"I hev been ter Shaftesville. I bided all night at Cousin Jane Scruggs's in Piomingo Cove, an' next day I footed it ter town."

This announcement would have surprised any one more than the roving Mrs. Purvine. Even she demanded, as in duty bound, with every intimation of deep contempt, "Laws-a-massy, what ye wanter go ter Shaftesville fur?"

"I went ter see Reuben Lorey in jail," replied Alethea.

Mrs. Purvine looked at her with an expression of deep exasperation. "Waal," she observed sarcastically, "I'd hev liked ter seen him thar, too. I ain't seen ez good a fit ez Mink Lorey an' the county jail fur this many a day. Kem hyar one night, an' tuk them bran' new front steps o' mine, an' hung 'em up on the martin-house. An' thar war a powerful deep snow that night, an' it kivered the consarn so ez nex' mornin' we could n't find out what unyearthly thing hed fell on the martin-house, an' we war fairly feared 't war a warnin' or a jedgmint till we missed them front steps. They ain't never been so stiddy sence."

Alethea had laid aside her bonnet and bathed her face. She was going about the house in a way which was a tribute to Mrs. Purvine's hospitality, for she felt much at home there. She had glanced toward the great fireplace, where the ashes piled on the top of the oven and the coffee-pot perched on the trivet over the coals told that the work of preparing supper was already done. She suddenly took down the quilting frame, suspended to the beams above by long bands of cloth, produced thread and thimble from her pocket, and, seating herself before it as before a table, began to quilt dexterously and neatly where Mrs. Purvine's somewhat erratic performance had left off long before. The smouldering firelight touched her fine, glistening hair, her pensive, downcast face; there was still light enough in the room through the pernicious glass window to reveal the grace of her postures and her slender figure. Aunt Dely, with some instinct for beauty native in her blood along with her "vagrantin' ways" and her original opinions, contemplated her for a time, and presently commented upon her.

"I 'm yer father's own sister," she averred. "I ain't denyin' it none, though he did go an' marry that thar Jessup woman, ez nobody could abide; an' I hate ter see a peart gal like you-uns, ez air kin ter me, a-sp'ilin' her eyes an' a-cryin' over a feller ez her folks don't favor noways. Yer elders knows bes', Lethe."

"Why, aunt Dely, you-uns *married* a man ez yer elders never favored; they war powerful sot agin him."

Mrs. Purvine was clad in logic as in armor.

"An' look how it turned out, — him dead an' me a widder woman!"

Alethea stitched on silently for a moment. Then she observed with unusual softness, for she feared being accounted "sassy," "I 'lowed I hed hearn ye say he war fifty-five year old, when he died."

"What 's fifty-five?" demanded Mrs. Purvine aggressively. "I knowed a man ez war a hunderd an' ten."

And so Alethea was forced to acquiesce in the proposition that Mrs. Purvine's consort had been cut off in the flower of his youth as a judgment for having some thirty years previous eloped with the girl of his heart.

Both women looked conscious when a sudden step sounded in cautious ascent of the flight before the door, which illustrated so pointedly the truism that pride goes before a fall, and a tall, lank, stoop-shouldered, redheaded fellow strode in at the door.

"Air yer eyesight failin' ye, Jerry Price?" Mrs. Purvine admonished him. He was her husband's nephew. "Thar 's Lethe Sayles."

Being called to order in this manner might well embarrass the young man, who had not expected to see Alethea, and who was rebuked for the dereliction before he was well in the room.

He shambled up to shake hands with her with a somewhat elaborate show of cordiality.

"Waal, Lethe," he exclaimed, "ye air a sight fur sore eyes! Ain't seen ye fur a month o' Sundays."

"Looks like she hed sore eyes herself, bound with red

ferretin'," commented Mrs. Purvine gruffly. She often had a disposition, as she averred, to knock these young people's heads together, — a sufficiently dangerous proceeding, for according to her account there were not two such hard heads in all Eskaqua Cove and Piomingo to boot. She had cherished an earnest desire to make a match between them, frustrated only by their failure to second the motion. They were well aware of this, and it impaired the ease of their relations, hampering even the exchange of the compliments of the season.

"Young folks take the lead!" Mrs. Purvine often exclaimed, oblivious of her own sentimental history. "Ef nobody war wantin' 'em ter marry they 'd be runnin' off with one another."

She had considered this breach of obedience on the part of her husband's nephew a special instance of filial ingratitude, and had begun to remind him, and in fact to remember, all that she had done for him.

"Folkses 'lowed ter me, whenst Jerry Price's mammy died, ez I hed better leave him be, an' his aunt Melindy Jane would keer fur him. An' I hed n't been merried but a few years, an' bein' ez I runned away my folks would n't gin me nuthin', an' me an' my old man war most o' the furniture we hed in the house. But law! we hed plenty arter a while, an' ter spare!" cried the rich aunt Dely. "An' they all 'lowed I hed better not lumber myse'f up with other folkses chill'n. Waal, I never expected ter, when I went ter the fun'el. But thar on the floor sot the hardest-featured infant I ever seen, red-headed, blinkin' eye, lean, an' sucked his thumb! An' all them folks war standin' 'round him, lookin' down at him with thar eyes all perverted an' stretched, like a gobbler looks at a deedie 'fore he pecks him on the noodle. An' they were all pityin' Melindy Jane fur hevin' ter keer fur him. Thar she war settin' wropped in a shawl, an' 'pearin' ez ef she could bite a ten-penny nail in two, sayin' she mus' submit ter the Lord! Waal, 'peared ter me ez I jes' could view the futur', an' the sorter time Red-head would hev along o' a woman ez war submittin' on account o' him ter the Lord! An' I jes' ups an' lied afore 'em all. I sez, 'That's the purties' child I ever see. Surely he is!' An' I sez right hearty ter the b'reaved husband, ' Ephr'im, ef ye 'll gin him ter me, I 'll keer fur him till he 's able ter keer fur me.' An' Eph looked up ez s'prised an' pleased, and says, '*Will ye, Dely?*' An' ef ye 'll b'lieve me, arter I hed called him 'purty' Melindy Jane 'lowed *she* wanted him, an' hed nuthin' ter say 'bout the Lord. But I jes' stepped inter the floor an' snatched him up under my arm, an' set out an' toted him five mile home. An' lean ez he 'peared, he war middlin' heavy. I rubbed some pepper on his thumb that night. He ain't sucked it sence."

Jerry Price used to listen, calmly smoking, hardly identifying himself — as what man would! — with the homely subject of the sketch; and yet with a certain sense of obligation to Mrs. Purvine, returning thanks in some sort in behalf of the unprepossessing infant.

"Ye an' me made a right good trade out'n it, ain't we, aunt Dely?" he would say.

She formerly accorded jocund acquiescence to this blithe proposition. But now she would exclaim, "Did ennybody think ye 'd grow up ter set yerse'f ter spite me, an' won't do nuthin' I ax ye? 'Kase I hev sot my heart on hevin' Lethe Sayles ter live along o' me, ye won't go courtin' her."

The specious Price would demand, "How d' ye know ez I won't?"

And hope would once more gleam from the ashes of Mrs. Purvine's disappointments.

"Lethe 's been ter Shaftesville," she said, nodding triumphantly, sure to impress Jerry with this statement, for he was as worldly as she. Then, with sudden animation, she turned to her niece: "Lethe, did ye see enny lookin'-glasses thar like mine?" She pointed to a cherry-framed mirror, some ten or twelve inches square, hung upon the wall at a height that prevented it from reflecting aught but the opposite wall. It was as well, perhaps, for glass of that quality could only return a corrugated image that might have induced depression of spirit in one gazing on the perversions of its surface. The walls were pasted over with pictures from almanacs and bright-tinted railway advertisements; for her husband had once been postmaster of the invisible neighborhood, and these were the most important trophies and emoluments of the office. They quite covered the mellow brown logs and the daubing between, and were as crude and gairish a substitute as well might be. They were the joy of Mrs. Purvine's heart, however, and as she dwelt upon them and committed them to memory they assumed all the functions of a literature. She valued hardly less a cheap clock that stood upon a shelf, and gave no more intimation of the passage of time than a polite hostess. Whether it had no works, whether it had sustained some internal injury, whether the worldly nephew and aunt had not sufficient knowledge of the springs of its being to wind it up, Alethea never speculated and Mrs. Purvine did not care. It was more than was owned by any one else in her acquaintance, and she rejoiced without stint in its possession.

"An' I'll be bound ye never seen no clock like mine!" she said.

"Naw 'm," said Alethea; "but I jes' went ter the jail."

"What fur?" demanded Jerry. He was leaning against the door, and did not notice that he kept the light from Alethea's work, but she was unwilling to remonstrate, and sewed on in the shadow.

"She went ter see Mink Lorey," said his aunt. "I hope he 'lowed he war sorry fur his sins, — 'though 't won't do him no good now; oughter hev been sorry fust."

"I never seen him," said Alethea.

Mrs. Purvine had knelt before the fire for the purpose of investigating the baking of the egg-bread; she held the lid of the oven up with a bit of kindling, while she turned half around to fix an astonished gaze on the girl.

"In the name o' — Moses!" — she produced the adjuration as if she thought it equal to the occasion, — "what did ye kem hyar lyin' 'bout'n it, Lethe, an' sayin' ye hed been ter see him? Ye'll git yer nose burnt, an' I'll be glad of it." She broke off suddenly, addressing a hound that, lured by the appetizing odor gushing out from under the lid of the oven, had approached with a sinuous, beguiling motion, and was extending his long neck. "Ye'd look mighty desirable with a blister on it."

"I never said I seen Reuben," returned Alethea, regardless of this interlude. "He would n't see me."

"What fur?" asked Jerry excitedly.

The lid fell from Mrs. Purvine's hand upon the oven with a crash. She was speechless with amazement.

Alethea sat, her hands clasped on the quilting frame, the glow of the firelight full on her golden hair; her beauty seemed heightened by the refined pathos which weeping often leaves upon the face when it is once more calm. It was hard to say the cruel words, but her voice was steady.

"He 'lowed I favored the harnt on Thunderhead what sp'iles folkses' prospects. I hed 'lowed ter him, when I las' seen him, ez he oughter gin what he hed ter old man Griff. An' he went ter Shaftesville. An' they jailed him."

Mrs. Purvine's moon face turned scarlet. "Now, ain't ye up an' down 'shamed o' yerse'f, Lethe Ann Sayles? Ter set store by a man ez talks ter you-uns like that!" She rose, with a toss of her head. "The kentry hev got my cornsent ter hang him!"

She began to move about more briskly as she placed the plates on the table. The fact of this breach between Alethea and Mink was auspicious to her darling scheme. "Naw, child," she said as the girl offered to assist, "ye set an' talk ter Jerry 'bout Mink; he wants ter hear 'bout Mink."

"I wisht I could be witness fur Reuben," said Alethea, feeling an intense relief to be able to mention this without revealing her secret. "I b'lieve I could holp Reuben some."

"Why n't ye go ter his lawyer?" asked Jerry. "Harshaw, they say, he hev got ter defend him."

"He would n't listen; he fairly run from me."

"In Moses's name!" cried Mrs. Purvine, with sibilant inversion of her favorite exclamation, "what ails them crazy bucks in Shaftesville? All of 'em got the jim-jams, in jail an' out!"

"Waal," said Jerry coolly, "ef ye want ter tell him sech ez ye know, I'll *make* him listen ter ye. I hev been summonsed on the jury fur the nex' term, an' I'll hev ter go ter Shaftesville or be fined. An' ef ye air thar I'll see Harshaw don't run from ye,—else he won't run fur, no mo'. He'll lack his motions arter that."

"Ai-yi! When Jerry talks he ain't minchin' his words!" cried aunt Dely admiringly.

Alethea was very grateful for this stalwart championship. She said nothing, however, for she had no cultured phrases of acknowledgment. Her spirits rose; her flagging brain was once more alert; she was eager to be alone,—to think what she would say to the lawyer, to Mink, on the witness-stand. She hardly noticed Mrs. Purvine's manner of self-gratulation, or her frequent glances toward her young people as they sat together before the dull fire. Alethea was very beautiful, and Jerry — Mrs. Purvine never deluded herself with denials of her adopted son's ugliness — was good and manly, and as sharp as a brier. Any man might be esteemed a poor match for looks, unless it were the worthless Mink, so safe in jail.

The feat a woman's imagination can accomplish in a given time is the most triumphant illustration of the agility of the human mind. Before either spoke again Mrs. Purvine had elaborated every detail of the courtship and engagement, pausing from time to time, as she placed the dishes on the table, and looking about the room in complete abstraction, planning how to arrange the furniture to give space for the dancing at the infair.

"Set out the supper in the shed-room, an' take these hyar two beds an' thar steads up-steers inter the roof-room," she muttered, measuring with her eye. "The loom kin jes' be h'isted out 'n the shed-room inter the yard — an' I don't keer ef I never see it agin — an' the spinning-wheels set in the bedroom." As to Satan, she had forgotten that he was quite capable of making himself small enough to hide in the fiddle.

The light was growing dull out of doors; the stridulous voices of the September insects sounded ceaselessly, scarcely impinging upon the sense of quiet, so monotonous was the iteration of their song. The strokes of an axe, betokening activity at the wood-pile, seemed to cleave the silence, and reverberated from the mountains, as if the echoes were keeping a tally. Alethea had rolled up the quilting frame, and it swung from the beams. Presently the children were trooping in, three great awkward boys, who evidently formed themselves upon Jerry Price's manner, except the youngest, a lad of fourteen, whose face had a certain infantile lower, saved over from his juvenile days, and concentrating readily into a pout. Even his mother admitted that he was "sp'iled some." Together they made short work of the egg-bread and "br'iled bacon."

They tarried not long afterward, but trooped noisily up the ladder to the roof-room; and as they strode about on the floor, which was also the ceiling of the room below, it seemed momently that they would certainly come through.

Jerry lighted his pipe and sat on the doorstep; the fashionable Mrs. Purvine lighted hers and took a chair near. All the doors stood open, for the night was sultry. The stars were very bright in the moonless sky. The dogs lolling their tongues, sat on the porch, or lay in the dewy grass; making incursions now and then into the room, climbing cavalierly over Jerry's superfluity of long legs, and nosing about among the ashes to make sure that none of the scraps had escaped.

"Don't ye know I never waste nuthin', ye grisly gluttons?" demanded Mrs. Purvine, the model housekeeper. But their fat sides did not confirm this statement, and, bating a wag of homage in the extreme tip of their tails, they paid no attention to her.

"What *I'm* a-honin' ter know," said Jerry Price presently, "air how them boys ez war along o' Mink an' war summonsed ez witnesses air goin' ter prove he war drunk. Ef they 'low Mink war drunk the 'torney-gin'al 'll try ter make out he war sober. He's a-goin' ter ax, 'Whar 'd he git the whiskey, bein' 's all the still thar is air a bonded still, an' by law can't sell less 'n five gallons. Then them boys 'll be afeard ter tell whar they got the whiskey, 'kase folks mought think they knowed who war makin' it. An' ef the moonshiners war raided, *they* mought declar' ez some o' them boys war aidin' an' abettin' 'em, an' the revenuers would arrest them too."

"Don't ye know who air makin' it?" Alethea asked, a vivid picture in her mind of Boke's barn, and Jerry Price and his cronies stalking their fantastic rounds about it.

"Naw, sir! an' don't wanter, nuther. I war along o' 'em in the woods that night. I holped tote the jug. We lef' it empty in Boke's barn an' fund it filled, but I dunno nuthin' mo'."

"Lethe," said Mrs. Purvine, handing her a ball of gray yarn, the knitting-needles thrust through an ill-knit beginning of a sock, "I wish ye 'd try ter find out whar I drapped them stitches, an' ravel it out an' knit it up agin. I hate ter do my work over, an' I hev ter be powerful partic'lar with Jerry's socks, — he wears 'em out so fas'. Ye 'd 'low he war a thousand-legs, ef ye could see the stacks of 'em I hev ter darn."

Alethea drew up a great rocking-chair, and now and then leaned over its arms toward the fire to catch the red glow of the embers upon her work, as her deft hands repaired the damages of Mrs. Purvine's inattention. Suddenly she said in a pondering tone, "Why would the 'torney-gineral ruther prove Reuben war sober?"

"'Kase ef he war proved drunk the jury would lean ter him," said Jerry.

She laid her work down in her lap, and gazed intently at him. His face had the transient glow of his pipe upon it, and then, as he took it from his lips, was as indistinct as his long, lank figure disposed in the doorway.

"They ought n't ter do it, — but they do. I ain't never seen nare jury hold a drunk man ez up an' down 'sponsible ez ef he war sober. They 'll lean ter him ef he could be proved drunk."

Alethea said nothing. Her mental attitude was one of intense receptivity. Her keen appreciation of how much depended on her comprehension, her desire that no point should escape her attention, were positive pain in their acute consciousness.

The discerning Jerry went on with that acumen and cogency which were such odd concomitants of his ignorance and uncouthness : —

"It makes me laff every time I see a witness sethere 'the truth, the whole truth, an' nuthin' but the truth.' Folks is so apt ter b'lieve the truth air jes' what they wanter b'lieve. Git them boys skeered up right smart 'bout the revenuers on one side an' the moonshiners on t' other, an' they 'll feel the truth war ez none o' we-uns hed ennythin' ter drink that night; mought hev hed a dram o' cider, or mebbe nuther stronger 'n yerb tea, but nobody war bodaciously boozy. Then they don't know sure enough whar the liquor kem from; mos' folks don't b'lieve thar 's no still round 'bout the mountings now."

Alethea leaned back in the rocking-chair, her nerveless hands falling idly upon the work in her lap. The crude mosaic of advertisements on the walls started out with abnormal distinctness, as a tiny flame rose from the embers and fell into sudden extinction among the ashes, leaving the only picture in the room the dusky night-scene dimly painted in purple and dove color upon the panes of the window.

It was only she who could remedy the deficiency in this valuable testimony. She knew full well the source of their secret supply. She it was who had seen the jug left in the barn by the roistering blades, and the moonshiner swing down from the loft to seize upon it. She had his full confession from his own lips. She appreciated the distinctions the jury would make between hilarious drunken sport and coolly intentional malice in the prisoner, and that it was in her hands to sacrifice one of these men to the other.

For the first time she was quick to distrust her own intuitions. Her tyrant conscience, hitherto always ready to immolate every cherished wish on the altar of the right, seemed now the suavest mentor, urging that her lover's liberty, his life for aught she knew, should not be jeopardized to protect a man whose vocation she accounted a curse to the community. She felt a secret amaze that her first vague project should expand into a fully equipped plan, with hardly a conscious process of thought to give it shape and detail. Her natural doubts, her efforts at alternatives, were flouted by some inner imperious determination. It was in the nature of a concession from this suddenly elate and willful power that she obtained her own consent, as she would have phrased it, to warn Sam Marvin, for the sake of his "houseful," that he might elude capture, and perhaps save his still and appliances from destruction. And she would warn Jerry, too, despite that triumphant, tumultuous consciousness which held all else so slight since she had knowledge that could aid in proving Mink's irresponsibility for what he had really done, and his innocence of the graver crime of which he was accused.

"Jerry," she said, observing that Mrs. Purvine had fallen asleep in her chair, her moon face all askew, her idle hands neatly rolled up in her apron, — "Jerry, I reckon ye would n't want me a-goin' testifyin' ter Shaftesville ef ye knowed I seen you-uns leave the jug that evenin' in Boke's barn. I sca'cely b'lieved 't war ye, at fust, all of ye acted so cur'ous; I 'lowed 't war sperits in yer likeness. An' I seen the distiller kem an' git the jug. An' he seen me."

"Look-a-hyar, Lethe!" exclaimed Jerry, seriously. "Don't joke 'bout sech ez that. Ye know the moonshiners mought fairly kill ye, ef they fund out ye knowed an' tole on 'em. They hev done sech afore now. Ye keep yer mouth shet an' yer tongue 'twixt yer teeth, ef ye knows what's healthy fur ye."

"I ain't jokin'," said Alethea.

"Ye mind what I say," declared Jerry. "I ain't afeard myself o' the moonshiners nor the revenuers, nare one, — ain't got no call ter be, — but words sech ez ye air speakin' air powerful ticklish au' techy kind o' talk. Ye better tend ter the cows an' sheep an' weavin' an' sech, an' leave the men's business alone. I hev never knowed," continued Jerry, a trifle acrimoniously, "a woman git ten steps away from home but what she acts ez ef she hed tuk off her brains an' lef' 'em thar along of her every-day clothes."

"I jes' went ter git the lam' out'n a hole," said Alethea, in no wise daunted, and ready with her retort. "His leg's mendin', though he hops some yit. An' I war in the cow-pen when the moonshiner kem an' talked ter me."

"Listen at ye, a-settin' talkin' 'bout law-breakers," said the fastidious Mrs. Purvine, who had abruptly waked. "I ain't kin ter none o' 'em. Naw, sir, an' I would n't own it ef I war. Mind me o' yer uncle Pettin Guyther, ez war always talkin' 'bout murder an' robbery: every tale he told they killed the folks a diff'ent way, — spilled thar blood somehows, an' cracked thar skulls bodaciously; an' whenever he 'd git hisself gone from hyar I useter be 'feared lawless ones would kem hyar of a night ter thieve an' kill, knowin' ez I hed consider'ble worldly goods. The Bible say riches ain't no 'count. Mebbe so, but I ain't so sure 'bout that."

Perhaps it was her clock which she had in mind, for — without any monition from it, however — she added, "Time ter go ter bed, chill'n, — time ter go ter bed."

She did not rise from her chair at once. She admonished Jerry to "kiver" the fire with ashes, and watched

him as he did it. Then he tramped up the ladder to the
roof-room, noisily enough to wake the dead, perhaps, but
not aunt Dely's boys.

She gave a long, mournful yawn of sleepiness and
fatigue, and stretched her arms wearily above her head.
Then with sudden cheerfulness she exclaimed, "Lethe,
ye hain't never hed a chance ter sleep in the bedroom!"

She spoke as if there were but one on the face of the
earth.

"Ye hev never been down hyar 'thout yer elders an'
sech, ez ye hev hed ter show respec' ter, an' stan' back
fur, — yer step-mam, an' Jacob Jessup's wife, an' sech;
but ye shell sleep in the bedroom one time, sure, instead
o' in this room, ez be het up so hot with cookin' supper
in it."

She rose bustlingly to stir up the fire, that there might
be light enough to make the requisite preparations. Alethea's heart failed her when she thought of the tiny apartment partitioned off at the end of the porch, and beheld
her aunt lighting a little tin lamp without a chimney at
the fire. The mountain girl, with all the conservatism of
her class, possessed the strength of prejudice against innovation which usually appertains to age. The characteristic of years seemed reversed as she looked on with
reluctance, and the old woman flustered about, full of her
experimental glories and her eager relish of a new fashion. "Ye kem along, child!" she exclaimed, her moon
face wreathed with a toothless smile and the redolent
emanations of the smoking and sputtering lamp. It was
placed on a shelf in the little room, and as Alethea buttoned the door it gave out less light than a suffocating
odor. It served, however, to reveal the timbers that
formed the sides of the room, for it was built after the
treasures of the post-office had been exhausted in the
decoration of the main house. Upon them hung an array
of Mrs. Purvine's dresses, suspended by the neck, and
suggesting the uncheerful idea of a row of executed
women. The bed was high, huge with feathers and
heaped with quilts. There were no means of ventila-

tion, unless sundry cracks incident to mountain architecture might be relied upon. Alethea made haste to extinguish the lamp. When she had climbed the altitudes of the feather bed she could not sleep. The roof-room at home, with its windows and its sweeps of high air, was not so fine, it might be, but as she smothered by slow degrees she thought poorly of fashion. Her brain was hot with the anxious, strenuous thoughts that seethed through it. She was much less cheerful as the hours wore on. The recollections of the sad day bore heavily upon her spirit. Over and again Mink's cruel words, the ridicule to which the lawyer had subjected her in her own estimation, the affront to her dignity, — she had no such fine name for it, she could only feel, — came back to her, and she could but marvel that the evening had passed so placidly; she wondered that she even lived, so acute were the pangs of her wounded pride. She had an ineffable repugnance to the idea of ever seeing Harshaw again; for herself alone, for her life, she felt, she would have made no further effort. "I'll do it fur Reuben, though," she said. The thought of him, too, was very bitter. Her wakeful eyes were hot, but they harbored no tears. Once she slipped down from the bed and unbuttoned the door, hoping to sleep with the influx of air. It came in fresh, sweet, full of the sense of dew. The night was not black; only a subdued gray shadow lay over all the land: how its passive, neutral aspect expressed the idea of rest! Looking out from the cavernous overhanging portal of the little porch, she could see the Great Smoky, darkly rising above the cove. She heard the stir of a bird roosting in an althea bush by the gate, and then a scuttling noise under the house. She had moved very softly, but the vigilant Towser bounded upon the porch. He knew her — for she spoke to him instantly — as well as he knew his name, but for some unexplained affectation of his nature he would not recognize her, and sat before her door and barked at her with a vehemence that made the roof ring, the sound reverberating from the mountains as if a troop of wolves were howling in the melancholy woods. Twice he tired of this pastime, and withdrew under the house, coming out once more to renew it. She shut the door, finally, and again and again he threw himself against it, at last lying down before it and growling at intervals. She fell asleep after a time, through sheer fatigue, regardless of the lack of air in the little dungeon; waking heavy-eyed and fagged in the morning, able to acquiesce only faint-heartedly when Mrs. Purvine triumphantly saluted her: "Waal, Lethe, now nobody kin never say ez ye ain't slep' in the bedroom."

All day she felt the effects of her vigil. She thought it was this which had touched her courage. She stood still with a quaking at her heart, when, climbing the Great Smoky, she reached the forks in the road where she should turn off to go to Sam Marvin's house. There was no view of the valley. The woods were immeasurable about her, all splendid with the pomp and state of autumn. Those great trees, ablaze with color, — the flaming yellow of the hickory, the rich, dull purple of the sweet-gum, the crimson of the oaks, — reached up in endless arches above her head, all boldly painted against the blue sky. An incredible brilliancy of effect was afforded by the long vistas, free of undergrowth, and carpeted with the poly-tinted leaves. Among the boughs often the full purple clusters of the muscadines hung, the vines climbing to the tops of the trees, and then trailing over to the ground. As she stood she heard a creaking and straining of the strong cables, — a fox in their midst as they lay tangled upon the earth. She noted, too, the translucent red globes of the persimmon hanging upon trees denuded of all but a few yellow leaves.

She sat down on a log at the forks of the road, feeling greatly perturbed and anxious. To do what she proposed to do was to take her life in her hands. Not her stepmother alone, but Jacob Jessup, had warned her, and Jerry Price had repeated what they had said, almost in their very words. But they had only sought to curb her foolish tongue. They had never dreamed of the reckless temerity of going into the moonshiner's den to defy him, proclaim herself the informer, and warn him to save himself. He had already threatened her; she remembered his stern, vehement face in the closing dusk. She wondered that her mind should balk from the decision so imperatively urged upon it. She seemed, as it were, to catch herself in lapses of attention. Often she looked, first at one, then at the other, of the roads,— neither visible for more than a few yards up the steep ascent, — as if she expected some diversion, some extraneous aid, in her dilemma, something to happen to decide it for her.

What, she said to herself, if never again she should behold this place? What if, in taking choice of the forks of the road, she should take a path she might never tread again?

And then she wondered that she should notice that the log on which she sat was a "lick log," should speculate whether the cattle often came here for salt, should look idly into the cleft within it to see if perchance there were still salt there.

It would be safer, it might be better for all, to give her testimony if it should be called for. and leave Sam Marvin to the law. "I'm fairly feared o' him, ennyways. I'm feared ter go thar an' let him know that he'll git fund out, mebbe, fur I'll tell on him ef I'm summonsed ez a witness. My step-mother's always sayin' I'm a meddler, an' mebbe I be."

She listened to the sound of an outgushing roadside spring. She looked up at the new moon, which seemed to follow the lure of the wind beckoning in the trees. They shook their splendid plumes together like an assemblage of bowing courtiers, gayly bedight.

She remembered the "houseful," the pinching poverty, the prison, the destruction of the still. She rose reluctantly and turned to the left. Her eyes were bright her cheeks were flushed; her red lips parted. She listened intently from time to time: not a sound but her own slow, light footfall. She had thought to hear

the dogs barking, for the place was now near at hand.
When she saw a rail-fence terminating the vista her
heart gave a great bound; she paused, looking at it with
dilated eyes. Then she went on, up and up, till the
house came in view, — a forlorn little cabin, with a clay
and stick chimney, smokeless! She stared at it amazed.
There was no creature in the hog-pen, which was large
for the pretensions of the place, — the distillery refuse
explained its phenomenal size, perhaps; the door of the
house swung loose in the wind. There were several slats
nailed across the entrance low down, evidently intended to
keep certain vagrant juveniles from falling out of the door.
No need for this now. The place was deserted. Alethea
walked up to the fence, — the bars lay upon the ground,
— and stepped over the slats into the empty room. The
ashes had been dead for days in the deep chimney-place;
a few rags in a corner fluttered in the drafts from
crannies; the whole place had that indescribable mournfulness of a deserted human habitation that had so pathetically appealed to her in the little house at Boke's
Spring. Here it pierced her heart. It was from fear
of her that they had fled, — and whither? A poor home
at best, where could they find another? She need not
have quaked, she said to herself; they had not sought to
still her tongue, lest it should wag against them. They
had uprooted their home, and had withdrawn themselves
alike from the informer and the law that threatened
them. The tears sprang into her eyes. She deprecated
their bitter feeling, their saddened lives, their deserted
hearthstone. And yet it was all wrong that they should
distill the brush whiskey, and could she say she was to
blame?

A faint scratching sound struck her attention. It
came from behind the closed door of the shed-room.
She stood listening for a moment, unable to account for
it. Then she went forward and unlatched the door.

A starved cat, emaciated and forlorn to the last degree, forgotten in the removal, shut by some accident
into the room, crept quivering out. It went through the

dumb show of mewing; it could not walk; its bones almost pierced its skin. Its plight served to approximate the date of the flitting. It had been there for days, weeks perhaps.

She picked up the creature, and carried it home in her arms.

X.

THE little brick court-house in Shaftesville had stood for half a century in the centre of the village square, as impassive as an oracle to the decrees which issued from it. Even time seemed able to make but scant impression upon it. True, the changes of the day might register on its windows, flaring with fictitious fires when the sun was in the west, or reflecting the moonlight with pallid glimmers, as if some white-faced spectre had peered out into the midnight through the dusty pane. Mosses clung to its walls; generations of swallows nested in its chimneys, soaring up from them now and then, bevies of black dots, as if the records below had spewed out a surplusage of punctuation marks and blots; decay had touched a window-sill here and there. But it was still called the "new court-house," in contradistinction to the primitive log building that it had replaced; and despite some inward monitions of its age once in a while, its long experience of various phases of life, its knowledge of the coming and going of many men who would come and go no more, it was enabled to maintain an air of jaunty unconsciousness, as it was still the handsomest edifice in Shaftesville and of a somewhat imposing architectural pretension. It had beheld many a "State's day" dawn like this, with fitful gusts of wind and rain, with a frenzied surging of the boughs of the hickory-trees about it as if some sylvan grief beset them, with a continual shifting of the mists that veiled the mountains and hung above the roofs of the straggling little town.

The few stores, all of which faced the square, were early full of customers clad in jeans, with heavy cowhide boots deeply bemired by the red clay mud of the streets, and with gruff faces that expressed surly disapproval of the frills and frippery of civilization as exhibited in Shaftesville. Canvas-covered wagons, laden with produce and drawn by oxen, stood before the doors, and among the piles of corn and bags of apples and chestnuts children's wide-eyed, grave faces looked out cautiously from behind the flaps at the inexplicable "town ways." In the intervals of the down-pour there was much stir in the streets. Men with long-skirted coats and broad hats and stern, grizzled faces rode about on gaunt mountain horses. Now and then one would be accompanied by an elderly woman in homespun dress, a shawl and sun-bonnet, wearing a settled look of sour disaffection, and chirruping a sharp warning rather than encouragement to her stumbling, antiquated gray mare. There were many horses hitched to the palings of the court-house fence, and numbers of men lounged about the yard, all crowding up the steps as the tuneless clangor of the bell smote the air. Around the door of the jail boys and rowdyish young men assembled, waiting with an indomitable patience, despite the quick, sharp showers, to see the prisoner led out.

The people of Shaftesville regarded the swarm of visitors as somewhat an encroachment upon their vested rights. "Leave *anybody* in the mountains?" was a frequent raillery.

"Ye town folks jes' 'lowed ye 'd hev all the fun ter yerselves o' seein' Mink Lorey tried, ye grudgin' half-livers," the mountaineers would retort; "but from what I kin see, I reckon ye air sorter mistook this time, sure."

And indeed the court-room was crowded as it had seldom been in the fifty years that justice had been meted out here. In the space without the bar the benches groaned and creaked beneath the weight of those who had taken the precaution to secure seats in advance, and had occupied them in dreary waiting since early in the morning. The forethought of one coterie had come to naught, for the bench succumbed beneath twenty stalwart mountaineers; its feeble supports bent, and as the party collapsed in a wild mingling of legs and arms, waving in frantic efforts to recover equilibrium, Shaftesville was "mighty nigh tickled ter death," for the first time that day. As the sprawling young fellows sheepishly gathered themselves together, a burst of jeering laughter filled the room, only gradually subdued by the sheriff's "Silence in court!"

The attorney-general was already piling his books and papers on the table, consulting his notes and absorbed in his preparations. He was a man of fifty, perhaps, with a polished bald head that might have been of interest to a phrenologist (for it had sundry marked protuberances), blunt, strong features, a heavy lower jaw, an expression of insistent common sense, and a deep bass voice. He was sonorously clearing his throat just now, and was wiping from his thick, short, grizzled mustache drops of some fluid that gave a pervasive unequivocal odor to his breath. It had only rejoiced his stomach, however, and did not affect the keen acumen for which he was famous, and he was settling to his work with an evident intention of giving the defense all they would be able to wrestle with. The old miller, in his rags and patches, sat beside him as prosecutor. His face wore a strange meekness. Now and then he lifted his bleared eyes with an intent look, as if hearing some unworded counsels; then shook his head and bowed it, with its long white locks, upon his hands clasped on his stick. There were many glances directed toward him, half in commiseration, half in curiosity; but these sentiments were bated somewhat by familiarity, for there was hardly a man in Cherokee County who had not visited the ruins of the mill and heard much gossip about the old man's uncharacteristic humility and submissive grief.

A stronger element of interest was added to the impending trial by the circumstance that it was a stranger on the bench. Comparatively few of the assemblage had been in attendance the preceding days, during the trial of the civil cases, and in the preliminary moments, throughout the opening of the court, the reading of the minutes, the calling of the roll, the miscellaneous motions, until the criminal docket was taken up and the case called, the judge sustained the fixed gaze of one half the county.

He did not embody the sleek, successful promise of his reputation. He had the look of a man who has fought hard for all that he has won, and, unsatisfied, is ready to fight again. It was a most unappeased, belligerent spirit expressed in his eyes. They were of a dark gray, and deeply set. He had straight black hair, cut short about his head. His face wore a repressed impatience; sharp lines were drawn about it, making him seem somewhat older than his age, which was thirty-five or six; his nose had a fine, thin nostril; his chin was round and heavy. He wore a long mustache; now and then he gnawed at the end of it. He sat stiffly erect before the desk, his elbow upon it, his chin resting in his hand. His blue flannel suit hung negligently on his tall, slender figure, and they were lean, long fingers that held his chin.

He was looking about with a restless eye. The great round stove in the room was red hot. Snow had been seen on the summits of the distant Smoky, and was not this sure indication that winter was at hand? The sheriff was a man of rigid rule and precedent, and the fire had been built accordingly.

The judge spoke suddenly. He had a singularly low, inexpressive voice, a falling inflection, and a deliberate, measured manner. "Mr. Sheriff," he said, "hoist that window, will you?"

All the windows were occupied by men and boys, some of them standing that they might obtain a better view of the prisoner when he should be led in. From the sill of the window indicated they descended with clumsy hops and thumps upon the floor, as they made way for the sheriff to admit the air. There was a half-suppressed titter from those more fortunately placed, as the dispossessed and discomfited spectators crowded together against the wall. The judge glanced about with displeasure in his eyes.

"I'll have you to understand," he said in his unimpassioned drawl, " that a trial before a court of justice is not a circus or a show. And if there's not more quiet in this court-room, I'll send one half of this crowd to jail."

There was quiet at once. The gaze fixed upon him was suddenly an unfriendly look. To be sure, he was not a visiting clergyman, but one expects a certain degree of urbanity from the stranger within one's gates, however lofty his mission and imperious his authority. Their own judicial magnate, Judge Averill, was a very lenient man, fat, and bald, and jolly. The frequenters of the place could but be impressed with the contrast. If Judge Averill found the room or the weather too warm, he took off his coat, and tried his cases clothed in his right mind, and in little else. Everybody in the county was familiar with the back of his vest, which had a triangular wedge of cloth let into it, for the judge had become more expansive than when the vest was a fit. He was a sound lawyer and an excellent man, and his decisions suffered no disparagement from his shirt sleeves.

The pause of expectation was prolonged. The stove was cracking, as it abruptly cooled, as if with inarticulate protest against these summary proceedings. The autumnal breeze came in dank and chill at the window. The spectators moved restlessly in their places. There was a sharp contrast between the townspeople — especially the lawyers within the bar, in their dapper store clothes, and with that alert expression habitual with men who think for a living — and the stolid, ruminative mountain folks, with unshorn beards and unkempt heads, habited in jeans, and lounging about in slouching postures.

There was a sudden approach of feet in the hall, — the feet, to judge by their nimble irresponsibility, of scuttling small boys. A thrill of excitement ran through the crowd as a heavier tramp resounded. The sheriff in charge of the prisoner, who was accompanied by his counsel, came into the room so swiftly as almost to impair the effect of the entry, and Mink and his lawyer sat down within the bar.

Oddly enough, Mink's keen, bright eyes were elate as he glanced about. He looked so light, so alert, so elastically ready to bound away, that those cautious souls, who like to be on the safe side, felt that it would conduce to the public weal if he were still ironed. He was visibly excited, too; his expression conveyed the idea of an inadequate recognition of everything that he saw, but he stood up and pleaded "Not guilty" in a steady, strong voice, and with his old offhand, debonair, manly manner. He held his hat in his hand, — a long time, poor fellow, since he had had need of it; his clothes still bore the rents of the struggle when he was captured; his fine hair curled down upon his brown jeans coat collar; and his face had an unwonted delicacy of effect, the refined result of the prosaic "jail-bleach." He seemed most thoroughly alive. In contrast any other personality suggested torpor. His strong peculiarities had a certain obliterative effect upon others; he was the climax of interest in the room. The judge looked at him with marked attention.

Harshaw had flung himself back in his chair, that quaked in every fibre beneath him. He mopped his flushed face with his handkerchief, sighed with fatness and anxiety, and pulled down his vest and the stubs of his shirt sleeves about his thick wrists, for he wore no cuffs. He leaned forward from time to time, and whispered with eager perturbation to the prisoner, who seemed to listen with a sort of flout of indifference and confident protest. Mink's conduct was so unexpected, so remarkable, that it attracted general attention. The members of the bar had taken note of it, and presently two or three commented in whispers on Harshaw's preoccupation. For he, a stickler at trifles, a man that fought on principle every point of his case, had allowed something to slip his notice. The names of the jury were about to be drawn. The sheriff, seeking, according to the law, that exponent of guilelessness, "a child under ten years of age," had encountered one in the hall, and came back into the room, beckoning with many an alluring demonstration some small person, invisible because of the density of the crowd. It once more showed a disposition to titter, for the sheriff, a bulky, ungainly man, was wreathing his hard features into sweetly insistent smiles, when there appeared, in the open space near the judge's desk, a little maiden, following him, beginning to smile, too, under so many soft attentions. Her blowzy, uncovered hair was of a sunny hue; her red lips parted to show her snaggled little teeth; her eyes, so fresh, so blue, were fastened upon him with an expression of blandest favor; her plump little body was arrayed in a blue-checked cotton frock; and despite the season her feet were bare. It was perhaps this special mark of poverty that attracted the attention of one of the lawyers. He was a man of extraordinary memory, a politician, and well acquainted in the coves. He looked hard at the little girl. Then he whispered to a crony that she was the miller's granddaughter. For it was "Sister Eudory." They watched Harshaw with idle interest, expecting him to identify the small kinswoman of the drowned boy, and to derive from the fact some fine-spun theory of incompetency. He did not recognize her, however, — perhaps he had never before seen her; he only gave her a casual glance, and then turned his eyes upon the jury list in his hands.

The scrolls bearing the names of the proposed jurors were placed in a hat, and the sheriff, bowing his long back, extended it to "Sister Eudory."

She held her pretty head askew, looked up, smiling with childish coquetry at the judge, put in her dimpled hand with a delicate tentative gesture, took out a scroll, and under the sheriff's directions, handed it to the clerk with an elaborate air of bestowal. He looked at it, and read the name aloud.

Her charming infantile presence, as she stood by the judge's desk among the grave, bearded men, drawing the jury with her dimpled hands, won upon the crowd. There were laughing glances interchanged, and no dissenting opinion as to the prettiness and "peartness" of "Sister Eudory." She was evidently under the impression that she was performing some great public feat, as she again thrust in her hand, caught up another scroll, and smiled radiantly into the face of the judge, who was visibly embarrassed by the blandishments of the small coquette. He hardly knew how to return her gaze, and instead he glanced casually out of the window close by.

The defense frequently availed themselves of their right of peremptory challenge. This was a matter of preconcerted detail with the jury list before them. Whenever it was possible they challenged " for cause " until the *venire* was exhausted. Then jurors were summoned from the by-standers. It was not exactly the entertainment for which the crowd had been waiting, but they found a certain interest in seeing Mink, no longer indifferent, lean forward, and with acrimonious eagerness whisper into the counsel's ear presumable defamations of the juror, who looked on helplessly and with an avidity of curiosity as to what was about to be publicly urged against him. Over and again the sheriff made incursions into the streets, summoning talesmen wherever he could lay his hands on suitable persons. Men of undoubted integrity and sobriety were scarce at the moment, for the good citizens of Shaftesville, averse to the duty, and hearing that he was abroad on this mission, disappeared as if the earth had swallowed them. Plunging into the stores, the baffled official would encounter only the grins of the few callow clerks — proprietor and customers having alike fled. Once he pursued the flying coat-tails and the soles of the nimble feet of one of the solid men of the town around a corner, never coming nearer. It was a time-honored custom to respond thus to one's country's call, and engendered no bitterness in the sheriff's breast. Perhaps he considered this saltatory exercise one of the official duties to which he had been dedicated.

The difficulty of securing a jury was unexampled in the annals of the county. Many, otherwise eligible, confessed to a prejudice against Mink, and had formed and freely expressed an opinion as to his guilt. One old codger from some sequestered cove of the mountains, never before having visited Shaftesville, and desirous of adding to the strange tales of his travels the unique experience of serving on the jury, dashed his own hopes when questioned as usual, by replying glibly in the affirmative. He said, too, that the "outdacious rascality of the prisoner showed in his face, an' ef they locked him up for life he 'd be a warnin' ter the other mischievious young minks, fur the kentry war a-roamin' with 'em." His look of blank amazement and discomfiture when told to "stand aside" elicited once more the ready titter of the crowd and the sheriff's formula, "Silence in court!"

As such admissions were made, Mink sat, his head thrust forward, his bright, intent eyes flashing indignantly, a fluctuating flush on his pallid cheek, his whole lithe, motionless figure seeming so alert that it would scarcely have astonished the community if he had sprung upon the holder of these aggressive views of his guilt. His lawyer sneered, and now and then exchanged a glance of scornful comment with him, — for Harshaw had recovered his equanimity in the exercise of that most characteristic quality, his pugnacity, during his wrangles with the attorney for the State in challenging the jurymen.

The crude gray light of the autumn day waned. A dim shadow fell over the assemblage. Gusts of wind dashed the rain against the grimy panes, the drops trickling down in long, irregular lines; the yellow hickory leaves went whirling by, sometimes dropping upon the window-ledges, and away again on the restless blast. The mists pressed against the glass, then quivered and disappeared, and came once more. Occasionally a great hollow voice sounded from the empty upper chambers of the building and through the long halls; the doors left ajar slammed now and then, and the sashes rattled as the wind rose higher.

It was not more cheerful when the lamps were lighted, for the court did not adjourn at the usual hour. A strong smell of coal oil and of ill-trimmed wicks pervaded the air; a bated suffusion of yellow radiance emanated from them into the brown dimness of the great room. The illumined faces were dull with fatigue and glistening with perspiration, for the stove was once again red-hot, — an old colored man, with a tropical idea of comfort, appearing at close intervals with an armful of wood. Old Griff's long white hair gleamed among the darker heads within the bar. He had fallen asleep, his forehead bowed on his hands, his hands clasped on his stick. Strange shadows seemed to be attending court. Grotesque distortions of humanity walked the walls, and lurked among the assemblage, and haunted the open door, and looked over the shoulder of the judge.

It began to be very apparent to the spectators, the bar, the prisoner, the attorney-general, and the sheriff, that Judge Gwinnan had the fixed purpose of sitting there without adjournment until the requisite competent dozen jurors should be secured. It was already late, long past the usual hour for supper, and although the lawyers and the crowd, who could withdraw and refresh themselves as they wished, might approve of this ascetic determination neither to eat nor to sleep until the jury was achieved, the sheriff, his deputy absent, felt it a hardship. He was a bulky fellow, accustomed to locomotion only on horseback. He had taken much exercise to-day on foot, a sort of official Diogenes, — searching for a mythical unattained man of an exigent mental and moral pattern, — with not even a tub as a haven to which he might have the poor privilege of retiring. When he next darted out with a sort of unwieldy agility into the hall, which was lighted by a swinging lamp, the wick turned too high and the chimney emitting flames tipped with smoke, he was not easily to be withstood. He seized upon a man leaning idly against the wall, his hands in his pockets, whom he had not seen before to-day. "Ye air the very feller I'm a-lookin' fur!" he cried, magnifying the accident into a feat of intention.

Peter Rood drew back further against the wall, with a shocked expression on his swarthy face and in his glittering black eyes. "I can't!" he cried. "Lemme go!"

"Why can't ye?" demanded the sheriff.

"I ain't well," protested Rood, more calmly.

"Shucks!" the officer incredulously commented. "Ef all I hev hearn o' that sort to-day war true, thar ain't a hearty, whoppin' big man in Cherokee County but what's got every disease from the chicken pip ter the yaller fever. Come on, Pete, an' quit foolin'."

Under the strong coercion of the law administered by a sheriff who wanted his supper, Rood could but go.

Despite his rapacious interest in all that concerned the tragedy, he had hitherto held aloof from the court-house; he had withdrawn himself even from the streets, fearing to meet the sheriff. Seeing the great yellow lights in the windows, each flaring in the rainy night like some many-faceted topaz, he had fancied that the trial must be well under way, for no gossip had come to him in his hiding-place of the difficulty of securing a jury. He could no longer resist his curiosity. He strode at his leisurely gait up the steps, meaning merely to glance within, when the sheriff issued upon him.

As he came with the officer into the room, Mink scanned him angrily, leaned forward, and whispered sharply to the lawyer. Rood was trembling in every fibre; the fixed gaze of all the crowd seemed to pierce him; his great eyes turned with a fluctuating, meaningless stare from one official to the other.

He was a freeholder, not a householder. He had expressed no opinion as to the guilt of the prisoner. Had he formed none? He had not thought about it. He was challenged by the defense on the score of personal enmity toward the prisoner, the peremptory challenges being exhausted. As he was otherwise eligible he was put upon his *voir dire.*

Harshaw looked steadily at him for a moment, his red lips curling, sitting with his arms folded across his broad chest. Mink's bright, keen face close behind him was expectant, already triumphant. His hand was on the back of his counsel's chair.

Suddenly Harshaw, tossing his hair from his brow, leaned forward, with his folded arms on the table before him.

"Did you not, sir," he said, smacking his confident red lips, and with an exasperatingly deliberate delivery, — "did you not on the twentieth day of August ascend a certain summit of the Great Smoky Mountains called Piomingo Bald, and there" — he derisively thrust out his red tongue and withdrew it swiftly — "shoot and kill a certain cow, believing it to belong to Mink Lo— to Reuben Lorey?"

The judge's eyes were fixed upon Rood. He seemed strangely agitated, shocked; his face assumed a ghastly pallor.

The attorney-general protested that the juror was not obliged to answer a question which tended to fasten disgrace, nay crime, upon him; Harshaw the while still leaning on the table, laughing silently, and looking with the roseate dimples of corpulent triumph at their discomfiture.

"The juror need not answer," said the judge.

"I'm mighty willin' ter answer, jedge," gasped Rood. "I never done no sech thing sence I war born."

In the estimation of all the crowd it was natural that he should say this; to accept the privilege of silence would be admission.

"Let me put another question in altogether another field," said Harshaw, smoothing his yellow beard. "If it please the court to permit us to cite the decision of an inferior court, perhaps, but altogether beyond the jurisdiction of this honorable court, I should like to refer to the dicta in the courts of Cupid. Were not you and the prisoner suitors for the hand of the same young lady?"

It tickled him, to use a phrase most descriptive of the enjoyment he experienced, to describe in this inflated manner the humble "courtin'" of the mountaineers. There was a broad smile on many of the faces within the bar, the townspeople relishing particularly a joke of this character on the mountain folks. The judge's discerning gray eye was fixed upon him as his pink laugh expanded, his peculiarly red lips showing his strong white teeth.

"Yes, sir, we war," Rood admitted. He was calm now; his agitation had excited no comment; it was to be expected in a man surprised, confounded, and dismayed by so serious a charge.

"You were! How interesting! Go where you may, the world's the same! The charmer spreads her snare even up in the cove! And you and Reuben Lorey fell together in it, two willing victims. And as he got the best of it, as the lady preferred him, it would be natural that you should have some little grudge against him, hey?"

"I dunno how he got the best of it," said Rood sharply. "I ain't got no grudge agin him fur that. 'T war jes' yestiddy she sent me word by her mother ter kem back; she war jes' foolin' Mink."

He was evidently glad to tell it; he did not care even for the giggle in the crowd.

The lawyer was abashed for a moment, and Mink, so long accustomed to be rated a breaker of hearts, a lady-killer, was grievously cut down. In all the episodes of that day which had so bristled with animosity this was the first moment that his spirit flagged, despite that he had never heretofore cared for Elvira, — did not care for her now.

Rood hardly was aware how the examination was tending; in the interests of self-defense he had overlooked its purpose. He stood staring with blank amaze when the judge's voice ended the discussion.

"The juror is competent," he said.

The two remaining talesmen being unchallenged, the jury was duly impaneled and sworn.

The court was adjourned. The sleepy crowd filed out into the streets, the lights in the court-house windows disappeared, and a dark and vacant interval ensued.

XI.

THE morning dawned with a radiant disdain of mists. The wind was buoyant, elated. The yellow sunshine, in its vivid perfection, might realize to the imagination the light that first shone upon the world when God saw that it was good. The air was no insipid fluid, breathed unconsciously. It asserted its fragrance and freshness in every respiration. It stirred the pulses like some rare wine; it seemed, indeed, the subtle distillation of all the fruitage of the year, enriched with the bouquet of the summer, and reminiscent of the delicate languors of the spring. The sky had lifted itself to empyreal heights, luminously blue, with occasional faint fleckings of fleecy vapors. The white summits of the mountains were imposed against it with a distinctness that nullified distance; even down their slopes, beyond the limits of the snowfall, the polychromatic vestiges of autumn were visible, with no crudity of color in these sharp contrasts, but with a soft blending of effect. Within the court-house great blocks of sunshine fell upon the floor through the dirty panes. Several of the sashes were thrown up to admit the air. The rusty stove stood cold and empty. Many a day had passed since the spider-webs that hung from the corners of the ceiling and draped the bare windows of the great room had been disturbed. They might suggest to the contemplative mind analogies to the labyrinthine snares of the law, where the intrusive flies perish miserably, and the spiders batten. On one of the window-panes a blue-bottle climbed the glass, intent on some unimagined achievement; always slipping when near the top, and falling buzzing drearily to the bottom, to recommence his laborious ascent in the sunshine. Sometimes he would fly away, droning in melancholy disgust, presently returning and renewing his futile efforts. He was a fine moral example of perverted powers, and might well be commended to the notice of human malcontents, — by nature fitted to soar, but sighing for feats of pedestrianism. In contrast with the day in its alertness, its intense brilliancy, yesterday was blurred, dim, like some distorted dream hardly worth crediting as a portent. It might need as attestation of its reality the jury which it had brought forth. They were all early in their places, having been sequestered in charge of the sheriff, and having slept as it were under the wing of the law. The privilege accorded by law, in phrase of munificent bestowal, — to be tried by a jury of one's peers, — seems at times a gigantic practical joke, perpetrated by justice on simple humanity. They were indeed Mink's peers so far as ignorance, station, — for most of them were mountaineers, — poverty, and prejudice might suffice. Few were so intelligent, but none so lawless. Most of them were serving under protest, indifferent to the dignity of the great engine of justice which they represented. The two or three who showed willingness were suspected, either by the defense or the prosecution, of occult motives. All looked unkempt, stolid, dogged, even surlily stupid, as they sat in two rows, chewing as with one gesture. Gradually, however, they visibly brightened under the bland courtesy of Mr. Kenbigh, the attorney for the State, who took early occasion to say — and he paraphrased the remark more than once in the course of the day — that he had never had the pleasure of trying a case before so intelligent a jury, or one to whom the sacred interests of justice could be so safely entrusted. Harshaw, too, deported himself toward them with a mollifying suavity which, to judge from his ordinary manner, would have seemed impossible. He had a very pretty wit, of a rough and extravagant style, that greatly commended him to them and relieved the irksomeness of their duress. Mink had evidently been tutored in regard to his demeanor toward them. He forbore to scowl at Pete Rood with the fierce dismay his face had worn when he saw his enemy sworn on the preceding night. But his dissembling was limited. He simply would not look at Rood at all. There was an unaffected confidence, almost indifference, upon his handsome face that occasioned much comment. It had already been rumored among the bar, thence percolating through the town at large, that the defense had discovered important testimony at the last moment, but that for some reason Harshaw had desired to apply for a continuance. The prisoner, it was said, had protested, and refused downright, declaring that by nightfall, by tomorrow at farthest, he would be on his way to his home in Hazel Valley. This rumor gave an added interest to the moment when the witnesses were brought in to be sworn and put under the rule. The crowd scanned each with a fruitless conjecture as to which possessed the potent and significant knowledge on which the defense relied. Several of them were women, demure as nuns in their straight skirts and short waists and long, tunnel-like sun-bonnets. The mountain men strode in, and stared about them freely, and were very bold, in contrast to these decorous associates, with their grave, downcast eyes and pale, passionless faces. The book was held toward the witnesses, two or three were instructed to put their hands upon it, and then the clerk, in a voice that might have proceeded from an automaton, so wooden was the tone and elocution, recited the oath with a swiftness that seemed profane. The group stood half in the slanting sunbeams, half in the brown shadow, close about the clerk's desk. Among the tall, muscular figures of the mountain men and the pallid, attenuated elder women was Alethea, looking like some fine illusion of the dusky shadow and gilded sunshine, with her golden hair and her brown homespun dress. How shining golden her hair, how exquisitely fresh and pure her face, how deep and luminous and serious her brown eyes, showed as never before. Somehow she was embellished by the incongruity of the sordid surroundings of the court-room, the great, haggard, unkempt place, and the crude ugliness of its frequenters. Her face was fully revealed, for she had pushed back her bonnet that she might kiss the book. As she took it from the clerk's hand and pressed her lips to it, Mink's heart stirred with a thrill it had never before known. He was entering as a discoverer upon a new realm of feeling. He experienced a subtle astonishment at the turbulence, the fierceness, of his own emotion.

The judge was looking at her!

Gwinnan's hand still held his pen. His head was still bent over the paper on which he wrote. The casual sideglance of those discerning gray eyes was prolonged into a steady gaze of surprise. He did not finish the word he was writing. He laid the pen down presently. He watched her openly, unconsciously, as she gave back the book, and as she walked with the other witnesses into the adjoining room to await the calling of her name.

Mink could hardly analyze this strange emotional capacity, this new endowment, that had come to him, so amazed was he by its unwonted presence. He had not known that he could feel jealousy. He could not identify it when it fell upon him. He had been so supreme in Alethea's heart, so arrogantly sure of its possession, that he had not cared for Ben Doaks's hopeless worship from afar; it did not even add to her consequence in his eyes. But that this stranger of high degree — he would not have phrased it thus, for he had been reared in ignorance of the distinction of caste, yet he instinctively recognized it in the judge's power, his isolated official prominence, his utter removal from all the conditions of the mountaineer's world — that *this* man should look at her with that long, wondering gaze, should lay down his pen, forgetting the word he was to write!

Mink felt a terrible pang of isolation. For the first time Alethea was in his mind as an independent identity, subject to influences he could scarcely gauge, perhaps harboring thoughts in which he had no share. Her love for him had hitherto served for him as an expression of her whole nature. He had never recognized other possibilities. Even her continual pleas that he should take heed of the error of his ways he had esteemed as evidence of her absorption in him, her eager, earnest aspiration for his best good; she would endure his displeasure rather than forego aught that might inure to his welfare. He had felt no gratitude that she had come to rescue him, as she had often done, never so sorely needed as now; it had seemed to him natural that she should bestir herself, since she loved him so. The first doubt of the permanence and pervasiveness of this paramount affection stirred within him. He wondered if she had noticed the man's look, if she were flattered by it. He sought to reassure himself. "Lethe jes' bogues along, though, seein' nuthin', studyin' 'bout suthin' else; mebbe she never noticed. But ef Mis' Purvine hed been hyar, or Mis' Sayles, I be bound, they 'd hev seen it, an' tole her, too, else they ain't the wimmen I take 'em fur." He marveled whether Gwinnan had thought she was pretty. He himself had always accounted her a fairly "good-lookin' gal," but no better favored than Elvira Crosby.

He had had no fear of the result of the case since he had known of Alethea's strange glimpse of Tad; he was, too, in a moral sense, infinitely relieved by the circumstance. Otherwise he might not have been able to entertain a train of thought so irrelevant to the testimony which was being given by the witnesses for the State. He heard it only casually, although he now and then languidly joined the general smile that rewarded some happy hit of Harshaw's. These pleasantries were chiefly elicited in cross-examining the witnesses for the State, and in wrangles with the attorney-general as to the admissibility of evidence. Kenbigh, with a determination of purple wrath to his bald head, would in his stentorian roar call aloud upon his authorities with a reverent faith as if they were calendared saints. More than once the court ruled against him, when it seemed appropriate in his next remark to drop his voice to a rumbling basso profundo. He maintained due respect for the judge and showed a positive affection for the jury, but the very sight of Harshaw would excite him to an almost bovine expression of rage, — the florid counsel being like a red rag to a bull. At first the only point which Harshaw seemed desirous to make was that none of the witnesses had attached any importance to Mink's threats, the afternoon of the shooting match, to "bust down the mill," until they heard of the disaster. He tried, too, to induce them to admit that Mink was a good fellow in the main. The tragic results, however, of his late mischief had given a new and serious interpretation to all his previous pranks, and the witnesses were more likely to furnish supplemental instances of freakish malice and the mischievous ingenuity of his intentional reprisals than to palliate his jocose capers. One old man, a by-stander at the shooting match, was especially emphatic, even venomous. Harshaw involved him in a sketch of what he considered a young man should be. When asked where he had ever known such a man he naively confessed, — himself, "whenst I war young."

Harshaw found it much safer to take the aggressive. He played upon the alternating fears which Mink's comrades entertained of the revenuers and the moonshiners. He seemed to question rather *pro forma* than with the expectation of eliciting serious results, and to amuse himself with the involutions and contradictions in which he contrived to enmesh them, in replying to his questions as to their sobriety that night in the woods, what they had to drink, how much it required to make them drunk.

To the witness it was not a reassuring playfulness. Harshaw looked very formidable as he sat, his chair tilted back on its hind legs, both hands clasping the lapels of his coat. Whenever he made a point he smacked his confident red lips.

"You were perfectly sober that night?"

The witness virtuously assented.

"And why should n't you be," said the crafty Harshaw, "when we all know there is no still but the God-fearing bonded still in the whole country! Look at the jury, and tell them that you were not drinking that night."

The unfortunate witness faltered that he *had* been drinking some.

"You had!" exclaimed Harshaw, with the accents of surprise. "And yet you say, on oath, that you were sober. Now what do you call sober? We must inquire into this. What do you take? I wish I could put that question as it should be between gentlemen, but" — he waved his fat hand — "some other day."

The witness stared dumbly at him, and the crowd grinned.

"Let me put the question in another form. How much of the reverend stuff is enough to settle you? A pint?"

The witness gallantly declared that he could stand a pint.

"A jugful?"

"Oh, naw, sir," — meaning a jugful would not be necessary.

In the staccato of affected amaze, *"Barrelful!"*

The badgered witness protested and explained, and Harshaw asked, lowering his voice, as if it were exceedingly important, "Now, did that whiskey taste like *brush* whiskey?"

As the quaking, shock-headed country lout replied, the facetious counsel recoiled.

"What! you tell this honorable court, and this intelligent jury, and this upright and learned and teetotaling attorney for the State, that you don't know the difference in the taste between the illicit corn juice of the mountains and the highly honorable, pure, rectified liquor, taxed and stamped, made and drunk, under the auspices of this great, good, and glorious government!"

The judge, who had watched Harshaw with a dilated, gleaming gray eye and a quivering nostril, spoke abruptly.

"The court will not longer tolerate this buffoonery," he drawled. "Counsel may cross-examine witness, and if he has *nothing* to say he may be silent."

Harshaw flushed deeply. He had always enjoyed certain privileges as a wit. Judge Averill, who loved a joke for its own gladsome sake, had often permitted him to transcend decorum. He had no idea, however, of figuring as the butt of his own ridicule. He was a quick fellow, and took what advantage was possible of the situation. "If it please your Honor," he said, rising to address the judge, and with an air of great courtesy, " I will waive the right of cross-examination, since my methods fail in satisfying the court."

Gwinnan looked at him with thinly veiled antagonism. Harshaw relapsed into his tilted chair, still lightly holding his lapels, that favorite posture of rural gentlemen, listening with an air of polite but incidental attention to the attorney-general's examination of the next witness, and declining with a wave of his fat hand to cross-examine.

A stir of excitement pervaded the bar; great interest was aroused in the audience. An old farmer, sitting on one of the benches, holding one treasured knee in both hands, put his foot on the floor to take care of itself, and leaned forward in breathless eagerness to lose no word. Others, who had been less attentive, were nudging one another, and asking what had been said. Again and again, as the successive witnesses were turned over to the defense for cross-examination, and the lawyer waved his pudgy hand, there was a suppressed sensation. His freak of silence had the effect of greatly expediting matters, and the attorney-general announced before the adjournment for dinner that he had no more witnesses to call.

In conducting the examination of the defendant's witnesses Harshaw was extremely grave. He had an excited gleam in his eye, a flurried, precipitate manner, as he went on. Now and then he nodded his head, and tossed back his mane of yellow hair as if it were heavy and harassed him. He still sat in the big, important posture he liked to assume, but every glance was full of an acute anxiety.

Mink strove again to fix his mind on the testimony. Over and over it wandered. He only knew vaguely that his best friends were assuring the jury that his escapades were all in mirth and naught in malice, and instancing as indications of his deeper nature all the good turns he had ever done. He was a loose-handed fellow. He had no thrifty instincts, and perhaps because he valued lightly he gave freely. But the habit, such as it might be, was displayed to the jury under the guise of generosity.

The sunlight now slanting upon the walls had turned to a deep golden-red hue, for the early sunset was close at hand. Through a western window one might see the great vermilion sphere, begirt with a horizontal band of gray cloud, and sinking down into the dun-colored uncertainties about the horizon. The yellow hickory-tree beside the window showed through its thinning leaves the graceful symmetry of its black boughs. The room was dropping into a mellow duskiness, hardly obscurity, for as yet the soft light was sufficient to make all objects distinct in the midst of the gathering shadow, — the lawyers, the prisoner, the tousled heads of the audience, the attentive jury, the unwearied judge. Harshaw could even read his own handwriting as he looked at the list he held, and said, "Mr. Sheriff, call Alethea Sayles."

"Alethea Sayles," roared Mr. Sheriff at the door, as if Alethea Sayles were "beyond the seas" and hard of hearing besides, instead of waiting expectantly in the adjoining room, ten steps away.

As she came in, Mink was quick to notice the interest on Gwinnan's face, — a sort of grave curiosity without any element of disrespect. She had a look in her eyes which Mink had often seen before, and which at once rebuked and angered him, — an expression of spiritual earnestness, of luminous purity; he had sneered at it as "trying to look pious." She sat down in the witness-chair, and pushed back from her forehead her long bonnet; under its brown rim her golden hair showed in lustrous waves. Her saffron kerchief was knotted beneath her round chin. Her face was slightly flushed with the excitement of the moment, but she was not flurried, nor embarrassed, nor restless, nor uncouth, as many of her predecessors had been. Her deliberate, serious manner gave her an air of great value, and as she began to reply to the questions, her clear-voiced, soft drawl pervaded the court-room, singularly silent now, and there was a growing impression that hers was the important testimony for which all had been waiting. Harshaw's manner served to confirm this. He was repressed, grave; only the quick, nervous glance of his opaque blue eye indicated his excitement; his questions were framed with the greatest care, and some of these were strange enough to excite comment. He asked her first to tell all that she knew about the party in the woods that night, — whether they were drinking and had access to any ample supply of liquor. She recited her adventure at Boke's barn, and detailed the subsequent interview with the moonshiner and her refusal to keep his secret, throughout scarcely suppressed excitement in the court-room, for every man knew that with the words she courted martyrdom and took her life in her hands. Harshaw seemed to prize this attestation of her courage and her high sense of the sacred obligations of her oath, and dexterously contrived it so that the judge and the jury should be fully impressed with the crystalline purity of her moral sense, with her immovable determination to tell the truth, the whole truth, and nothing but the truth. He persevered in the examination of this point with great pertinacity, despite many stormy wrangles with the attorney for the State as to the pertinence and admissibility of the evidence, and the occasional ruling of the judge against him. Enough was secured, however, to prove that despite the limitations of the bonded still, Mink had had the opportunity to get drunk if he chose, and his habits were not those of a teetotaler.

The lawyer's questions then became more inexplicable.

"When you discovered that you could give some testimony in this case, what did you do?"

Alethea pushed back her bonnet still further, and stared at him.

"Why, you-uns know," she said.

"Tell the jury."

Like many rural witnesses, she persisted in addressing the judge. She would fix her serious brown eyes on the stolid wooden faces in the jury-box, then lift them to the judge and answer.

"I kem down ter the jail ter see Reuben, an' tell him."

"And did you see him?"

She looked at Harshaw, with a deep humiliation and resentment intensifying the flush on her delicate cheek to a burning crimson. His gravity, the respect of his manner, reassured her. She replied with her deliberate dignity, —

"You-uns know mighty well he would n't see me."

"Then what did you do?"

She seemed for a moment doubtful if she would answer.

"I dunno how ye hev forgot," she said slowly. "*I* hain't."

"I want you to tell the jury," he explained.

"I tried to make you listen."

"And what did I do?"

Once more she pushed her brown bonnet further from her golden head, and looked at him silently.

The pause was so long that the attorney-general remarked that really he could not see the pertinence of the examination.

The judge spoke presently: "Counsel would do well not to harass the witness with unnecessary questions."

What new life was in the man's tones! He had forgotten to drawl. There had been many a badgered witness on the stand to-day whom he had not interfered to protect. Mink eyed him narrowly through the closing dusk. He was leaning forward upon the desk. He was listening with no impartial judicial interest. A personal concern was expressed in his face.

The sympathetic cadence in his voice struck on other ears than Mink's. It was like an open sesame to Alethea's heart. The pent-up indignation burst forth. She was all at once eager to tell the affronts she could not resent. "He would n't listen ter me, jedge!" she cried. "He ran from me,— actially ran down the street. An' I did n't know what ter do. An' nobody knowed 'bout 'n it but me. An' I dassent tell nobody 'ceptin' the lawyer. An' Jerry Price,— him ez air on the jury,— he 'lowed ef I knowed suthin' I wanted ter tell in court, he 'd *make* the lawyer listen, an' so he did. An' I tole him."

"When was that?" asked Harshaw.

"Yestiddy mornin'."

"So that was the reason you did n't tell it before?"

"I war feared ter tell ennybody but the lawyer, 'kase Reuben's enemies mought fix it somehows so 't would n't be no 'count."

"Well, what was this you wanted to tell?"

Her face was growing dim among the glooms. The dusky figures within the bar, the shadowy judge, the indistinct mass of the crowd, the great windows, — indefinite gray squares, — seemed for a moment the darker because of a dull suffusion of yellow light in the halls, falling through the doorways, and heralding the coming of the lamps.

"I wanted to tell that I seen Tad Simpkins arter they 'lowed he war drownded."

There was absolute silence for a moment; then, wild commotion. Men were talking loudly to each other in the crowd. The lights came in with a flare. Several of the jury requested to have the answer repeated. The attorney-general began to ask a question, left off, and bent his head to his notes. A sudden shrill, quaking voice pierced the tumult.

"I know it air a true word!" cried the old miller, clasping his hands. "God would not deliver my soul ter hell. I fund him in my youth, but my age air the age o' the backslider. He would not desert me, though! An' I hev been gin ter do my good works o' faith anew. I 'll find my boy. I 'll make amends. I 'll" —

The sheriff's insistence, "Silence in court!" had no coercion for him. He began to sob and cry aloud, and to call the idiot's name, and was finally taken by the deputy and led out of the court-room, the officer promising to come and let him know as soon as Alethea had disclosed the boy's whereabouts.

Mink glanced around him in triumph. His lip curved. A brilliant elation shone in his eyes. He tossed back, with an arrogant gesture, his long, red, curling hair, gilded by the lamplight to a brighter hue. He joyed to see the discomfiture of his detractors, who had given their testimony with all the gusto that appertains to stamping on a man, literally and metaphorically, who is already down. He noted, too, the surprise and pleasure in Ben Doaks's eye, in Jerry Price's freckled, ugly face, and, strangely enough, Peter Rood looked transfigured. His surly scowl was gone, as if it had never existed. His swarthy face was irradiated by his great excited eyes. A flush dyed his cheek. His breath came in quick gasps. He seemed inordinately relieved, delighted. What! because the forlorn little idiot was not dead? Mink could not understand it. With not even a surmise to explain the demonstration, he stared in suddenly renewed gravity at his old enemy on the jury.

As soon as order was restored, Harshaw resumed his questions.

"Tell the jury when and where you saw him, and how you are sure it was after he was reputed to be drowned."

"'Kase 't war on the Monday o' the camp-meetin' in Eskaqua Cove, an' that war n't begun till arter the mill war busted down," said Alethea.

She detailed the scene at the little school-house in her uncouth phrasings, every syllable carrying conviction to her hearers. Her bonnet had fallen quite back on her shoulders. Her face was delicately ethereal in the lamplight, — so much of the sincerities of her nature it expressed, so fine and true an intelligence, that, beautiful as it was, it was still more spiritual. The strange story she had told was improbable. Looking upon her face it was impossible to doubt it.

"That night, what did you do?"

"I let Buck an' the rest o' the fambly go by ter aunt Dely's house, an' whenst they war out o' sight I called Tad, but he would n't answer. An' then I climbed over the fence, an' sarched an' sarched fur him. But I could n't find him, — not in the house, nor under it, nare one. Then I went on ter aunt Dely's, — Mis' Purvine's," she added, decorously, remembering that her relative was a stickler for etiquette, and might not relish the familiar appellation of kinship in a public assembly. "I never tole nobody, 'kase I war feared ez whoever hed Tad a-hidin' of him fur spite agin Reuben would hear 'bout'n it, an' take him so fur away ez we-uns could n't never ketch him agin. I went back ter the schoolhouse over an' over, a-sarchin' fur him, hopin' he 'd take a notion ter kem thar agin. An' at last I 'lowed I 'd tell the lawyer."

It had become very plain to the listeners that it was in the interests of his client that Harshaw had permitted his own rude conduct to be made public. The prosecution could not now reasonably demand why a hue and cry had not been raised, and why the boy was not brought into court, as it was very evident that because of the witness's mistaken secrecy and the lawyer's purblind folly the facts had not become known to the defense until the preceding day, when it was futile to search a place where the fugitive had been glimpsed three months before.

The attorney-general, about to cross-examine the witness, cleared his throat several times on a low key. He began with a deliberation and caution which indicated that he considered her formidable to the interests of the State. He sat with his side to the table, — the rural lawyer seldom rises save to address the court, — with one elbow upon it, and the other hand twirling his heavy gold watch-chain that festooned his ample stomach. More than once he desisted in this operation, and passed his hand soothingly over his bald head, as if he were encouraging his ideas. He at once sought to show an interested motive in the testimony.

Was she a relation of the prisoner? Was she not interested in him? Was he not her lover? Ah, he had been! And he was not now? And why?

Alethea's simple and modest decorum in answering these questions abashed the ridicule that the mere mention of the tender passion always excites in a rural crowd. She only threw added light upon her character when she replied:

"Reuben did n't like folks ter argufy with him. I useter beg him not ter play kyerds, an' be so powerful gamesome, an' drink whiskey, an' git in sech a many scrapes. An' he 'lowed 't war n't my business. An' I reckon 't war n't. But it never 'peared-like ter me ez sech goin's-on war right, an' I could n't holp sayin' so. An' so he 'lowed ez me an' him could n't agree, an' thar war no use a-tryin'."

Mink glanced up at Gwinnan to note the impression of this plain statement. The judge was looking at *him*.

The attorney-general went on, hoping to find a discrepancy in her testimony, yet hardly knowing how he had best approach it. The court-room had relapsed into absolute silence. One could hear in the pauses the slight movement of the branches of the trees without as the light wind stirred. They were distinctly visible beside the windows, for the night was fair. All the long upper sashes gave upon a sky of a fine, pure azure, seeming more delicate for the dull yellow lamplight flooding the room. The moon with an escort of clouds was riding splendidly up toward the meridian; now and then they closed jealously about her, and again through their parting ranks she looked out radiantly and royally on her realms below. The frost touched the panes here and there with a crystalline sparkle. The attorney-general fixed his eyes upon the moon as he pondered; then, his fingers drumming lightly upon the table, he asked, "It was at the little school-house on the road to Bethel campground?"

"Yes, sir," said Alethea.

"Were you ever there before?"

"A many a time," said Alethea. "The folkses in Eskaqua Cove goes thar ter preachin'."

He glanced again absently at the moon, his fingers still drumming on the table.

"It's a church-house, then," he said, adopting the vernacular, "as well as a school-house?"

"Yes, sir," assented the witness.

"Well, is this fence by which you were standing the fence around the play-yard?"

"Naw, sir," said Alethea, amazed at the idea of this civilized provision for youthful sports. "The palin's air round three sides o' the house, leavin' out the side whar the door be, ter pertect the graves."

The drumming fingers of the attorney-general were suddenly still. "It is a graveyard, then?" he said, in a sepulchral undertone, overmastered himself by the surprise.

"Yes, sir. Folks air buried thar. It's a graveyard."

There was a pause.

"There's no place more appropriate for a boy in poor Tad's predicament to be!" cried the lawyer. "Look here," squaring himself before the table and placing his elbows upon it, "do you believe in ghosts?"

Harshaw had changed color; he had been fiercely biting his red lips and stroking his yellow beard throughout these interrogatories, seeing their drift more clearly, perhaps, than the prosecuting officer did. Now he sprang to his feet, and insisted that the attorney for the State should not be permitted to play upon the superstition of the witness. She had seen no ghost. The court would not, he hoped, permit the questions to take the form of an attempt to persuade a witness — of great native intelligence, indeed, and of the highest moral worth, but densely ignorant, and doubtless saturated with the ridiculous superstitions of the uneducated — that in seeing this fugitive lad she had beheld a supernatural manifestation. "In one moment, sir," he interpolated, addressing Peter Rood, who sat in the back row of the jury, and who had suddenly bent forward, pointing a long finger at the witness, as if he were about to ask a question. "The boy doubtless swam out of the river, and being a maltreated little drudge ran away, and is now somewhere held in hiding by persons inimical to the prisoner. The witness had a glimpse of him. There is no man here ignorant enough to believe that she saw a ghost, — least of all the learned and astute counsel for the State."

"I don't believe she saw a ghost," said the attorney-general, still seated, cocking up his eyes at his vehement opponent. "I do believe, however, most firmly, that the witness had an illusion, hallucination."

There was a stir in the audience and the jury as he uttered these big words. They seemed to represent something more vaguely formidable than a ghost.

"Counsel must conduct the examination on a reasonable basis," remarked the judge.

"I will do so, your Honor," in the basso profundo of deep respect.

Mink, agitated, trembling with the sudden shock, leaned forward and looked with burning eyes at Alethea. How was she discrediting the testimony she had given for him? How was she jeopardizing his fate?

She was almost overcome for a moment. Her nerves were shaken; she was appalled by the sudden revolution her simple disclosure had wrought. Her lips trembled, her eyes filled, but she made a gallant struggle for self-control, and answered in a steady voice the attorney-general's next question.

"Did the boy wear a hat, or was he bare-headed?"

There was suppressed excitement in the audience, for Tad's hat and coat, recovered from the river, had been shown to the jury while she was in the ante-room with the other witnesses.

"I didn't notice, — 't war so suddint."

"How was he dressed?"

"I did n't see," faltered Alethea.

"What *did* you see?"

"I seen his face, ez clear ez I see yourn this minit."

"How did he look, — hearty?"

"Naw, sir; he looked mighty peaked. His face war bleached," — a thrill ran through the crowd, — "an' I reckon he war skeered ez he seen me, fur he 'peared plumb tarrified."

"How long did you see his face?"

"A minit, mebbe; the fog passed 'twixt us."

"Ah, there was fog!"

The attorney-general cast a triumphant sidelong glance at the jury.

He paused abruptly, and turned toward them.

"I beg your pardon, sir," he said, addressing Peter Rood. "I had quite forgotten you wanted to ask a question."

It did not immediately strike him as odd that the man was still in the same position, — in the shadow, leaning forward, supported on the back of the chair of the juryman in front of him, and still pointing at the witness with a long finger.

The judge took note of the lapse of time. "Mr. Sheriff," he said, irritably, "wake that juror up. The man 's asleep."

There was a stir in the jury-box among the attentive eleven men. The juror on whose chair the immovable figure leaned turned his head, and met the fixed gaze of the eyes so close to his own.

He sprang up with a loud cry.

"The man is dead!" he shrieked.

XII.

THE finger of the dead man still pointed at Alethea. His ghastly eyes were fixed upon her. The chair of the juryman in front of him had sustained his weight in the same position in which he had fallen when the first shock of the idea that the witness had seen a spectre instead of the boy, alive and well, had thrilled through the room.

For a few moments it was a scene of strange confusion. The crowd rose from their seats, and surged up to the bar. New-comers were rushing in from the halls. Some one was calling aloud the name of the principal physician of the place. Many were clamoring to know what had happened. The judge's voice sounded suddenly. "Look out for your prisoner, Mr. Sheriff!" he exclaimed sharply; for the officer still stood as if transfixed beside the dead man, on whose shoulder he had laid hold. No hand, however heavy, could rouse him from the slumber into which he had fallen.

The sheriff turned toward the prisoner. The proud mountaineer, keenly sensitive to an indignity, burst out angry and aggrieved. "I hain't budged a paig!" he cried. And indeed he had not moved. "It's jes' 'kase you-uns set thar in jedgmint, an' I hev ter set hyar an' be tried, ez ye kin say sech ez that ter me!"

Harshaw had vehemently clutched his client's arm as a warning to be silent. To his relief, he perceived that Gwinnan had not heard. He was absorbed in directing a physician to be called, and formally adjourned court until nine o'clock the following morning. The reluctant jurymen, quivering with excitement and consumed with curiosity as to the subsequent proceedings, were led off from the scene in charge of an officer, — himself a martyr to duty, — with many an eager backward glance and thought. The crowd hung around outside with unabated excitement. Often it effected an entrance and surged through the doors, to be turned out again by the orders of the physicians. Many climbed on the window-ledges to look through. The lower branches of the hickory-trees swarmed with the figures of nimble boys. The wind now was high. The boughs swayed back and forth with a monotonous clashing. Leaves continually fell from them like the noiseless flight of birds. The moon showed the pale, passionless sky; a planet swung above the distant mountains, burning with the steadfast purity of vestal fires; the inequalities of the hills and dales on which the rugged little town was built — very dark beneath the delicately illumined heavens — showed in the undulating lines of lighted windows, glimmering points stretching out into the gloom. Constantly the weighted gate clanged as men trooped into the court-house yard. The shadows seemed to multiply the number of the crowd.

Suddenly there was a cry: "He's comin'! They're bringin' him! He's comin'!"

The expectation had been so strong that the physician would pronounce it some transient paroxysm of the heart, which he was known to often suffer, that the crowd was stricken into a shocked silence to recognize the undertaker among the men coming out and bearing a litter on which the motionless figure was stretched. One glance at it, and there seemed nothing so inanimate in all nature. The moon, the trees, even the invisible wind, were endowed with redundant life, with identity, with all the affirmations of speculation, of imagination, in comparison with the terrible nullity of this thing that once was Peter Rood. It expressed only a spare finality.

It was strange to think he could not hear the wind blow, straight from the mountains, the dull thud of the many feet that followed him through the gate and down the street; could not see the moon which shone with a ghastly gleam upon his stark, upturned face. He was dead!

He was so dead that already his world was going on with a full acceptation of the idea. He had no longer an individuality as Peter Rood; he was only considered as a dead man. Considered as a dead man, he furnished the judge with a puzzle which irritated him. Gwinnan could not remember any case in which a man had died upon a jury, and he debated within himself whether this instance came under the statute leaving it to the discretion of the court, in the case of a sick juror, to discharge the jury and order a new one to be impaneled, or to excuse the juror and summon another in his place from the by-standers. He went into one of the lawyers' offices, and turned over a few books in search of precedent.

The attorney-general utilized the respite. He had lingered at the scene for a time, animated by curiosity. But when one of the physicians who had been summoned to the court-house, returned to his office, after the vain efforts to resuscitate the man, he found the attorney for the State seated before the wood fire, his hands clasped behind his head, his feet stretched out upon the hearth, his chair tilted back upon its hind legs, waiting for him in comfortable patience.

There was no carpet on the floor. The small windows were lighted by tiny panes of glass. The hearth was broken in many places, but painted a bright red with a neat home-made varnish of powdered bricks mixed with milk, commonly used in the country. There were several splint-bottomed chairs, an easy-chair, and one or two tables; book-cases covered the walls from the floor to the ceiling. It was the doctor's professional opinion that tobacco was the ruin of the country; on the high mantelpiece were ranged several varieties of pipe, from the plebeian cob and brier-root to the meerschaum presented by a grateful patient, all bearing evidences of much use.

Kenbigh looked up quietly as the owner of the appropriated quarters walked in. Dr. Lloyd was a tall, spare man of sixty odd, with a back that never bent, dressed punctiliously in black broadcloth and the most immaculate linen of an old-fashioned style. His thick hair was white. He wore a stiff mustache; his shaven chin was square and resolute; his features were singularly straight. His gray eye expressed great cleverness and goodness, but there was a refined sarcasm in the curl of his lips, and he affected a blunt indifference of manner, not to say brusqueness.

"What's the matter with you?"

"Nothing, doctor,—nothing with my vitals, or I would n't have trusted myself near you. The instinct of self-preservation is strong. I have come for some information."

"An aching void in the regions of your brain, eh? Well, at your time of life that's incurable."

"I want you," said the lawyer, his eyes roaming around the medical library, ranged upon the wall, with a gloating, gluttonous gleam at the idea of the feast of information within the covers of the volumes, "to lecture me, doctor."

"Where's your Medical Jurisprudence?"

"It does n't teach me all I want to know about ghosts."

Surprise was something Dr. Lloyd was never known to express or imply. He sat looking at the visitor with his calm professional eye, as if it were the most habitual thing in the world for sane lawyers to come into his office at night, wanting to know about ghosts.

"I want to know all about absurd illusions,—in people of undoubted sanity."

"Subject of some scope," dryly remarked the doctor.

"I want to know all that *you* know about hallucinations, visions. I want an elaborate exposition of the visual apparatus as connected with the brain, and of the derangement of its nervous functions."

"Upon my word, you're a pretty fellow!"

"And then I want you to lend me *all* your books." And once more he gazed around on the coveted treasures of the shelves.

One of the great logs had burned in two, the chunks falling forward upon the other blazing sticks. The doctor had made a move toward the tongs, but the lawyer arose, and with a sort of cumbrous agility kicked first one and then the other into the space between the dogs. Dr. Lloyd watched this proceeding with silent disapproval. Far be it from him to put his dapper old-fashioned foot-gear to any such purpose.

The warmth of the fire was grateful, for it had grown much colder without. The wind surged down the street like the passing of many feet, some tumultuous human rush. The fir-tree beside the door was filled with voices, sibilant whisperings, sighs. Clouds were scudding through the sky; Kenbigh could see them from where he sat listening to the doctor's monologue. The moonlight lay on the old-fashioned garden without, all pillaged by the autumn winds, — the rose-bushes but leafless wands; the arbors, naked trellises; the walks, laid off with rectangular precision, showing what the symmetry of its summer guise had been, as a skeleton might suggest the perfection of the human form. The lights in the two-story frame house beyond — for the doctor's office was in the yard of his dwelling and the garden lay a little to the rear — were extinguished one by one. A dog close by barked for a time, with echoes from the hills and depressions, and then fell to howling mournfully. The doctor talked on, now and then taking down the books to illustrate; marking the passages with a neat strip of paper in lieu of turning down a leaf, as Kenbigh seemed disposed to do. He piled the volumes beside his apt pupil on the candle-stand, and as the lawyer fell to at them he himself read for a time, as a light recreation, from a history in some twelve volumes. To a country gentleman of ample leisure and bookish habit, this lengthy work was but as a mouthful.

Dr. Lloyd rose at last, knocked the ashes out of his

pipe upon the head of one of the fire-dogs, glanced at the absorbed lawyer, and remarked, "You'll come over to my house to go to bed after a little more, won't you?"

"Reckon so," responded Kenbigh, without lifting his head.

The fire flared up the chimney in great white flames; they emanated from a lustrous, restless, pulsing red heart. The sparks flew. The faint and joyous sounds from the logs were like some fine fairy minstrelsy which one is hardly sure one hears. A sylvan fragrance came from the pile of wood in the corner, the baskets of chips, the pine knots.

The doctor left the room, opened the door and looked back.

"Don't you set the house afire and burn up these books," he said, with the first touch of feeling in his tones that night.

The results of the attorney-general's vigil were abundantly manifest in his speech to the jury the following day. For that body was recruited by summoning another talesman in Rood's place, and the trial perforce began anew; Gwinnan apparently thinking this alternative served better the ends of justice than to risk the delays and vicissitudes of again securing a competent jury. This decision encouraged Mink, who had been tortured by the fear that by some disaster the case would be continued to the next term. He was not now greatly perturbed by the strange turn which the attorney-general had contrived to give to Alethea's testimony. Since Harshaw had found that any one claimed to have seen Tad after the report of the boy's death he had felt confident of an acquittal, laying much stress on the necessity of proving the *corpus delicti*, as he phrased it; and Mink accepted his lawyer's opinion and relied upon it. He had not been greatly affected by Rood's fate, so absorbed was he by his own interests; but it was a moment of tense excitement when the testimony again reached the juncture at which, on the preceding day, the unfortunate juror had leaned forward and pointed at the witness, his question failing on his lips in the dumbness of death. Nothing further was elicited from Alethea except that she did believe in ghosts, but that she was sure she had seen Tad alive, albeit he had stood among the graves with a blanched face, disappearing in a moment, lost in the mist.

The whole testimony occupied much less time than on the previous day, and as the afternoon progressed it began to be apparent that the case would go to the jury before the court adjourned.

The surprise of the day was the speech of the attorney-general. It opened simply enough. He sought to show that it was impossible for Tad to be alive. The poor boy was doubtless at the bottom of the river. How could it be otherwise? Assume, as his learned opponent would have them believe, that he had swum ashore. Where was he now? The suggestion that he was in the custody of some enemy of the prisoner, who sought by concealing him to effect the incarceration of Reuben Lorey in the penitentiary for a long term, was so absurd that he hesitated to argue such a foolish position before so intelligent a body of men as the jury whom he had the pleasure of addressing. Who would, for revenge, encounter the hazards of such a scheme? The boy was as well known throughout the section as Piomingo Bald. Any chance glimpse of him by a casual visitor would fling the conspirators themselves into the clutches of the law, that would be loath to lightly loose its hold on such rascals. Who would voluntarily burden themselves with the support of an idiot? If anybody had found Tad, he would have been mighty quick to carry the boy back to old man Griff. Say that no one had detained him,— what then? He was an idiot, incapable of taking care of himself. If he were wandering at large, starving, half clad, would not some one have seen him besides Alethea Sayles, in all these weeks, gentlemen, in all these months? It was a remarkable story that the witness had told,— a remarkable story. (The counsel seemed to find fit expression of his sense of its solemnity by sinking his basso profundo to a thunderous mutter.) No one for a moment could doubt the sanity of that witness. She was evidently a girl of fine common sense; an excellent girl, too, — no one could for a moment doubt the truth of any word she uttered. The fact was, Alethea Sayles saw a strange thing that night. She thought she saw Tad. It was only his image, not himself. "The forlorn boy is dead, gentlemen," he continued. "She saw the fantasy of her own anxious, overwrought brain. He was in her mind. She had pondered long upon him, and upon the plight of her lover, who had killed him. What wonder, then, that in the mist, and the flickering moonlight, and the lonely midnight, she should fancy that she saw him!"

He told the gaping and amazed jury that this was not an isolated instance. He mentioned other victims of hallucination; he detailed the strange experiences of Nicolai, of Spinoza, of Dr. Bostock, of Lord Londonderry, of Baron de Géramb, of Leuret, of Lord Brougham.

Harshaw, who had sat listening, with his hands in his pockets and his legs crossed, a smile of ostentatious derision upon his face, grew grave upon the mention of the last name. He had never heard of the others, but to attempt to bolster a theory of spectral apparition by this name, revered in the profession, was, he felt, a juridical sacrilege that should cause the attorney-general to be at the very least stricken from the rolls.

As Kenbigh went on, expounding the relative and interdependent functions of the brain and eye, the fine and subtle theories of spiritual and physical life, its vague boundaries, its unmeasured capabilities, — the deductions, the keen analysis of science, all reduced to the vernacular in the mouth of a man trained by years of practice to speak to the people, — Harshaw sat in blank dismay. He had never heard of any spiritual manifestation but the vulgar graveyard ghost, usually headless, stalking in its shroud to accomplish missions of vengeance upon the very ignorant in the deep midnight. But Kenbigh's account of sundry ethereal-minded and mild-mannered spectres, with a preference for high company, singing, appearing at dinner-tables, conversing agreeably, arrayed in conventional garb, as decorous and reasonable and as mindful of etiquette as if still bound by all the restraints of the world, the flesh, and the devil, disappearing as noiselessly as they had come, with no appreciable result of the visit, — it shocked every sense of precedent within him. He was country-bred and did not know that when ghosts are fashionable they conduct themselves as fashionable people do. He noted keenly the discrepancies in the scientific explanations. Always, despite its show of learning, its systems, its terminology, its physiology, its psychology, and its persistent reference of supernatural appearances to natural causes, Reason retires from the spectral exhibition with some admission of occult influences, not fully understood, — in effect making a bow to the ghost in question, "Saving your presence." He noticed, too, that the jury were listening with that intentness and eager interest which characterize every mind, even the most ignorant, in considering things of the other world, manifestations of hidden agencies. When he rose to reply he felt at a loss. The sound, however, of his own hearty voice ringing against the walls, instead of the sepulchral basso profundo of the attorney for the State, the motion of his own stalwart arm sawing the air, — for he was in the habit of impressing his views with a good deal of muscular exertion, — had an invigorating effect upon him, and brought him back to his normal state of confidence and bluster. He found words for his ready scorn. He sought to discredit the attorney-general's phantoms. He did not know where the counsel got these old women's tales; they were an insult to the intelligence of the jury. The learned counsel knew mighty well he was n't going to be called upon for his authorities, — medical books can't be produced as evidence in a court of justice, much less ghost stories, "Raw-head and bloody-bones"! For his own part, he did n't believe a word of them. A fact is a thing that can be proved. The law requires authentication. "Henry Brougham, Lord Chancellor, saw visions, did he? And may be Lord Coke dreamed dreams," he sneered indignantly. "And Lord Mansfield perchance walked in his sleep. And who knows they did? And what drivel is this! Gentlemen, *we* live in the nineteenth century!"

The aspersion of Lord Brougham — for thus he considered the anecdote — was very bitter to him. He was a man of few enthusiasms, and such hero-worship as was possible to him had been expended upon the great lights of his profession whose acquaintance he had formed in his early reading of law, some twenty years ago. He so dwelt upon this point that the jury received the valuable impression that Henry Brougham was a chancellor and a "valley man," hailing from Knoxville, perhaps, and was held in high esteem by the lawyers in Shaftesville, and that Harshaw seemed to think the attorney-general had slandered him. He wrenched himself from this phase of the subject with some difficulty. "Gentlemen," he said sarcastically, "the attorney-general is a mighty smart man. He's got a heap of learning lately about visions." He glanced down obliquely at his opponent; he would have given a good deal to know how the counsel for the State came by his information. He could have sworn that it was not indigenous. "But there are plenty of folks in this town could have told him just as much and more. He's mighty particular to show the difference between *il*-lusion and *de*-lusion, and hallucination and mania. Visions! That ain't what *we* call 'em, gentlemen. Down here in the flat woods we call 'em — 'snakes'!" The hit told, and he went on, encouraged. "Right over yonder in Tim Beeker's saloon they keep every assortment of vision. Men have seen green rabbits there, and black dogs, and snakes, and whole menageries of hallucinations. Is anybody going to believe Alethea Sayles had the jim-jams that night, coming from camp-meeting? She had no call to see visions! This girl had her head in her hands; she was leaning on the fence; she felt some one touch her; she looked up, and saw the boy before her. Mighty few of the ghosts that we have heard of had such consistency of entity as to make their presence perceived by the sense of touch; on the contrary, it is thus that their unreality is often demonstrated in these same fables. A lady passes her fan through one immaterial image. A man thrusts his knife vainly into the misty heart of another. And why does this instance differ? Because, gentlemen, there was no phantom. It was Tad Simpkins in flesh and blood. The fugitive boy sees Alethea Sayles, whom he knows well; he is about to appeal to her; he lays his hand on her hand. She lifts her head, and at the unexpected appari — sight, she screams, and the foolish boy is frightened, and flees!"

He went on to say that he would impose upon the patience of this court and jury only for a few moments longer. He wanted to contradict the statements of the attorney-general that no one would voluntarily burden himself with the support of a useless member of society. "How many yaller dogs at your houses, gentlemen? I'd be afraid to count how many at mine. How many of your wife's relations? No, gentlemen, none of us are so rich in this world's goods as we deserve to be, but we ain't got down to dividing bread and meat that close yet. As to the reckless crime of keeping the boy in hiding in order to put Mink Lorey in the penitentiary for involuntary manslaughter, — why, gentlemen, if there were not just such reckless people continually committing crimes, the consequences of which they cannot escape, the attorney-general and I would have nothing to do. We'd have to suck our paws for a living, like a bear in the winter, and look at one another, — a profitless entertainment, gentlemen."

He sat down, his pink smile enlivening his countenance, well satisfied with his efforts and with the prospects of the case.

The attorney-general, who had the last word, was very brief in saying it. The judge charged the jury, and he, too, was brief. The long slant of sunshine falling athwart the room was reddening when the jury were led out by the officer to their deliberations, noisily ascending the stairs to the jury-room above, assigned to their use.

XIII.

They slouched into their lair, looking more like offenders detained against their will than the free and enlightened citizens of a great country in the exercise of the precious privilege of serving on the jury. They were all tired. They had undergone much excitement. They felt the mental strain of the arguments and counter-arguments to which they had listened.

"It hev fairly gin me a mis'ry in my head ter hev ter hear ter them red-mouthed lawyers jaw an' jaw, like they done!" exclaimed one, flinging himself in a chair, and putting his feet up against the round sides of the stove, which was cold and fireless, the day being warm and genial. The windows were open, the sunlight streaming over the dusty floor and chairs and benches. Two or three of the jurymen, looking out, laughing, and making signs to the people in the streets, were smartly remonstrated with by the officer in charge.

His objections had the effect of congregating them in the middle of the room, where the discussion began, most of them lighting their pipes, and tilting their chairs on the hind legs. Two or three lifted their feet to the giddy eminence of the backs of other chairs; several stretched themselves at lank, ungainly length upon the benches. They were mostly young or middle-aged men; the senior of the party being a farmer of fifty, with a pointed, shaven chin, newly sprouting with a bristly beard, over which he often passed his hand with a meditative gesture. His eyes were downcast; he leaned his elbows on his knees; his mien was depressed, not to say afflicted. "I ain't hearn ten words together," he remarked. "I never knowed when they lef' off, sca'cely, bein' so all-fired oneasy an' beset 'bout them cattle o' mine." He turned to explain to the new juror whom they had taken on that morning. "Ben Doaks hed my cattle a-summerin' of 'em up on Piomingo Bald, an' when the cattle war rounded up I went thar ter pick out mine, an' I druv 'em down an' got ez far ez Shaftesville, an' I let 'em go on with Bob, my son, 'bout fifteen year old. An' I stopped hyar ter git a drink an' hear a leetle news. An' durned ef they did n't ketch me on the jury! An' Bob dunno what's kem o' me, an' I dunno what's kem o' Bob an' the cattle, nor how fur they hed traveled along the road 'fore they fund out I war n't comin' arter."

"Waal, I reckon they be all right," said the new man, a hunter from the mountains, just come into town with game to sell.

"Lord knows! *I* don't!" said the old fellow, sighing over the futility of speculation. "Ef Bob war ter draw the idee ez I got hurt, or robbed, or scrimmagin' in them town grog-shops, — I hev always been tellin' him a all-fired pack o' lies 'bout the dangers in sech places, bein' ez I war n't willin' ter let him go whar I'd go myself,— he'd leave them cattle a-standin' thar in the road, an' kem back ter town ter s'arch fur me. He hain't got much 'speriunce, an' he ain't ekal ter keerin' fur them cattle. They'll stray, an' I'll never see 'em agin."

"I reckon they hev strayed back ter the mountings by this time; must be wilder 'n bucks, ef they hev been out all summer," suggested a broad-faced twinkling-eyed young fellow, with a jocose wink at the others.

"Bob dozes, too; sorter sleepy-headed, ye know," said the old man, taking note of all the contingencies. "I hev seen him snooze in the saddle, ef the cattle war slow. He's growin', an' runs mighty hard, an' ef he sets still, he falls off. Ef he got tired, he's apt ter lie down in a fence-corner ter rest; an' he mought go ter sleep thar, an' somebody mought toll the cattle off. Or else he mought ax somebody ter keer fur the cattle till he could kem back an' find me. Lord A'mighty, thar's no yearthly tellin' what Bob mought do!"

"Then, again, he *mought n't*," said Jerry Price. "Ye hev jes' got ter gin up yer hold on worldly things when ye air on a jury, like ye war dead."

"Yes; but when ye air dead ye ain't able ter be pestered by studyin' 'bout what yer administrator air a-doin' with yer yearthly chattels an' cattle."

"How d' ye know?" demanded Price. "Arter all we hearn ter-day, a body mought b'lieve a real likely harnt air ekal ter ennything in motion an' looks, an' ye dunno *what* they air studyin' 'bout. But time's a-wastin'. 'Less we air wantin' ter bide hyar all night agin, we hed better be talkin' 'bout our verdict on Mink Lorey. The jedge's waitin', an' from all I hev seen o' him he ain't handy at patience."

"Waal, sir," said the man with his feet on the stove, who was the foreman of the jury, taking his pipe from his mouth, "I ain't settin' much store on Gwinnan. I don't b'lieve he acted right an' 'cordin' ter law about this jury. Thar's thirteen men on this jury!"

They all sat motionless, staring at him.

"Yes, sir," he declared, reinserting his pipe between his teeth, and speaking with them closed upon it. "I know the law! My uncle war a jestice o' the peace fur six year, 'bout ten year ago. An' he hed a Code o' Tennessee! An' I read in it! Some mighty interestin' readin' in the Code o' Tennessee. Sure 's ye born, thar is! The law say the juror, ef he be ailin', kin be excused, an' another summonsed. But Peter Rood war n't excused, nor discharged nuther. He's on this jury yit."

"Waal, fur Gawd's sake, don't git ter jawin' 'bout Peter Rood!" cried Bylor, the man on whose chair the dead juror had fallen, and who had turned his face to the close encounter of the stare of death in those glassy eyes. Bylor's nerves were still unstrung. He looked as ill as a broad-shouldered, sunburned, brawny fellow could look. "I never slep' a wink las' night; an' that thar cussed 'torney-gineral a-tellin' them awful tales 'bout harnts all day, an' that thar solemn Lethe Sayles purtendin' she hed seen that drownded idjit, — I felt ez ef I'd fall down in a fit ef they did n't quit it."

"I don't b'lieve she seen Tad's harnt," said Ben Doaks, instinctively adopting her view.

"Then what war it in the *graveyard* fur?" demanded the foreman conclusively.

There was momentary silence. The sunshine was dying out on the floor; the dim tracery of the boughs of the hickory-tree was the only manifestation of its presence. The rural sound of the lowing of cattle came in on the soft air, — the village kine were returning from their pastures. The voices of men in the rooms below rose and fell fitfully; they were trying another case, in the interim of waiting for the verdict.

"An' how kem nobody hev seen him sence, 'ceptin' Lethe Sayles?" he supplemented his question.

"The jedge hinted ez much ez we-uns oughter be powerful keerful o' not convictin' a man fur killin', when a witness claimed ter hev seen the dead one sence," argued Jerry Price, ambiguously.

"She never seen nuthin' but his ghost," said the foreman.

"Ben, how'd that leetle red cow o' mine git her hawn bruk?" interpolated the bereaved cattle-owner, meditating on the vicissitudes experienced by his herds in their summer vacation.

"Gawd A'mighty, man, quit talkin' 'bout yer cattle, interruptin' we-uns jes' ez we war a-gittin' ter the p'int!" exclaimed the foreman.

"I'd heap ruther hear Mr. Beames talk 'bout his cattle 'n hear 'bout harnts, an' sech," said Bylor, as he lay on the bench. He was still feeling far from well. He got up presently, and went to the officer, who was at the door, and petitioned for something to drink. But that worthy, determined upon the literal performance of duty, withstood his every persuasion, even when he declared he was "plumb sick;" and the rest of the jury, alarmed lest he should be excused, another juror summoned, and the whole performance of the trial begin anew, the agony of their detention thus lengthening indefinitely, pleaded for him. The officer's devotion to what he considered his duty did not save him from some abuse.

"'T would sarve ye right ef we war ter lay a-holt o' ye an' fling ye outer this winder," said Ben Doaks.

"Ye mis'able leetle green gourd, ye dunno nuthin' 'bout nuthin'," declared the foreman, the much informed because of the Code.

"Waal, ye kin say what ye wanter," retorted the official. He was a young man; he had a resolute eye and a shock head. "But ye ain't goin' ter git out'n here till ye find yer verdict." He withdrew his tousled head suddenly, and shut the door on them.

Rebellion availing nothing, they resorted to faction.

"Ye need n't be so powerful techy 'bout harnts; ye ain't seen none ez.I knows on," said the foreman, turning upon the sick juror.

"Naw, an' I don't wanter hear 'bout none o' 'em till my stommick feels stronger."

"Shucks! that air nuthin' oncommon, seein' harnts an' sech. Plenty o' folks hev seen the same one. Thar's ever so many o' them herders on Thunderhead hev seen the harnt ez herds up thar. Rob Carrick seen him. I have hearn him tell 'bout'n it arter he got his mind back. Hain't you, Ben?"

The moon was at the eastern windows. The white lustre poured in. The great room seemed lonely and deserted, despite the group of deliberating jurymen, and the colorless double with which each had been furnished, to ape his gesture, and caricature his size, and dog his every step. An owl was hooting in some distant tree. The voices from the street were faint.

"Ain't that thar weasel of a constable goin' ter hev no lamps brung hyar ter-night?" exclaimed Bylor.

But the lamps which came in almost immediately were inadequate to contend with the solemn, ethereal, white pervasion of the night that still hung in the window, and lay upon the floor, and showed the gaunt bare tree outside. They only gave a yellow cast to the circle in which the party sat, and made their faces seem less pallid and unnatural.

"Yes, I hev hearn Carrick tell it a many a time. He used ter herd with Josh Nixon in life." Ben Doaks paused a moment. "I seen the Herder wunst myse'f, though I never felt right sure about it till ter-night. I 'lowed I mought jes' hev fancied it."

"What made ye sure 'bout it ter-night?" demanded Bylor, starting up from the bench.

"'Count o' what the 'torney-gineral said 'bout *hell*ucination. I know now ez 't war a vision sent from hell, an' I reckon that air one reason I hev fund it air so hard ter git religion. My mind hev got too much in league with Satan."

"Waal, Carrick 'lowed ez Josh Nixon kem back from hell ter herd on Thunderhead 'kase all his bones war n't buried tergether," said the foreman.

"Law, Ben," broke out the owner of cattle, "I wonder ef them beef bones we seen on the top o' Piomingo Bald war n't the bones o' that thar leetle black heifer o' mine ez could n't be fund, an' ye 'lowed mus' hev been eat by a wolf."

"I knocked off the vally o' that thar heifer in our settlin' up, an' I hed hoped ter hear no mo' o' her in this mortal life!" cried Ben Doaks, lifting his voice from the bated undertone in which he had discussed the spectral phenomena to an indignant worldly resonance. "I did n't know ez ye branded yer beastis on her bones," sarcastically; "the las' time I seen her she war too fat ter show 'em. I never looked fur yer mark on them bones on the bald."

"Waal," said a slow, measured voice, with that unnatural tone one has in speaking to one's self, "Tad hev got no call ter kem back."

"Who air ye a-talkin' ter?" cried Bylor, starting up, his nerves quivering at the slightest provocation.

"Somebody told me just then 't war Tad's harnt," said Price, rousing himself with an effort.

"They never!" cried Bylor. "Old man Beames

hain't got done moanin' 'bout his cattle, like they war the ornymints o' the nation. Nobody never opened thar mouths ter ye. Ye jes' answered ter nuthin'."

"Harshaw never b'lieved Lethe Sayles seen no harnt," declared one.

"He *hed* ter say that," observed the foreman, evidently of spectral tendencies, "no matter what he believed. The 'torney-gin'al war powerful sure she seen a harnt."

"He 'lowed it war a *hell*ucination," protested Bylor, being extremely averse to any theory involving supernatural presence.

"Waal," argued the logical Price, "he 'lowed ez a *hell*ucination war suthin' ez looks like a person, but 't ain't him. Now ain't that a harnt? Ain't Tad's harnt suthin' that looks like Tad, an' ain't Tad?"

"Oh," cried Bylor, springing from the bench, "I feel obligated ter git away from sech talk! I jes' look ter see Peter Rood a-stalkin' round hyar direc'ly, with that awful stare he hed in his eyes when he war stone dead fur ever so long, with his face so close ter mine. I can't abide it no longer! Let's toss up. Heads, acquit! Tails, convict!" He produced a coin from his pocket.

"Naw, ye won't," said the foreman quickly. "Naw! We'll delib'rate on this hyar question, an' decide it like a jury oughter."

Bylor cast a glance at the windows, each with its great white image upon the floor below; at the dim faces about him; at the lamps, dull and yellow, making the moonlight seem more pallid and vaguely blue. He threw himself upon the bench, and for a long time was silent.

"Look hyar," said Jerry Price, "it hev jes' got down ter this,—harnt or no harnt. Ef Lethe Sayles seen *Tad*, Mink never killed him, an' hev ter be acquitted. Ef Lethe Sayles seen Tad's harnt, Mink killed him whilst doin' a unlawful act, an' he hev ter go ter the pen'tiary fur involuntary manslaughter, ez the jedge 'lows sech be a felony."

The wrangle over the question, which bristled with

difficulties enough, began anew. They were even more illogical and irritable than before. They were utterly unused to debate, to reason. The mental strain of laboriously applying their attention to each detail, striving to master circumstance and argument, throughout the two days during which the case had been tried twice before them, had resulted in a certain degree of prostration of their faculties. The singular surprise in the evidence and the sudden death of one of their number had unnerved them all, more or less. Being ignorant men, untrained to discriminate and differentiate, while they could accept the strange occurrences which the attorney-general had brought to their knowledge, they were not able to perceive and apply the scientific explanations. And in fact many of these were lame and inadequate. They had heard these seemingly supernatural instances from a man of education and acumen, and it had fallen to their lot to probe the probabilities, and possibilities, and decide an important question based upon them. They were no nearer a conclusion when Ben Doaks, who had been sitting with his arms folded, silently meditating for a time, broke out abruptly, "That's it! Tad's harnt kem back 'kase *his* bones ain't buried."

. Bylor once more started up. "Who tole ye that? Who said it fust?"

"I dunno," replied Ben Doaks quietly. "Some o' them boys."

"They never!" cried Bylor. "I hev been listening ter every one. Some o' ye answers the words o' a man who never speaks aloud! Thar's a harnt on this jury! I know it! I feel it!" He stood up at his full height, trembling like a leaf. He was in a nervous panic. "Gentlemen, we hev got" — he faltered at the name — "him with us yet. Thar's thirteen men on this jury. For Gawd's sake, let's go down an' tell the jedge we can't agree. I'll see Rood d'rec'ly, an' ye will too."

"Laws-a-massy!" cried old Beames, interested for the first time in aught save his cattle. "I'll make a break an' run" — he did not say where, the obdurate officer being on the other side of the door. He too rose, agitated, his toothless jaw shaking. "I could n't abide ter see him, like he looked las' night!"

"Thar 's thirteen men on the jury. Thar 's no use denyin' it," said the foreman, "whether Pete Rood's sperit 's in the panel or no."

A great shadow suddenly flapped awkwardly across the floor. Every man of them started. But it was only the owl they had heard in the distance, now flying past the window. The situation was not more cheerful when the ill-omened bird settled itself on the branch of the hickory-tree, and shrilled its nerve-thrilling cry and convulsively chuckled aloud.

The foreman rose, too. "Thar 's no use a-tryin'," he said: "we can't agree, an' we hev got a right ter disagree. Le's go down an' tell the jedge, an' git discharged. I ain't easy shook, but this hyar whole case hev been powerful cur'ous, an' I hev mighty nigh petered out."

"Look hyar, ought n't we ter hold on a while longer? Fur Mink Lorey will hev ter stay in jail fur four months more, till he kin git tried at the next term," suggested Jerry Price.

"I 'm willin'," said Ben Doaks reluctantly. He looked doubtfully over his shoulder as he spoke. "Eh?" he said, as he turned his head back again.

"Nobody never said nuthin'," declared the foreman.

"I 'lowed I hearn somebody call my name."

"I 'll be bound ye did!" cried Bylor. "But nobody called it ez we kin see — yit."

He rushed to the door and summoned the officer. The court was notified, and the twelve men were conducted down the stairs, each conscious of the presence of the unseen thirteenth.

It was like a transition from the conditions of delirium to the serene atmosphere of right reason. The windows were all flaring with lights, as if the court-room were some factory that ran all night. The lawyers looked fagged and worn out; they had the air of working by momentum aggregated during the day rather than by immediate exertion. It was a contrast to Averill's leisurely procedure, and they regarded the innovation with exasperation and the judge with some personal animosity. He had his pen still in his hand; there was a moment's silent waiting while he finished the line he was writing. Mink had been brought out from jail. He sat feverishly impatient and bright-eyed.

Harshaw and the attorney-general turned expectant and interested faces toward the jury.

The judge laid down his pen and looked kindly at them. He viewed them as a bit of completed work. He had a great respect for completed work.

When they were asked if they had agreed upon their verdict, the foreman answered that they could not agree.

The prisoner's countenance changed instantly. It had upon it an expression of blank amaze, then of sharp distress. Harshaw's face fell. The attorney-general pricked up his ears. The judge looked grave, concerned.

"Do you desire any further instructions, — any point of difficulty explained?"

The foreman interpreted this formula as a general inquiry into the nature of the trouble. He began precipitately, the quaking men behind him feeling all the despair of being the members of a responsible corporate body of which he was the mouthpiece.

"Ye see, jedge, we-uns can't but feel thar 's thirteen men on this jury."

They felt the judge's quick gray eye counting them. Perhaps at that moment they were all indifferent to the terrors of their spectral associate, so much more substantial a source of terror being presented to them.

The man who had read the Code went on: "Pete Rood — him ez died las' night — war neither excused nor discharged, so thar 's thirteen men on this jury; an' we hearn him talkin' up-stairs along o' the rest o' the jurors, sometimes interruptin' us, an' we-uns can't agree 'count o' thar bein' a harnt on the jury."

Even he faltered before the look in the face of the

judge, whose decisions were thus frankly criticised. There was something terrible in the fury that his eyes expressed. He sat motionless, with an air of great calmness and dignity. His face, however, crimsoned to the roots of his hair. The veins in his forehead stood out swollen and blue. There was an intense silence for a moment. Then his voice, as always, singularly low and inexpressive, broke the pause.

"Mr. Sheriff," he said, "conduct those thirteen — those twelve men to the county jail, and keep them there for contempt of court until ten o'clock to-morrow morning, permitting no communication with others."

He directed that a fine of ten dollars should be entered against each, and forthwith adjourned the court.

This high-handed proceeding had no parallel in the annals of the circuit. Harshaw, swelling with rage, found knots of men eagerly discussing it, as he pushed his way out into the hall. Some one was advancing the opinion that a jury in jail was no longer a jury, but merely twelve culprits. Another found a hearty laugh in the reflection that they would not probably discover so many harnts in jail as in the jury-room. A third demanded of Harshaw, "Why did n't he discharge the jury, and imprison them as men?"

"Too afraid of the S'preme Court," Harshaw hissed between his teeth. "Wish he had! On appeal a premature discharge would operate as an acquittal of the prisoner."

He regarded the action of the judge as an outrage, and he did not hesitate to express this opinion. He had expended much time and force upon his case, and looked for no compensation but the satisfaction of success. He had that excellent quality in a lawyer, the faculty of making his client's cause his own. He felt the hardship of this extension of the prisoner's jeopardy scarcely less deeply than Mink himself. A little remonstrance with the ignorant men, a little pocketing of personal and judicial pride, a few coaxing. explanatory words, might have sent them back refreshed and invigorated to their deliberations, with a good hope of agreement. Now, there was no prophesying what effect these strong measures would have upon them. He believed that Gwinnan had transcended all the authority of his office. "By God," he cried, "if he keeps on like he's started he'll get impeached some day! And if I could see my way to it, I swear I'd introduce the resolution in the House myself!"

He walked off, his head swimming a little. He had said this rash thing before a motley crowd, and at any time it might be repeated to Gwinnan, who was himself a politician in some sort, and a man of great force.

XIV.

IMPRISONMENT proved an efficacious method of exorcising the "harnt" upon the jury. Much of the sojourn in the county jail was expended in criminations and recriminations. Not one of the jurymen would admit any responsibility for their plight. Not one had entertained the slightest belief in their ghostly associate. The mere contact with that practical, prosaic mundane force, the law of the land, had so restored them that they were emboldened to roundly denounce the harnt. And the name of poor Peter Rood, which had been whispered with bated breath in the jury-room, came smartly enough from the tongue even of Bylor. In fact, he was the most persistent in disavowing susceptibility to spectral influence.

"I begged an' begged ye ter shet up talkin' 'bout sech," he cried, which was indeed the truth. "An' ye jes' kep' it up an' kep' it up, till ye skeered yerse'fs out'n yer boots, an' then I could n't do nuthin' with ye."

They had all been locked temporarily into one room of the jail, while the sheriff and jailer consulted in regard to the accommodations for so unusual a number of prisoners. In their close quarters the jurymen leaned against the wall or walked the floor, jostling each other in the shadow, for the room was dark save for the moonbeams slanting through the bars of the window. The foreman hung about in the obscure places, freely addressed,—for they knew, without seeing, that he was there,—and required to bear the brunt of all the reproaches for the calamity. Once he plucked up spirit to retort.

"Ye war the very man ez yapped fur the dep'ty," he

said to Bylor, who allowed himself to be drawn into argument.

"How'd I know ez you-uns war a-goin' ter traipse down them steers an' 'low ter the jedge ez you-uns knowed mo' law 'n he do? Ye dad-burned aged idjit, ef ye war n't older 'n me I'd lay ye out on this floor."

"I felt jes' like the tail of a dog in a fight, — could neither holp nor hender the critter ez toted me ahint him, but war jes' ez apt ter git gnawed ez him," said Jerry Price disconsolately.

"I looked ter see the jedge fetch him a pop 'side the head, myself," said the new juryman, evidently unacquainted with judicial methods. He had regarded his capture to serve on the jury as a woful disaster, and could hardly bear up under this aggregation of misfortunes. "Ef I hed knowed what war comin', I would n't hev followed him down them steers."

"Six spry young steers 'mongst my cattle, — I'll never see 'em agin!" cried old man Beames from out the darkness, reminded anew of his journeying herds under the insufficient guidance of Bob. "I hev never done no wrong in my life. I hev tuk heed ter my feet ter walk in the right way. An' hyar in my old age, through another man's fault, the door of a jail hev been shet on me."

His voice dropped. They were all feeling the poignant humiliation of the imprisonment. They were honest men, to whom it could scarcely have come but for this mischance. At every contortion of wounded pride they turned upon the unlucky foreman.

"I 'lowed I'd drap in my tracks," cried Ben Doaks, "whenst he jes' tuk the Code o' Tennessee by the hawns an' tail, an' dragged it up afore the jedge."

And Jerry Price was fain to sneer, too.

"Did the Code hev nuthin' in it 'bout cuttin' out the tongue of a foreman of a jury?" he demanded.

But the Code was an unabated fact still, and the nephew of the ex-justice alone could say what was in it. "Naw, sir!" he retorted, emboldened by the allusion to his superior knowledge, " nor about jailin' a jury, nuther. I don't b'lieve the jedge hed the right ter jail the jury."

" Waal," drawled Jerry, satirically, " we-uns hed better make up our minds powerful quick how we air a-goin' ter pay him back fur it."

The foreman was saved the mortification of acknowledging the hopelessness of reprisal. A voice without sounded suddenly.

" I wanter see how many thar air," said the jailer.

"On a jury? Shucks! ye 're funnin'. Twelve," in the familiar tones of the sheriff.

" I jes' wanter look at 'em agin."

" Ye sha'n't," retorted the sheriff.

He did not reckon on the fact that although he, as sheriff, had the legal authority and control of the jail, the jailer was possessed of the material keys, and locked and unlocked the doors at will. He opened this one now, gingerly, and the men within felt the grin they could not see.

" Brung 'em byar 'kase they could n't count," he said, jocosely. " They air the fust boarders we hev hed fur sech ez that."

The sheriff, who was holding a lamp in the hall, pulled the door to, still animated by his sense of duty, and the jury heard the lock click as the facile jailer turned the key.

"They 'lowed thar war a harnt in the jury-room," said the officer.

Within all were silent, that they might hear.

" I ain't s'prised none," said the jailer; "plenty o' harnts hyar. Men ez war hung, ye know, — liked our accommodations better 'n them they got arterwards; that brings 'em back. Tim Jenkins war dragged right out'n that thar room whar the jury be now, when the lynchers kem an' tuk him. Hed me tied down-steers, ye 'member."

He went off gayly down the hall, jingling his keys. Presently his voice was heard in another mood, swearing at the judge and demanding, " What sorter man is this hyár Gwinnan, ennyhow, ez you-uns hev got out thar on the bench? Send me twelve men ter eat an' sleep, an' the jail ez full ez it air! Does he think I keep a tavern? Thar ain't room enough hyar fur twelve fleas!"

He compassed the problem somehow, for the jurymen, smarting with the indignity and hardship, were led forth the next morning, having slept as well as was possible considering the united grievances of the accommodations and the mortification, and eaten as their reduced appetites and the prison fare permitted.

They resumed their deliberations in the jury-room, and it argues much for their earnest desire to do right and their respect for their oath that they did not find a verdict at hap-hazard. They reported again and again that they could reach no decision. They were held over Sunday, and after nightfall on Monday they came into the court-room, and in guarded phrase and with some perturbation of manner announced once more that they could not agree as to the guilt or innocence of the prisoner.

In answer to the usual question, the foreman was eager to explain that they had experienced no difficulty other than a difference of opinion, and felt no want of further instructions. He forbore to offer criticisms upon judicial methods, and the men behind him, all acutely realizing the position of the dog's tail, breathed more freely. The judge looked at them with a certain resentment in his eyes. He leaned back in his chair, gnawing the end of his mustache. Mink sat beside his lawyer, eager, intent, hardly appreciating at the moment the significance of the disagreement. Harshaw had turned aside with a pettish mutter to his yellow beard, for the final adjournment for the term impended, Gwinnan being compelled to leave on the train that night to hold court in a remote county in his own circuit.

How Gwinnan could infuse into his impassive mien and his soft, expressionless drawl so caustic a suggestion of displeasure is one of those mysteries of manner addressed to a subtle and receptive sense which can take account of so fine and elusive a medium of communication. The jury, in receiving their discharge, felt like culprits until they were once more at large and in the outer air, when they swore at the judge with the heartiest unanimity, — on this point they could agree, — and promised themselves, taking note of his character as politician, that if ever they were vouchsafed the opportunity they would retaliate. Then among the loungers about the tavern they fell to asking the news with the hungry interest of travelers who have been long absent.

They experienced a certain surprise to find that their accountability as jurors had not ceased with their discharge. There was a manifest inclination on the part of public opinion, as embodied in the idlers about the hotel, to hold them individually responsible for the mischances of the trial. Perhaps the impression that they had been long absent was strengthened by the revolution which popular prejudice had accomplished in the interval. Its flexibility could hardly be better illustrated than by the fact that the prankish Mink had suddenly risen in its estimation to the dignity of a public martyr.

"He's a tremenjious wild scamp, the Lord knows," said one, "but folks ain't jailed fur bein' gamesome, an' by rights ye oughter hev turned Mink out'n that jail this evenin'."

"Yessir," assented another. "Mink oughter be mighty nigh Hazel Valley by now, ef he had been gin a fair trial."

That conclusive formula, "'This is a free country, by the Lord!'" was often insistently reiterated in the discussion, for the bewildered jury discovered that the persuasion of the prisoner's innocence had never wavered after Alethea Sayles had sworn that she had seen Tad Simpkins since the disaster. The community at large had not been subjected to the morbid influences of seclusion, and mental stress, and the nervous shock which the jury had sustained upon the death of Peter Rood, and the necessity of persistent consideration of spiritual and spectral phenomena forced upon them by the attorney-general.

"You see, gentlemen," said a young sprig of a lawyer, glad to air his information, "you went off on the wrong road. 'T war n't the business o' the defense to account for Tad. 'T was the prosecution's business to prove that he was dead and that Mink killed him. And they did n't do it; they just proved he was missing, for that girl swore she saw him afterward. They 've got to prove the *corpus delicti*, gentlemen, in a case like this."

The jurymen were laughed to scorn when they suggested their doubts of the genuineness of Tad's appearance.

"Now did n't the attorney-general stuff you as full of lies as an egg of meat!" cried the young lawyer, divided between admiration of the attorney-general's resources and contempt for their credulity.

"Ye air the only folks in Cherokee County ez b'lieves sech," said another by-stander. "Old man Griff an' all his gran'chil'n lef' town yestiddy evenin' plumb sati'fied Tad's alive, an' goin' ter hunt him up. An' then I reckon the old man 'll furgit all about his repentance, an' club an' beat him same ez he always done."

"Waal," demanded the ex-foreman, who was disposed to maintain the difficulty of the question, "how could a idjit keer fur hisself all this time?"

"Tad never war sech a idjit; could run a mill, an' plough, an' pull fodder, an' feed stock! I'll be bound thar's a mighty differ round old man Griff's diggins now, sure. He 'peared a idjit mos'ly when he war beat over the head. Mos' folks would look miser'ble then. He air lackin', I know, but I reckon he kin work fur hisself ez well ez he done fur old man Griff. It's a plumb shame ter jail Mink Lorey fur fower month more till he kin git another fool jury ter try him, an' mebbe send him ter the Pen'tiary fur five year. I dunno what oughter be done ter sech a jury ez you-uns."

It was probably well for the public peace that events of general interest had taken place during the seclusion of the jury which the by-standers found a certain gloomy satisfaction in detailing; their attention was thus readily enough diverted from the disagreements of the jury-room to the circumstances of Peter Rood's funeral, — who preached the sermon, and who were in attendance. They all sat, solemnly chewing, tilted back in their splint-bottomed chairs on the front gallery of the little hotel. The lights which came from the doors and windows of the building, slanting out in wide shafts, seemed to sever the gloom in equal sections. The figures of the men were dimly seen in the dusky intervals. The stars, in infinite hosts, were marshaled in the black sky, for the moon was late to-night. Only about the horizon were melancholy desert spaces. The summit line of the distant mountains was indistinguishable in the gloom. The landscape was all benighted. The presence of invisible trees close at hand was perceptible only to some fine sense of the differing degrees of density in the blackness. A horse trotted through the slant of light, falling into the road and showing the sleek roan of the steed and the impassive face under the drooping hatbrim of the rider, — then loomed an indeterminate centaur in the alternate glooms. The sounds of the town were shrill, then faint, with lapses of silence. One forlorn cricket was piping somewhere between the bricks of the pavement.

"'Pears ter me," said Bylor, "toler'ble cur'ous ez they wagoned deceased" — he had adopted the word from the reports of the sermon — "way up yander ter Eskaqua Cove, ter be buried in the graveyard thar."

"Waal," explained a by-stander, "his mother 'lowed he 'd feel mo' lonesome down hyar 'n he would 'mongst the mountings, — an' I reckon he would."

"Ennybody ez air dead always looked lonesome ter me," suggested Ben Doaks.

"I don't b'lieve thar 's a man in the Newnited States, alive or dead, ez lonesome ez me!" cried the cattle-owner. "I wisht that thar durned moon would heft over the mountings. Ez soon ez she shows her aidge I 'm a-goin' ter light out arter my cattle an' Bob."

"'Pears ter me," said Doaks, reflectively, "ez things

hev turned out mighty cur'ous, ez he war buried in the same graveyard whar Lethe Sayles seen Tad's harnt."

"I would n't go by thar of a dark night fur nuthin'," declared Bylor. "Mought see both of 'em."

"I reckon," said Ben Doaks, "ez Peter Rood knows all 'bout'n it now, — whether it war Tad's harnt or no."

Something at a distance sounded sharply and fell into silence.

"I reckon folks ez air dead hev got suthin' mo' ter tend ter 'n studyin' 'bout folks they knowed in this life," said Bylor, nodding his head with grim conviction.

"Yes, sir-ee!" exclaimed the ex-foreman, as he chewed vigorously, and spat at the post which upheld the floor of the gallery above; he was an effective marksman. "They hev got a verdict in the courts of the t'other world on Peter Rood by now. They ain't got no failin' human jury thar," he continued sanctimoniously. "I reckon he's burnin' in Torment before now." He offered this suggestion with that singular satisfaction in the symmetry of the theory of fiery retribution characteristic of the rural religionist.

Ben Doaks stirred uneasily. "I dunno 'bout that," he said, dubiously. "Rood war a perfessin' member." He himself laid great stress upon this unattained grace.

"I know that," said the ex-foreman, "but 't ain't done him no good. I hearn him 'low at camp ez he war a backslider, an' ef the truth war knowed I reckon he war a black-hearted sinner."

Once more that strange sound, half smothered by the distance, smote upon the air. Then the regular hoof-beat of a horseman riding by on the red clay road interposed and rattled against the stones, and echoed from the bridge below with hollow reverberations.

"What war that cur'ous noise?" demanded Ben Doaks.

"Sounded ter me like cattle a-bellerin'," said old man Beames.

The attentive pause was illustrated by the red spark of each man's pipe, dulling as it was held motionless for a moment in the hand; then restored to the smoker's lips, it glowed into subdued brilliancy, sometimes giving an elusive glimpse of the delicate and shadowy blue vapor curling from the bowl. They heard nothing but a vague murmur, dropping presently into silence.

"I b'lieve," said Bylor, "ez Peter Rood hed suthin' on his mind."

"Me, too," spoke up another man. "He sot next ter me, an' he looked troubled an' tried, somehows, an' wunst in a while he sighed mightily. I dunno what ailed him."

"I reckon he war sick," suggested a by-stander.

"He did n't 'pear ter be sick. He turned an' looked at me plumb pleased ter death when that Lethe Sayles 'lowed Tad war alive. An' then when the 'torney-gineral made it out ez 't war jes' Tad's harnt he jumped for'ards, an' pinted with his finger, an' next thing I knowed the man war a harnt hisself."

The sound in the distance had become continuous, louder. Once more it broke upon the conversation. "Boys," said Jerry Price, in a tone of conviction, "suthin' is a-goin' on somewhar."

The vocation for the *rôle* of spectator is strong in humanity. Each of the long, lank mountaineers started up with unusual willingness, under the impression that he was balked of some entertainment at which nature intended that he should be dead-headed. The distant murmur was once more lost in the sounds nearer at hand. A sudden resonant, brazen clangor challenged the dark stillness. It had a vibratory, swaying iteration, for it was the court-house bell, rung as an alarum to the law-abiding population. As the group started swiftly in the direction of the sound, a man came running at great speed down the pavement, almost overturning old Beames, and called loudly to the proprietor of the hotel, asking if Judge Gwinnan were within. They recognized the deputy sheriff as he rushed into the bar-room.

"'The old man's been hevin' hell with Mink Lorey, down yander at the jail," he explained in breathless gasps. "He kerried on like a crazy idjit when we tuk him back,—fout like a wild-cat every foot o' the way. An'. now thar's a crowd at the jail a-batterin' the doors, an' breakin' the winders, an' swearin' they'll take Mink Lorey out."

In pursuit of the promise of excitement their feet did not lag. They heard, as they set out, the deputy's rasping voice behind them renewing his anxious demand for Judge Gwinnan; then it was lost in the ceaseless thud of their own feet, and the insistence of the bell filling the darkness with its deliberate alternations of tone, till the night rocked and swayed with the oscillating, remonstrant sound. Approaching the court-house, they could hear those fainter and continuous vibrations of the bell-metal, the turbulent but bated undertones, that set the air a-trembling and seemed some muttered affirmation, some reserve of clamors, that should presently break out, too, and utter wrath and measured menace. The darkness seemed unparalleled, since there was something to be done and at hazard. Only at long intervals in the blackness, windows of dwellings were opened, and here and there a venturesome female head was thrust out in baffled and hopeless curiosity. But most of the houses had closed blinds and barred doors, for the alarum of the court-house bell had told the inmates all that the prudent might care to learn. The streets of Shaftesville, grass-grown as they were, had known the tread of lynchers, and distrusted any lawless mission. It was so dark that men, meeting at intersections of the streets, ran blindly against each other, recoiling with oaths,—sometimes against trees and posts. A few provident souls carrying lanterns, and looking in the blackness like fleet fire-flies, were made aware when they encountered the rescuers, in pressing in among the crowd in the jail-yard,—the posse and the mob otherwise indistinguishable,—by having the lanterns struck out of their hands. The jail was silent; its very vicinity had a suggestion of glum resistance. Some consciousness of a darker and solid mass in the air was the only cognizance that the senses could take of its propinquity, except, indeed, the sound of breaking glass. A rail had been dragged from a fence, and, in the hands of unseen parties, after the manner of a battering-ram, the glass in the lower panes was shattered. This was wanton destruction, for the bars withstood the assault. The working of some instrument at them, ever and anon, was an evasive bit of craft, for follow the sound as they might, the sheriff and his posse could never locate it. A light showing in an upper window was saluted by a volley of stones, and quickly disappeared. The missiles fell back in the dense, panting, nameless, viewless crowd, eliciting here and there a howl, succeeded by jeering laughter.

Once, as the glass crashed in a lower window, a child's voice within whimpered suddenly; a soothing murmur, and the child was silent.

"Mis' Perkins," called out a voice from among the mob to the jailer's wife, "make Jacob open the do'! Tell him we'll string him up ef he don't, when we git holt o' him."

There was intense silence in the closely jammed, indistinguishable crowd without, for who could say who was the posse or who the mob, helpless against each other?

A murmur of remonstrance within. An interval. A sharp insistence from the crowd, and a quavering response.

"I *can't*, gentlemen!" cried a shrill feminine voice. "Jake's sech a bull-headed fool, he *won't!*"

The summit line of the distant mountains was becoming vaguely visible; the stars were not less bright, the black earth was as dark as ever, but the moon-rise was imminent.

There was suddenly a surging commotion in the crowd; it swayed hither and thither, and rushed violently upon the door. The point of attack being plain enough, there was some feeble resistance, offered presumably by the posse. A pistol was fired in the air —

another — a wild turmoil; all at once the door crashed and gave way; half the assailants were carried over its splintered ruins by the force of their own momentum. There were lights enough now springing up in every direction. Men with torches dashed through the halls, holding them aloft with streaming clouds of flame and smoke, as erratic as comets. It required only a moment, with the united exertions of half a dozen stalwart young fellows, to break the door of Mink's cell; it offered no such opposition as the main entrance.

There was no cry of joy as they rushed in; no fraternal embrace for the liberators who had risked so much in the cause of natural justice.

The cell was empty. The bars at the window were firm as ever. The locked door was broken but a moment ago. And he was gone!

The word rang through the building. The infuriated crowd pervaded the cell in a moment, like some tumultuous flood. The jailer himself was not to be found. His wife and children had sought refuge elsewhere.

The doors were guarded against the sheriff, while a select party searched every room in the house. Some serious fright was occasioned to certain malefactors, who had reason to fear the people more than the law, and esteemed the jail in some sort as a haven, but there were many who appealed for liberation. One of these, a victim of the federal court, Big Brandy Owen by name, made so earnest an insistence that his case was considered. But he was no genuine moonshiner, it was argued; he was only a saloon-keeper who had fallen a victim to the liquor laws. "We dunno ye," they prevaricated. "Ye ain't labeled Brandy, ye see." And so they locked his door upon him.

They did as much damage as they could, in default of accomplishing their object, and on retiring they dispersed without recognition among the peaceful citizens who had weakly striven, half-heartedly, to uphold the law.

The moon was up. The Great Smoky Mountains, in magnificent immensity. clasped the world in the gigantic curve about the horizon east and south. The trees seemed veiled in some fine, elusive silver gauze, so gleaming a line of light came to the eye from their boughs. Frost sparkled upon the grass-fringed streets. The shadows were sharp and black. The stars — few now — faintly scintillated in empyreal distances. The town was so still, not even a dog barked. The rescuers experienced a luxury of bravado in the realization that it was for fear of them that it was fain to hold its breath and lie in darkness, save for the light of the moon. Perhaps it was as well, and spared further mischief, that they exulted in riding their horses at a gallop through the streets, breaking now and then into wild fantasies of yells, with a fantastic refrain of echoes.

The rioters after a time disappeared. A long interval, and perhaps a single equestrian figure would ride down the straggling street and whoop aloud, and turn in his saddle to listen for a comrade's response, and then ride on.

Finally silence fell. The waning moon was high. The night was well-nigh spent. Sundry movements of shadows on window blinds, sundry dim yellow lights showing through them, despite the lustre of the moon, indicated that the inhabitants considered that the drama had been played, and were betaking themselves to bed. Alethea Sayles, crouching in the dormer window of the cottage where the witness fee had sufficed to lodge her, looking with dilated eyes over the little town enmeshed in the silver net of its frosted trees, strained her ears in the silence, and exclaimed in the anguish of suspense, "They mus' hev tuk him out, Aunt Dely, or they would n't hev been so gamesome."

She knew little of town ways. Had the mob been successful, the frost itself could not vanish more silently.

Mrs. Purvine, her wise head pillowed, for the first time in her life, as she remarked, on "town folkses' geese," sleepily assented.

The moon looked down in Alethea's upturned eyes. The pine that stood by the window tapped upon the pane.

She felt as if it were a friendly and familiar thing, here where there were so few trees; for the sight of houses — crowded, indeed, they seemed — overwhelmed her in some sort, and embarrassed her. It was all a-shimmer with the frost; even an empty bird's-nest on a bough was a miracle of delicate interweaving of silver gleams. Her hair in its rich dishevelment fell in coils and tangles half-way to her waist. She clasped her hands over one knee. It was an interval of peace.

"Lethe!" said Mrs. Purvine, rousing herself. "Ain't that gal kem ter bed yit!" The admonition was a subterfuge. She was about to impart information. "Lethe, ef ye b'lieve me, these hyar crazy muskrats o' town folks hev got *sun-bonnets ready-made* in these hyar stores."

The vicissitudes of the trial had been the veriest trifles to her. She had utilized the metropolitan sojourn. She had pervaded the stores, as women of her sort do elsewhere. Mighty little there was in these stores that Aunt Dely had not rummaged.

"Ye tole me that afore," said the absorbed Alethea.

Mrs. Purvine chuckled aloud as she reviewed the fact. It afforded her an occult complacence, yet she laughed at it.

Presently she recurred to it.

"My cracky! Lethe," she exclaimed, "*who* makes 'em?"

And with this problem in her mind, she fell asleep among the comforts of "town folkses' geese."

XV.

THE fires of discontent smouldered throughout the next day. Although many of the country people had left town, there was more than the usual stir upon the streets. Idle knots of men strolling about or standing on the corners neglected their avocations in eager discussion of the events of the previous evening. There was very general reprehension of the action of the mob, — so general that it might suggest a wonder as to whence came its component elements, and an unpleasant feeling that perhaps a satirical ringleader might be advancing these rebukes, and watching with secret laughter their effect. Many rumors prevailed, some so fantastic as to balk the credulity that sought to accept them, and others probable enough to be a solution of Mink's disappearance. Some maintained that he had been liberated by the mob. Others said that at the time of the onslaught he had been hidden in the cellar with the jailer and the jailer's family; and this was again roundly denied, for the cellars were reported to have been thoroughly searched.. It was said, too, that the prisoner had been gagged, bound securely, and boldly carried forth from the back door through the crowd in the intense darkness, and that he was now held in retreat at the sheriff's house. However it might have been, that officer received about noonday two or three threatening letters signed, "The men that elected you."

He had since been disposed to exonerate himself, and he bore a troubled, anxious face about the town, and talked in a loud, strained, remonstrant falsetto. It was through some words which he let fall, in the perturbation of the discovery that he was liable to be held to account personally by this unknown and numerous enemy, that it became public he had applied to Judge Gwinnan, not in his judicial capacity, but for advice in this emergency, and that it was Gwinnan who had devised the ruse which had baffled the rescuers.

The curiosity as to Mink's fate grew so pronounced as the day wore on that a party of young roughs went openly to the jail and interrogated the jailer. For that functionary had returned. He showed himself at the window of his stronghold jauntily enough. He had a jovial expression, a black mustache that turned cheerfully upward,— for he laughed often and usually laughed last, — quick brown eyes, and a bushy, unkempt head; he was unshaven and in his shirt-sleeves. He seemed to care not an atom for the illogical views of his fellow-citizens.

"I 'm appinted by the sher'ff o' Cherokee County ter keep folks in jail, an' by Hokey, I 'm a-goin' ter do it."

They begged him to let them in; they had come to see him sociably, — a-visitin', they protested.

"Can't git in hyar, 'thout ye steal a horse or kill yer gran'mother, one." He shook his keys jocosely at them, and vanished.

At noon, when the train was due at the little station, the mystery was solved. The jailer was strolling up and down the platform, grave enough for once in his life, and with apparently no purpose. Asked if he were going to Glaston he replied, with an effort at his usual manner, "Not in these clothes, if the court knows itself, an' it rather think it do!"

It was a day of doubtful moods, of sibilant gusts of wind and intervals of brooding stillness. There was a pervasive suggestion of moisture in the air, but as yet no rain. The odor of decaying leaves came from the woods on the other side of the road. The sunshine was uncertain. White clouds were silently astir in the upper regions of the atmosphere; among the distant blue ranges the intervenient valleys could be distinctly located by the mist rising from them, elusively showing, then veiling the farther heights, and anon falling like some airy cataract over a mountain side, seeming to cleave it in twain, and simulating a gap, a pass, in the impenetrabilities of the massive clifty range. The little stream that flowed along on the other side of the rails reflected the vacillating sentiments of the sky: now a cloud driving faster than its current showed upon its lustrous olive-green surface among the reflections of the crimson sumach bushes that lined its banks; and now it glittered in a burst of sunshine and emulated the azure of the changing heavens. The little town lay at a considerable distance; whether it hoped to grow up to the depot, or desired the advantages of civilization without its close contact, one might speculate in vain. Its clustering roofs were quite distinct among the thinning red and yellow and brown leaves of the trees.

A number of loungers waited to watch the train pass; for it was only a short time since the road had been completed, and the engine was still a mechanical miracle in the estimation of many of the country people, who came sometimes great distances to see it. Harshaw was going down to attend the court at Glaston. He was much smarter than usual, although he wore on his yellow head a soft wide hat, which gave him a certain highwayman-like aspect. A gay necktie of blue shot silk showed beneath his yellow beard; his stiffly starched cuffs, already much crumpled, protruded beneath his coat-sleeves.

"What are you about, my friend? Going to jump the country?" he demanded of the deputy-sheriff, who was embarrassed, and replied evasively that he was waiting to see a man. Harshaw turned to greet Gwinnan, who was also going off, having adjourned the court a few moments too late the preceding evening and thereby failing to catch the night train. Harshaw accosted him with a full expression of his large, bluff, familiar manner. It was received with a certain coolness, which may have been Gwinnan's normal social temperature, but Harshaw was keenly alert to descry significance, and was disposed to refer it to the hasty threat at the courthouse door. Gwinnan's impassive inexpressiveness gave him no intimation whether or not it had been repeated, and as the judge stood looking about the little unpainted wooden depot, all its business easily to be comprised in the two rooms, Harshaw began to detail to him how much the road had cost, how it was hoped it would aid in developing the resources of the country, how it had already begun to conduct itself like a sure enough grown-up railroad, and had got into law. Suddenly the two shining parallel rails trembled with a metallic vibration. A distant roar growing ever nearer and louder impinged upon the air. A cloud of smoke appeared above the trees, and with a glitter of burnished metal, a turmoil of sound, a swift gliding rush, the overpowering imperious presence of the engine gladdened the sight of the simple country folks.

Gwinnan was silent as Harshaw talked, until suddenly that worthy broke off, "Hello! what's going on here?"

Some distance up the red clay road from the direction of the town, a buggy was driven at a furious rate, with the evident intention of forestalling the departure of the train.

All the loungers saw it. The conductor saw it, and yet he cried out, "All aboard!" and sprang upon the platform as the train began to move. The by-standers understood the ruse the next moment. There were two men in the buggy: one was handcuffed; the other was the sheriff. The deputy and two guards dragged the prisoner across the platform and upon the slowly moving train, which forthwith rattled away around the curve at the greatest speed of which it was capable, leaving the suspected rescuers gazing blankly at it, and realizing that because of the insecurity of the county jail Mink was to be lodged in the metropolitan prison of Glaston.

It is said that nothing so expands the mental horizon as the experience of emotion. In this sense Mink was becoming a wise man. He knew despair not as a word, a theory, a sentiment, but in its baffled, futile finality.

He had conned all the fine vacillations of suspense. He had exhausted the delusions of hope.

Only the passion of rage had as yet unsated capacities. As he sat in the car, shackled, among his guards, he fixed his shining eyes, full of suppressed ferocity, on Gwinnan's face, who was absorbed in a book and heedless of his fellow-travelers. The guards did not notice the prisoner's gaze, and after a moment it was diverted for a time. For Mink had quick enough perceptions and no mean power of deduction. He divined that his guards and fellow-passengers were in much perturbation lest the train should be stopped. At every intersection of the country roads with the track there was a perceptible flurry amongst them, an anxious outlook to descry mounted and armed men.

He had himself no further expectation of deliverance.

"Nobody's goin' ter resk ten year in the Pen'tiary fur rescuin' me in broad daylight whar they could be knowed. Ef the mob wanted ter hang me, though, *they would*," he said, with the cynicism of the truth.

"Nobody wants ter hang you-uns, Mink, nor hurt ye no-ways. All ye need is a leetle patience ter wait fur another trial," said the deputy.

"I ain't got no mo' patience," said Mink drearily.

His fatigued faculties, that had almost sunk into stupor under the strain of excitement and suspense, roused themselves to take note of the surroundings. The motion of the train filled him with amaze. He held his breath to see the fantasies of the flying landscape without. The panting snorts and leaps of the engine, like some great living monster, the dull rolling of the wheels, the iterative alternating sound of the clanking machinery, each registered a new estimate of life upon his intent, expressive face. His eyes rested on the lamp fixtures shining in their places as if he beheld enchantment. The tawdry ornamentation, the paneling of light and dark woods with occasional glimmers of gilding, the red velvet of the seats, were to his unaccustomed eyes unparalleled magnificence. He asked no questions. He accepted it all simply, without comment, without consciousness. His fine head, with its rich coloring of complexion and eyes and hair, looked as if it might have been painted upon the panel of maple on which it leaned, he sat so still. His hat lay on the seat beside him; he was well used now not to wear it. It may have been because he was innocent, it may have been because he felt no shame, but the handcuffs on his wrists seemed not more ignominious than a wild creature's captivity.

He had been so docile, so unresisting all the morning, that the deputy, who had grown to like the young fellow in their constrained intercourse, and valued him far more than a duller and a better man, was disposed to treat him as gently as was consistent with duty. The guards were jolly and they joked with him; but he had little to say, and presently they talked to each other, and looked over their shoulders at the rest of the company, covertly entertaining themselves with such fragments of the conversation as the roaring and clangor of the train permitted to be audible. They noticed after a time that the surroundings had ceased to interest him, and that he was looking with lowering and surly ferocity at Judge Gwinnan, intent upon his book.

"Look-a-hyar," said one of the guards, nudging Mink violently, "ye 'pear like some wild varmint. Ye look ez keen an' wicked an' mean ez a mink. Quit eyin' Jedge Gwinnan like that, else I'll blindfold ye, — sure's ye born, I will."

Mink's dilated eyes rested upon the unconscious, half-averted face for a moment longer. Then they turned to the face of the deputy in front of him.

"That thar man," he said between his set teeth, and for all his voice was low it was distinct, even in the rumbling and noise of the train, so charged it was with the emphasis of intention, the definiteness of a cherished revenge, — "d 'ye know what he hev done ter me? He put Pete Rood on the jury, though he knowed Pete hated me, an' why. He put the jury in jail, 'kase they war fools, an' 'lowed they hed a harnt on the panel, an' bein' jailed conflusticated 'em so they could n't find a verdict. *He* knows an' *they* know Tad 's alive, but I hev got ter bide in jail fower month longer an' resk the Pen-'tiary agin, account o' a drownded boy ez hev run away. An' when my friends wanted ter take me out'n jail, — God A'mighty! I did n't know I hed sech friends, — he goes out'n his way ter tell the sher'ff how ter flustrate 'em. An' I war gagged an' ironed, an' toted out'n the back door, an' kep' at the sher'ff's house, an' am tuk off on the train. 'T war n't his business. Ye know thar war n't ez much ez that done whenst the lynchers kem fur Tim Jenkins, — *not ter save the man's life.*"

"Waal, he hed ter be hung some time, ennyhow," said the deputy indisputably.

"What did this hyar Jedge Gwinnan do all this hyar fur?" continued Mink.

"Waal, Mink, he war obleeged ter, by his office. Ye know I don't hold no grudge ter ye, yit I 'm 'bleeged ter iron ye an' gyard ye. I could n't set no mo' store by ye ef ye war my own blood relation," said the deputy.

"Naw, sir! naw!" exclaimed Mink. "This hyar man have tuk a notion ter Lethe Sayles, — I seen it; an' he 'lows I ain't good enough fur her, an' he be doin' sech ez he kin agin me on account o' her."

The deputy sheriff broke into a horse-laugh. The others laughed, too, more moderately. "Ye air teched in the head, Mink," one of them remarked.

"Mebbe so," Mink responded quietly enough, but with a glancing gleam in his dark eyes. "But I 'll remember what he hev done ter me. An' I 'll git even with him fur it. By the Lord, I 'll git even with him fur it. An' ye shell see the day."

He leaned back against the window, with his eyes bright, his lips curving, tossing his tangled hair with a quick, excited gesture, as if he saw his revenge an accomplished fact.

Somehow his look impressed the guards.

"Naw, ye won't," said one of them. "Ye won't do nuthin' like it. Ye air goin' ter jail *fower* month, an' arter that ter the Pen'tiary *five* year, an' time ye git out'n thar ye 'll be so powerful pleased ter be foot-loose ye 'll mind yer manners the rest o' yer days, an' ye will hev clean furgot Jedge Gwinnan."

He evidently thought some harshness salutary. Mink made no reply, and they presently fell to talking together of their town affairs and gossip, excluding him from the conversation, in which, in truth, he desired to take no share.

XVI.

In contrast with the steam-cars, the old ox-cart was a slow way of getting through the world, and had little of that magnificence which forced itself upon Mink's jaded and preoccupied faculties. But as Alethea turned her face toward the mountains, it seemed the progress into Paradise, so happy was she in the belief that the rescuers had prevailed. For she, aunt Dely, and Jerry Price had left town early that morning, before doubts and contradictions were astir. The waning yellow moon still swung high in the sky, above the violet vapors of the level west. Long shadows were stalking athwart the fields and down the woodland ways, as if some mystic beings of the night were getting them home. A gust of wind came shivering along the road once and again, — an invisible, chilly presence, that audibly rustled its weird garments and convulsively caught its breath, and was gone. Above the Great Smoky Mountains the inexpressible splendors of the day-star glowed and burned. She walked behind the cart much of the time with Jerry, while aunt Dely sat, a shapeless mass, within it. A scent of tar issued from its clumsy wheels, heavy with the red clay mire of many a mile; a rasping creak exuded from its axles, in defiance of wagon-grease. The ox between his shafts had a grotesque burliness in the moonlight. The square, unpainted little vehicle was a quaint contrivance. Four of the dogs ran beneath it, in leash with their nimble shadows. And aunt Dely's sun-bonneted head, nodding with occasional lapses into sleep, was faithfully reproduced in the antics of the silhouettes upon the ground that journeyed with them.

Now and again the Scolacutta River crossed their

way in wide, shining curves scintillating with the stars,
and then Alethea would perch upon the tail-board, and
Jerry would clamber into his place as driver, and the
dogs would yelp and wheeze on the bank, reluctant to
swim, and the ox would plunge in, sometimes with a
muttered low of surprise to find the water so cold.
Fording the stream was slow work; the wheels often
scraped against great hidden bowlders, threatening dislo-
cation and destruction to the running gear. The transit
was attended with a coruscation of glittering showers of
spray, and left a foaming track across the swift current.
Sometimes it was a hard pull up the steep, rocky bank
opposite. The old ox had a sober aspect, a resolute
tread, and insistently nodding horns. His sturdy rustic
demeanor might have suggested that he was glad to be
homeward bound, and to turn his back upon the frivoli-
ties of civilization and fashion. Not so aunt Dely. It
seemed for a time as if her enforced withdrawal from
these things had impaired her temper. She woke up
ever and anon with caustic remarks.

"I reckon now, Lethe Ann Sayles, ye be goin' ter
bide along o' yer step-mother?"

"Ye know that's my home. I hev ter, aunt Dely."

The girl's voice was clear, sweet, thrilling with gladness, like some suddenly awakened bird's singing a stave
before dawn.

"I b'lieve ye!" satirically. "Ennybody but you-uns
would be 'shamed ter own up ez ye hev got no home.
Old ez ye be, an' ye ain't married yit! How old be ye?
Lemme see," — with a tone intimating that she would
give no quarter, — "nineteen year, five month, an' fower
days. It's plumb scandalous," she muttered, arranging
her shawl about her. "Ye Bluff!" addressing the ox
in a querulous crescendo, "ye goin' ter jolt the life
out'n me, a-tryin' ter ape the gait o' the minchin' sinners
ye seen in Shaftesville! Actially the steer hev got the
shuffles! I tell ye, Sodom an' G'morrah war n't nowhar
fur seethin' sin ter Shaftesville. The devil be a-gatherin'
his harvest thar. His bin an' barn air full. Them folks

will know some day ez store clothes ain't no defense agin fire. They hev bartered thar salvation fur store clothes. But I do wisht," she broke off suddenly, dropping her voice from her sanctimonious whine to her cheery drawl, "I hed one o' them ready-made sun-bonnets. I hed traded off all my feathers an' truck for store sugar an' sech afore I seen 'em. I was so full o' laff that I could n't keep my face straight whenst I viewed the contrivance."

The darkness had fled; the moonlight had failed; the fine, chastened pallor of the interval — the moment's pause before the dawn — showed the colorless sky, the massive dusky mountains, the stretches of woods below, almost leafless now, the gaunt, tawny fields here and there, the zigzag lines of the rail fences, the red clay road. There were gullies of such depth on either side that the ox, who received so little supervision that he appeared to have the double responsibility of drawing and driving the cart, demonstrated, in keeping out of pitfalls, ampler intellectual capacities than are usually credited to the bovine tribe. But indeed his gifts were recognized. "I ain't s'prised none ef some day Bluff takes ter talkin'," his mistress often averred, with her worldly pride in her possessions.

The wind freshened; the white frost gleamed; a pale flush, expanding into a suffusion of amber light, irradiated the sky; and the great red wintry sun rose slowly above the purple ranges.

They had barely passed through a gap of the mountains and entered Eskaqua Cove, when they saw riding along an intersecting road close to the bank of the river a girl in a yellow homespun dress, with a yellow bonnet on her head, and mounted on a great white mare. She had the slaie of a loom in her hand which she had borrowed of a neighbor, and which served to explain her early errand.

Alethea, in her joy, had forgotten Elvira Crosby's sneers and gibes the night she had brought to the Hollow the raccoon which Mink had given her. All other considerations were dwarfed by the rapturous idea that he was at liberty. Eager to tell the news, she sprang forward.

"Elviry!" she cried. The girl drew up her mare and turned about. Alethea ran down the road and caught the bridle. "Elviry," she reiterated, "Reuben air out o' jail! He's free! He's free!"

The news was not received as she expected. Elvira put back her bonnet from the soft rings of short hair that lay about her head. She fixed her dark eyes on Alethea in doubting surprise.

"Waal," she demanded, as if herself sitting in judgment, "who killed Tad?"

"Tad be alive ez I be!" cried Alethea, harried by the reawakening of those questions which she had thought were forever set at rest.

"An' did the jury say sech?" Elvira asked. It might have seemed that with the breach between her and Mink irreparable, she was not rejoiced to hear of his good fortune.

"The jury could n't 'gree," said Alethea breathlessly. "The rescuers tuk him out."

"Sech ez that be agin the law," said Elvira staidly.

"I ain't keerin' fur the law!" cried Alethea. "He hev done no harm, an' all the kentry knowed it. An' 't war n't right ter keep him cooped in jail. So they tuk him out."

She lifted her head and smiled. Ah, did she indeed look upon a wintry landscape with those eyes? So irradiated with the fine lights of joy, so soft, they were, it might seem they could reflect only endless summers. The gaunt, bleak mountains shivered in the niggardliness of the averted sun; the wind tossed her loose locks of golden hair from beneath her brown bonnet as if they were flouts to the paler beams.

Elvira looked down at her with the pitiless enmity of envy.

"Waal," she said, "'twixt ye two ye hev done me a powerful mean turn. Mink kep' a-tryin' ter cut out Pete

Rood till I did n't know my own mind. An' then ye a-tellin' them tales 'bout harnts till Pete drapped dead, — ye knowin' he hed heart-disease! Yes, sir, he 's dead; buried right over yander in the graveyard o' the church-house in the cove. An' I reckon ye be sati'fied now, — ef *ye kin* be sati'fied."

She looked away over the swift flow of the river, and began to fleck her shoe with the hickory switch she carried.

Alethea's face fell. She still stood holding the mare's rein, but aunt Dely's voice had broken upon the silence. For Bluff had followed Alethea when she turned from the main road, and had refused to be guided by Mrs. Purvine's acrid remonstrance. As to Jerry, he was stalking on ahead, unaware that the others were not close on his steps. Sawing upon the ropes on Bluff's horns which served for reins, Mrs. Purvine succeeded in drawing him up when she reached the spot where the two girls stood. She suddenly joined in the conversation with an astute intention.

"Yes, sir, Mink 's out," she said, confirming her niece's statement. "An' ye 'll hev ter do mighty little tollin' ter git him back agin, Elviry," she added beguilingly.

"I don't want no jail-bird roun' me," said Elvira, with a toss of her head.

"Mebbe ye air right, child!" cried Mrs. Purvine. "That 's edzacly what I tole Lethe." She nodded gayly, and her head-gear, swaying with the expressive gesture, could not have seemed more jaunty had it been a ready-made sun-bonnet from the store. "Ye mark my words, Lethe air goin' ter marry a man she seen in Shaftesville." Elated with this effort of imagination, she continued, inspirationally, "He 'lowed she war a plumb beauty, beat ennything he ever dreampt could hev kem out'n the mountings. He air a town man, an' he be a fust-rate one."

"Oh, aunt Dely!" faltered Alethea, amazed and almost speechless.

But aunt Dely, charmed with the image she had conjured up, had no mind to relinquish this mythical man, and added another touch of verisimilitude: "He's well off, too. Lethe, she don't keer nuthin' 'bout riches, but bein' ez I hev 'sociated so much with town folks, I sorter set store by worldly goods,—though not enough ter resk my soul's salvation, nuther."

Aunt Dely's evident desire was to combine spiritual and material welfare, and in this she was not unlike more sophisticated religionists.

The opinionated Bluff being induced to turn around at last, Mrs. Purvine let fly a Parthian dart: "But ez ter you-uns, Elviry, I dunno whether ye hed better be lookin' down on fust one boy, an' then another. Ye'll git lef' hyar a lonesome single woman, the fust thing ye know, — *the only one in the cove!* But then, mebbe ye'd better jes' bow yer mind ter the dispensation, fur arter all ye mought n't be able ter ketch Mink. The gals honey him up so ez he air toler'ble sp'iled; they 'low he air special good-lookin', though I hev never been able ter see good looks in him sence he kem ter my house, one night, an' bedeviled my front steps so ez they hev never been so stiddy sence."

"Aunt Dely," cried Alethea, when they were once more on their homeward way, "what ailed ye ter tell Elviry sech a pack o'"— Respect for her elders restrained her.

"I war prompted by my conscience!" replied the logical Mrs. Purvine, unexpectedly. "I can't be at peace with my conscience 'thout doin' all I kin ter purvent a spry, good-lookin' gal like you-uns from marryin' a wuthless critter sech ez Mink Lorey." She made no secret of her designs. "He be good a plenty an' ter spare fur that thar snake-eyed Elviry Crosby, but I want ye ter marry Jerry Price, an' kem an' live along o' me."

The immaterial suitor evolved by Mrs. Purvine's conscience dwelt in Alethea's mind with singular consistency and effect afterward. When she was once more in

Wild-Cat Hollow, and day after day passed, — short days they were, of early winter, — and Mink did not come, expectation was supplanted by alternations of hope and disappointment, and they in their turn by fear and despair. Was it possible, she asked herself, that he could have heard and credited this fantastic invention of Mrs. Purvine's affection and pride; that Elvira had poisoned his mind; that he was jealous and angry; that for this he had held aloof? Then the recollection of their old differences came upon her. His sorrows had obliterated them in her contemplation. It did not follow, however, that they had brought her nearer to him. He had long ago fallen away from her. Why should she expect that he would return now? She remembered with a new interpretation his joyous relief the morning that she had told to him and his lawyer in the jail the story of her glimpse of Tad; although she had shared his gratulation, it was for his sake alone. She remembered his burning eyes fixed with fiery reproaches upon her face in the court-room, when the disclosure was elicited that it was in a graveyard she had seen the missing boy. After all, she had done nothing for him; her testimony had fostered doubt and roused superstition, and other and stronger friends had effected his release.

She became silent, sober-eyed, and absorbed, and went mechanically about the house. Her changed demeanor occasioned comment from Mrs. Jessup, who sat idle, with a frowzy head and an active snuff-brush, by the fireside instead of on the porch, as in the summer days. "When Lethe fust kem back from Shaftesville she 'peared sorter peart an' livened up. Her brain war shuck up, somehow, by her travels. I 'lowed she war a-goin' ter behave arter this like sure enough folks, — but shucks! she 'pears ter be feared ter open her mouth, else folks 'll know she hev got a tongue 'twixt her teeth." For Alethea found it hard now to reply to the continued queries of Mrs. Sayles and Mrs. Jessup, who had relished her opportunity, and in the girl's observation of village life were enjoying all the benefits of travel without impinging upon their inertia or undertaking its fatigues. The elder woman sat smoking in the corner, her pink sunbonnet overhanging her pallid, thin face, ever and anon producing a leaf of badly cured tobacco, and drying it upon the hearthstone before serving her pipe. Now and then she chuckled silently and toothlessly at some detail of the gossip. It had hurt the girl to know how little they cared for the true object of the expedition. Mink Lorey was naught to them, and they did not affect a picturesque humanity which they did not feel.

"Waal, sir!" Mrs. Sayles would say, "I'll be bound them town folks air talkin' 'bout Dely Purvine yit. I jes' kin view in the sperit how she went a-boguein' roun' that town, stare-gazin' everything, like she war raised nowhar, an' war n't used ter nuthin'. Did n't the folks laff powerful at yer aunt Dely?"

"I never seen nobody laffin'," protested Alethea, loyally.

Jacob Jessup, sober enough, but surly, was wont also to sit in these days idle by the fire. The farm work, such as it was, had been done. The stock he fed when he liked. He chose to consider Alethea's metropolitan trip as a bit of personal self-assertion, and sneered whenever it was mentioned, and sought to ignore it as far as he might. For his own part, he had never been to Shaftesville, and he grudged her the distinction. He would not recognize it; he treated the fact as if it were not, and thus he extinguished it. He seemed somehow, as he sprawled idly about, to take up much more room by the fire than the women, despite their skirts, and he was often engaged in altercations with the dogs, the children, and the pet cub as to the space they occupied. The bear had been reared in a bad school for his manners; he had grown intelligent and impudent and selfish in captivity among his human friends. He would stretch himself along the hearth in front of the family, absorbing all the heat, snarling, and showing his teeth sometimes, but steeling himself in his fur and his fat and his fortitude, and withstanding kicks and blows till his persecutor was tired. Sometimes Jessup would catch him by the rolls of fat about his neck and drag him to the door, but the nimble beast would again be stretched upon the hearthstones before the man could reach his chair. Jessup did the brute no great hurt, for, lowering and ill-natured as the fellow was, he was kindly disposed toward animals, and this made the more marked a sort of spite which he seemed to entertain toward the raccoon which Mink had given Elvira, and which she had brought to Alethea. The grotesque creature was in some sort a domestic martyr. As it scuttled about the uneven puncheon floor, he would affect to stumble over it, swear at it, seize it by the tail, and fling it against the wall. But the coon's griefs were readily healed. It would skulk away for a time, and then be seen eating stolen delicacies in its dainty fashion, washing the food between its two fore-paws in the drinking pail. Old man Sayles, silent, subdued, sat a sort of alien at his own fireside, sorting seeds, and bits of tobacco, buttons, herbs, tiny gourds, which went by the name of "lumber" with him, in a kind of trough beneath the window that served in lieu of sill. Now and then he passed his hand over his head and sighed. Perhaps he regretted his second matrimonial venture; for the domestic scene was one of frowzy confusion, very pronounced when crowded into one small room, instead of being shared with the porch, which the wind swept now and shook, and where the mists congregated in the evenings or the frosts convened. The Jessup children were shrill at play. The baby had got on its feet, and was walking into everything, — unwary pans and kettles and tubs of water. Tige's overbearing disposition was very manifest in his capacity as fireside companion. And when the chimney smoked, and L'onidas preferred his complaints at Alethea's side as she sat and carded wool, and the cub leaned his weight against her as he contemplated the fire with his head upon her knee, and her step-mother scolded, and Jacob Jessup fumed and contradicted, and the experimental baby brought down the churn with a crash, while the cat lapped amidst the waste, Mrs. Jessup would shift her snuff-brush to the other corner of her pretty mouth, and demand, "Now ain't Lethe a plumb fool ter live hyar along o' sech cavortin' ways up on the side o' a mounting, a-waitin' fur a pore wuthless scamp like Mink Lorey, when she could hev a house ter herself in Piomingo Cove, with no hendrance but Ben Doaks, a quiet respectable boy, ez I don't look down on 'kase he ain't got religion! I know some folks ez religion itself can't holp."

Sometimes, however, — it was at long intervals, — even Mrs. Jessup would be summoned to rouse herself from the heavy sluggishness that made all exertion, beyond the necessary routine, positive pain. The code of etiquette that prevails in the mountains, simple as it is, has yet its rigorous requirements; and when the death of a kinsman in Eskaqua Cove presently occurred, the graceless creature deplored it less than the supervening necessity of attending the obsequies. There was no snow, nor ice, nor rain, to urge as an excuse. The weather was singularly fine and dry. It was easier getting down the mountain now than in the summer. And so she was constrained to go.

The sunshine was still, languid; the air was calm. Wild-Cat Hollow wore its wintry aspect, although below in the cove one might have glimpses of red and yellow, as if the autumn yet lingered. Everywhere there was a wider outlook because of the denudation of the woods, and the landscape was the more gaunt, the more rugged. It was like a mind stripped of the illusions of youth; the stern facts are the plainer, and alas! more stern. The purplish-garnet hue of the myriads of bare boughs in the forests covering the mountain slopes contrasted with the indeterminate blue of the sky. There was a fibrous effect in their fine detail; even the great mass, seen at a distance, was like some delicate penciling. Singularly still it was, the air very dry; the dead leaves on the ground did not rustle; the corn-stalks, standing withered and yellow in the fields, did not stir.

The only motion was the slow shifting of the shadows as the day went on, and perhaps high, high even above the Great Smoky, a swift passing of wild geese flying southward, their cabalistic syllable *Houk! houk!* floating down, seeming in the silence strangely intoned and mysterious. At night a new moon looked through the rigid, naked trees. The feeble glimmer from the little log cabin was solitary. The stars themselves were hardly more aloof from the world. The narrow vista through the gap only attested how darkly indistinguishable was the cove, how annihilated in the blackness were the mountains.

No sound of cattle drifted down now from the bald; the herds were gone; sometimes in the midnight the howl of a wolf echoed and re-echoed in all the tortuous ways of the wilderness; then silence, that seemed to tremble with fear of the reiteration of the savage cry. Alethea was prone to be wakeful and sad and anxious, so perhaps it was well that she had much to occupy her thoughts during the day. The baby fretted for his mother. Mrs. Jessup was not a model mother, but she was the only one the baby had, and he was not recreant to filial sentiment. He exacted a vast number of petty attentions from Alethea which he had never before required. Tige and the cub resented the pampering she gave him; they were jealous and made their feeling known in many dumb manifestations: they kept themselves sadly in the way; now they were hungry and now they were thirsty, and they whined continually about her.

She hardly noticed at first that a thick haze had appeared over the cove, but as yet did not dim the sky. It climbed the mountain sides, and hung like a gauze veil about the cabin and the sheds. Suddenly she became aware of the pungent odor of smoke. She put the child away from her, as he clung to her skirts, and stepped out upon the porch. The dog and cub pressed close after her, fancying that they had scored one against the baby, who had sunk, squalling because of his desertion, upon the floor.

She looked about for a moment at the still white presence that had usurped the earth, the air, the sky.

"Somebody hev set out fire in the woods!" she cried.

"Hev ye jes' fund that out?" drawled Jacob Jessup, as he sat on the porch. Her father and he were languidly discussing whether they should fire against it. It was far enough away as yet, they thought, and with the annual conflagrations in the woods they had become experts in judging of the distance and of the emergencies of fighting fire with fire.

She listened as they talked, thinking that Sam Marvin's home, miles away, would presently be in danger, if they were right as to the location of the fire. The cruel flames would complete the desolation she had wrought. Her conscience winced always at the recollection of its bare, denuded plight. Some small reparation was suggested in the idea that she might save it; she might go thither now and fire the dead leaves on the slopes below. Above there was a desolate, barren stretch of rocks, covering many acres, which the flames could hardly overleap. There was no wind, but a slight stir was now in the air. Its current was down the mountain.

She set out, Tige and the coon with her: the wild thing ambling demurely along with all the decorum of cultivated manners; the domestic animal barking and leaping before her in mad ecstasy for the simple privilege of the excursion. The cub looked after them from the doorway, whined, and crept within to the fire.

As she went she was vividly reminded of the day when she had journeyed thither before, although the woods had then worn the rich guise of autumn, and they were now austere and bleak and silent, and shrouded in the white smoke. She even noted the lick-log at the forks of the road, where she had sat and trembled and debated within herself. She wondered if what she had said in the court-room would pursue the moonshiner in his hiding place. Would it harm him? Had she done right or wrong?

Still walking on up the steep slant to the moonshiner's

house, seeing only a yard or two before her, she at last came upon the fence. She paused and leaned upon the rails, and looked about her. The corn-field comprised more acreage than is usual in mountain agriculture. The destination of the crop was not the limited legitimate market of the region. It was planted for use in the still. She experienced another pang when she realized that it too was a grievous loss; for Sam Marvin had been forced to leave the fruit of his industry when it stood immature. Now, early in December, the full crisp ears leaned heavily from the sere stalk. She wondered that the abandoned crop, a fine one, had not been plundered. Then she bethought herself how deep in the wilderness it stood secluded. All at once she heard a rustling among the corn. Her first thought was the bear. In amaze she discerned a wagon looming hard by in the smoke. Then the indistinct figures of a man, a woman, and a half-grown girl came slowly down the turn row. To judge from their gestures, they were gathering the corn.

XVII.

ALETHEA stood motionless for some little time, still leaning on the fence. A stalk of golden-rod, brown and withered, its glory departed, touched the rails now and then. Its slight, infrequent swaying was the only intimation of wind, except that the encompassing smoke, filling the vast spaces between heaven and earth, shifted occasionally, the dense convolutions silently merging into new combinations of ill-defined shapes, — colorless phantasmagoria, dimly looming. It might have seemed as if all the world had faded out, leaving only these blurred suggestions of unrecognized forms, like the vestiges of forgotten æons.

Even the harvesters did not maintain always a human aspect. Through the haze they were grotesque, distorted, gigantic; their hands vaguely visible, now lifted, now falling, in their deliberate but ceaseless work. They looked like vagrants from that eccentric populace of dreams, given over to abnormal, inconsequent gestures, to shifting similitudes, to preposterous conditions and facile metamorphoses of identity. Alethea felt a strange doubt, in recognizing Sam Marvin, whether it were indeed the moonshiner whom she saw.

An insistent silence possessed the air, broken only by the rustle of the crisp husks as the three dim figures pulled the corn. Suddenly there sounded a mad, scuttling rush, shrill canine yelps, and a series of nimble shadows vaulted over the fence. The coon ran up a tree, while the moonshiner's dogs ranged themselves beneath it, with upturned heads askew, and gloating, baffled eyes, and moans of melancholy frustration, punctuated ever and anon with yaps of more poignant realization of the coon's inaccessibility. Tige, irresolute, showed fight at first to the strangers; then he too sat down, and with quivering fore-paws and wagging tail wheezed and yelped at his fireside companion, as if he had no personal acquaintance with the raccoon, had held with him no relations of enforced amity, and could not wait one moment to crunch his bones.

The half-grown girl, desisting from her work, turned her head in the direction of the noise, and caught a glimpse of Alethea. She had an excited eye, high cheekbones, and a thin, prominent nose. Her face looked peculiarly sharp inside her flabby sun-bonnet. She was at the "growing age," and her frock was consequently short for the bare, sun-embrowned legs which protruded from it. Her bare feet were long and bony. She seemed to be growing lengthwise only, for her shoulders were narrow, her arms slim. She had a callow, half-fledged look, not unlike a Shanghai pullet. Her manner was abrupt and fluttered, and her voice high and shrill.

"Laws-a-massy!" she exclaimed, jumping precipitately backward on her long, attenuated legs, "yander's Lethe Sayles!"

Both the man and the woman started violently, — not because of the matter of the disclosure, but of its manner, as was manifested in his rebuke.

"By Gosh, Sereny! ef ye ain't mighty nigh skeered me ter death!" he cried angrily. "S'pose it air Lethe Sayles?" He bowed his body grotesquely amidst the smoke, as he emphasized his reproof. "Air she ennything so powerful oncommon ez ye hev ter jump ez sprightly ez ef ye hed stepped on a rattlesnake, an' squeech out that-a-way? Howdy, Lethe," he added, with an odd contrast of a calm voice and a smooth manner, as if Alethea were deaf to these amenities. "Thrivin', I s'pose?"

Alethea faltered that she was well, and said no more. The imperative consciousness of all that she had done against him, of all for which she feared him, prevailed for a time. She knew that it would have been wiser to venture some commonplace civility, and then go. But that insistent conscience, strong within her, forbade this. She was all unprepared now for the disclosure of her testimony in the court-room, but the fact that she had ever intended to warn him made it seem as if this were due. She felt as if she had missed a certain fortification of her courage in that she had not had the privilege of trembling over the prospect, of familiarizing herself with it, of approaching it slowly, but none the less surely, by lessening degrees of trepidation. She wondered that he did not look at her with more of the indignation which she knew he must feel toward her. Bitterness, however, was acridly manifested in the woman's manner, her averted head, her sedulous silence. She continued industriously pulling the corn, as if no word had been spoken, no creature stood by. The gallinaceous girl, silent too, returned to her work, but often looked askance at Alethea over her shoulder.

The man spoke presently. His face and figure were blurred now in the smoke. It was as if a shadow had purloined a sarcastic voice. Alethea's nerves were unstrung by the surprise of the meeting, and the fact that she could see only this elusive suggestion of his presence harassed and discomposed her.

"Waal, Lethe, I dunno ez I be s'prised ter see ye. I hev seen ye sech a many times whenst I never expected ye, — startin' up yander at Boke's barn ez suddint ez ef ye hed yer headquarters in the yearth or the sky. An' jes' at this junctry, whenst we air a-tryin' ter steal our *own* corn away from hyar, ye kem a-boundin' out'n the smoke, like ye hed no abidin' place more 'n a witch or that thar Herder on Thunderhead, or sech harnts. I never see yer beat ez a meddler. Satan ain't no busier with other folkses' souls."

She made no reply. The shifting vapor hid the tree where the bright-eyed coon hung fast by his claws, and the wheezing yapping of the foiled dogs besieging his stronghold seemed strangely loud and near since they were invisible.

The shucks rustled sibilantly. The ears of maize fell with a monotonous sound upon the heaps in the turn row.

"What did the revenuers do when they kem up the mounting?" Marvin asked suddenly. His tone was all alert now with curiosity. He could reserve his rebukes till his craving for gossip should be satisfied. Conversation, a fine art elsewhere, assumes the dignity of a privilege in these sparsely settled wilds, where its opportunities are scant.

"They ain't never kem, ez I knows on," said Alethea tremulously. They might come yet, and here he was still unwarned and at the mercy of accident. She had climbed the fence, springing lightly down on the other side, and had mechanically begun to assist them in their work,—the usual courtesy of a guest in the mountains who finds the host employed.

"Slip-shuck it, Lethe," he remarked, calling her attention to the fact that the outer husks were left upon the stalks, and the ear, enveloped merely in its inner integuments, was thrown upon the heap. "I hates powerful ter be obleeged ter leave all this hyar good roughness;" he indicated the long rows of shucks upon the stalks. "My cattle would be mighty thankful ter hev sech fedded ter 'em. But the corn itself air about ez much ez I kin haul so fur"—

"*Don't* ye tell her wharabouts we-uns lives nowadays," broke out the woman.

She was standing near Alethea, and she turned and looked at her. The girl's fresh and beautiful countenance was only more delicate, more sensitive, with that half-affrighted perturbation on it, that piteous deprecation. The elder woman's face was furrowed and yellow in contrast; her large, prominent eyes, of a light, hazel color, were full of tears, and had a look as if tears were no unfamiliar visitants. She wiped them away with the curtain of her pink sun-bonnet, and went on pulling the corn.

"I dunno whar Sam Marvin lives, myself," the moonshiner declared, with reckless bravado. "I don't go by that name no.mo'."

He straightened up and set his arms akimbo, as he laughed.

"Ye need n't send no mo' o' yer spies, Lethe, arter me," he declared. "My neighbors way over yander dunno no sech man ez Sam Marvin."

Alethea's lifted hand paused upon the shuck on the sere stalk. As she turned half round he saw her face in the smoke; her golden hair and fresh cheek, and the saffron kerchief tied beneath the round chin. He was not struck by her beauty; it always seemed a thing apart from her, the slightest incident of her personality, so much more forceful were the impressions of her character, so much more intimately her coercive opinions concerned those with whom she came in contact. But in her clear eyes he detected a surprise which he hardly understood at the moment. And he paused to look at her, wondering if it were only simulated.

Her heart throbbed with a dull and heavy pain. So angry were they because she would not promise to keep their secret. She shrank from their rage when she should tell that she had voluntarily disclosed it.

"Ye 'll be purtendin' ez 't war somebody else ez sent the spy ter make sure o' the place whar we kep' our still. I *know ye!*" He wagged his head in more active assertion that her machinations could not avail against his discernment.

"I never sent no spy," faltered Alethea.

"'Thar now! What did I tell ye!" he broke out, laughing disdainfully; the woman added a high, shrill, unmirthful refrain; even Serena the pullet, stepping about in the smoke on her long, yellow feet and in her abbreviated garments, cackled scornfully.

"Ye may thank yer blessed stars," cried the woman scathingly, — she could hold silence no longer, — "ez ye done nuthin' agin we-uns. An' the revenuers never raided our still, nor got nare drap o' our liquor, nor tuk nuthin' o' ourn. Yer bones would be a-bleachin' on the hillside ef they hed! Jes' afore yer spy kem them white-livered men — Sam thar, an' the t'other distillers — war a-talkin' 'bout how they could make ye hesh up yer mouth, ez ye would n't keep it shet yerse'f. They 'lowed it never seemed right handy ter them ter shoot a woman same ez a man, an' I jes' up-ed an' tole 'em ez ye desarved no better 'n a bullet through that yaller head o' yourn, an' they could git a shot at ye enny evenin' whenst ye war a-drivin' up the cow. An' I 'lowed ez whenst a woman went a-meddlin' an' informin' like a man, let her take what a man hev ter take. Naw, sir! but they mus' run away, 'count o' a meddler like you-uns, an' go live somwhar else! An' I hed ter leave my home, an' the three graves o' my dead chill'n, yander on the rise, ez lonesome an' ez meagre-lookin' ez ef they war three pertater hills."

She burst into a tumult of tears. The smoke wafted down, obscuring her, — there was commotion in its midst, for the wind was rising, — and her sobs sounded from out the invisibility that had effaced the earth as if some spirit of grief were abroad in it.

"Shet up, M'ria! Ye talk like ye hed no mo' sense 'n a sheep. The chill'n ain't in them graves," Marvin said, with the consolations of a sturdy orthodoxy.

"Thar leetle bones is," said the spirit of grief from the densities of the clouds.

And he could not gainsay this.

She wept on persistently for the little deserted bones. He could not feel as she did, yet he could understand her feeling. His under-jaw dropped a little; some stress of melancholy and solemnity was on his face, as if a saddened retrospection were evoked for him, too. But it was a recollection which his instinct was to throw off, rather than to cherish as a precious sorrow, jealously exacting for it the extremest tribute of sighs and tears.

"Lethe," he said suddenly, with a cheerful note, "bein' ez they never cotch us, did they pay ye ennything ez informer? I ain't right sure how the law stands on that p'int. The law 'pears ter me ter be a mighty onstiddy, contrariwise contrivance, an' the bes' way ter find out ennything *sartain sure* 'bout'n it air ter 'sperience it. Did they pay ye ennything?"

"I never informed the revenuers," declared Alethea, once more.

He turned upon her a look of scorn.

"I knowed ye war a powerful fool, a-talkin' 'bout 'what's right,' an' preachin' same ez the rider, an' faultin' yer elders. But I never knowed ye war a liar an' a scandalous hypocrite. The Bible say, 'Woe ter ye, hypocrites!' I wonder ye ain't hearn that afore; either a-wrastlin' with yer own soul, or meddlin' with other folkses' salvation." It occurred to him that he preached very well himself, and he was minded, in the sudden vanity of the discovery, to reiterate, " Woe unto ye, hypocrite!"

"What makes ye 'low ez I gin the word ter the revenuers?" demanded Alethea.

"'Kase the spy kem up thar with yer name on his lips. 'Lethe Sayles,' he sez, — 'Lethe Sayles.'"

The girl stared wide-eyed and amazed at him.

Marvin's wife noted the expression. "Oh, g'long, Lethe Sayles!" she cried impatiently; "ye air so deceivin'!"

"The spy!" faltered Alethea. "Who war the spy? I never tole nobody 'bout seein' ye at Boke's barn, nor whenst I war milkin' the cow, nuther, till a few weeks ago. Ye hed lef' hyar fur months afore then."

The woman, listening, with an ear of corn in her motionless hand, turned and cast it upon the heap with a significant gesture of rejection, as if she thus discarded the claims of what she had heard. She sneered, and laughed derisively and shrill. The pullet, too, broke into mocking mirth, and then both fell to pulling corn with a sort of flouting energy.

"Oh, shucks!" exclaimed Marvin, with a feint of sharing their incredulity. But he held his straggling beard in one hand, and looked at Alethea seriously. To him her manner constrained belief in what she had said.

"Why, Lethe," he broke out, abruptly, "'t war n't long arter that evenin' whenst I seen ye a-milkin' the cow when the spy kem. We-uns war a-settin' roun' the still, — we kep' it in the shed-room, me an' my partners, — an' we war a-talkin' 'bout you-uns, an' how ye acted; an' M'ria, she war thar, an' she went agin ye, an' 'lowed ez we hed better make ye shet yer mouth; an' some o' the boys were argufyin' ez ye war jes' sayin' sech ez ye done ter hear yerse'f talk, an' feel sot up in yer own 'pinion. They 'lowed ye'd be feared ter tell, sure enough, but ye hankered ter be begged ter shet up. 'T war a powerful stormy night. I never hear a wusser wind ez war a-cavortin' round the house. An' the lightnin' an' thunder hed been right up an' down sniptious. A lightnin' ball mus' hev bust up on Piomingo Bald, 'kase nex' day I see the ground tore up round the herders' cabin, though Ben Doaks war n't thar, — hed gone down ter the cove, I reckon. Waal, sir, it quit stormin' arter a while, but everything war mighty damp an' wet; the draps kep' a-fallin' off'n the eaves. We could hear the hogs in the pen a-squashin' about in the mud. An' all of a suddenty they tuk ter squealin' an' gruntin', skeered mighty nigh ter death. An' my oldest son, Mose, he 'lowed it war a varmint arter 'em; an' he snatched his gun an' runned out ter the hog-pen. An' thar they war, all jammed up tergether, gruntin' an' snortin'; an' Mose say he war afeard to shoot 'mongst 'em, fur fear o' hittin' some o' them stiddier the varmint. An' whilst he war lookin' right keerful, — the moon hed kem out by then, — he seen, stiddier a wolf, suthin' a-bowin' down off'n the fence. An' the thing cotch up a crust o' bread, or a rind o' water-million, or suthin', out o' the trough fur the hogs, an' then sot up ez white-faced on the fence, a-munchin' it an' a-lookin' at him. An' Mose 'lowed he war so plumb s'prised he los' his senses. He 'lowed 't war a harnt, — it looked so onexpected. He jes' flung his rifle on the groun' an' run. It 's mighty seldom sech tracks hev been made on the Big Smoky ez Mose tuk. We-uns ain't medjured 'em yit, but Mose hev got the name 'mongst the gang o' bein' able ter step fourteen feet at a stride."

He showed his long, tobacco-stained teeth in the midst of his straggling beard, and as he talked on he gnawed at a plug of tobacco, as if, being no impediment to thought, it could be none to its expression.

"Mose lept inter the house, declarin' thar war a harnt a-settin' on the fence. Ye know Jeb Peake? — hongry Jeb, they useter call him." Marvin broke off suddenly, having forgotten the significance and purpose of the recital in the rare pleasure of recounting. Even his wife's face bore only retrospective absorption, and Serena had lifted her head, and fixed an excited, steadfast eye upon him. "Waal, hongry Jeb war a-settin' thar in the corner, an' bein' toler'ble sleepy-headed he hed drapped off, his head agin the chimbley. An' when Mose kem a-rampagin' in thar, with his eyes poppin' out, declarin' thar war a harnt settin' on the fence, eatin', — '*Eatin' what?*' sez hongry Jeb, a-startin' up. Ha! ha! ha!"

"Jeb ain't never forgot the bottom o' the pot yit," chimed in the wife.

"I ain't a-grudgin' him ter eat, though," stipulated the moonshiner, "nor the harnt, nuther. I jes' 'lowed ez that thar white-faced critter a-settin' on the fence, a-thievin' from the hog, mought take up a fancy ter Mose's rifle, lef' onpertected on the ground. So I goes out. Nuthin' war n't settin' on the fence, 'ceptin' the moonlight an' that thar onregenerate young tur-rkey ez nuthin' could hender from roostin' on the rails o' the hog-pen, stiddier on a limb o' a tree, 'longside o' the t'other tur-rkeys."

"An' thar a fox cotch her afore daybreak," interpolated Mrs. Marvin, supplying biographical deficiencies.

"I always *did* b'lieve 't war them thar greedy old hogs," said Serena.

Marvin went on, disregarding the interruption: —

"I picked up Mose's gun, an' in I kem. I barred up the door, an' then I sot down an' lighted my pipe. An'

Jeb, he tuk ter tellin' tales 'bout all the folks ez he ever knowed ter be skeered haffen ter death" —

"Nare one of 'em war Jeb," remarked the observant Mrs. Marvin, seizing the salient trait of the romancer. "In all Jeb's tales *he* comes out'n the big e-end o' the hawn."

"An' ez I sot thar, jes' wallin' my eyes round the room, I seen suthin' that, ef the t'others hed said they seen, I 'd hev tole 'em they war lyin'. 'T war a couple o' eyes an' a white face peekin' through the holes in the chinkin' o' the walls, whar the daubin' hed fell out. 'T war right close ter me at fust, — that war how I kem ter see it so plain. I 'lowed ter jes' stick my knife right quick inter one o' them eyes. I 'lowed 't war a raider. 'Fore I could move 't war gone! Then all of a suddenty I seen the face an' eyes peekin' in close ter the door. I jes' flew at it that time, — war n't goin' ter let nuthin' hender" —

"I war 'twixt him an' the door, an' he jes' run over me," interpolated the pullet. "Knocked me plumb over, head fust, inter a tub o' beer. Hed ter set in the sun all nex' day fur my hair ter dry out, an' I smelt like a toper."

Sam Marvin not ungenially permitted his family thus to share in telling his story. He resumed with unabated ardor: —

"An' I jumped through the door so quick that the spy jes' did see me, an' war steppin' out ter run when I cotch him by the collar. I don't reckon thar ever war a better beatin' 'n I gin him. I hed drapped my knife a-runnin', an' I hed no dependence 'ceptin' my fists. His face war so bloody I did n't know him a-fust, when I dragged him in the house, with his head under my arm. An' when I seen him I knowed he never kem of hisself, but somebody had sent him. An' I say, 'What did ye kem hyar fur?' An' he say, 'Lethe Sayles.' An' I say, 'Who sent ye?' An' he say, 'Lethe Sayles.'"

"Now, Lethe, see what a liar ye hev been fund out ter be!" said the woman, scornfully. "Lord knows I never 'lowed ye would kem ter sech. I knowed ye whenst ye war a baby. A fatter one I never see. Nobody would hev b'lieved ye 'd grow up sour, an' preachified, an' faultin' yer elders, an' bide a single woman, ez ef nobody would make ch'ice o' ye."

Alethea looked vaguely from one to the other. Denial seemed futile. She asked mechanically, rather than from any definite motive, " Did ye hear o' enny revenuers arter that ? "

" Did n't wait ter," said Marvin. " We hed hearn enough, knowin' ez ye hed tole, an' the word hed got round the kentry, so ez the spy hed been sent up ter make sure o' the place. We-uns war too busy a-movin' the still an' a-hustlin' off. Ef thar hed been time enough fur ennything, I reckon some o' them boys would hev put a bullet through that thar sandy head o' yourn. But the raiders never kem up with we-uns, nor got our still an' liquor, — we-uns war miles an' miles away from hyar the night arter Tad kem a-spyin'."

Alethea stood staring, speechless. " Tad ! " she gasped at last. " *Tad !* "

They all stopped and looked at her through the wreathing smoke, as if they hardly understood her.

" Lethe, ye air too pretensified ter be healthy ! " Mrs. Marvin exclaimed at last.

" O' course ye knowed, bein' ez ye tole him," said the moonshiner. He did not resume his work, but stood gazing at her. They were all at a loss, amazed at her perturbation.

Her breath came fast; her lips were parted. One lifted hand clung to the heavily enswathed ear of corn upon the tall, sere stalk ; the other clutched the kerchief about her throat, as if she were suffocating. Her face was pale ; her eyes were distended.

" I would n't look so pop-eyed fur nuthin'," remarked the pullet, in callow pertness ; she might not have been suspected of laying so much stress on appearances.

" I 'm tryin' ter think," said Alethea, dazed, " ef that war afore Tad war drownded or arterward."

Marvin turned, and leered significantly at his family.

"Mus' hev been afore he war drownded, I reckon," he said satirically.

"Lethe Sayles," observed Serena reprehensively, "ye air teched in the head."

She tossed her own head with a conviction that, if not strictly ornamental, it was level. Then, like the sane fowl that she was, she went stepping about on her long, yellow feet with a demure, grown-up air.

"Oh," said Alethea, fixing the dates in her mind, "it mus' hev been arterwards" —

"Likely," interrupted Sam Marvin.

— "'kase that very evenin' arter I seen ye at the cowpen Elviry Crosby kem an' tole ez how Reuben Lorey hed bust down old man Griff's mill, an' his nevy Tad war in it, an' war drownded in the ruver."

"Laws-a-me!" exclaimed Mrs. Marvin, clutching her sun-bonnet with both hands, and thrusting it backward from her head, as if it intercepted the news.

"Waal, sir!" cried the moonshiner, amazed.

"Oh," cried Alethea, clasping both her hands, "ef I hed called ye back that evenin', an' promised not ter tell, like I war minded ter do" —

"Ye 'lowed 't war n't right," suggested the moonshiner.

— "ye would hev knowed ez Tad war n't no spy, but war jes' vagabondin' round the kentry, a runaway, houseless an' hongry; an' ye would hev tuk him back ter old man Griff, an' Reuben would n't hev been tried fur killin' him!"

"Shucks, Mink war n't tried fur sech sure enough?" said Marvin, uneasily. His face had changed. His wife was turning the corner of her apron nervously between her fingers, and looking at him in evident trepidation.

"He hev been in jail fur months an' months," said Alethea. "An' when he war tried, I told on the witness stand 'bout glimpsin' Tad one night whenst I kem from camp, — mus' hev been the same night whenst he went up the mounting ter yer house, 'kase thar war a awful storm. An' when I seen him suddint I screamed, bein' s'prised; an' I reckon that war the reason he said 'Lethe Sayles.' An' at the trial they 'lowed I hed seen nuthin' but Tad's harnt, an' the jury disagreed."

"An' — an' — an' air Mink in jail yit?" demanded the moonshiner, his jaw falling in dismay.

"The rescuers tuk him out," said Alethea.

"Waal, sir," he exclaimed, with a long breath. "Ye see," — he seemed to feel that he must account for his excitement and interest, — "bein' hid out, I hain't hearn no news, sca'cely, sence we-uns lef'."

"Whar be Tad now?" Alethea asked suddenly, realizing that here was the man who had seen him last.

He glanced quickly at her, then in perplexed dubitation at his wife. In common with many women, she was willing enough to steer when it was all plain sailing, but among the breakers she left him with an undivided responsibility. She fell to pulling corn with an air of complete absorption in her work.

He made a clumsy effort at diversion. "By Gosh," he declared, waving his hand about his head, "ef this hyar smoke don't clar away, we-uns 'll all be sifflicated in it."

But the smoke was not now so dense. High up, its sober, dun-colored folds were suffused with a lurid flush admitted from the wintry sunset. The black, dead trees within the inclosure stood out distinctly athwart the blank neutrality of the gray, nebulous background. The little house on the rise was dimly suggested beyond the cornfield, across which skulked protean shapes of smoke, — monstrous forms, full of motion and strange consistency and slowly realized symmetry, as if some gigantic prehistoric beasts were trembling upon the verge of materialization and visibility. The wind gave them chase. It had lifted its voice in the silences. Like a clarion it rang down the narrow ravine below. But Sam Marvin, expanding his lungs to the freshened air, declared that he felt "plumb sifflicated."

"Whar be Tad now?" persisted Alethea.

He spat meditatively upon the ground. "Waal, Lethe," he said at last, "that's more 'n I know. I dunno whar Tad be now."

She detected consciousness in the manner of the woman and the girl. She broke out in a tumult of fear:—

"Ye did n't harm Tad, did ye?" with wild, terrified eyes fixed upon him. "Ye did n't kill Tad fur a spy? — 'kase he war n't."

"Shet up, ye blatant fool!" exclaimed Mrs. Marvin, "layin' sech ez that at we-uns's door."

"An' shet up yerse'f, M'ria. Least said, soonest mended," Marvin interposed. "Look-a-hyar, Lethe Sayles, ye hev done harm enough; it may be 'kase it war right. Take sech satisfaction ez ye kin in yer notion. It never turned out right,— turned out mighty wrong. I ain't goin' ter answer ye nare nuther word. I hev got a question ter ax you-uns right now. Who war it ye tole 'bout findin' out 't war me a-moonshinin'?"

She detailed tremulously the scene in the court-room, and the impression it produced was altogether at variance with her expectations. Perhaps, however, it was only natural that Sam Marvin should feel less interest in the belated disclosure, which he had thought was made months previous, than in the circumstances of the trial, Peter Rood's death, the imprisonment of the jury, and the riot of the rescuing mob. As to his wife, she was chiefly shocked by the publicity attaching to testimony in open court.

"An' ye jes' stood up thar, Lethe Sayles, ez bold-faced ez a biscuit-block, an' lifted up yer outdacious voice afore all them men? Waal, sir! Waal! I dunno what the wimmen air a-comin' ter!"

"I war obligated ter tell sech ez I knowed," Alethea contended against this assumption of superior delicacy. "I never felt no more bold-faced than in tellin' 'speriunce 'fore the brethren at camp."

"Oh, child!" cried Mrs. Marvin. "It's the spirit o' grace movin' at camp, but at court it's the nimbleness o' the devil."

Alethea argued no further, for conversation was impeded by the succeeding operations of gathering the crop. Marvin was leading the team of the great wagon from one to another of the heaps of corn. The huge creaking wheels crushed the ranks of stalks that fell in confusion on either side; the white canvas cover had been removed from the hoops, in order to facilitate the throwing of the corn into the wagon. Through the wreaths of smoke appeared the long ears of a pair of mules. Sam Marvin had apparently found his new home in a thirstier locality than his old, for he was evidently thriving. The pair of mules might have been considered a sorry team in point of appearance: their sides were rubbed bare with the friction of the trace-chains; they were both unkempt, and one was very tall and the other small, but they were stalwart and sure-footed and fleet, and a wonderful acquisition in lieu of the yoke of slow oxen she remembered. The continuous thud, as the ears of corn were thrown into the wagon, enabled Marvin to affect not to hear Alethea's reiteration as to Tad's fate.

"I wisht ye 'd tell me suthin' 'bout'n Tad," she said piteously. "I wisht I knew ye hed n't hurt him, nor — nor" —

She paused in the work, looking drearily about her. The wind tossed her garments; she was fain at times to catch her bonnet by the curtain, to hold it. The smoke had taken flight; dragons, winged horses, griffins, forgotten myths, all scurrying away before the strong blast. And still they came and went, and rose once more, for the wind that lifted the smoke fanned the fire. The flames were in sight along the base of Big Injun Mounting, writhing now like fiery serpents, and now rising like some strange growth in quivering blades; waving and bowing, appearing and disappearing, and always extending further and further. They seemed so alive, so endowed with the spirit of destruction, so wantonly alert, so merciless to the fettered mountain that tossed its forests in wild commotion, with many a gesture of abject despair, and spite of all could not flee. Their strong, tawny color contrasted with the dull garnet of the bare boughs and the deep, sombre green of the solemn pines. The smoke carried from the fire a lurid reflection, fading presently in the progress across the landscape of the long, dun-colored flights. The wintry sunset was at hand. The sky was red and amber; the plains of the far west lay vaguely purple beneath. On Walden's Ridge, rising against the horizon, rested the sun, from which somehow the dazzling fire seemed withdrawn, leaving a sphere of vivid scarlet, indescribably pure and intense, upon which the eye could nevertheless gaze undaunted.

Pensive intimations there were in its reduced splendors; in the deep purple of Chilhowee, in the brown tints of the nearer ranges. Something was gone from the earth, — a day, — and the earth was sad, though it had known so many. And the night impended and the unimagined morrow. And thus the averted Future turns by slow degrees the face that all flesh dreads to see. The voice of lowing cattle came up from the cove. The fires in the solitudes burned apace.

"I hev axed ye time an' agin, Sam Marvin, whar Tad be. Ef ye don't tell, I'll be bound ter b'lieve ye moonshiners hev done suthin' awful ter him."

They were about to depart on their journey. Already Serena was on her uneasy bed of corn in the ear. But the pullet's life had been made up chiefly of rough jouncing, and never having heard of a wagon with springs, she was in a measure incapable of appreciating her deprivation. She had wrapped a quilt of many colors about her shoulders, for the evening air was chill, and she looked out of the opening in the back of the canvas-covered wagon in grotesque variegation. Mrs. Marvin was climbing upon the wheel to her seat on the board in front. The moonshiner stood by the head of one of the mules, busy arranging the simple tackling. He looked with a sneer at Alethea over the beast's neck.

"An' I hev tole ye, Lethe Sayles, ez I dunno whar Tad be now. I'm a mighty smart man, sure enough, but 't would take a smarter one 'n me ter say whar Tad be now, an' what he be a-doin'."

He looked at his wife with a grin. She laughed aloud in tuneless scorn. The girl, gazing out of the back of the wagon as it jolted off, echoed the derision in a shrill key. And as the clumsy vehicle went creaking down the precipitous slope, beyond which could be seen only the flaming base of the opposite mountain, all luridly aflare in the windy dusk, they seemed to Alethea as if they were descending into Tophet itself.

XVIII.

FOR a long time that night Alethea sat on the cabin porch in Wild-Cat Hollow, absently watching the limited landscape seen through the narrow gap of the minor ridges superimposed upon the great mountain. The sky was dark but for the light that came from the earth. The flames were out of sight behind the intervening ranges. Weird fluctuating gleams, however, trembled over the cove below, and summoned from the darkness that stately file of peaks stretching away along the sole vista vouchsafed to the Hollow. Sometimes the illumination was a dull red suffusion, merging in the distance into melancholy gradations of tawny yellow and indeterminate brown, and so to densest gloom. Again it was golden, vivid, fibrous, divergent, like the segment of a halo about some miraculous presence, whose gracious splendor was only thus suggested to the debarred in Wild-Cat Hollow. The legions of the smoke were loosed: down in the cove, always passing in endless ranks what way the wind might will; along the mountain side, marshaled in fantasies reflecting from the fires subtle intimations of color, — of blue and red and purple; deploying upward, interposing between the constellations, that seemed themselves upon the march. There were clouds in the sky; the night was chill. Alethea gathered her shawl over her head. Now and then Tige, who sat beside her, wheezed and glanced over his shoulder at the door ajar, as if to urge her to go in. Sometimes he ran thither himself, looking backward to see if she would follow him. Then, as she continued motionless, he would come and sit beside her, with a plaintive whine of resignation. Tige was pensive and humble to-night, and was making an edifying show of repentance. On the homeward walk he had been disposed to follow the example of the moonshiner's dogs and harass the coon, thereby becoming acquainted with the teeth of the smiling creature, and incurring Alethea's rebukes and displeasure.

It was a cheerful scene within, glimpsed through the half-open door, contrasting with the wild, dark world without, and its strange glares and fluctuating glooms and far-off stars and vast admeasurements of loneliness. The old woman knitted and nodded in her rocking-chair; Jessup and Mr. Sayles smoked their pipes, and ever and anon the old man began anew to detail — the pipestem between his teeth — the legends that his grandfather had learned from the Indians of the hidden silver mines in these mountains, found long ago, and visited stealthily, the secret of the locality dying with its discoverer, who thus carried out of the world more than he brought with him. Their eyes gloated on the fire as they talked, seeing more than the leaping yellow flames or the white heats of the coals below. It might seem as if the craving for precious metal is a natural appetite, since these men that knew naught of the world, of the influence of wealth, of its powers, of its infinite divergences, should be a-hungered for it in their primitive fastnesses, and dream of it by night.

"On the top of the Big Smoky Mountings, on a spot whar ye kin see the Tennessee River in three places at once," said the old man, repeating the formula of the tradition.

Jessup puffed his pipe a moment in silence, watching the wreathing smoke. "I know twenty sech spots," he said presently.

The old man sighed and shifted his position. "Me too," he admitted. "But thar it be," he observed, "fur the man ez air a-comin'."

They fell silent, perhaps both projecting a mental ideal of the man of the future, and the subservient circumstance that should lead him to stand one day on these stupendous heights, with sunshine and clouds about him and the world at his feet, and to look upon the mystic curves of the river, trebly visible, strike his heel upon the ground, and triumphantly proclaim, "It is here!"

The dogs lay about the hearth; one, a hound, in the shadow, with his muzzle stretched flat on the floor between his fore-paws, had saurian suggestions, — he was like an alligator. Leonidas and Lucinda had gone to bed, but the baby was still up and afoot. The fiat of nursery ethics that gentry of his age should be early asleep had been complied with only so far as getting him into his night-gown, which encased his increasing plumpness like a cylinder. He wore a queer night-cap, that made him look incongruously ancient and feminine. He plodded about the puncheon floor, in the joy of his newly acquired powers of locomotion, with reckless enthusiasm. His shadow accompanied him, magnified, elongated, — his similitude as he might be in years to come; he seemed in some sort attended by the presentiment of his future. The energy, however, with which he had started on his long journey through life would presently be abated. In good sooth, he would be glad to sit down often and be still, and would find solace in perching on fences and whittling, and would know that hustling through this world is not what one might hope. He had fallen under the delusion that he could talk as well as walk, and was inarticulately loquacious.

Alethea's errand outside was to gather chips from the wood-pile hard by, to kindle the morning's fires. It had been long since rain had fallen, but the routine of spreading them upon the hearth, to dry during the night, was as diligently observed as if the reason that gave rise to the habit now existed. The splint baskets filled and redolent of the hickory bark, stood at her feet, yet she did not move.

She was solitary in her isolated life, with her exalted moral ideal that could compromise with nothing less than the right. She had known no human being dominated by a supreme idea. The reformers, the martyrs, all who have looked upward, sacrificed in vain for her — not even as a tradition, an exemplar might they uphold when she failed. Religion was vague, distorted, uncomprehended, in the primitive expoundings to which she was accustomed. Her inherent conscience prevailed within her like some fine, ecstatic frenzy. It was of an essence so indomitably militant that in her ignorant musings it seemed that it must be this which marshals the human forces, and fights the battle of life, and is unconquered in death, and which the stumbling human tongue calls the soul. And yet so strange it was, she thought, that she could not always recognize the right, — that she must sedulously weigh and canvass what she had done and what she might have done, and what had resulted.

She dwelt long on the moonshiner's story. She was heart-sore for the hungry idiot, filching from the hogs, — and what forlorn fate had he found at last! She drew her shawl closer about her head, and shivered more with her fears than with the wind. She was very tired; not in body, for she was strong and well, but in mind and heart and life. Somehow, she felt as if she were near the end, — surely there was not enough vitality of hope to sustain her further, — the frequent illusion of sturdy youth, with the long stretches of weary years ahead. There was even a certain relaxation of Mink's tyrannous hold upon her thoughts. It was not that she cared for him less, but she had pondered so long upon him that her imagination was numb; she had beggared her invention. She could no more project scenes where he walked with all those gentler attributes with which her affection, despite the persistent contradictions of her subtler discernment, had invested him. She could no longer harass herself with doubts of his state of mind, with devising troublous reasons why he had avoided her, with fears of harm and grief menacing him. She had revolted at last from the thrall of these arid unrealities. She felt, in a sort of grief for herself, that they were but poor delusions that occupied her. He must come, and come soon, her heart insistently said. And yet so tired was her heart that she felt in a sort of dismay that were he here to-night there would be no wild thrill of ecstasy in her pulses, no trembling joys. All that she had suffered — despair, and frantic hope that was hardly less poignant, and keen anxieties, and a stress of care — had made apathy, quiet, rest, nullity, the grave, seem dearer than aught the earth could promise.

"He oughter hev kem afore," she said to herself, in weary deprecation.

And then she thought that perhaps now, since he was at liberty again, he was happy with Elvira, and she experienced another pang to know that she was not jealous.

The clouds had obscured the few stars. The wind was flagging; the smoke grew denser; the forest flames emitted only a dull red glow; the file of peaks that they had conjured from the blackness of night was lost again in the deepening gloom.

She was roused suddenly to the fact that it was intensely quiet in-doors. She could even hear the sound of the fire in the deep chimney-place; it was "treadin' snow," the noise being very similar to the crunch of a footfall on a frozen crust. She rose, looking upward and holding her hand to the skies; the glow from within fell upon her fair face, half hooded in the shawl, and upon her pensive eyes. Flakes were falling; now, no more; and again she felt the faint touch in her palm.

Her first thought was of Mrs. Jessup, and the impediment that a snow-storm might prove to her return; and thus she was reminded that the pedestrian within was still, for she no longer heard the thud of his bare feet on the floor. He had fallen asleep in a corner of the hearth, with a gourd in one hand, and in the other a doll, made, after the rural fashion, of a forked twig arrayed in a bit of homespun. Tige watched him as he was borne off to his cradle with an envy that was positively human.

It was for the baby's sake that Mrs. Jessup returned the next day, despite the deep snow that covered the ground. She had had a dream about him, she declared, — a dreadful dream, which she could not remember. It had roused all the maternal sentiment of which she was capable. She had endured some serious hardship in coming to assure herself of his well-being, for she was obliged to walk much of the way up the mountain, — the snow and ice making the road almost impracticable, and rendering it essential that there should be as little weight as possible in the wagon; to a woman of her sedentary habit this was an undertaking of magnitude. After her wild-eyed inquiry, "Air Ebenezer well ez common?" she seemed to hold him responsible for the deceit of her dream, as if he were in conspiracy with her sleeping thoughts, and to be disappointed that the trouble which she had given herself was altogether unnecessary.

"Ye fat gopher!" she remarked, contemptuously, eying his puffy red cheeks. "Don't lean on me. I'm fit ter drap. Lean on yer own dinner. I'll be bound Lethe stuffed ye ez full ez a sassidge."

She addressed herself to bewailing that she had curtailed her visit, having enjoyed it beyond the limits which the lugubrious occasion of the funeral might seem to warrant.

"Mis' Purvine war mighty perlite an' sa-aft spoken. I never see a house so fixed up ez hern air, — though I don't b'lieve that woman hev more 'n two or three hogs ter slarter fur meat this year, ef that. I slep' in the bedroom; 't war mighty nice, though colder 'n 't war in the reg'lar house, through hevin' no fire. I reckon that's what sot me off ter dreamin' a pack o' lies 'bout that thar great hearty catamount, fairly bustin' with fatness. I wisht I hed bided in the cove! Mis' Purvine begged me ter bide. We-uns went ter the fun'el tergether, an' the buryin', an' we went round an' seen my old neighbors, an' traded ter the sto'. An' I spun some fur Mis' Purvine."

"Mighty little, I'll bet," declared her husband inopportunely, "ef what ye do hyar be enny sign."

Whereupon Mrs. Jessup retorted that she wished she had made an excuse of the snow to remain with Mrs. Purvine until the thaw, and retaliated amply by refusing to tell what hymns were sung at the funeral, and to recite any portion of the sermon.

This resolution punished the unoffending members of the family as severely as Jessup himself; but it is a common result that the innocent many must suffer for the guilty unit, — justice generally dealing in the gross. The old man's lower jaw fell, dismayed at the deprivation. He had relinquished sorting his "lumber," and had roused himself to listen and note. The details would long serve him for meditation, and would gradually combine in his recollection in dull mental pictures to dwell on hereafter, and to solace much lonely vacant time. Mrs. Sayles was irritated. Alethea had looked to hear something from Mink, and Jessup was unexpectedly balked.

Nothing could be more complete than Mrs. Jessup's triumph, as she held her tongue, — having her reason. Her blue eyes were bright with a surface gleam, as it were; there was a good deal of fresh color in her face. She was neater than usual, having been "smartened up ter meet the folks in the cove." Her snuff-brush, however, was very much at home in the corner of an exceedingly pretty mouth. As they all sat before the fire, she took off the socks which Aunt Dely had lent her, and which she had worn up the mountain over her shoes, because of the snow; and she could not altogether refrain from remark.

"Ef these hyar socks hed n't been loant ter me," she said, holding one of them aloft, "I could n't holp noticin' how Mis' Purvine turned them heels, knittin' 'em. I do declar', ef these hyar socks fits Jerry Price, he hev got a foot shaped like Buck's, an' no mistake."

It jumped with her idle humor to keep them all waiting, uncertain whether or not she would relent and disclose the meagre gossip they pined to hear. Nothing was developed till Jacob Jessup, retaliating in turn, flatly refused to go and feed Buck, still harnessed in the wagon.

Alethea rose indignantly.

"I don't lay off ter do yer work ginerally, but I ain't goin' ter let the steer go hongry," she said, "'kase ye air idle an' onfeelin'."

"Don't ye let him go hongry, then," said Jessup, provokingly.

It had ceased to snow. When Alethea opened the door many of the traits of Wild-Cat Hollow were so changed amid the deep drifts that one who had seen it only in its summer garb might hardly recognize it. Austere and bleak as it was, it had yet a symmetry that the foliage and bloom, and even the stubble and fallen leaves of autumn, served only to conceal. The splendid bare slope down the mountain, the precipitous ascent on either side of the deep ravine, showed how much the idea of majesty may be conveyed in mere lines, in a gigantic arc. The boles of the trees were deeply imbedded in drifts. On the mountain above, the pines and the firs supported great masses of snow lodged amongst the needles. Sometimes a sharp crack told that a branch had broken, over-burdened. The silence was intense; the poultry had hardly ventured off their roosts to-day; the gourds that hung upon a pole as a martin-house were whitened, and glittered pendulous. Once, as Alethea stood motionless, a little black-feathered head was thrust out and quickly withdrawn. Down in the cove the snow lay deep, and the forests seemed all less dense, lined about as they were with white, which served in some sort as an effacement. Through the narrow gap of the ridges was revealed the long mountain vista, with the snowy peaks against the gray sky. Very distinct it all was, sharply drawn, notwithstanding that there lacked but an hour, perhaps, of the early nightfall. For a moment she had forgotten her errand; the next she turned back in surprise. "Whar's Buck an' the wagin?"

"Oh," said Mrs. Jessup, still serenely casual, "he's a-kemin' up the mounting along o' Ben Doaks. I met Ben, an' I 'lowed ez I did n't know how I 'd make out ter drive sech a obstinate old steer up the mounting in all this snow. Buck hev fairly tuk ter argufyin' 'bout the road ter go, till ye dunno whether ye air drivin' the steer or the steer air drivin' you-uns. I mos' pulled off his hawns sence I been gone. So Ben, he 'lowed he'd like ter kem an' spen' a few days along o' we-uns, ennyhow."

"Why n't ye tell that afore?" demanded her mother-in-law angrily. "Ye want him ter 'low ez we air a-grudgin' him victuals. Lethe, put in some mo' o' them sweet 'taters in the ashes ter roast, an' ye hed better set about supper right now."

For Mrs. Sayles had been accounted in her best days a good housekeeper, for the mountains, and she cherished the memory of so fair a record. Perhaps her reputation owed something to the fact that she entertained a unique theory of hospitality, and made particularly elaborate preparations when the guests were men. "Wimmen don't keer special 'bout eatin'. Show 'em all the quilts ye have pieced, an' yer spun truck, an' yer gyardin, an' they'll hev so much ter study 'bout an' be jealous 'bout ez they won't want nuthin' much ter eat."

Now she proceeded to "put the big pot into the little pot," to use a rural expression, singularly descriptive of the ambitious impossibilities achieved. She did it chiefly by proxy, directing from her seat in the chimney corner Alethea's movements, but wearing the absorbed, anxious countenance of strategy and resource. The glory of the victory is due rather to the head that devised than to the hands that executed; as in greater battles the pluck of the soldiery is held subordinate to the science of the commander.

It was no mean result that smoked upon the table when the sound of Buck's slow hoofs was heard on the snow without, and a warm welcome was in readiness besides. A cheerful transition it was from the bleak solitudes: the fire flared up the chimney; the peppers and the peltry hanging from the rafters might sway in draughts that naught else could feel; the snow without was manifested only by the drifts against the batten shutters, visible in thin white lines through the cracks, and in that intense silence of the muffled earth which appeals to the senses with hardly less insistence than sound.

Ben's aspect was scarcely so negative, so colorless, as usual, despite his peculiarly pale brown hair and beard. The sharp sting of the cold air had brought a flush to his face; his honest, candid gray eyes were bright and eager. His manner was very demure and propitiatory, especially to Mrs. Sayles, who conducted herself with an ideally motherly air, which was imbued with many suggestions of approval, even of respect.

"Howdy, Ben, howdy? We-uns air mighty glad ter see ye, Ben."

"Don't ye git too proud, Ben," said Mrs. Jessup, roused from her inertia by the unwonted excitements of her journey to the cove, and, since she was not too lazy to exercise her perversity, thoroughly relishing it. "They 'd be jes' ez glad ter see ennybody,—it air so beset an' lonesome up hyar. They fairly tore me ter pieces with thar questions whenst I kem."

And this reminded old man Sayles that the details of the funeral could be elicited from Ben Doaks. Upon request the young man lugubriously rehearsed such portions of the sermon as he could remember, prompted now and then by Mrs. Jessup, who did not disdain to refresh his recollection when it flagged; he even lifted his voice in a dolorous refrain to show how a certain "hyme chune" went. But his attention wandered when supper was over, and he observed Alethea, with a bowl of scraps in her hand and a shawl over her head, starting toward the door.

The dogs ran after her, with voracious delight in the prospect of supper, and bounded up against the door so tumultuously that she had difficulty in opening it.

"Goin' ter feed the dogs, Lethe?" said Ben Doaks, seizing the opportunity. "I'll keep 'em back till ye kin git out."

He held the door against the dogs, and when he shut it he too was on the outer side. It was not yet quite dark; the whiteness of the snow contended with the night. The evening star showed through the rifts in the clouds, and then was obscured. The dogs were very distinct as they ran hither and thither on the snow at Alethea's feet, while she leaned against the post of the porch and threw to them scraps from the bowl.

Ben knew that his time was short. "Lethe," he said, with a lamentable lack of tact, "I hearn ez how ye hev done gin up waitin' fur Mink."

Her lustrous eyes seemed all undimmed by the shadows. The sheen of her hair was suggested beneath the faded shawl, drawn half over her head. What light the west could yet bestow, a pearly, subdued glimmer, was on her face. She said nothing.

He lifted his hand to the low eaves of the porch, — for he was very tall, — and the motion dislodged a few flakes that fell upon her head. He did not notice them.

"I hearn Mis' Purvine 'low ye air all plumb outdone with Mink, an' would n't hev him ef he war ter ax ye agin, — an' I reckon ye won't see him no mo'. 'T ain't likely, ye know. An' Mis' Purvine 'lowed ye hed been mightily struck with a man in Shaftesville, — a town cuss" (with acrimony), " ez war mighty nigh demented 'bout yer good looks an' sech. Now, Lethe, ye dunno nuthin' 'bout'n them town folks, an' the name they hev got at home, 'mongst thar neighbors."

She looked steadily at him, never moving a muscle save to cast more scraps to the hounds, who, when their tidbits became infrequent, or were accidentally buried in the snow by inopportune movements of their paws, gamboled about to attract her attention; rising upon their hind legs, and almost dancing, in a manner exceedingly creditable to untrained mountain dogs.

"An' I 'lowed I war a tremenjious fool ter hev kep out'n the way 'count o' Mink, — jes' 'kase ye seemed ter set so much store by him. T'other folks mought kem in whilst I war a-holdin' back. Nobody ain't never goin' ter keer fur ye like I do, Lethe. Mink don't — never did. An' my house air ready fur ye enny day ye'll walk in. I got ye a rockin'-cheer the t'other day, an' a spinnin'-wheel. It looks like home, sure enough, down thar, Lethe. I jes' gazed at that thar rockin'-cheer afore the fire till I could fairly see ye settin' in it. But shucks, I kin hear ye callin' chickens roun' thar, — 'Coo-chee, Coo-chee!' — enny time I listens right hard." He laughed in embarrassment because of his sentimentality. "I reckon I mus' be gittin' teched in the head."

It was snowing again. From those stupendous heights above the Great Smoky Mountains down into the depths of Piomingo Cove the flakes steadily fell. Myriads of serried white atoms interposed a veil, impalpable but opaque, between Wild-Cat Hollow and the rest of the world. Doaks looked about him a little, and resumed suddenly: —

"I ain't purtendin' I'm better 'n other men. I never *could* git religion. I ain't nigh good enough fur ye, — only I think mo' of ye. I'm mean 'bout some things. I couldn't holp but think, whenst I hearn 'bout Mink, ez now ye'd gin him up. I war n't *bodaciously* glad, but I could n't *holp* thinkin' 't war better fur ye an' me. Ye'd be happier married ter me, Lethe, than ter him, enny time."

"I ain't never goin' to marry you-uns, Ben," she said drearily. "An' now ye hev hed yer say, an' thar's no use a-jawin' no mo' 'bout'n it."

She turned to go in. Tige was already scratching at the door, as eager for the fire as he had been for his supper. She glanced at Ben over her shoulder, with some appreciation of his constancy, some pity for his disappointment.

"Ye hed better go make a ch'ice 'mongst some o' them gals in the cove," she suggested.

He cast a glance of deep reproach upon her, and followed her silently into the house. Their return was the occasion of some slight flutter in the home circle, in which had prevailed the opinion that the young folks out in the cold "war a-courtin'."

All relics of the supper were cleared away; the fire leaped joyously up the chimney. L'onidas and Lucindy were asleep. The baby in his night-gown, all unaware that he cut an unpresentable figure before company, pounded up and down the floor, unmolested. The pipes were lighted. As Ben Doaks leaned down to scoop up a coal from the fire, his face was distinct in the flare, and Mrs. Jessup noted the disappointment and trouble upon it. Mrs. Sayles too deduced a sage conclusion. A glance was exchanged between the two women. Then Mrs. Jessup, with a view to righting matters between these young people, whom fate seemed to decree should be lovers, asked abruptly, " Did ye tell Lethe the news 'bout Mink ? "

" Naw," Doaks responded, somewhat shortly. " I 'lowed she knowed it long ago."

" Naw, she don't," said Mrs. Jessup; " none o' we-uns hyar on the mounting knowed it."

She paused to listen to the wind, for it was astir without. A hollow, icy cry was lifted in the dark stillness, — now shrill and sibilant, now hoarsely roaring, then dying away in the distance, to be renewed close at hand. The boughs of the bare trees beat together. The pines were voiced with a dirge. The porch trembled, and the door shook.

" Why, Lethe," resumed Mrs. Jessup, turning toward the girl, as she sat in a low chair in the full radiance of the fire-light, " Mink ain't out'n jail. The rescuers never tuk him out."

The color left Alethea's face. Her doubting eyes were dilated. Mrs. Jessup replied to the expression in them.

" Mis' Purvine, she 'lowed ez she an' you-uns hearn everybody sayin' the rescuers tuk him out afore ye lef' Shaftesville that mornin'. That war town talk. But 't war n't true. The jailer an' the sher'ff tied an' gagged him, an' tuk him out tharse'fs in the midst o' the dark, whenst nobody could see 'em. Makes me laff ter think how they fooled them boys! They jes' busted up the jail

so ez 't war n't safe ter try ter keep him thar no mo',
an' the nex' day the dep'ty an' two gyards tuk him down
ter the jail at Glaston, — an' thar he 's safe enough."

Alethea's first thought, charged with vague, causeless
self-reproach, was that she had let Sam Marvin, who had
seen Tad since the disaster at the mill, go in the belief
that Mink had been released. But how could she have
detained him? And would he, a moonshiner, suffer himself to be subpœnaed as a witness, and thus insure his
own arrest?

Her lips moved without a sound, as if she were suddenly bereft of the power to articulate.

"Glaston, that 's a fac'," reiterated Mrs. Jessup, noticing the demonstration. "'kase I see 'Lijah Miles, ez
war one o' the gyards. He kem up ter the cove ter the
fun'el, bein' ez his wife war kin ter the corpse. She
war one o' the Grinnells afore she war married, — not
the Jer'miah fambly, but Abadiah's darter; an' Abadiah's gran'mother war own cousin ter the corpse's
mother" —

"I dunno 'bout'n that," said Mrs. Sayles, following
this genealogical detail with a knitted brow and a pains-
taking attention.

"Corpse war 'bleeged ter hev hed a mother wunst, ef
ever he war alive," said Mrs. Jessup, recklessly.

"I reckon I know *that*," retorted Mrs. Sayles. "But
'Lijah Miles's wife's father's grandmother war the aunt
o' the corpse, stiddier his mother's cousin," — she tossed
her head with a cheerful sense of accuracy, — "sure ez
ye air a born sinner."

Mrs. Jessup paused in her recital, leaned her elbows
on her knees, and fixed her eyes on the fire, as if following some abstruse calculation. The wind swept about
the house and whistled down the chimney, till even Tige
roused himself, and lifted his head to listen and to
growl.

"Waal, hev it so," said the young woman, unable to
contradict. "Howbeit he war kin ter the corpse, he
kem ter the fun'el, an' arterward, ez he war goin' back

ter Shaftesville, he stopped at Mis' Purvine's an' stayed all night. An' he tole us 'bout'n takin' Mink ter jail in Glaston. An' 't war the fust Mis' Purvine knowed ez Mink war n't out. But she 'lowed she 'd miss him less in jail 'n out."

"I reckon everybody feels that-a-way 'bout Mink," interpolated Mrs. Sayles. "Folks never knowed what *could* happen onexpected an' upsettin' till Mink's capers l'arned 'em."

"Waal, none o' his capers ever war like this las' one o' his'n," said Mrs. Jessup, nodding seriously. "They tuk him ter Glaston, an' 'Lijah Miles war one o' the gyards. They tuk him on the steam-kyars."

"I'll be bound Mink war fairly skeered by them steam-kyars!" exclaimed Mrs. Sayles, with all the assumption of superior experience, although she herself had never had a glimpse of them.

"Waal, I reckon not, from the way he kerried on 'cordin' ter 'Lijah," said Mrs. Jessup, clasping one knee as she talked, eying the fire. "'Lijah 'lowed he never seen sech a fool. Mink got ter talkin' ter the gyards an' dep'ty 'bout this hyar Jedge Gwinnan" —

"Need n't tell me nuthin' 'bout Jedge Gwinnan. 'Jeemes' air what they call him over yander in Kildeer County. An' 'Jim,' too," said Mrs. Sayles. "I knowed a woman ez knowed that man's mother whenst he war a baby."

"Waal, he's changed some sence then. He ain't a baby now. Mink kep' a-talkin' ter his gyards 'bout Gwinnan, an' swearin' Gwinnan had spited him in the trial, — put Pete Rood on the jury an' sent 'em ter jail, an' tole the sher'ff ter look arter his prisoner or he'd escape the night Pete Rood fell dead, an' tole 'em how ter keep the crowd from rescuin' him, an' all sech ez that. An' what d' ye reckon Mink 'lowed Gwinnan hed done it fur? 'Kase Gwinnan hed tuk a notion hisself ter Lethe Sayles, an' 'lowed Mink war n't good enough fur her."

The incongruity of the idea impressed none of them.

They all looked silently expectant as Mrs. Jessup went on: —

"Waal, Mink swore ez some day he 'd git his chance, an' he 'd git even with Gwinnan, sure. An' 'Lijah, he seen ez Mink war a-lookin' at Jedge Gwinnan, — the jedge, he war a-goin' down on the train ter Glaston, an' then out ter wharever he war a-goin' ter hold court, an' he war a-smokin' in the 'smokin'-kyar,' 'Lijah say they call it, whar they hed Mink. An' 'Lijah say Mink looked at Gwinnan with his mouth sorter open, an' his jaw sorter drapped, an' his eyes ez set ez ef he war a wild beastis."

Once more the wind, tumultuous, pervasive, with all the vast solitudes given over to it, swept down the mountain with shrill acclaim.

"Goin' ter hev some weather arter this, — ye mind my words," said Mrs. Sayles, listening a moment.

"Waal, 'Lijah never thunk nuthin' mo', an' Mink kep' his eyes ter hisself the rest o' the way. When they got ter Glaston the gyards sorter waited fur the t'other folks ter git out fust, an' then they started. Waal, 'Lijah say the dep'ty he jumped off'n the platform fust, an' tole Mink ter kem on. An' the dep'ty — 'Lijah say the dep'ty set a heap o' store by Mink — he war a-tellin' Mink ter look how many tracks an' locomotives an' sech thar war in the depot, an' not noticin' Mink much. An' 'Lijah say he seen Mink dart ter one side; he 'lowed Mink war makin' a bust ter git away. Naw, sir! Gwinnan hed stopped by the side o' the kyar ter speak ter a man. 'Lijah say he felt like he war a-dreamin' when he seen Mink lift up both his handcuffed hands an' bring the irons down on the jedge's head. 'Lijah say him an' the dep'ty an' the t'other gyard hed thar pistols out in a second. But they war feared ter shoot, fur the jedge, stiddier drappin' on the groun', whurled roun' an' grabbed the man ez hit him. He got Mink by the throat, an' held on ter him same ez a painter or sech. He nearly strangled Mink ter death, though the jedge war fairly blinded with his own blood. Mink writhed an' wriggled so they could n't tell one man from t'other.

The gyards war feared ter shoot at Mink, 'kase they mought kill the jedge. They tore Mink loose at last. They 'lowed his face war black ez ef he hed been hung. He won't tackle Gwinnan agin in a hurry. Ye 'lowed Gwinnan war a feeble infant, mother; he ain't very feeble now. Though he did faint arterward, an' war hauled up ter the tavern in a kerridge. They hed ter hev some perlice thar ter holp keep the crowd off Mink, takin' him ter jail. Waal, 'Lijah say they dunno whether the jedge will live or no, — suthin' the matter with his head. But even ef he do live, 'Lijah say we ain't likely ter see Mink in these parts no mo' fur a right smart while, 'kase he hearn thar ez assault with intent ter c'mit murder air from three ter twenty-one year in the pen'tiary. An' I reckon enny jury would gin Mink twenty" —

"Yes, sir, he needs a good medjure!" exclaimed the negative Mr. Sayles, with unwonted hearty concurrence.

"Mink will be an old man by the time he do git back," computed Mrs. Sayles.

"Now, Lethe," argued Mrs. Jessup, "ain't ye got sense enough ter see ez Mink ain't nobody ter set sech store on, an' ef ye like him it's 'kase ye air a fool?"

The girl sat as if stunned, looking into the fire with vague distended eyes. She lifted them once and gazed at Mrs. Jessup, as if she hardly understood.

"Look-a-hyar, Lethe, what sorter face air that ye hev got onter ye?" cried Mrs. Sayles. "Ye better not set yer features that-a-way. I hev hearn folks call sech looks 'the dead-face,' an' when ye wear the 'dead-face' it air a sign ye air boun' fur the grave."

"Waal, that's whar we all air boun' fur," moralized old man Sayles.

"Quit it!" his wife admonished the girl, who passed her hand over her face as if seeking to obliterate the obnoxious expression. "Ye go right up-steers ter bed. I'm goin' ter gin ye some yerb tea."

She took down a small bag, turning from it some dried leaves into her hand, and looked at them mysteriously, as if she were about to conjure with them.

The girl rose obediently, and went up the rude, uncovered stairs to the roof-room. After an interval Mrs. Jessup observed the babbling baby pointing upward. Among the shadows half-way up the flight Alethea was sitting on a step, looking down vacantly at them. But upon their sudden outcry she seemed to rouse herself, rose, and disappeared above.

XIX.

GWINNAN, upon recovering consciousness, showed no retrospective interest in the scene at the depot. He remarked imperatively to the physician whom he found in attendance that it was necessary for him to leave during the afternoon, — in fact, as soon as possible, — to hold court in a distant county. He added, for the instruction of the doctor, that the clerk could open court, and had no doubt done so on Monday and Tuesday, and would be obliged to repeat this on Wednesday, without the presence of the presiding judge, but Thursday was the last day for which the statute had provided the alternative. He evidently expected that if the physician had any flimsy objections he would withdraw them before this grave necessity, understanding that this was no time for the indulgence of professional whimseys.

There was something so arrogantly disregardful of any other claims upon his attention, so belittling of merely corporeal considerations, that the physician would have been a little less than medical had he been able to repress a certain sense of domination as he answered, "Well, that happened more than two weeks ago, judge, and I reckon court was adjourned over to the next term."

Gwinnan became aware with a sort of amaze that the hands he lifted did not seem his own; that his head was light and giddy, or dully aching; that he was fretful and helpless; that no manner of respect was paid to his views. He was hardly pleased by the exchange of identity with this ill-adjusted, listless, forlorn being; the less when he finally grew able to stand upon his feet again, and was informed that for the next month or so he must do nothing but seek to interest and entertain the invalid, to see that he forbore to dwell on business, to seek to occupy his attention with passing events, to divert him with trifles.

It might have seemed even to others an arduous task to amuse with incidents a man whose every waking moment was occupied by principles. So completely had his rarefied, judicial ambition, his pride of office, his solicitous reverence of its dignity, attenuated his personality that he cared little for Gwinnan as a man; he respected him as a judge. He had held himself sedulously to his aspirations; as it were on his knees, he had served his vocation day and night. It was to him as essential an organic constituent of his being as the lungs; he could ill live without it, even for a time. Perhaps he might not have made the effort had not the physician warned him that he might never be fit for business, never again sit upon the bench, should he overexert himself now, before recovering from the effect of those terrible blows upon the skull. He became suddenly tractable, wistful, and turned mournfully to the search of light entertainment. He assented with a dreary docility to the prescription of a change of air and scene. He accepted without demur, with a dull sense of endurance, the plan briskly devised for him to spend a week or two in Nashville, and if he did not recuperate rapidly, to go thence South for the winter. He was not given to scanning his own mental poses and adjusting them to some theory of symmetry; he could but feel, however, as if he were already dead, stalking among scenes in which he had no interest, half-heartedly mingling with men whose every instinct was as far removed from the spirit that swayed him as if some essential condition of existence divided them. It was with a truly post-mortem indifference that he listened to the talk of his friends who sought him out during his stay in Nashville, — very interesting talk, doubtless, but purposeless, inefficacious; they cited neither case nor section. He preferred to sit alone and idle before the blazing coal fire in his own room, — expressionless with the stereotyped hotel furniture; now and then he roused himself, with a conscientious start, when he found his mind revolving like a moth around some *scintilla juris* which had a special attraction for him.

He had experienced a sense of reluctant relinquishment to find how the weeks had fled during his illness. Winter had advanced; the Cumberland River was full of floating ice; the town had the shrunken, deserted, torpid aspect common to every southern city when the snow is on the ground. No one was abroad without absolute necessity except the English sparrow, prosperous exile. In the hope of varying the tedium, one evening, Gwinnan sat down in one of the arm-chairs drawn close to the balustrade of the corridor overlooking the rotunda. It was a coigne of vantage from which all the life of the hotel was visible. Below, at the desk, the in-coming travelers were registering their names; the click of billiards was a cheerful incident of the atmosphere, with the rising of the fumes of many a cigar. On the opposite corridor the clatter of dishes could be heard from the dining-room, and occasionally there emerged gentlemen and toothpicks. The rumble of the elevator sounded ceaselessly, and now and then fluttering flounces issued from its door which was visible down a cross-hall.

Behind Gwinnan the great windows opened upon the snowy street. He could see the white roofs opposite gleam dimly against the nebulous sky. Carriage-lamps sometimes flashed past, yellow, lucent with jeweled effects. An electric light hard by flamed with a fibrous radiance, and empurpled the black night, and conjured circles, mystically white, far-reaching into the snow. The plate-glass gave a reflection of his long lank figure and the red velvet arm-chair, and of the innumerable children of the place, racing about, unrestrained, in white frocks, much bedizened. There was a dog among them, a poodle, in his white frock too, accoutered also with a sharp, shrill cry, and swiftly gamboling despite much fat. He had as independent an aspect as if he knew that all the legislators crowded into all the caucuses in the city could not, compass a dog-law that would interfere with his pretty liberty, or place a tax on his frizzy head. The sovereign people would have none of it. And so the obnoxious law stands repealed, and the dog-star is in the ascendant. Now and then he came and sat at Gwinnan's feet, with a lolling tongue and panting sides.

There had been a caucus in the reading-room of the hotel, and presently the doors opening upon the corridor began to disgorge knots of men, some of whom walked off together, others stood in discussion. Now and then one was seized by a lobbyist, lying in wait. Gwinnan was aware of Harshaw's presence before he saw him: a liquid, gurgling, resonant laugh, and then the floater, accompanied by a colleague into whose arm he had hooked his own, came through the door. His hat was thrust on the back of his yellow head; he stroked his yellow beard with a gesture of self-satisfaction; his face was broad and animated, and pink with prosperity.

Fortune was favoring Mr. Harshaw, and few men have ever basked in her smiles so appreciatively. He had the reputation of being very influential in the House. His coöperation was eagerly sought. In truth, as a wire-puller he had developed marked dexterity, and there were precious few things that Mr. Harshaw could not accomplish in a caucus. He did a little "log-rolling," but he was chary of the interchange of favors, carrying his point usually by persistence and pugnacity, and he possessed tremendous staying power as a debater. He had a certain barbaric delight in oppression; having become possessed of the opportunity, he used it often when neither he nor his constituents had anything to gain. He took advantage of his ascendency to pay off many old grudges, some of them of a purely arbitrary construction and æsthetic nature. He was in some sort aware that his colleagues were ashamed of his rough manners, his bullying, his coarse onslaughts, in which, being of the same political party, they were often constrained to appear as his supporters. He continually alluded to himself as if he were of peculiarly humble origin, representing himself as being *of* the People, *from* the People, and FOR the People, and forcing the conclusion that the other members from his region were bloated aristocrats. Nevertheless, whoever would go to the State Senate next session, it seemed safe to say that the demagogue had assured his own nomination; for merit had a fine chance to be modest, as behooves it, while Mr. Harshaw was shaping the future by manipulating the present.

And now suddenly he was not quite sure that he wanted the nomination. In these days, while he divided his time between the beautiful Capitol building and one of the hotels of the town, he meditated much upon Mink's assault upon Judge Gwinnan in the depot of Glaston. Not in the interest of his client, however; even the most solicitous of counsel could not be expected to occupy his attention with the fate of the wayward Mink, who had passed beyond his aid. Mink's deed did not in truth seem to Harshaw so very much amiss. Of course he recognized its iniquity, being one of those cognizable by the law, but he also perceived in it the finger of Providence, — laid somewhat heavily, it must be confessed, on Gwinnan. He speculated deeply, despite his other absorptions, on who would probably be elected to supply Gwinnan's place, in case of the death of the wounded incumbent, and he reflected that he himself as a lawyer was highly esteemed in that circuit, for he had a large practice throughout the region, and that moreover, by a certain fortuitous circumstance, he was eligible for the position; although his law office was in Shaftesville, he lived on his farm which was several miles distant, just within the boundaries of Kildeer County, one of the judicial circuits over which Gwinnan presided. Apart from his repute at the bar, he was well known to the people at large through certain popular measures he had advocated. He devoted himself to these with renewed ardor. He never allowed himself to view with a vacillating mind any course, however obviously salutary, when he had once discovered with a keen instinct that it was unlikely to secure the approval of the masses. Nevertheless, he applied his tact with such success that this foregone conclusion was not readily apparent, and he was continually beset for his influence. He had a secret gratulation that he was held in special veneration by the lobbyists. He could ill maintain the aspect of unwilling captive, when he was waylaid and button-holed, and his attention eagerly entreated for certain measures. As an anxious-faced man, who had evidently been awaiting him, stepped forward now, glancing with a casual apology at his friend, who walked on, Harshaw's reluctant pause, his frown, his important bored sufferance, were as fine histrionically as if he were playing at being a statesman on a stage, — which, indeed, he was.

He listened with a divided mind to the outpouring of the lobbyist, his opaque blue eyes fixed in seeming deliberation upon the chandelier hanging down into the rotunda below, his exceedingly red lips pursed up in a pucker of dubitation. Now and then he patted the toe of one boot on the floor meditatively. Occasionally he looked his interlocutor full in the face, asking a question, presumably a poser; then his triumphant, resonant, burly laugh would vibrate above the dancing of the overdressed children, and the riotous barking of the dog, and the tinkling waltzes played by a band of musicians ranged about the fountain in the rotunda. His entertainment in his own self-importance and posings was so absorbing that the lobbyists and the advocates of many measures were often at a loss to know how best to reach Mr. Harshaw's desire to serve his country; for he did not love money, and his integrity, as far as it was concerned, was above suspicion.

All at once genuine interest usurped these feignings on his face. His eye fell on Judge Gwinnan walking along the corridor, and leaning upon a stout cane. He looked very thin, very pale, taller than before, and somehow his face was more youthful with the wistfulness of illness upon it, his hair clipped close, and the eyes hollow and luminous. He moved slowly, and with little spirit.

Harshaw stepped briskly forward, with a curt "Excuse me" to the lobbyist, taking no reproach for leaving him with his mouth open, for it seemed his normal condition.

"Why, judge," Harshaw exclaimed, with his bluff familiarity, "you look bloomin'!" He was about to stretch out his hand, but desisted, noticing that Gwinnan held his hat in one hand, and leaned upon his stick with the other. He took the judge by the elbow, as he walked a few steps with him. A dim image of the pair paced along in the plate-glass windows, as if their doubles were stalking without in the snow in scenes of which they were unconscious. "I had no idea you were pulling together so fast," he continued, scanning the face which was almost spectral in its attenuation and pallor, in close contrast to his own fat floridity of countenance, his red lips, his gleaming white teeth, his mane of yellow hair, and his dense yellow beard. His wide, black soft hat stuck on the back of his head accented his high color. "But I declare, it's worth while for a man to get hit over the head to find out how important he is, and how he is esteemed. I never knew more profound sympathy and indignation than the affair excited. As to myself, I felt it especially, as I had taken so much stock in that rascally client of mine."

Gwinnan made no reply. His face was turned toward Harshaw with a certain unresponsiveness, an inscrutable questioning, a cadaverous gravity. His hollow eyes were very bright and large. Somehow they put Harshaw out of countenance. Something there was in their expression beyond his skill to decipher. He became a trifle embarrassed, and yet he could not have said why. He went on at random. He had observed that a number of people were remarking them. There was nothing uncommon in the peripatetic method that the interview had taken, but suddenly he found it odd that Gwinnan had not paused.

"That fellow, Mink Lorey, is a most extraordinary and unexpected kind of scamp," Harshaw proceeded uneasily, making talk. "To my certain knowledge, he cared so little about the girl that he refused to see her when she came to visit him in jail. But the idea that another man admired her seemed to set him wild."

Gwinnan stopped short.

"What girl?" he asked, in his soft, inexpressive drawl.

"The girl that testified, — Alethea Sayles," said Harshaw, relieved that Gwinnan had spoken, and striving for his old bluff assurance, but still conscious that he had lost his tact. "She was pretty, very pretty indeed, and you were not alone in having the good taste to notice it. The rest of us didn't have to pay for it with a broken head, though, eh, judge? Ha! ha!"

There was a moment's pause.

"Mr. Harshaw," said Gwinnan, leaning against one of the great pillars, the reflection in the plate-glass duplicating the posture on the snowy sidewalk, as if that other self, liberated and in isolated independence, busied in different scenes, now meditated, and now spoke and now lifted a fiery glance, "I will take this opportunity to tell you that I believe you to be an egregious liar, and I know you for an arrant hypocrite."

"Sir!" cried Harshaw, starting back, tingling from the words as if they were blows. He made an instinctive gesture toward his pistol pocket; it was empty. He was acutely conscious of the spectators who pressed a little nearer, noticing the excitement.

Gwinnan's voice had a singular carrying quality, and every deliberate, low-toned word was distinct.

"I repudiate your professions of friendship. I despise your protestations of sympathy. If your threats at the court-house door in Shaftesville had been earlier repeated to me, ludicrously impotent as they are, you should never have approached me again. Now," — his voice broke suddenly, in his feebleness and excitement, and was thin and tremulous and shrill, — "keep out of my way, or I will beat you with this stick like a dog!"

Gwinnan had lifted the stick, and shook it threateningly in his trembling hand. Harshaw, with his own reasons for declining to give the first blow, could only shrink and wince in anticipation. The stick did not descend on him, however, for Gwinnan turned, and, leaning on it, made his way down the corridor among the wondering men, who slowly opened an aisle for him in their midst.

XX.

It was a confused scene which Gwinnan had left. Harshaw's friends pressed about him, animated equally, perhaps, by curiosity and surprise. His self-restraint had given way. He swore with every breath he drew, repeating, in answer to questions, the unlucky threat over and again. "I said that he would be impeached, and that I would introduce the resolution in the House myself. And so, by God, I will!"

His face was hot and scarlet. The perspiration stood out on his forehead. He ground his teeth and clenched his hands. He would walk forward a few unsteady steps, then pause to reiterate and explain, and swear that if Gwinnan were not at death's door he would cowhide him within an inch of his life. The progress of the group, slow as it was, with these frequent interruptions, was in the direction of the stairs. It was chiefly composed of members of the legislature, and, there being a night session, they mechanically took their way to the Capitol. A few gentlemen lounging about the corridor were watching their exit with the gusto of disinterested spectators, as they disappeared down the staircase, reappearing below in the rotunda, — Harshaw still in the van, his florid face bloated with rage, his hat on the back of his head, his hands thrust in the pockets of his trousers. His friends wore a becoming gravity, but Harshaw was too thoroughly a man of this world not to suspect that they valued more the diversion he furnished than his interests as affected by the episode. They all crossed the office, and disappeared finally through the street door, and the spectators on the corridor shifted their postures, and tipped off the ash grown long on their cigars, and commented.

"Biggest blatherskite out of hell, Harshaw is," remarked a young fellow, who flung himself diagonally into a seat, hanging his long legs over one arm of the chair and resting his back against the other. He put his cigar into his mouth, and puffed at his ease. He had a pale face, thin dark hair, irregular features, straight black eyebrows, and wide, black eyes, quickly glancing, but with a suggestion of melancholy. He was handsomely dressed, although he wore his clothes with a slouching, irreverent air, as if he gave his attire scant heed. Despite their cut and quality, there was nothing dapper about him. He had a lank, listless white hand, and a foot singularly long and narrow. His forehead was remarkably high, austere, and noble; one might look in vain for correlative expressions in the other features. He was languid and inattentive, but this manner suggested affectation, for it did not eliminate the idea of energy. He smoked a great deal, and drank not much, but discriminatingly; he was proud of seeming reckless, and of being more reckless than he seemed. He had other qualities more genial. He knew a good dog when he saw him. He knew a good horse, and he loved him. He was the possessor of a liberal hand and a long purse. He had an enthusiastic admiration of fine principles, and he had — the pity of it! — his own definition of fine principles. He entertained a horror of anything base, and he had a command of very strong language to characterize it. He arrogated to himself the finer attributes. He strained for the heroic poise. He would feel nothing, believe nothing, do nothing, that was unbecoming of what he esteemed the noblest expression of man and gentleman. Nevertheless he had no serious objects in life, no absorbing ambition, no ability to originate. But he could espouse another man's cause with a fervor of unselfishness. The excitements and vicissitudes of the affairs of others rejoiced the voids of his capacities for emotion. He was of the stuff of which adherents are made, essentially a partisan. His prototypes have ridden in the ranks of every losing cause since the world began. He was of the essence of those who are born for freaks of valor, for vagrant enthusiasms, for misguided fantastic feuds, for revolution.

"Do you think, sir, that Mr. Harshaw had no foundation for his threat," said an elderly granger, who leaned against a pillar, — "no foundation for this charge against Judge Gwinnan?"

"Gwinnan may have ruled against him a time or two," said Kinsard. "That's about the size of it."

He had a pedigree as long as his favorite colt's, but this was the way he talked.

"It is a gross slander, then : it implies a stealage, or taking a bribe, or some malfeasance in office, — the judicial office," said one of the by-standers.

"It was very shabby in Harshaw to say it; then, thinking Gwinnan had never heard of it, to go fawning up, pretending to be so mighty friendly," rejoined another.

Kinsard's black eyes turned slowly from one speaker to the other.

"If I had been Judge Gwinnan, I would have killed him for it," he said, with his cigar held tightly between his fingers. "I would have spilt his brains, not his blood; and I would have had some scientific man to find the precise section of the brain structure which ideated that theory, and I would have had it comminuted, and vaporized, and transmuted into nothingness."

He spoke with calmness, as if these things were done every day for the vengeful in Tennessee.

The granger took off his spectacles suddenly. He wanted to see this extraordinary young man, who he had an idea was too dangerous to be at large.

The others looked at him with a less serious air. They had before heard him talk.

"Well," said a certain Mr. Forsey, also a young man, who had dropped upon the broad window-seat and lounged there, holding one knee in his clasped hands, and smoking too, "do you think Harshaw would have ventured to say it if there were no foundation for it, — if Gwinnan had done nothing to suggest such a proceeding? What motive had Harshaw?"

He was a different manner of man. He had close-cut fair hair, a face broad across the cheek-bones and narrow at the chin, sparse whiskers and a light gray, wide-open eye. He had a sedulously neat appearance, a soft tread, and delicate white hands, in one of which he held his hat.

"What motive? What motive for slander? Go to first principles. Gwinnan has got something that Harshaw wants." Kinsard put his cigar into his mouth and went on talking as he held it fast between his teeth. "What fools we all are! We make laws against predatory beasts and decree their extermination. Pay a bounty for the scalps of the marauding men, I say, — the sharp fellows who ravage and pillage and have contrived so far to keep the law on their side. But pshaw!" he shifted his legs over the arm of the chair impatiently. "He can't hurt Gwinnan. Talk can't compass the impeachment of a judge. Gwinnan is one of the strongest men on the bench. Made the stiffest show that ever was seen when he ran against old Judge Burns, who had sat on the bench in that circuit till everybody thought he owned it. Old man could have mortgaged the bench, — could have raised money on it, I have n't a doubt. Gwinnan could n't have beat Burns, if he had n't been above reproach and suspicion; it's a tremendous thing to upset an old fixture like that."

Mr. Kinsard's views, as his colleagues in the legislature had discovered to their confusion, were apt to confirm his hearers in the opposite opinion. A bill was much safer when he arrayed himself against it. Mr. Forsey was not convinced that so serious a charge would have been made with absolutely nothing to support it. The idea of the blurtings of an uncontrolled rage occurred to neither of them. Forsey sat looking so steadily at the dapper toe of his boot for a time, and yet with so stealthy a stillness, that his manner might have suggested the bated exultation of a cat that had had a glimpse of a frisking mouse in that neighborhood, and was waiting to pounce upon it.

"Judge Gwinnan has the reputation," gravely remarked the granger, who looked as if he might be a pillar of the church, "of being a very upright man, a most worthy man, and a Christian gentleman."

"Of course he is," said Kinsard; "no question about it, and nobody but a fool would have thought of anything else. I am going to introduce a bill," he added seriously, "to make the fool-killer a State officer. We need him more than a geologist, or a governor, or anybody but a sheriff. A fool-killer ought to be on the State pay-roll."

No one said anything further, for Kinsard was lazily pulling himself out of the contortions into which he had sunk in the chair.

He was very striking when he stood at his full height. There was an air of dash and bravery about him engaging to the imagination. His high, broad forehead gave nobility and seriousness to a face that would otherwise have been only sparkling, or sneering, or melancholy, as his mood dictated. One might have hoped that should he wear out his fantastic, aimless, erratic spirit, should some blow subdue it and give it into his control, he would develop great gifts hitherto dwarfed and denied. He was aware of them in some sort; he bore himself as a man endowed with some splendor of pre-eminence. And others accorded it. Youth has much credit given to its promise, despite that it so often falls in the bud or fails in the fruit. But it rarely has so brilliant a prospect as here; and after he had strolled off at a leisurely, swinging gait, saying that he was going to the House, where a bill was coming up that he wanted to kill, they all looked after him, and commented on him, and called him a fine, high-minded young man, and said that it was a good thing for young fellows to have political ambition, and that it was dying out among that class generally, who was too fond of making money and of using their time to their own advantage.

He stood for a moment on the steps of the hotel, drawing on his gloves. Despite the snow, there was a faint suggestion of spring in the air. A thaw had set in. He heard drops slowly pattering down from the cornice above. The blue-white splendors of the electric light, with its myriad fine and filar rays whorled out into the darkness, showed a deserted street. A carriage, looking with its two lamps like some watchful-eyed monster, pulled up in front of the door, and the colored driver, with a wide display of a toothful grin, alighted with a "Want a hack, boss?"

"Jim, Tom — oh, it's Dick," said Kinsard, glancing at the dusky face in the lamplight; he knew all the colored folks in town. "Well, drive me to the Capitol, and don't be all night about it, either."

He flung himself upon the seat, lifted his long, slender feet to the opposite cushions, and with a complete collapse of anatomy resigned himself to the transit. The vehicle moved from the curb with something of the sound of a boat pushing off from shore, so splashing was its progress through the deep slush of the streets. The hoof-beats of the horses were muffled; the voice of the driver sounded, and was still again. Kinsard smoked in idle abstraction, hardly thinking, perhaps, even of his mission and the slaughter of the "innocent William," as he slangily called the bill which he intended to kill. When the carriage had climbed the Capitol hill, on which the fair edifice towered, glimmering vaguely white against the purple night, its rows of illuminated windows all gleaming yellow, and casting dim shafts of light adown the snowy slopes of the grounds below, he roused himself and looked out. Even after he had alighted and ascended the long flights of stone steps, between the groups of great figures that stand beneath the flaring gas lamps, he turned, and more than once walked the length of the stately portico, gazing down with a vague attraction which he could hardly have explained at the snowy roofs of the city, on its many hills, amidst the dun-colored intervals of the streets and the misty depressions. The heavens were purple above it; the stars palpitated in the infinite distances; a late moon was rising. He recognized the outline of Fort Negley to the south against the sky; he saw the steely gleam of the river. Spires, long glancing lines of light, domes, turrets, mansard roofs, mingled in picturesque fantasies of architecture. A bell rang out a mellow note; the icy air had crystalline vibrations. Here and there the aureola of an unseen electric light, the mere fringes of lustre, seemed the rising of some more cheerful orb; for melancholy hung upon the progress of the moon. In the tower of a public building Time lifted a smiling face in an illuminated dial, and far away to the west he saw a planet touch a spire, in an unprophesied conjunction. The lights of homes, yellow, steady, gleaming in some fantasy of form, seemed themselves a constellation of more genial suggestion than the pallid keener clustered scintillations of the chimeras of the skies. The gilded cross of the cathedral held aloft over the city was sublimated in the moonbeams and the fair nocturnal influences; it was mystic, effulgent, seeming to radiate light like the consecrated sign in a vision. He did not feel the cold; he stood for a long time, with his hands in his pockets, his overcoat falling back on his shoulders, watching with his restless eyes the quiet snowy town suffused with dreamy yellow light and pervaded by long, pensive shadows. Suddenly he turned and went within.

The House of Representatives presented a spectacle not altogether unprecedented in his experience. A spirited debate was in progress. Sixteen men were trying to speak at once. The seventeenth earnest orator was forcibly held in his chair by his friends. The speaker's gavel sounded continuously, but produced little effect upon the incoherency of the discussion. Other members were talking in low tones of alien matters; one had fallen asleep. His snores might have been generally noticed but for the commotion. Kinsard glanced at him as he took his seat close by.

"That's the best oratorical effort I ever heard McKimmon make," he said to a friend. "Observe how he sticks to the point: iterative, it is true; tautology might be urged against it as mere diction; but I admire its simplicity, its comprehensibility, its continuity. There are no digressions; nothing is done for effect; plain, cogent, impressive. It is a fine display of natural eloquence." His colleague burst out laughing, and Kinsard looked at him in apparent surprise, lifting his straight black eyebrows a little. Then he asked if the bill to remove the county seat of Kildeer County had yet been reached.

"No," said his friend, "but Harshaw has been around here after you three or four times."

The speaker's gavel had succeeded in securing order, and now the sixteen men's statements and counter-statements were elicited in decorous routine. The sudden cessation of noise roused Mr. McKimmon, whose somnolency ended in a snort and a conviction that he had not closed his eyes. He perceived a suspicion to the contrary in the minds of his nearest neighbors, and he could not account for it.

After the House had voted upon the question of public policy which had so agitated it, various minor bills were taken up, and there was a good deal of quiet movement, groups of two or three colloguing together here and there, and Harshaw came up again to talk to Kinsard.

"I want to know whether you'll coöperate with us against the bill for moving the county seat of Kildeer County."

He stood leaning one arm upon Kinsard's desk; the other was akimbo. He knitted his brow meditatively, and pursed up his red lips, and looked not at Kinsard, but at his inkstand. He had not altogether recovered from the rebuff so publicly given in the hotel corridor.

It is always a misfortune when a man of Harshaw's stamp has to contend with any degree of injustice. He had repeated to Gwinnan the truth, and for it he had been given the lie direct in circumstances under which he could not resent it; even the original threat was only the blurtings of an honest rage and for another man's sake. He was clever in adroitly justifying means and ends. To be armed with the truth, a genuine grievance endowed him with a force, a self-respect, all-potent in their way, and a wonderful driving-wheel to an already lubricated and too alert machinery. He had an imperative serious air which seemed to intimate to Mr. Kinsard that this was no time for fooling.

Kinsard was eccentric, ill-balanced. He was made up of prejudices, and he obeyed the impulse of the moment as other men obey interest or law. He was not predisposed in Harshaw's favor. He took a different view of the scene upon which Harshaw presumed. He looked up, a whimsical light in his grave eyes, as he allowed Harshaw to waste his breath in urging him to vote against a bill which he was already pledged to kill.

"The county line of those portions taken from Cherokee and Kildeer counties to form a new county in no instance approaches the county seat of Kildeer within eleven miles. There is no use for the people of Kildeer to commit the extravagance of a new court-house when they already have one, — a frame building, it is true, but spacious."

He looked very spacious himself, as he stood erect and waved his arm, the mental vision of the commodious Temple of Justice of Kildeer before him.

"Then, sir, it is thought there may be a railroad to the present county seat, a branch of the T. C. V., which will aid in developing the resources of the country."

"Well, I don't believe in railroads," said Kinsard, unexpectedly. "Whenever they get to talking about running a railroad from one little town where there is nothing to another little town where that nothing is not wanted, I understand it as developing the resources of the country."

Harshaw was not in a mood to be bantered.

"Mr. Kinsard," he said, "you are either a fool absolute, or you think I am."

"As far as you are concerned," said Kinsard with mock courtesy, "I have the highest opinion of your intelligence; ergo, it is more than probable that I *am* a fool."

Harshaw endeavored to recover himself. He reassumed his more genial manner. "Admit thât we are a choice brace. Well, now, we want you on our side; all the solid, substantial people of Kildeer County are arrayed against it."

"Oh, there are some solid citizens for it," said Kinsard perversely, "or you 'd be willing for it to be put to the popular vote."

Harshaw looked keenly at him. "Judge Gwinnan has been talking to you, has n't he? We 've had to fight his influence all the way through."

"Well, Judge Gwinnan is a prominent citizen of that county and a very sensible man, and if he is in favor of the change he must have good reasons," said Kinsard, seriously. "That 's enough to take it through."

Harshaw cast an indignant glance upon him. "Well, before I 'm done with it I 'll show you that this General Assembly is n't run by Judge Gwinnan's influence and by his myrmidons. I am glad you have let me know at last whose mouthpiece you are!"

He walked away with that extraordinary quickness and lightness so incongruous with his portliness. Kinsard's black eyes, that seemed kindled with actual flames, followed him for a moment. Then, as comprehension slowly dawned upon him, and with a wrench as if he broke from actual physical restraint, he started from his seat to follow.

"No, you won't, now; no, you won't." His nearest neighbor had locked his arm into Kinsard's, and held it like a vise. He was a square-built, slow, muscular man, solid as granite. His eyes were fixed upon Harshaw, who was already speaking against the bill. "What is that man saying?"

Kinsard at once lapsed into attention. Harshaw was a clear and forcible speaker, and with lucid arguments ranged upon the side of conservatism and economy he was giving the advocates of the measure a very stiff fight. They got on their feet time and again, and came at him. He had a great fund of pugnacity, and on principle fought every point. His face was flushed; his eyes were grave and intent; his frequent gestures ponderous and forcible. Now and then he tossed back his mane of yellow hair, as if its weight vexed him. He sought to show the ephemeral nature of the advantages urged, the solid interests relinquished. Presently his old slogan was resounding on the air. He was representing that the sacred interests of the people were imperiled by the machinations of the bloated plutocracy of Kildeer County. He wanted it to be distinctly understood that he did not charge any nefarious practices, any corrupt influences; only that most subtle, insidious, and pervasive sway always exerted by the views of men of position, men of family, men of "prawperty," against the simple will and simple needs of the Plain People. The high-toned folks, the few rich folks, wished the county seat moved to Damascus, because they had "prawperty" there. (He pronounced "prawperty" with so contemptuous an intonation that one felt one could never take pleasure in paying taxes again.) They had "prawperty," and railroad stock, and thus from the people, the many of moderate means, who had built up the present county town and made it what it was, who spent their money right there instead of going off to patronize merchants and schools in Glaston, as was the habit of the wealthy, — from this class would be wrenched those privileges which they had made valuable. All those advantages which had been nursed for years, which were so much actual materialization of the efforts of the Plain People, would go to — not to Tophet, as one might have expected from the tone, but to — Damascus!

But he would champion their rights; he would be heard; he would not heed the ostentatious reference of the gentleman from Cherokee to his watch. Why, he could tell the speaker that these same influential men had their personal representation in this House. A member confessed to him that because one of these little great men wanted a thing it had to go through this General Assembly. "And so his mouthpiece repeats his wish, his tool does his will!"

A murmur arose.

Kinsard was on his feet in an instant.

"Mr. Speaker," he thundered, "the member means *me!*"

There was sudden silence.

He stood at his full height, his head thrown back, his brilliant eyes fixed angrily on Harshaw.

Harshaw was dumfounded. He had expected Kinsard to quake silently and secretly under the lash; to quiver in terror lest his identity be hinted. This open avowal had routed him. He was in an ill-humor, but he had no desire to seriously attack Kinsard on a point like this. He wanted to punish him, to intimidate him; to threaten that most sensitive possession of the young and spirited, his reputation, or, as Kinsard would have phrased it, his "sacred honor." He had the usual contempt of a man of forty for youth, — its self-assertion, its domineering. He intended the chance allusion as discipline. He had fallen under his own lash. He stood in dismay as Kinsard reiterated, "He means *me!*"

There was a general laugh; the imputation, in view of his character, his prominence, his wealth, his very eye, was so absurd.

"But," — Kinsard's tones were grandiloquent, — "in view of the publicity of this charge, I consider that I am wounded in my reputation, and I demand reparation."

"I can make no formal retraction," said Harshaw, hastily, "for I have imputed no discredit, except being easily dominated."

Kinsard fixed upon him a look of amazement. He turned again to the chair. "Mr. Speaker," he said, "the member from the floterial district of Cherokee and Kildeer "— he sedulously avoided the word "gentleman"

— "labors under a mistake. I do not demand the retraction of a word. Perhaps he will understand this token." He took his glove, and cast it in the open space before the speaker's desk.

Only a nineteenth-century kid glove, with two porcelain buttons at the wrist, but it was flung down with as splendid and gallant a gesture as if it were a gauntlet of mail.

The old fellows, who had outlived folly such as this, were grinning at the revival of their ancient manners. The younger men, profiting by the traditions of their elders, were grave and quivering with excitement. Harshaw was in a quandary, conscious of being ridiculous in the eyes of one class, and of being defied in the eyes of the other. He would not do so absurd a thing as to lift Kinsard's glove. Yet with the significance of the "token" he was ashamed to let it lie.

And the speaker had a big job on his hands.

The gavel sounded now and again. Some one, with a pious view of making bad worse, was calling attention to the anti-dueling legislation. Another reminded Mr. Kinsard of his "sacred obligations" to his constituents, to the people of Tennessee, to the House, all of which seemed to have escaped him for the moment. Kinsard's colleague had sprung forward, recovered the somewhat ridiculous glove, and, crumpling it up, put it into his own pocket. He succeeded in attracting the attention of the chair and of the House. He wished — he spoke in a labored way, with a pause between each phrase, and a rising inflection — to remark that the House was disposed to take a great deal on trust. The gentleman had not given any challenge. Did a member ask what that glove meant, then? Why, defiance! Dueling was with a *deadly* weapon; *deadly* weapon was of the essence of the offense. The gentleman might have preferred to have a round or two at fisticuffs, or, perhaps, simply to engage in debate. (Derisive cries and laughter.) Defiance only! It was a breach of all the proprieties to mention the anti-dueling laws in this connection. Too much taken for granted, Mr. Speaker. If I should be heard to say to a man that I would see him before dinner, it would be highly preposterous to have me arrested. We might be going to kill each other, it is true, but then, again, we might be only going to " smile."

The speaker sat listening gravely, much wishing to further the acceptance of this view, for he considered the demonstration mere boyish wrath and folly. He made strong efforts for the adjustment of the difficulty. Harshaw rose presently, and begged to call attention to the fact that he had named no names, had given no intimation as to identity. He had spoken indefinitely, and the gentleman had insisted upon revealing himself. He would say that he desired to provoke no quarrel; he had no ill-will to the gentleman in question. He begged to withdraw what he had said, and he tendered his apologies.

Kinsard, under the pressure that was brought to bear, could hardly do less than accept them, and thus, it seemed at the time, the matter ended.

It had been a stormy evening for Harshaw. He was, however, well accustomed to contention. It was not this that irked him; he writhed under the sense of disadvantage, of being brought in propinquity to defeat. He was a man not susceptible of the finer emotions of success, of gratulation because of the thing attained rather than the plaudits of attainment. His sensibility to achievement was manifested in a certain sordid inversion of values. He made popularity, position, social opportunity, political preferment, the end of mental supremacy, rather than its humble incident. And thus it was that, rough as he was, courageous, obstinate, full of rugged nodules of traits, hard, strong, but limited, there was no solid substratum of absolute sincere purpose in his nature, no bed-rock impervious to all infiltration of temptation, all extraneous influence; whatever he might build would fail at the foundation.

His world had changed to him in some sort during the short hours since the darkness had fallen. He strode into the hotel feeling a different man. He found it necessary to assert himself. All the fight in him was on the alert. He cared little for Kinsard or for the scene itself in the House, but it was peculiarly obnoxious to him that it should have been another chance allusion to the man he hated which precipitated the collision. He revolted from the fact that it might seem a reiteration of the lesson received earlier in the evening. He knew that many commented upon the coincidence, and that doubtless he was recommended to leave Gwinnan alone. Now submission was not what he was prepared to offer. He preferred that it should seem a persistent attack on Gwinnan. Once more he returned to the charge.

He was serious, lowering, formidable. He did not go at once to his room, as the lateness of the hour might have impelled him. He was quick to observe the faces of the legislators about: some were merely curious; others held a half-cloaked triumph; and still others an open gloating satisfaction. It was with a manner which was a distinct replication to all three manifestations that he lounged about the reading-room with a striding gait, his hat on the back of his head, his hands in his pockets, and his cigar fast between his teeth. He finally threw himself into a chair by the table before the open fire in the inner room, and said in a meditative undertone to a gentleman with whom he had sufficient association to make it seem a confidence to a friend, "I reckon I'll have to write to Judge Gwinnan." The others heard it, however, and it was to several that he read the letter when it was completed. They thought it very bold; to show that it was not empty bluster, but written with all the sincerity of immediate intention, he rang for a bell-boy, and dispatched it in their presence to Gwinnan's room.

That gentleman's physician still urged his patient to cultivate a more vivid interest in life, in passing events; to seek to absorb himself; to rouse himself. Mr. Harshaw's letter very effectually compassed this result.

The writer begged to call Judge Gwinnan's attention

to sundry facts which he proceeded to set forth in due detail. He premised that he would endeavor to take no other notice of an insult offered him by a man who was virtually at death's door, and who might uncharitably, perhaps, be supposed to have taken advantage of that circumstance; such as the advantage was, he made Judge Gwinnan most heartily welcome to it. In defense of his reputation for veracity, however, he felt it necessary to state his authority, besides his own observation, for saying that Judge Gwinnan had taken such notice of a very beautiful girl, who was a witness, as to render her lover, who was the prisoner, wildly jealous, and to result in the injuries from which Judge Gwinnan was now unfortunately suffering. His authority was the deputy sheriff and the two guards, to whom the prisoner stated these facts, swearing that he would get even with Judge Gwinnan. Mr. Harshaw begged to remark in addition that he fully realized that he was ill advised in saying he would like to introduce a resolution to impeach Judge Gwinnan. He knew that the action of a court in a matter of contempt committed in the presence of the court is wholly a matter of judicial discretion not liable to be reviewed by the court above, and therefore it should have been free from impotent criticism, which could avail naught to either counsel or prisoner, who have absolutely no resource nor recourse. He deeply regretted his words, and their futility.

The mock apology, which had been highly appreciated by the coterie in the reading-room, the whole tenor of the letter, the revelation which it made, had important results to Judge Gwinnan, who was accustomed to deal with larger motives and finer issues than Harshaw's wrath or satire could furnish.

He had such exceeding confidence in the dignity and decorum of Gwinnan as judge that at first it seemed almost impossible that he should have taken such notice of the witness as to attract the attention of others. But there was a sort of coercive evidence in the circumstance that the girl's face had lingered in his mind with

a luminous distinctness, a surprised pleasure, a newly
awakened sense of beauty, which he had associated with
no other face that he could remember. He was not a
sentimental man. He had had few romantic experiences,
and the flavor they had left was vapid and foolish.
Alethea had not primarily impressed him as beautiful.
She looked so noble, so true, so radiantly good. It was
altogether an abstract sentiment, a tribute to the lofty
qualities which he revered and she embodied.

He cared so little for Gwinnan as Gwinnan that he
entertained the mildest resentment toward the man who
had struck him on the head with his iron shackles. The
indignity offered by the foreman of the jury, and afterward by Harshaw, to Gwinnan the judge had burned
into his consciousness, and the scars would be there on
the judgment day. The knowledge that the attack was
not in revenge for some fancied wrong in the trial, but
that it was the frenzy of a madly jealous lover in chains
and in expatriation, altered the whole aspect of the case
for Gwinnan as Gwinnan.

The judge could not, perhaps, have sufficiently condemned Gwinnan's state of mind as he sat down and
wrote to Mr. Kenbigh, the attorney for the State at Glaston, requesting that no action should be taken in regard
to the assault, as he was not willing to prosecute.

XXI.

ALETHEA SAYLES awoke early the morning after the momentous news of Mink's journey had come to Wild-Cat Hollow; such an awakening as a barn-swallow might know, the familiar of the rafters and the clapboards. There was no other ceiling to the roof-room. She might put up her hand and touch it where she lay, but in the centre it was higher, — high enough for many pendent uses: bags of cotton swung from the ridge-pole; hanks of yarn; bunches of pepper; gourds; old hats and garments, of awry, distorted, facetious aspect in their caricature of the habit of humanity. The snow pressed heavily without; through the crevices vague white glimpses of the drifts might be seen, for the dull glow from the fire in the room below penetrated the cracks between the boards of the flooring, which served as the ceiling of the lower story. Light came in, too, from the rifts between the wall and the great stick-and-clay chimney, which bulged outward, being built outside the house, as is the habit in the region. It was the light of the waning moon, fitful, fluctuating, for clouds were astir. Now and then, too, Alethea could see the great morning star with its tremulous glister, seeming nearer, dearer, than all the others, — splendid, yet tender and full of promise. She looked wistfully at it for a moment, feeling the dull aching wound in her heart, and forgetting what dealt it. Then it all came back to her, and she wondered she had awakened again. She could not understand how she lived. She felt as if she could rise no more. But the cow was to be milked; she listened to the cocks crowing. The baby, who had developed a virulent habit of early rising, was already astir. She heard his thumping bare feet on the floor of the room below; he would be cold, and she thought of the danger of the embers, and remembered that the sluggard his mother still drowsed. The breakfast must be cooked, the dishes must be washed. Her physical strength was asserting itself agaiust the shock to her mind. Her collapsed energies were recuperated by sleep, albeit the slumber induced by the primitive narcotics of the "yerb bag." Ah, the world of Wild-Cat Hollow, small though it was, was full of work, and she must lay hold. And so she rose once more, and joined hands with joyless duty.

Ben Doaks sojourned with them for a time, and went hunting with Jessup, and brought back game, and made Mrs. Sayles presents of the peltry. As he sat by the fire at night he told the news from the cove in great detail, and discussed it freely with Mrs. Jessup, and developed remarkable capacities for acquiescence. Old Griff, he said, was having a mighty hard winter. His mill had proved a sore loss, for he was bereft of his tolls, and he had planted little corn. "He mought make out, though. His meat looks thrivin'; he hain't killed yit." Ben spoke of the miller's hogs afoot as if they held their fat in trust and were stewards of their own bacon. The old man seemed failing, and talked much about Tad; sometimes as if he had already returned, sometimes as if he momently expected him. The children, too, "'peared thrivin'," though Ben did n't believe Sophy would ever be good for much except to look at, and the little ones "all 'peared ragged ez ef she did n't study 'bout them much."

"Too many peart, spry boys in the cove fur her ter study 'bout, stiddier them," said Mrs. Sayles, with a scornful toss of the head, histrionically seeing the situation from Sophy's standpoint.

"Jerry Price 'pears ter set a heap o' store by Sophy's looks," submitted Ben, with the implication of the remark.

"Waal, 't would be a jedgmint on Dely Purvine fur all her onwholesome vanity an' slack-twisted sort o' religion, ef that thar Jerry Price, ez she hev brung up ez ef he war her own son, — though his looks air enough ter tarrify a mole. — war ter marry Sophy Griff."

"Waal, sir, one thing,— her housekeepin' could n't 'stonish him none arter Mis' Purvine's," remarked Mrs. Jessup, with an elaborate semblance of seeing the brighter side of things.

"Shucks!" Mrs. Sayles commented. "He'd miss mightily the show and the shine he hev been used ter along o' Mis' Purvine."

"Waal," said Ben, "I don't b'lieve ez Mis' Purvine would mind much who Jerry marries, so long ez he keeps clar o' Elviry Crosby. Mis' Purvine air mightily outdone with her. She hev been mournin' fur Peter Rood same ez ef she war a widder-woman. An' ye know she would n't speak ter him ez long ez Mink war out'n the grip o' the sher'ff. She tried ter toll Pete back arterwards. I hearn him 'low sech when they war drawin' the jury. I dunno how she made out."

Mrs. Sayles gazed at the fire solemnly from under her pink sunbonnet. "Death tolled him," she said lugubriously.

"I'd jes' ez lief Death as Elviry Crosby," said Mrs. Jessup, in calm superiority to the wiles of feminine fascination.

Old man Sayles shook his head in negation.

"Mighty dark under the ground," he said, with terror of the termination of life; which for him signified so little that a sponge with a vocable or two might have seemed his correlative.

But when Ben was gone,— and the sight of Alethea, silent, absorbed, pallid, broken-hearted, gave him little wish to prolong his stay,— the scene at the fireside was less amicable and cheerful. The elder women, bereft of gossip, bickered over the trifling mishaps of the day. The old man sorted his "lumber." Jessup slouched and lazed and smoked. Only the weather varied the aspect of the world. The snow slipped away in the thaw, leaving mud and ooze and intervals of blackened ice. Then the rains descended, and the scene without was dimly visible through the long, slanting, dun-colored fringes of the cloud. The roof clamored with the resonant fall of the drops, the clapboards leaked, and puddles formed even in the ashes of the chimney corner. The sun might shine vaguely for a day. The chill splendors of the wintry constellations scintillated icily in the dark spaces of the night. But the clouds, rallying from every repulse, closed once more about the Great Smoky, and ravine and peak and cove were again deeply covered with snow.

Mrs. Jessup bewailed the change. "I war a-hopin'," she remarked, "ez we would hev no mo' fallin' weather, so Lethe could go ter the meetin' at the church-house in Eskaqua Cove, an' fetch up some word o' what's a-goin' on down thar ter this benighted roost. *I* war raised in the *cove!* I ain't used ter sech a dwindlin' sort o' life ez this hyar."

"What ailed ye, then, ter marry a mounting boy?" Mrs. Sayles would demand in resentment.

"'Kase I war the mos' outdacious an' astonishin' fool in Cherokee County."

Mrs. Jessup was not a woman of great abilities, but she had an uncommon gift of conclusiveness in retort.

Mrs. Sayles could only knit off her needle with a sort of whisking scornfulness of gesture.

And presently, not to be silenced, she demanded when the meetin' was to be held.

"To-morrer's the day; this be Sat'dy. Ter-morrer's Sunday."

"The snow's a dry snow," remarked Mrs. Sayles. "I dunno what's ter hender Lethe, ef she feels minded ter go ter meetin'."

It never occurred to either of them to undertake themselves the hardships and dangers of the excursion. Even Mrs. Jessup, pining for the fuller development and richer social opportunities of life in the cove, did not covet them to the extent of exertion.

Alethea was glad to be alone. The burden of the work, however mechanically accomplished, had pressed heavily upon her consciousness. The acrimony, the continual talk, the trivial stir, had impinged jarringly upon her deeper absorption. The infinite solitude of the wilds, the austere dignity of their silence, harmonized with her mood. She had craved to hear the preaching. She was spiritually an hungered. She turned to the consolations of religion. Now and then she drew a deep sigh as she went, and paused and looked about her with eyes that felt as if they had wept long; but they were dry, and tears for a time had been strangers. She was fain to note closely to-day the aspects of the outer world, or, woodland creature though she was, she might have missed her way in the tortuous intricacies that the road had followed in striving to make and keep a footing among the steeps. Icicles still hung to the dark faces of the crags, grim and distinct upon the snowy slopes about them. On every side towered the great trees, their gigantic proportions more incredibly imposing when fully revealed in bare bole and branch than when the foliage had veiled them. Now and then she met a mist, stealing softly, silently along, or lurking like some half-affrighted apparition in the depth of ravines, or peering down from over unmeasured heights. As the road turned abruptly she saw a mass of white vapor against the sky, — nay, it was Thunderhead, the great cloud-mountain. There was movement upon the slopes of the peak. The mists shifted to and fro, with vague gray shadows mysteriously attendant upon them. Sudden gusts of wind swept through the forest, rousing it to motion, to weird murmurs. She gathered her brown shawl about her and drew her bonnet forward. And then the wind would slip away, and she would hear it repeating its mystic apostrophe far off among the ravines of Thunderhead, or Big Injun, or another of the mighty company of the border. Through rifts of the clouds came sometimes a pallid glimpse of the midday moon. It had a strange ghastly gleam on this sad gray day, above the great legendary mountain. She stood and gazed at it for a moment in vague fascination, then she turned and went on. She saw occasionally the footprints of small animals in the snow. Often she looked after them, for she had the com-

passionate tenderness of a compatriot for these little
mountaineers. Once she noticed a rabbit that crouched
chilled and trembling for an instant, and then went leaping through the frozen weeds.

She was not cold. It was growing warmer as she
made her way down to lower levels, and much of the time
she walked rapidly. Only when she cautiously crossed
the mountain torrent, icy and motionless save that in its
crystal heart a stream like a silver arrow swiftly and
silently glided, glancing in the light, she felt the chill of
the day. For the foot-bridge was hung with icicles and
enveloped in deceptive snow that fell at the touch of her
foot, and she began to be afraid she would lose so much
time here that she might be late and miss some part of
the sermon. When the cove became visible, one might
fail to discern any expression of the social opportunities
for which Mrs. Jessup valued it. In its wintry guise it
was peculiarly open to the eye: its forests were bare;
the unbroken snow lay in its broad fields in lieu of its
harvested crops; its road was distinguishable by the narrow interval between the zigzag fences; the serpentine
lines of the river were defined by its snow-fringed
laureled banks; here and there a curl of blue smoke
arose from the chimney of a little house heavily thatched
with drifts.

The church had for Alethea many melancholy associa-
tions. She paused at the palings, remembering the night
when she had stood here in the silent moonshine, in the
full summer-tide, and the vapors had shifted about, and
in their midst she had seen the boy whom they had said
was dead. How much had come into her life since then,
and, alas, how much had gone forth forever! The snow
hung heavy in the pine-trees; the faint moon was in the
fretted gray sky above the mountains. The little house
was dark and drear under its whitened roof. The snow
was melting close to the chimney. She heard the drops
trickling down. The mounds in the inclosure were very
distinct. Some of them had a square of palings close
about: those were the graves of the well-to-do people of

the cove. She could hardly have said, but for her lifelong knowledge of the place, which was the new-made grave where lay the man who had pointed at her with his last living impulse, whose last word was intended for her, becoming dumb on his lips as his life died in him, — a word never to be heard, never to be answered. Here they all were, little ephemeral mounds in the midst of the great eternities of the mountains. She wondered if there were words to be said buried with the others; deeds to be done or undone; hopes unrealized; promises deferred until now when time was no more for them. Life was transitory, and so' she was minded anew of the preacher.

He was already in the pulpit when she entered the low, dark little building, with its scanty congregation huddled on the few benches. He was a long-haired, wild-eyed, jeans-clad mountaineer, with a powerful physique and an admiration of prowess. He was a worthy and a well-meaning man, and there are those of his profession wiser than he who forget that they are apostles of peace. The circumstantial account of various feuds detailed in the Old Bible proved of intense interest to the majority of his congregation, who listened with eager faces and spellbound attention. The methods of slaughter in those days seem to have had phenomenal diversity, and certainly exceeded anything of the sort that had ever been heard of in Eskaqua Cove.

Alethea's mind was too closely held in subordination to reverence for her to acknowledge, even to herself, how little this discourse met her peculiar needs. She endeavored to fix her attention humbly upon the harrowing details of barbarity; now and then an expression of wincing sympathy was in her clear eyes.

The application of the sermon — for it had an application — was to be found in the thankfulness which every professing member should experience because his lot was cast in Eskaqua Cove, where such practices did not obtain, and the fear which the unregenerate should harbor, since these tortures were nothing in comparison to what would happen to him in the next world, unless he forthwith mended his ways.

It left a certain trace of meditative astonishment among the heavy mountaineers, slouching out to their horses and wagons, slowly commenting while chewing hard on their great quids of tobacco. The women lingered and talked in a lack-lustre fashion to one another of their ailments, and interchanged inquiries concerning absent members of the family. Sophy Griff stood by the palings, debating whether she should accept the proffer of one of the youths to take her home on his horse behind him.

She was looking about doubtfully. "I brung two o' the chil'ren along o' me, but they 'pear ter hev runned off somewhar. I dunno ez I wanter leave 'em."

"They'll be home 'fore supper-time," urged the gallant. "Trest 'em ter git thar ef thar's enny eatin' goin' on."

With this logic she suffered herself to be persuaded, mounted his horse behind him, and they rode away after the manner of a cavalier and his lady-love of the olden time.

Alethea trudged along the road to Mrs. Purvine's house, for the journey up the mountain was hardly a possible achievement after the fatigues of the descent. The sun had come out. It scintillated on the snow. The cascades in the half-frozen river glittered iridescent. The bluffs were outlined with drifts in all their fissures; icicles clung to them at every jutting point, and the stunted trees of their summit, whose insistent roots seemed to pierce the stone, were encased in ice, and sparkled as the wind moved them. In the midst of all this splendor Mrs. Purvine's house was dark and humble, despite the porch, and the front steps, and the glass windows. In the half-buried garden a bevy of dark figures sped this way and that over the snow. They were aunt Dely's boys chasing rabbits. The creatures, half famished and bold with necessity, — fatally distinct on the whitened ground, — were deftly knocked on the head with a stick, and one blow from such experts was sufficient. In the party was a smaller boy, whom, at first, Alethea was puzzled to remember. Presently she recognized 'Gustus Tom, and this prepared her to see, when she entered, "sister Eudory," sitting in front of Mrs. Purvine's fire.

The pernicious glass in the windows added much cheerfulness to the apartment in weather like this. It aided the firelight in revealing sister Eudory's tangle of flaxen hair and beguiling plumpness, as she sat, looking demure and wise, in one of the large rickety chairs. She was nearly five years of age now, and a great girl, and when she got down and went and stood behind the churn, in an affectation of shyness because of Alethea's presence, she was not hidden by the article, and the handle of the dasher was insufficient to obscure her downcast face and her finger in her mouth.

"Yer aig will pop an' bust, fust thing ye know," said aunt Dely, the politic.

And Eudora forthwith came briskly out to investigate an egg which she was roasting in the ashes, the kind present of Mrs. Purvine. The hen that laid it was stalking about the room in unconscious bereavement. Now and then there was a shrill piping from a basket on the floor, from which overflowed, as it were, a downy collection of fall "deedies," hatched too late to stand any chance of weathering the winter except by being reared into those obnoxious animals, house-chickens. A matronly feathered head would occasionally be thrust out with a remonstrant cluck, and the assemblage, miraculously escaping the heedless human foot, would climb into the basket, and there would ensue a soft sound of snuggling down and drowsy pipings. All of which excited sister Eudory almost to ecstasy.

Mrs. Purvine experienced less complacence. "Ef ennybody ain't got no baby, an' feels like adoptin' one ter take trouble about, jes' let 'em git 'em a settin' o' aigs an' hatch out some fall deedies. They'll be ez much trouble ez twins!"

"Why n't you-uns stay ter the meetin' ter the church-house, Eudory?" demanded Alethea.

The little girl, kneeling on the hearth, anxiously adjusted a broom straw on the egg to see if it were done, — when, according to culinary tradition, the straw would turn; she glanced up with her charming smile showing her snaggled little teeth.

"'Gustus Tom would n't bide," she declared.

"Waal, now, 'Gustus Tom oughter begin ez early ez he kin," said Mrs. Purvine. "Sech ez 'Gustus Tom hev a mighty wrastle with Satan 'fore they git grace. 'Gustus Tom hev got a long way o' wickedness afore him. He oughter be among them in early youth convicted o' sin an' afeard o' Satan."

"Naw," said the child, sitting upright and staring steadily at the straw. "He be 'feared o' Pete Rood. An' he wou't bide a-nigh the church-house."

The light of the fire was on her face. Its breath stirred her bright hair. Her chubby hand hovered about the egg in the ashes. Surely the straw was turning at last.

"Pete Rood is dead, Eudory," said Mrs. Purvine, rebukingly.

"In the groun'," said Eudory unequivocally.

The mention of him recalled to Alethea that momentous day of drawing the jury, the mystery of Tad's fate, the hardships of Mink's duress, and finally the calamity which he had brought upon himself.

Alethea had taken off her bonnet, and sat down in the rocking-chair before the fire, her eyes fixed reflectively upon the great burning logs. The interior of Mrs. Purvine's house always had a leisurely aspect; to-day it wore the added quiet and ease of Sunday stillness. It was evident that here no anxious female heart was "harried ter death," in yearnings for the perfecting of a theory of housekeeping.

Mrs. Purvine, sitting with her empty hands in her lap, once more rebuked sister Eudory, the decorums of the day giving a more stringent interpretation to her code of manners.

"Ye must n't say 'Gustus Tom air 'feard o' Pete Rood, 'kase he air dead."

"That 's what 'Gustus Tom say — he say don't talk 'bout'n it." Eudora looked up gravely. "He be wusser 'feard now 'n he war when Pete Rood war 'live."

There was a sudden hand on the latch, and 'Gustus Tom came hastily in.

"Look-a-hyar, sister Eudory!" he cried remonstrantly, seizing her by the arm, "what ails ye ter let yer tongue break loose that-a-way? Shet up! Ye promised ye would n't tell."

He had an excited, grave, frightened look that was incongruous with the roguish cast of his features; his torn old hat was jauntily askew; his clothes were ragged; a single suspender seemed quite adequate to support so many holes; his shoes were broken. There was a distinct deprecation and anxiety in his face more pitiable than poverty, as he looked from one to the other of the women. He was evidently wondering how much of his secrets the faithless sister Eudory had told. He could not control his fears. He broke out suddenly:

"Hev she tole 'bout'n what I done?"

Mrs. Purvine, who was jocose with children, and who could not appreciate at this stage of the disclosure that anything of moment impended, folded her arms slowly across her bosom, looked at him over her spectacles, a great deal of the whites of her blue eyes showing, and with mock solemnity nodded assent.

"Waal, waal — did she tell 'bout'n the — the mill, too?"

Aunt Dely shook her head in burlesque reproach. "She hev tole on ye, 'Gustus Tom. Yer wicked ways air made plain."

His eyes were wildly starting from his head; he caught his breath in quick gasps. The little girl first detected the genuine terror which he was suffering, and as she held his hand she began to whimper and to lay her head against his ragged shirt-sleeve.

"Oh, Mis' Purvine," cried 'Gustus Tom, "I never

knowed aforehand how 't war goin' ter turn out, else I'd never hev gone thar that night, an' I would n't hev knowed no mo' 'bout who bust down the mill 'n nobody else ! "

" Did n't Mink bust the mill down ? " asked Mrs. Purvine, staring.

" Naw," said 'Gustus Tom, miserably, " Mink never."

Aunt Dely suddenly sat upright, and took her spectacles from her astonished eyes. She was about to speak sharply, but met Alethea's warning glance, and desisted.

XXII.

CONSCIENCE, the great moral inquisitor, whose sessions are held in secret, whose absolute justice is untempered by mercy, whose processes are unrelated and superior to the laws of the land, makes manifest its decrees only at such long intervals that we are prone to consider their results exceptional. Although its measures are invariably meted, they are seldom so plainly set forth as in Peter Rood's fate. Alethea, listening to 'Gustus Tom's story, saw in aghast dismay how he had been pursued by those terrible potencies of the right which he had sought to disregard. Many things that had been vague were made distinct. She understood suddenly the meaning of the strange words he had spoken at the camp-meeting, when his spiritual struggles had nearly betrayed him. She divined the mingled fear and self-reproach, and at the same time the cowardly gratulation he experienced because of his fancied security, when entrapped to serve on the jury. She remembered with a new comprehension his joyous excitement when it appeared that the idiot boy had not been drowned, and the pallid anguish on his face as the lawyer dexterously reversed the probabilities. It might seem that he had expiated his deed, but the extremest penalties were not abated. He had been a pillar in the church, renowned for a certain insistent piety, and zealous to foster good repute among men; and this last possession that he held dear upon earth, which may be maintained even by a dead man, who can carry naught out of the world, was wrested from him.

The truth which he had so feared, which he had so labored to hide, over which the grave had seemed to close, was at last brought to light by very simple means.

On the eventful morning, the miller's erratic grandson, awaking early, he knew not why, had sought to utilize the occurrence by robbing an owl's nest in the hollow of a tree beside the mill. The day had not yet dawned, and he hoped that one or the other of the great birds would be away on its nocturnal foragings, so that he might the more easily secure the owlet, which he had long wanted for a pet. It was very still, 'Gustus Tom said. The frogs by the water had ceased their croaking; the katydids were silenced long ago; he heard only the surging monotone of the gleaming cascade falling over the natural dam. He had climbed the tree to the lower limbs, and had perched on one of them to rest for a moment, when there broke upon the air the sound of the galloping of a horse far away, approaching at a tremendous rate of speed. Presently he came into view, his head stretched forward, his coat flecked with foam, his rider plying both heel and whip.

This rider was Peter Rood, whom 'Gustus Tom knew well, as he often came to the mill. He dismounted hastily, close to the water-side. He walked uncertainly, even pausing sometimes to steady himself by holding to the supports of the old mill. He was evidently very drunk, and thus it appeared to 'Gustus Tom the less surprising that he should drag two or three fence rails stranded on the margin of the river,— which was high and full of floating rubbish, — and laboriously place them in a position to cumber the wheel; an empty barrel, too, he found and put to this use, some poles, driftwood. He paused after a careful survey of his work, and held up his head, looking away toward the east, as if he were listening. It seemed to 'Gustus Tom, all veiled by the dew-tipped chestnut leaves, that Rood was strangely intent of purpose for a drunken man. He heard, long before the boy did, some monition of approach in the distance, for he caught eagerly at his horse's bridle. Yet he was drunk enough to find difficulty in mounting. As the animal swerved, he was obliged to grasp the stirrup with one hand in order to steady it, so that he could put his foot in it; then he flung his right leg over the saddle, and away he went along the grassy margin of the road, — noiseless, swift, dark, like some black shadow, some noxious exhalation of the night.

'Gustus Tom explained at this point, with tears and many anxious twistings of the button on his shirt front, — which was quite useless, the correlative button-hole being torn out, — that he understood so little of what all this meant at the time that it seemed to him the only important point involved was to remember to tell his grandfather early in the day of Pete Rood's drunken freak of clogging the mill-wheel. He did not call out and make his presence known, because he was frightened by the man's strange conduct and terrible look. As he still sat meditating on the limb of the tree, the sound which had aroused Peter Rood again broke upon the silence. Once more the regular thud of hoofs — of many hoofs. The pace was far slower than the rattling gallop at which Pete Rood had come. There were several men in the group that presently appeared. 'Gustus Tom knew some of them, — he could n't help knowing Mink Lorey from far off; he looked so wild and gamesome; the moonlight was on his face and all his hair was flying. He knew Mink well. Mink it was who climbed the timbers of the race and lifted the gate. And once more 'Gustus Tom, with quivering lips and twisting the futile button on his shirt front, began to exculpate himself. He did not understand what Mink was about to do until the gate was lifted and the water surged through. The wheel, turning with its curiously contrived clogs, jerked spasmodically, gave sudden violent wrenches, finally breaking and crashing against the shanty, that itself tottered and careened and fell. He heard Tad scream, for the idiot, having incurred the miller's displeasure during the day, had been locked in the mill, supperless, to sleep. 'Gustus Tom did not see the boy in the river, because of the falling timbers, the clouds of dust and flour and meal, and the commotion of the water. The men galloped away, Mink among them. For the house had been alarmed by the noise; old Griff ran out, wringing his hands and crying aloud, first for the loss of the mill, then for the fate of the idiot. The others of the family came, too. 'Gustus Tom easily slipped down unobserved from the tree, in the midst of the excitement, and no one was aware, except sister Eudory, that he knew more than the rest. Lately she had noticed that he was afraid of the dark and would not sit alone; and she had begun to say so much of this that he was alarmed lest she might excite the suspicions of others. And so, thinking she would keep his secret, — he would have divulged it to no one else, — he told her that he was afraid of Peter Rood, who was dead, and who perhaps had found out in the other world that he knew the secret, and would come and haunt him to make sure that he did not reveal it. And at the renewal of these ghastly terrors 'Gustus Tom bent his head upon his arm, and began to sob afresh.

"Why did n't ye tell at fust, 'Gustus Tom?" asked Alethea, her mind futilely reviewing the complications that circumstance had woven about Mink Lorey.

'Gustus Tom lifted his head, a gleam of this world's acumen shining through the tears in his eyes.

"He 'd hev walloped the life out'n me, ef I hed told. He kem nigh every day ter the mill arterward, whenst they war a-s'archin' fur the body. An' his eyes looked so black an' mad an' cur'ous whenst he cut 'em round at me, I 'lowed he knowed what I knowed. An' I war afeard o' him."

Aunt Dely could not be altogether repressed. "Waal, 'Gustus Tom, ye air a bad aig," she remarked, politely. "Ye ter know all that whenst ye war down thar at Shaftesville, along o' yer gran'dad, an' seen them men a-talkin' by the yard-medjure, an' a-cavortin' 'bout in the court, ez prideful ez ef thar brains war ez nimble ez thar tongues; an' ye look at 'em try Mink fur bustin' down the mill an' drowndin' Tad, an' ye ter know ez Pete Rood done it, — an' ye say nuthin'!"

"Waal," said 'Gustus Tom, sorely beset. "he war a-settin' thar in the cheer; he could hev told hisself."

"Why n't ye tell arter he drapped dead?" suggested the politic Mrs. Purvine.

The boy winced at the recollection. "He looked so awful!" he said, putting up his hand to his eyes as if to shut out the image presented. "I war 'feared he'd harnt me."

It occurred to sister Eudora that this investigation was degenerating into a persecution of 'Gustus Tom. She had looked from one to the other in grave excitement and with a flushing face, as she stood on the hearth, the breath from the fire waving her flaxen hair, hanging upon her shoulders.

Suddenly, with an accession of color, she stepped across the broad, ill-joined stones, and, fixing a threatening eye on Mrs. Purvine's moon-face, she lifted her fat hand, and retributively smote that lady on the knee.

'Gustus Tom had never manifested any special desire to suit his own conduct to a high standard of deportment, but he appeared to entertain the most sedulous solicitude concerning sister Eudory's manners, and to be jealous that she should be esteemed the pink of juvenile propriety. His mortification at the present lapse was very great. It expressed itself in such unequivocal phrase, such energetic shakings of his tow-head, which seemed communicated, with diminished rigor, however, to her plump little shoulders, — for he went through all the motions of discipline, — that Mrs. Purvine, beaming with injudicious laughter, was forced to interfere. Her indulgence did not serve to reassure sister Eudory, who stood dismayed at the fullness of fraternal displeasure. She presently put her hands before her eyes, although she did not shed tears, and thus she was led toward the door, to be taken home as unfit for polite society. Mrs. Purvine hurried after her, carrying the roasted egg — which was very hot, in its shell — between two chips, and further pressing upon her a present of a sweet-potato, an ear of pop-corn, and a young kitten, all of which sister Eudory, regardless of the animate and the inanimate, the hot and the cold, carried together in her apron. The affront was but a slight matter to aunt Dely, whose lenient temperament precluded her from viewing it as an enormity; but as the brother and sister went away in humiliation, one could well guess that sister Eudora would be a woman grown before she would be allowed to contemplate with indifference the dreadful day when she "hit Mis' Purvine."

In whatever manner it might have seemed judicious to make use, in Mink's interest, of the disclosures of Peter Rood's agency in the destruction of the mill, anything like caution, or reserve, or secrecy was rendered impossible by the circumstance that it was Mrs. Purvine who shared in the discovery of the fact. For weeks no one passed the house, going or coming on the winding road, whom she did not descry through the worldly glass windows, — which thus demonstrated an additional justification for their existence, — and whom she did not hail with a loud outcry from the unsteady flight of steps, and bring to a not unwilling pause as she hurried out to the fence, with her glib tongue full of words. There was no weather too cold for the indulgence of this gossip. Sometimes aunt Dely would merely fling her apron over her head, if the exigency suggested haste; or she would hood herself with her shawl, like a cowled friar, and stand in the snow, defiant of the rigors of the temperature. More often, however, the passer-by would suffer himself to be persuaded to come in and sit down by aunt Dely's fire, and discuss with her all the details so tardily elicited. Pete Rood's death, considered as a judgment upon him, was a favorite point of contemplation, offering that symmetrical exposition of cause and effect, sin and retribution, peculiarly edifying to the obdurate in heart and acceptable to the literalist in religion. So much was said on this subject at the store, and the blacksmith-shop, and the saw-mill, — those places where the mountain cronies most congregated,—that it came to the ear of Rood's relatives with all the added poignancy of comment. They indignantly maintained that only the ingenuity of malice could feign to attach any special meaning to the moment or manner of his death, for it was widely known that he had for years suffered from a serious affection of the heart; they stigmatized the whole story as an effort to blacken his name in order to clear Mink Lorey. Their attitude and sentiment enlisted a certain sympathy, and it was only when they were not of the company that the counter-replication was made that it was a supremely significant moment when Peter Rood's doom fell upon him, and that it behooves those who sit in the shadow of death to be not easily diverted from the true interpretation of the darkling signs of the wrath of God.

It was a scene of pathetic interest when his aged mother, resolved upon forcing a recantation, came herself to the miller's home. A dark, withered, white-haired crone she was, with a hooked nose and a keen, fierce, intent eye that suggested strength of mind and purpose defying age and ailments. She shrewdly questioned the boy, and sought to involve him in discrepancies and to elicit some admission that the story had been prompted by Alethea Sayles. Her dark-browed sons stood about the great white-covered ox-wagon, their bemired boots drawn high over their trousers, their broad hats pulled down to their lowering eyes, maintaining a sedulous silence. So strong a family resemblance existed between them and the dead man that 'Gustus Tom was greatly perturbed as from time to time he glanced at them; looking away instantly with a resolution to see them no more, and yet again with a morbid fascination turning his eyes to meet theirs, before whose dark and solemn anger he quailed. Now and then the sobs would burst from him, and he would lay his head on his arm against the rails, as he cowered in the fence corner; for the old woman would not enter the miller's house, but stood upon the frozen crust of snow by the roadside, and looked upon the denuded site of the mill, and the turbulent river, and the austere bleak bluffs on the opposite bank. The miller peered out from his door, himself the impersonation of winter, his snowy locks and beard falling about his rugged face; the desolate little shanty was plainly to be seen among the naked and writhen boughs of the orchard, that bore only snow and icicles in the stead of the bloom and fruit they had known.

Cross-questioning, threats, all the devices of suggestion, availed naught. The terrible story once told, 'Gustus Tom found the pluck somehow to stand by it without other support than the uncognizant affection of sister Eudory; for the shallow Sophy cared for none of it. She came to the door once to lead the old man within from the piercing wind, and she lingered for a moment, her golden hair flying in the blast; her placid blue eyes and superficial smile underwent no change when the old woman turned away, baffled and hopeless and stricken.

"I 'lowed my son war dead," she said to the cluster of gossips who had assisted at the colloquy. She shook her head as she leaned upon her stick, and hobbled down across the frozen ruts of the road toward the wagon. "I 'lowed my son war dead, an' I mourned him. But I said the words of a fool, for he war alive; the best part of him, his good name, war lef' ter me. An' now he air beset, an' druv, an' run down ter death, — fur ye air a-murderin' of him in takin' his good name. Lemme know, neighbors," — she turned, with her hand upon the wheel, — "when the deed air fairly done, so ez I kin gin myself ter mournin' my son, fur then he'll be plumb dead."

The two dark-browed brothers said never a word; the slow oxen started; the wagon moved creaking down the road toward the snowy mountains, with their whitened slopes and black trees, and gray shadows.

The public sentiment excited in favor of Mink Lorey by the developments during his trial, and which had expressed itself in the riot and attempt at a rescue, had sustained a rebuff consequent upon his assault on Judge Gwinnan. Nevertheless, it is difficult to nullify a popular prepossession, and the discovery that the young mountaineer had been the victim of the machinations of the true criminal, that he had been placed in jeopardy, had suffered many months' imprisonment, had still longer duress in prospect, served to justify him in some sort, and reinstated him in the feelings of the people, never very logical. All the details of the trial were canvassed anew with reviviscent interest. Now that the veil of mystery was torn from it, there seemed still other inculpations involved. It would appear to imply some gross negligence, some intentional spite, some grotesque perversion of justice, that the criminal should have been one of the jury impaneled to try an innocent man. The fact itself was shocking. It was significant that only through accident had it come to light, and it augured grievous insecurity of liberty, life and property.

Mr. Harshaw, who had returned to Shaftesville upon the adjournment, for a few days, of the Legislature, was not slow to note the direction and progress of popular favor. In the state of his feelings toward Gwinnan, he had no great impulse to combat the position taken by the unlearned that it was a grave dereliction on the part of the court that Pete Rood had been admitted to the panel. Why should he expound the theory of judicial challenges, the conclusiveness of the *voir dire*, in instances of general eligibility? He truly believed that in the incarceration of the jury Gwinnan had sacrificed the interests of the defense and a favorable verdict, and as he felt much reminiscent interest in the details of his cases, he could listen with all the relish of mental affirmation to the denunciations of the stranger judge, who was often profanely apostrophized and warned to show his head no more in Cherokee County.

"Somebody besides Mink Lorey 'll try ter beat some sense inter it, ef he do," said Bylor. The bitterness of the affront offered to the jury by their imprisonment had grown more poignant as time went on, for while the general excitement had gradually subsided, the fact remained. Not one of the unlucky panel, venturing from time to time into town with peltry, or game, or produce for sale, could escape the gibes and laughter of retrospective ridicule. The dignity of the interests involved had ceased to be a shield to them. Even the acrimony excited by their failure to agree had yielded to light sarcasm and jocose scorn, — not ill-natured, perhaps, but sufficiently nettling to proud and sensitive men whom accident had succeeded in immuring behind the bars. Everywhere the subject lurked in ambuscade, — in the stores, at the tavern, on the streets. The jailer was the most hospitable man alive. "When 'll ye kem an' take pot-luck agin, gentlemen?" he would hail them in chance encounters. "My door air easy ter open — *from the outside.*" Or he would call out, with a roguish twinkle in his brown eyes. "How's 'rithmetic up in the cove?" in allusion to the unlucky thirteen on the panel. It seemed to them that humiliation was their portion, and the festive and gala occasion known as "goin' ter town," which had hitherto been so replete with excitement and interest, and was in the nature of a tour and a recompense of toil, had resolved itself into a series of mortifications.

Harshaw's law-office proved in some sort a refuge to the coterie, as it had always been more or less a resort. It had some of the functions of a club-house, and its frequenters felt hardly less at home than its proprietor. He was a man difficult to be taken amiss by his country friends. He had a sonorous, hearty greeting for whoever came. If he were at work, half a dozen sprawling fellows talking about his fireside were no hindrance to the flow of his thought, the scratch of his pen, or the chase of some elusive bit of legal game through the pages of a law-book. More often he bore a part in the conversation. The bare floor defied the red clay mire that came in with the heavy boots; the broken bricks in the hearth were not more unsightly in his eyes for the stains of tobacco juice. The high mantelpiece was ornamented by a box of tobacco, a can of kerosene, and an untrimmed lamp that asserted its presence in unctuous odors. There were some of the heavy books of his profession in a case, and many more lying in piles on the floor, near the walls, defenseless against the borrower. There was a window on one side of the office, and another opening upon the street. At this a face was often applied, with a pair of hands held above the eyes to shut out the light, that the passer-by might scan the interior, perchance to see if some one sought were within; perchance merely to regale an idle curiosity. The unique proceeding occasioned no comment and gave no offense. An open door showed an inner apartment, where consultations were held when too important for the ear of the indiscriminate groups in the main office, and where there was a lounge, on which he slept during court week, or when political business was too brisk to admit of his driving out to his home on his farm, some miles from the town.

"Well," said Harshaw, tilting his chair back upon its hind legs until it creaked and quaked with the weight, and clasping both hands behind his yellow head, "I wonder you ain't willing for Gwinnan to be a fool, considering what Mink got for beating his skull into a different shape."

The county boasted no weekly newspaper, and without it the news was a laggard. Ben Doaks looked up with interest; Bylor paused expectant. Jerry Price, too, was present, for there was an unusual number from the coves in town — this was county court week, and the crowd assembled offered special facilities for trading stock and small commodities.

The hickory logs crackled on the hearth above the gleaming coals, and the white and yellow flames were broadly flaring; great beds of gray ashes lay beneath, for they were seldom removed; the murmurous monotone of the fire filled the pause.

"Yes, sir," said Harshaw, taking his pipe from his lips and knocking the ashes from the bowl, "Mink got a sentence for twenty years in the penitentiary for assault with intent to commit murder."

There was dead silence. The clay pipe that Jerry Price was smoking fell from his hands unheeded, and broke into fragments on the hearth. This knowledge affected the group more than the news of Mink's death might have done. That at least was uncertain. The mind flags and fails to follow in the journey to the unknown the spirit that has quitted the familiar flesh, — the entity for which it has merely a name, an impression, an illusion of acquaintance. But this sordid, definite fact, this measure of desolation bounded by four walls, this hopeless rage, this mental revulsion from ignominy, all were of mortal experience and easily imagined.

"Yes, sir," resumed Harshaw. his florid face grave but firm. He had the air of a man whose feelings have been schooled to calmness, but who protests against a fact. "I did what I could for Mink. I could n't defend him myself, — could n't leave the interests of my constituents in the House for the sake of an individual; but I put the case in Jerome Maupert's hands. Maupert could n't help it. Mink was locking the door of the state prison and double-locking it every time he lifted his hand to strike Gwinnan. A *judge*, you know," — he rolled his eyes significantly at the group, — " a judge is a mighty big man, and Mink is just a poor mountain boy."

He stuck his pipe into his mouth again, and vigorously puffed it into a glow.

" The crowd in court cheered when the jury gave their verdict," he said.

The group looked at each other with quick, offended glances; then lapsed into gazing at the fire and contemplating the circumstances.

" 'Pears like ez nobody kin git even with Gwinnan right handy," said Bylor. " Ef 't war n't fur makin' bad wuss fur Mink, I 'd wisht ez he hed killed him."

" Shucks ! " said Harshaw scornfully. " Gwinnan thinks he 's mighty popular with the people. He 's always doing the humbugging and bamboozling dodge. Just before I left Glaston the attorney-general — Kenbigh, you know — showed me a letter from Judge Gwinnan asking him to take no notice of Mink's assault, as he was n't willing to prosecute."

He brought his chair down with a thump on its forelegs, and looked about the circle, his roseate plump face full of bantering sarcasm.

"What war his notion fur that?" demanded Doaks, slowly possessing himself of the facts.

"To impose on the people — so good — so lenient" —

"Mighty lenient, sure!" interpolated Bylor. He rubbed his wrist mechanically; he never was quite sure that he had not been shackled.

"Letter dated just about two weeks after Mink was sentenced," Harshaw sneered.

"Waal, who war the prosecutor, then?" demanded Jerry Price, at a loss.

"Why, of course they did n't wait for a prosecutor. Mink was tried on a presentment by the grand jury; and as the criminal court came on right straight, Kenbigh just hurried him through. He's a regular blood-hound, Kenbigh is."

There was a silence for a few moments. Several of the sticks of wood had burned in two and fallen apart, and were sending up dull columns of smoke, some of which puffed into the room, — an old trick of the chimney's, if the testimony of the blackened ceiling be admitted.

"As if," cried Harshaw, suddenly uncrossing and crossing his legs, reversing their position, "Gwinnan, of all the men in the world, would n't know and think of that! But Kenbigh seemed to take it *all* in, — seemed to think 't was Gwinnan's modesty. He showed me the answer he wrote to the judge." Harshaw cast up his eyes meditatively to the ceiling, as if seeking to recall the words. "He begged to express his admiration of Judge Gwinnan's modesty in thinking that so serious an injury to one of the most brilliant ornaments of the State judiciary could fail to be summarily punished, or would need his personal interposition as prosecutor."

They all listened with an absent air, as if the refusal to hear the compliments nullified them.

Harshaw gave a short, satirical laugh, showing his strong white teeth.

"I wisht ter Gawd that thar Gwinnan wanted ter go ter Congress, or sech, ez would fling him 'fore the vote o' Cher'kee County, — it be in the same congressional deestric' whar he hails from, — I'd show him," said Bylor, shaking his head with the savagery of supposititious revenge, and in the full delusion of unbridled power characteristic of the free and independent American unit. "*I'd* show him."

"I reckon everybody don't feel like we-uns do," said Jerry Price, who, although he smarted under the unmerited disgrace he had experienced at the hands of Gwinnan, had submitted to it as a judicial necessity. Its rankling pangs were manifested only when, chancing to meet the foreman, Jerry would ask, in a manner charged with interest and an affectation of mystery, whether he had had his tongue measured yet, and how many joints it had been ascertained to have.

"They're a little more disgruntled over in Kildeer than you are here," Harshaw declared. "You'd allow the court-room was a distric' school, if you could know the way he domineers over there. I always look to see the learned counsel put his finger in his mouth and whine when Gwinnan gets on the rampage."

"Why, look-a-hyar, Mr. Harshaw," demanded Bylor, "do you-uns call this a free country? Ain't thar no way o' stoppin' him off? Goin' ter hev five mo' years o' him on the bench?"

"He'll be impeached some day, mark my words," Harshaw declared; and then he fell to eying the smoking fire with slow, sullen, vengeful speculation, and for the rest of the day he was not such jovial company as his general repute for good-fellowship might promise.

In this interval of leisure which the recess afforded him, both as legislator and lawyer, Harshaw devoted himself to furthering his political prospects and strengthening his hold upon the predilections of the people. He was a man of many mental and moral phases: he sang loud and long at the revival at the cross-roads church; he attended rural merry-makings; he connived at having his own house "stormed" by a surprise party, the preparations being profuse and exhilarating, and the flavor of his hospitality was not impaired by his shaking hands with his guests, and violently promising to vote for them at the next election, each enlightened and independent citizen being himself not quite clear as to who was the prospective candidate: but the whole episode faded from recollection with the evening, mingling with the vain phantasmagoria of wild elation, and subsequent drowsiness, and retributive headache, and physical repentance. He went on a camp hunt with a party of roaring blades. The weather in the changeful Southern winter had turned singularly fine and dry; the air had all the crisp buoyancy of autumn and all the freshness of spring; fires drowsed on hearths; doors stood ajar; the sunshine was pervasive, warm, languorous, imbued with pensive vernal illusions. One might wonder to see the silent sere grass; were there indeed no whirring songs, no skittering points of light, hovering in mazy tangles, and telling the joy that existence might prove to the tiniest insect life? Birds? The trees were empty, but one must look to make sure: only the rising quail from the clumps of withered weeds; only the infrequent cry of the wild turkey down the bare, sunny vistas of the woods. The shadows of the deciduous trees were spare and linear, distinctly traced on the brown ground or upon the gray rock. In these fine curves and strokes of dendritic scripture a graceful sylvan idyl might perchance be deciphered by the curious. But the dense masses of laurel and the darkling company of pines cloaked themselves in their encompassing gloom, in these bright days as ever, and in their shade the dank smell and the depressing chill attested the winter. Vague shimmers hung about the mountains, blue in the distance, garnet and brown and black close at hand. The terrible heights and unexplored depths, the vast, sheer, precipitous descents, the titanic cliffs, the breadth, the muscle, the tremendous velocity of the torrents hurling down the gorges, gave august impressions of space unknown to the redundant richness of the summer woods. There were vistas of incomparable amplitude, as still, with the somnolent sunshine and the sparse shadow, as if they were some luminous effect on a canvas, painted in dark and light browns, graduated through the tints of the sere leaf in ascendant transition to the pale gold of the sunbeams; affording, despite the paucity of detail, an ecstasy to the sense of color.

It was a moment of preëminent consequence to Harshaw one day, when far up a stately avenue a deer appeared with the suddenness of an illusion, yet giving so complete a realization of its presence that the very fullness and splendor of its surprised eyes left their impression. Then, as in some jugglery of the senses, the animal with consummate grace and lightness, vanished, bounding through the laurel.

The wind was adverse and the hounds did not readily catch the scent. A few tentative, melancholy yelps of uncertainty arose; then a deep, musical, bell-like bay, another, and the pack opened with a great swelling, oscillating cry, that the mountains echoed as with a thousand voices, and in a vast compass of tone. The mounted men, hallooing to one another, dashed off in different directions, making through the woods towards various "stands" which the deer might be expected to pass. Now and then the horn sounded to recall the stragglers, — inexpressibly stirring tones, launched from crag to crag, from height to height; far-away ravines repeated the summons with a fine and delicate mystery of resonance, rendered elusive and idealized, till one might believe that never yet did such sound waves float from the prosaic cow-horn of the mountaineer.

Harshaw's pursuits had not been those of a Nimrod, and although a good horseman and a fair marksman, he had found himself at a grievous disadvantage with others of the party who were mountaineers and crack shots. Stimulated by rivalry, they had achieved prodigies in instances of quickness of sight and unerring aim in unpropitious, almost impossible circumstances. They had already had some good sport, in which he had acquitted himself creditably enough; but his inexperience and ignorance of the topography of the country had given him some occasion to perceive that without more familiarity with the localities he could not fully enjoy a camp hunt. He was not surprised when, becoming involved in an almost impenetrable tangle of the laurel, he lost his companions, who got over the broken ground with an amazing swiftness, divination of direction, and quickness of resource. He drew rein upon emerging, and listened to the baying hounds: now loud, now faint and far away; now sharply yelping for the lost trail, and again lifting the exultant, bell-like cry of bated triumph. He despaired of rejoining his friends till the deer was lost or killed, and, remembering the pluck of the *personnel* of the diversion, of the deer, the hounds, and the mountaineers, he reflected that this result might not soon ensue.

The echoes infinitely confused the sounds, giving no reliable suggestion of the direction which the hunt was taking. He pushed on for a time — a long time, his watch told him — in the complete silence of the wintry woods. He began to experience a dull growing apprehensiveness. He had no faint approximative conjecture concerning the locality; there was no path, not even a herders' trail. He could himself establish no landmark by which he might be guided. There was a lavish repetitiousness in the scene: grand as it might be with scarred cliffs and sudden chasms and stupendous trees, it was presented anew with prolific magnificence forty yards further, and ride as he might he seemed to make no progress. As time passed, there recurred to his recollection instances — rare, it is true, but as uninviting to the imagination as infrequent — of men who have been lost in these fastnesses, trained woodsmen, herders, the familiars of the wild nature into whose penetralia even they had ventured too far. A handful of bleaching bones might tell the story, or perhaps the mysterious disappearance would be explained by much circling of birds of prey. Mr. Harshaw felt a sudden violent appreciation of the methods and interests and affluent attractiveness of the civilized world. He could not sufficiently condemn his folly in venturing out of its beaten track; in leaving, even for a space, the things he loved for the things he cared not for. The scene was inexpressibly repugnant to him; the woods closed him in so frowningly; his mind recoiled from the stern, Gorgon-like faces of the crags on every hand. The wintry sunlight was reddening; he could see only the zenith through the dense forest, and upon its limited section were interposed many interlacing outlines of the bare boughs; nevertheless, he was aware that the sky was clouding. The wind did not stir; the woods were appallingly still; there was no sound of horn or hounds; the chase had gone like a phantom hunt, — suddenly evoked, as suddenly disappearing.

XXIII.

As Harshaw paused to let his mare breathe, an abrupt sound smote his ear; he lifted his head to listen. It was the fitful clank of a cow-bell — and again; nearer than he had thought at first. He experienced infinite relief. The prosaic jangling had a welcome significance. It intimated the vicinity of some dwelling-place, for at this season the cattle are not at large in the withered pasturage of the mountain. He heard the bushes cracking at a little distance; he pressed his reluctant mare in that direction, through a briery tangle, over the trunks of fallen trees, pausing now and then to listen to the sound. Suddenly there was a great thwack; a thick human tongue stammered a curse. There was something strange and repellent and unnatural in the mouthing tones. The next moment he understood. The laurel gave way into the open aisles of the brown woods; a red suffusion of the sunset lingered among the dark boles on the high slopes, contending with, rather than illuminating, the lucent yellow tints on the dead leaves. A red cow shambled along at a clumsy run amidst the pervasive duskiness, that was rather felt than seen; and driving her with a long hickory sprout was a tall mountain boy, who turned his head at the sound of the hoofs behind him, showing under the bent and drooping brim of an old white hat a pale and flabby face, on which pitiless nature had fixed the stamp of denied intelligence. He gazed, with open mouth and starting eyes, at the horseman; then, regardless of Harshaw's friendly hail, he dropped his stick, and with a strange, unearthly howl he fled along the woodland ways like a frightened deer. He plunged into the laurel, and was out of sight in a moment.

Harshaw began to drive the cow along, hoping she

would take the familiar barn-yard way. He could hardly gauge his relief when, almost immediately, he saw before him a rail-fence; and yet he had an accession of irritation because of the folly, the futility, of the whole mishap. His consciousness was so schooled to the exactions of political life that he experienced a sort of grotesque shame as if the misadventure were already added to the capital of a political opponent expert in the art of ridicule.

No one was visible in the little clearing. Smoke, however, was curling briskly from the chimney of a log hut; there was a barn of poles hard by, evidently well filled. Harshaw hallooed, with no response save that his hearty voice roused the dogs; they came trooping from under the house and from out of it, sharply barking, although two or three, still drowsy, paused to stretch themselves to a surprising length and to yawn with a vast dental display. The cow went in by the way, doubtless, that she had come out, stepping over the fence, where a number of rails had been thrown off. Harshaw, thinking it as well to encounter the dogs within the inclosure as without, followed her example, the mare resisting slightly, and stumbling over those of the rails that lay upon the ground. He saw that his approach had occasioned a commotion within the house; there was a vague flutter of skirts elusively appearing and disappearing. Across the doorway, low down, were nailed wooden slats, doubtless to restrain the excursiveness of a small child, who suddenly thrust his head over them, and was instantly snatched back by some invisible hand.

Nevertheless, the inhabitants were presently induced to hold a parley, perhaps because of Harshaw's manifest determination to force an entrance, despite the dogs that leaped and yelped about his stirrup irons, their vocal efforts more shrilly keyed as his whip descended among them; for although he held his revolver cocked, he was too shrewd a politician to present its muzzle to a mountaineer's dog save in the direst emergency. A woman suddenly appeared at the door. She looked at him with so keen and doubtful a gaze, with a gravity so forbidding, a silence so significant, that, accustomed as he was to the hospitable greeting and smile of welcome that graces the threshold of every home of the region, however humble, he lost for the moment his ready assurance. When he told her of his plight, she received the statement with the chilling silence of incredulity. Nevertheless, upon his request for shelter for the night and a guide the next morning, she did not refuse, as he had feared, but told him in a spiritless way to "'light and hitch," and that the boy would look after his horse. He strode up to the house, the dogs, suddenly all very friendly, at his heels, and stepped over the barricade that restrained the adventurous juvenile who was now hanging upon it, looking with eager interest at the world of the door-yard, which was a very wide world to him. He followed Harshaw to his seat by the fire, eying with great persistence his boots and his spurs. The latter exerted upon him special fascinations, and he presently stooped down and applied a small inquisitive finger to the rowel. The interior was not unlike the other homes of the region, — two high beds, a ladder ascending to a chamber in the roof, a rude table, a spinning-wheel, at which a gaunt, half-grown girl was working as industriously as if oblivious of the stranger's presence. The woman sat with her arms folded, her eyes on the fire, pondering deeply. A young man came to the back door, glanced in, and turned away.

When the woman fixed her grave, wide, prominent eyes upon Harshaw, there was something in their expression so unnerving that his refuge seemed hardly more comfortable than the savage wilderness without. But he said bluffly to himself that he had not stumped Kildeer and Cherokee for nothing; he rallied his traditions as a politician. Surely, he reflected, he who could so beguile other men's adherents to vote for him could win his way to a simple woman's friendship, if he tried.

He looked at the child and smiled, and said that the boy was "mighty peart." He dropped into the vernacular as a conscious concession to the habits of the "plain people."

The woman's fierce face was transfigured. "That's a true word, stranger," she said, beamingly. "An' Philetus ain't three year old yit, air he, Sereny?"

The girl in an abrupt, piping way confirmed the marvel, and Harshaw looked again at Philetus, who had no sort of hesitancy in seeking to take off the spurs and convert them to his own use.

His mother went on: "Philetus, though, ain't nigh so pretty ez three others I hed ez died. Yes, sir, we-uns lived up higher than this, on a mounting over yander thar."

"You haven't been living here long?" said Harshaw, merely by way of making talk.

The woman instantly resumed her stony, impassive manner. "'T ain't long nor short by some folkses' medjure," she said equivocally. She looked watchfully at him from time to time. An old gray cat that sat on the warm stones in the corner of the hearth, purring, and feigning to lift now one of her forepaws and then the other, eyed him with a round, yellow, somnolent stare, as if she too had a charge to keep him under surveillance. She got up suddenly, arching her back, to affectionately rub against the great booted feet of the idiot, who came and leaned on the chimney and gazed solemnly at the stranger. He was overgrown and overfat, and had a big, puffy, important face and a cavalier, arrogant manner.

"Don' wanter," he said, in his thick, mouthing utterance, as the woman, once more seeming flustered and anxious, told him to take the basket and go out to the wood pile and fill it with chips.

The whir of the spinning-wheel was suddenly silent, and the girl, who officiated as a sort of echo of her mother's words, a reflection of her actions, came and emptied the basket of the few bits of bark within it, and handed it to him.

"G' way, Sereny," he said good-naturedly, but declining the duty.

The unfathomable dispensation of idiocy, its irreconcilability with mundane theories of divine justice or mercy, its presentment at once repellent and grotesque, has its morbid effect when confronted with sanity. Harshaw was a man neither of delicate instincts nor of any subtle endowment, but the contemplation of the great vacant face grimacing at him, coupled with the singular influences of his reception, required a recollection of the anguished anxiety he had experienced, the sound of the rising wind without, the sight of the whirling dead leaves, the gathering gloom of the cloudy dusk, to reconcile him to the conditions of his refuge.

"Well, my man," he said, looking at the boy, "what's *your* name?"

The idiot grinned importantly. "Tad," he stuttered thickly, — "Tad Simpkins. What's yourn?"

Harshaw sat for a moment in stunned surprise. Then all the discomforts of the situation vanished before the triumphs of this discovery. This — this great, well-fed, hearty creature, the forlorn, maltreated idiot depicted by the evidence in Mink Lorey's trial; this, the pitiable boy drowned in the mill like a rat in a trap; this, the elusive spectre of the attorney-general's science! The next moment it occurred to him that he must use special caution here; the motives that had led these people to harbor the idiot, if not to conceal him, were suspicious, and favored his theory in the trial — which he had adopted more from the poverty of his resources than a full credulity — that the retirement of the boy reputed drowned was prompted by a deep-seated enmity to Mink Lorey.

He turned to the woman, all his normal faculties on the alert.

"Well, that's a fact, Mrs. Simpkins; your son ain't plumb bright, — I can see that, — but he's right there. I ought to tell you *my* name."

"Mine ain't Simpkins," said the woman suddenly, responding quickly to his clever touch, "an' Tad thar ain't my son." She was mixing corn-meal batter for

bread in a wooden bowl; she stirred it energetically as
she went on with a sort of partisan acrimony: "Mebbe
he ain't bright, ez ye call it, but I ain't never hearn o'
Tad doin' a mean thing yit,—not ter the chill'n, nor
dogs, nor cats, nor nuthin'. He may be lackin' in the
head, but he ain't lackin' in the heart; thar's whar's
the complaint o' mos' folks ez ain't idjits. I dunno
which air held gifted in the sight o' the Lord. 'T ain't
in human wisdom ter say. Tad 'll make a better show
at the jedgmint day 'n many folks ez 'low they hev hed
thar senses through life."

"Ain't no idjit, nuther," protested Tad, gruffly.

"Well, my name's Harshaw — Bob Harshaw." The
guest leaned forward, with his elbows on his knees, looking steadily at her as he talked. She held her head on
one side, listening eagerly, almost laboriously, sedulous
that she should lose no point, showing how sharp had
been her desire for him to give an account of himself.
As he noticed this, he was more than ever sure that the
household had some cause to fear the law. His vanity
received a slight shock in the self-evident fact that she
had never before heard of him. "I 'm a lawyer from
Shaftesville. I defended Mink Lorey when he was
tried for drowning that chap."

"Flung me in the water!" exclaimed Tad parenthet-
ically.

"I hearn 'bout that," said the woman. She had knelt
on the broad hearth-stone, depositing the bowl beside
her while she made up the pones in her hands, tossing
them from one palm to the other, then placing them
upon the hoe which smoked upon the hot live coals
drawn out from the bed of the fire. "I war glad the
rescuers tuk him out," she continued, "fur Tad ain't
drownded."

"The rescuers did n't take him out," said Harshaw,
sharply.

The woman looked up, surprised; her hand shook a
little with the bread in it; she was evidently capable of
appreciating the weight of responsibility.

"Why, Lethe Sayles told me so," she said.

"Lethe Sayles!" he exclaimed, perplexed. Her name instantly recalled Gwinnan — incongruous association of ideas! — and Mink's persuasion of Gwinnan's enmity toward him for her sake. Had she known the judge before? he wondered. Had Mink some foundation for his jealousy beyond the disasters of the trial? Somehow, this false representation to the people who knew that the lad was not drowned had, he thought, an undeveloped significance in view of that fact. Harshaw resolved that there should be no question of the substantiality of Tad's apparition when the case should come up to be tried anew. He forgot himself for the moment. "I'll produce you in open court, my fine fellow," he said, swaggering to his feet and striking the boy on his fat shoulder. "That's what I'm bound for!"

He had naught in mind save the details of his case. He regarded the incident only as the symmetrical justification of his conduct of the evidence and his evolution of the theory of the crime. He did not pause to reflect on its slight and ineffective value to Mink himself, to whom an acquittal could only mean that a few years were not to be added to the long term of imprisonment which already impended for him. He did not even notice that the woman rose suddenly from her knees, went toward the door, and beckoned in the burly young fellow who had appeared on the porch at intervals, covertly surveying the scene within.

"Naw, sir," she exclaimed, with an agitated, accelerated method of speech and a fierce eye, "ye won't! Ye ain't a-goin' ter kem in hyar an' spy us out an' perduce us in court, fur yer profit an' our destruction." Harshaw turned and gazed at her, with a flushing, indignant face. The young man had his rifle in his hand; she herself was taking down a gun which lay in a rack above the fireplace. "Ye war n't axed ter kem in hyar, but it be our say-so ez ter when ye go out."

The surprise of it overpowered him for a moment; he stood blankly staring at them. The next, he realized that his pistols were in the holster with his saddle, and his gun that he had placed beside the door had been removed. He was not, however, deficient in physical courage.

"Take care how you attempt to detain me!" he blustered.

She laughed in return, shrilly, mirthlessly; as he looked at her he was sure that she would not hesitate to draw the trigger that her long, lean fingers, bedaubed with the corn-meal batter, already touched..

The idiot put his hands before his eyes, with a hoarse, wheezing moan of horror and remonstrance. The girl looked on with the tranquillity of sanity.

Harshaw could rely only on the superiority of his own intellectual endowments.

"Why, look here, madam," he said bluffly, rallying his wits, "what do you want of me, — to stay here? I have got no notion of going, I assure you; not till daybreak, anyhow."

He flung himself into his chair, and looked up at her with an exasperating composure, as if relegating to her all the jeopardy of the initiative and the prerogatives of action.

She quailed before this unexpected submission. She could have had no doubts as to her course had he shown fight; the tall and subsidiary young man also wore an air of sheepish defeat. Harshaw stifled his questions; he gave no sign of the anger that seethed within him. the haunting fear that would not down. He stretched out his booted legs to the warm fire, feeling in the very capacity of motion, in the endowment of sensation, a relief, an appreciated value in sheer life which is the common sequence of escape, and remembering that by this time, but for his quick expedient, he might be in case to never move again. He thrust his broad hat far back on his yellow head, put his hands into his pockets, and looked in his confident fashion about his surroundings, while the woman lowered her weapon, and presently went mechanically about her preparations for sup-

per, evidently attended by some lurking regret for her
precipitancy. She looked askance at him now and then,
and after a time ventured upon a question.

"Ye say yer name be Harshaw?" she asked.

"I said so," Harshaw replied. So alert were her
suspicions that she fancied significance in the simple
phrase. She exchanged a quick glance with the young
man, who appeared at once lowering and beset with
doubt.

Even Tad apprehended the meaning in the look.

"Ye know my name, 'pears like, better 'n yourn," he
grinned, with a guttural, foolish laugh.

As the boy spoke Harshaw was impressed anew with
the change in his fate; the creature of cuffs and curses,
who had been the very derision of perverse circumstances, was a marvelous contrast to the well-fed, fat,
kindly-tended lad who leered good-humoredly from
where he lounged against the great chimney. Yet despite this attestation of benignant impulses harbored
here, there was the rifle, which had had such importunate concern for his attention, standing ready at the
woman's right hand.

"Well, madam," said the politician, "I have been
about right smart in the mountains, and I have partaken
of the cheer around many a hearth-stone, but this is the
first time I have ever been invited to look down the
muzzle of a rifle."

She winced visibly at this reflection upon her hospitality, as she knelt on the hearth, slipping the knife under the baking pones on the hoe, and turning them
with a dexterous flip.

"I wouldn't have believed it," continued Harshaw.
"I have never heard of anybody but law-breakers giving
themselves to such practices, — moonshiners and the
like."

The woman suddenly lifted her face, her dismayed
jaw falling at the significant word. Harshaw could have
laughed aloud. The simple little riddle was guessed.
And yet the situation was all the graver for him. There

was a step outside; the door opened for only a narrow space; darkness had fallen; the room was illumined by the flaring flames darting up the chimney; he knew that he was scrutinized sharply from without, and now and then he heard the sound of voices in low conference.

It was well, doubtless, that the secret petitions he preferred to the powers of the earth and the air for the utter confusion and the eternal destruction of the mountain hunters who had made so slight and ineffective a search for him — or perhaps none at all — could not be realized, or his misfortune might have engendered far-reaching and divergent calamity, disproportionate in all eyes save his own.

He knew now that he had stumbled upon a gang of moonshiners, and had been taken for a revenue spy, or a straggler from a raiding party. How to escape with this impression paramount, or indeed how to escape at all, was a question that bristled with portentous dubitation. He was content to pretermit it in the guarded watchfulness that absorbed his every faculty, as one by one the men strode in to the number of four or five, each casting upon him a keen look, supplementing the survey through the door.

One of them he suddenly recognized. "I have seen you before," he said, with a jolly intonation. "This is Sam Marvin, ain't it?"

The owner of the name was discomfited when confronted with it, and seeing this, Harshaw was sorry that he had, with the politician's instinct, made a point of remembering it.

He could with difficulty eat, despite the fatigues of the day, but he sat down among them with a hearty show of appetite and with his wonted bluff manner. His sharpened attention took cognizance of many details which under ordinary circumstances he would not have noticed. He could have sworn to every one of the rough faces — and right welcome would have been the opportunity — grouped about the table. The men ate in a business-like, capacious fashion, especially one lean, lank fellow, with unkempt black hair and a thin face, the chin decorated with what is known as a goatee. Notwithstanding their roughness they were not altogether unkind. Philetus could not complain of disregarded pleas as he begged from chair to chair, under the firm impression that there was something choice in the *menu* not included in the contents of the pan placed for him on a bench, which should serve as table, while he was to be seated on an inverted noggin. And the dogs spent the time of the family meal alternately in a petrified expectancy and sudden elastic bounds to catch the bits flung liberally over the shoulders.

When the repast, conducted chiefly in silence, was concluded, the group reassembled about the hearthstone, the pipes were lighted, and conversation again became practicable. It required some strong control of his faculties to bear himself as an honored guest instead of a suspected informer, trapped, but Harshaw managed to support much of his wonted manner as he lighted a pipe that he had in his pocket and pulled it into a strong glow. Nevertheless, he was beset with a realization of how easy it would be for them to rid themselves of him without a possibility that his fate would excite suspicion. As he looked into the flaming coals of the fire, his quickened imagination could picture a man lying lifeless at the foot of a great wall of rocks, — lying motionless where he had fallen, but with an averted face, — and another vista in which his horse, with an empty saddle, with pistols in the holster, cropped the grass on a slope. He thought of it often afterward, — the man lying lifeless beneath the crags, with a face he did not see! This was the doom that persistently forced itself upon him as most obviously, most insistently, his; naught else could so readily release these desperadoes from the peril that threatened them. He began to remember various stories of Marvin's old encounters with the "revenuers:" on one occasion shots had been exchanged; one or more of the posse had been killed; he could not remember accurately, but he thought this was accredited to Jeb

Peake, — "hongry Jeb," who could, according to the popular account of him, "chaw up five men of his weight at a mouthful an' beg for more." They had much at stake; perhaps, as they looked into the fire with that slow, ruminative gaze, they also saw a picture, — a halter wavering in the wind. The room alternately flared and faded as the flames rose and fell. It bore traces of renovation: the door was new, the floor patched. He made a rough guess that Marvin had taken possession of one of the long-deserted huts seen at intervals in the mountains. Raindrops presently pattered on the roof; then ceased, as if waiting breathlessly for some mandate; and again a fusillade; and anon torrents. The melancholy elements in the wild wastes without seemed not uncheerful companions in lieu of the saturnine group about the fire. Alack, for liberty, the familiar thing! Harshaw sought to reassure himself, noting their kindness to the idiot and to the little child. Philetus climbed over their feet, and made demands, of a frequency appalling to a mind less repetitious than the one encased in the downy yellow head, to be ridden on their great miry boots.

Suddenly Marvin spoke: "My wife 'lows ez how ye defended Mink Lorey when he war tried."

"I did," said Harshaw jauntily.

"Waal, did this hyar gal, — this Lethe Sayles, ez lives yander at the t'other eend o' the county, — did she up an' tell in court ennything 'bout me?"

Harshaw was not a truthful man for conscience' sake; but in the course of his practice he had had occasion to remark the inherent capacity of the truth for prevailing. He was far too acute to prevaricate.

"Yes," he said, sticking two fingers into his vest-pocket and swinging the leg he had crossed over the other, "she swore that you were moonshining and told her so; she had told me as much before. We wanted to prove that Mink was drunk, and had somewhere to get whiskey besides the bonded still. We couldn't get in all the evidence, though."

The fire snapped and sparkled and flared. The pendent sponge-like masses of soot clinging to the chimney continually wavered in the strong current of air; now and then fire was communicated to it, and a dull emblazonment of sparks would trace some mysterious characters, dying out when half realized.

Harshaw could but see that his frankness had produced its impression: there was a troublous cast in all the stolid countenances around the hearth; but he was glad to be regarded as a problem as well as a danger.

"In the name o' Gawd," exclaimed Marvin irritably, "why did ye kem hyar ter this hyar place fur? Ain't Shaftesville big enough ter hold ye?"

Harshaw repeated the account of himself which he had already given to Mrs. Marvin. "I ain't ready to go yet," he remarked. "But when your wife thought I wanted to, by George, she got down the gun and said I should n't."

"Ye know too much," suddenly put in "hongry Jeb," who looked as cadaverous and as melancholy as his name might imply.

"I know enough to shut my mouth," said Harshaw bluffly, "and keep it shut."

He looked eagerly at "hongry Jeb," as he threw this out tentatively.

The mountaineer's face was distinct in the firelight, and he gazed at the leaping flames instead of at the speaker.

"I ain't able ter afford ter resk it," said "hongry Jeb." He made a sudden pass across his jugular toward his left ear, exclaiming "Tchisk!"—the whites of his eyes and the double row of his shining teeth showing as he smiled horribly on Harshaw.

The lawyer turned sick. How could he hope that these moonshiners would jeopardize aught for his sake? He could trust only to himself.

There was some drinking as the evening wore on; the monotony of this proceeding was beguiled by the fact that one of the dogs took a drop occasionally, at the instance of the youngest of the moonshiners — a mere boy of twenty — and Marvin's son Mose. It was desired that he should extend his fitness as a boon companion by the use of a pipe, but he revolted at fire and distrusted smoke, and displayed much power of shrillness when snatched by the ears and cuffed. He was finally kicked out, to crawl wheezingly under the house, debarred from the hearth-stone which unaccomplished dogs who were not even bibulous, much less smokers, were privileged to enjoy.

But the evening was not convivial. The moonshiners brooded silently as they drank and smoked. Among them, unmolested, Tad sat. He had never been so happy as now, poor fellow. He goggled about and laughed to himself till he fell asleep, his grotesque head dropping to one side, his mouth open, snoring prosperously.

Marvin glanced at him presently. Then he looked at Harshaw, showing his long tobacco-stained teeth as he laughed. "I hearn ye hev all been in a mighty tucker ter know what hed kem o' Tad, down yander in the flat-woods," he said. He sat in a slouching posture as he smoked, his legs crossed, his shoulders bent, his head thrust forward. "Lethe Sayles tole me 'bout'n it."

"Old Griff has nearly lost his mind about Tad," said Harshaw.

"What?" demanded Marvin, with an affectation of deep surprise. "Can't he find nuthin' else ter cuss an' beat?"

"Pore — old — man!" exclaimed "hongry Jeb," wagging his black head, and showing the gleaming whites of his eyes in his characteristic sidelong glance.

"Well, I expect Tad has been a good deal better off along of you," Harshaw admitted. "But that don't make it right for you to have kidnapped him."

"Lord knows, we-uns did n't want him," said Marvin. "We-uns ain't gifted in goadin' sech a critter ez him, like old man Griff. We can't git work enough out'n him ter wuth the stealin'. He jes' kem up ter whar we-uns lived, one night. I reckon 't war several nights arter he war flung in the water. He looked mighty peaked."

"An' I never see a critter so hongry," put in the pullet boldly from her seat in the chimney corner, her long yellow feet dangling beneath her short homespun skirt, her hair, which was luxuriant, gathered in a sort of topknot on her head, "'thout 't war Jeb thar." She gave a cackling laugh of elation at this thrust, as she knitted off her needle in a manner that might make one wonder to see a pullet so deft.

Jeb good-naturedly grinned, and Marvin went on: —

"We reckoned he war a spy for the revenuers, 'kase they 'lowed we would n't suspect sech ez him, sent ter find out edzac'ly whar the place be, an' we war 'feared ter let him go back."

Harshaw winced.

"So we jes' kerried him off along o' we-uns. Mebbe 't war n't right, but folkses sech ez we-uns air can't be choosers."

"Naw, sir; else we can't be folkses," said "hongry Jeb."

How could he grin, with that lean, ghastly countenance, whenever he contemplated his terrible jeopardy!

"Ef Tad hed been well keered fur at home I'd hev felt wuss, but 't would n't hev made no differ," said Marvin; "but I know'd I could do better by him 'n old Griff."

"Mink's in jail now to be tried again for drowning him," said Harshaw, surprised at his own boldness.

"Waal, stranger," said Marvin satirically, evidently going to make the best of it, "the court air gin over ter makin' mistakes, an' we pay taxes ter support a S'preme Court ter make some mo'. Man's human, arter all; he can't be trested ter turn from everything else, an' take arter the right an' jestice. He ain't like my gran'dad's dog, ez would always leave the scent of deer or b'ar an' trail Injun. That dog knowed what war expected of him, an' he done it. But man's human. Man's nuthin' but human."

"Ho! ho! ho!" laughed "hongry Jeb," in appreciative elation.

A pause ensued.

The sound of the rain on the roof was intermitted at intervals, and the wind lifted a desolate voice in the solitudes. The sense of the vast wilderness without, measureless, trackless, infinitely melancholy, preyed upon the consciousness. Perhaps Harshaw, in the quick transition from the artificial life of the world, was more susceptible to these influences, more easily abashed, confronted with the grave, austere, and august presence of Nature. He had a fleeting remembrance of life in the city: the gush of soft light; the mingled sound of music and the babbling of the fountain in the rotunda of the hotel; the Capitol building, seen sometimes through morning fogs and contending sunshine, isolated in the air above the roofs of the surrounding town, like a fine mirage, some turreted illusion; and again its white limestone walls ponderously imposed, every line definite, upon the deep blue midday sky.

That other sphere of his existence seemed for the moment more real to him; he had a reluctance as of awakening from a trance, as he gazed at the unkempt circle of mountaineers about the dying fire.

They were beginning to yawn heavily now. Marvin was laying the chunks together and covering them with ashes, to keep the coals till morning. Harshaw looked on meditatively. Once, as he lifted his eyes, he became aware that they were all covertly watching him with curiosity and speculation.

XXIV.

QUIET did not immediately ensue. After Harshaw had been ushered up the rickety ladder to the roof-room he heard voices below in low-toned conference. Occasionally he noted the peculiar chuckle of "hongry Jeb," suppressed even beneath its usual undertone; for it was a sort of susurrus of laughter, never absolutely vocal, — a series of snorts and pantings. It was not jocular at best, and now conveyed sinister suggestions to Harshaw, as he listened to the vague sound of words he could not distinguish. He had not been conscious of an effort of close observation during the evening, and he was surprised to discover how definitely he could differentiate the murmurs, the mere methods of speech, of the various members of the household. As they discussed his fate, he knew who urged measures, who was overpowered in argument, who doubted. Now and then a word or two in the woman's shrill voice broke from the huskiness of her whisper, for she was the most insistent of the group. He divined that her views were not mild, and he took hope from the intimations of opposition in the tones of the men as they gruffly counseled quiet. She it was, he felt sure, whom most he had to fear.

He had thrown himself, dressed as he was, on the sorry couch, which was made by placing two poles between the logs of the house, supported at the other end by a cross-bar laid in two crotched uprights on the floor. It was not a stable contrivance, nor, although it upheld a heavy feather bed, conducive to slumber, but Harshaw cared little for sleep.

The rain came through the leaks in the roof, now in an intermittent, sullen pattering, and now the drops falling in quick succession, tossed by the wind that whistled through the crevices, and piped a shrill refrain to the sonorous cadences trumpeted by the great chimney. Once, in a sudden flash of lightning, which was far distant and without thunder, he saw through gaps in the chinking, the white clouds pressing close to the house.

Again and again his courage would reassert itself, of its own sheer force, and he would experience a sort of affront that it had ever lapsed. He hardly knew how he could hereafter face that fact in his consciousness. Then, in arguing to reinstate his self-respect, he would review the dangers of his position,— and thus rouse anew the fears he had sought to still. He would wonder that he did not die of fright; that he made no effort to escape, to fire the house and force his way out in the confusion,— his fingers even fumbled the matches in his pocket; that he could lie still and listen to the sound of words impossible to distinguish; that he could turn, with the heavy gesture of one roused from sleep, when he heard a footfall on the rude stairs, and look yawning over his shoulder, and demand in a slumbrous voice, "Why in the hell do you make such a racket?"

A glimmer of light quivered on the brown rafters; it grew momently less flickering; it revealed the wretched apartment, the slanting floor, one or two pallets rolled up against the wall. And finally, as from a trap-door of a theatre, through the rude aperture in the floor, Jeb's gaunt black head appeared among the shadows which the tallow dip, that he carried in his hand, could not dispel.

He came in, and placed the sputtering light on a strut that supported one of the rafters, and was converted to shelf-like utility. Marvin followed, sitting down on the foot of Harshaw's bed. His face was more lowering than that of the other man; he leaned his hands ponderingly on his knees, his elbows turned outward, and bent his eyes on the floor in deep meditation.

There was a short silence.

"Hello?" said Harshaw interrogatively, raising himself on his elbow and boldly taking the initiative. "Anything the matter?"

Jeb sat down on a keg close to the chimney, and the perturbed hosts glanced at one another.

"Waal, stranger," said Marvin, "ye hev gone an' put us in a peck o' troubles, ter kem interruptin' us in this fur place, whar we hev been hunted an' hounded ter."

"Yes, sir," remarked "hongry Jeb," "same ez the varmint, ez be specially lef' out'n salvation by the Bible."

Marvin cast a glance over his shoulder at Harshaw. Then he continued, evidently striving to put the worst possible interpretation on the situation and to work himself into a rage: "We-uns air a-thinkin' ez ye mought be a spy fur the revenuers."

Harshaw let his head fall back on the pillow. His resonant, burly laugh rang out, jarring the rafters, and rousing in its hearty jocundity the reciprocity of a smile on "hongry Jeb's" cadaverous face. Even Marvin, casting another hasty look over his shoulder, was mollified.

"Ye 'd better be keerful how ye wake Philetus up, with his nap haffen out; ye 'll 'low ye air neighborin' a catamount," he admonished his guest.

"I tell you," said Harshaw, clasping his hands behind his yellow head as he lay at length, "you fellows live up here in these lonesome woods till your brains are addled. Why on earth would I, single-handed, mind you, a lawyer, a member of the legislature, with a good big farm of my own and half a dozen houses in town," (he had never before thought to brag of them,) "risk myself here, for the little reward I could get *if*—mighty big *if*, folks — if I could get away again?"

He lifted his eyes, with a bluff challenge of fair play.

"You know who *I* am. You 've seen me in Shaftesville. You know my farm down there in Kildeer County, on Owl Creek. Spy! Shucks! it makes me laugh. Do the quality often come spying for the revenuers in this neighborhood?"

Ten days ago he could not have believed that, however closely harried, his tongue would ever so forget its formula as thus to repudiate his alignment with the Plain People, and to claim to rank with "the quality."

Under other circumstances the two mountaineers might have resented this arrogation of superiority. They were, however, by virtue of their law-breaking, a trifle more worldly-wise than their stolid compatriots of the hills. It had been in some sort an education; had familiarized them with the springs of commercial action, the relations of producer and consumer, the value of money or its equivalent; had endowed them with an appreciation of emergency and an ingenuity in expedients and makeshifts; had forced upon their contemplation the operations of the law; and their great personal risk had superinduced care, thoughtfulness, and the exercise of a certain rude logic.

As they unconsciously sought to realize Harshaw's position in the world, resources, opportunity, their suspicion that he was a spy gradually waned.

There was a pause. The candle sputtered on the timber where it had been placed, the flame now rising apparently with an effort to touch a resinous knot in the wood just above it, and now crouching in a sudden gust from a crevice hard by. The rain came down with redoubled force for a few moments, then subsided again into its former steady, monotonous fall. Harshaw's senses, preternaturally keen now, detected an almost imperceptible stir on the ladder that ascended to the loft. He knew as well as if he had seen the coterie that Marvin's wife and the rest of the moonshiners were sitting on the rounds, listening and awaiting the announcement of his fate. Perhaps it was this which prompted his reply, when Marvin said pettishly, —

"It air all M'ria's fault. Ef she hed n't been so powerful quick ter git down the gun, ye'd hev never knowed nor axed whar ye war, nor s'picioned nuthin'."

"Yes, I would, though," Harshaw declared.

Marvin once more looked over his shoulder, and the lawyer quaked at the risk he ran.

"I saw Tad, you know, and I was figurin' round, big as all-out-of-doors, how I was going to produce him in court, and she thought I meant right off. Then, the minute I saw *you* I knew you, — and I had heard that girl say you were moonshining."

"Ai-yi! Sam Marvin!" cried a shrill feminine voice from the primitive stairway, "that's what ye got fur tryin' ter put the blame on me!"

Sam Marvin turned his bushy head toward the aperture in the floor. It might seem that Mrs. Marvin had left him nothing to say, but the versatility of the conjugal retort is well-nigh limitless, and he could doubtless have defended himself with an admirable valor had not Jeb "the hongry" interfered.

"Shet up, Sam," he said, looking positively famished in his lean anxiety. "We-uns hed n't thunk o' that. Mink Lorey hev got ter be tried agin."

It was all that Harshaw could do to restrain some expression of despair at this infelicitous turn given to the consultation, at which he seemed to assist to devise his own doom. He found a certain relief in shifting his position, and still, with his hands clasped under his head, briskly participated in the conversation.

"Yes," he assented in a debonair way which caused Marvin to look at him in lowering amazement, "I'm Mink's lawyer, but I could n't testify for him. I could n't swear of my own knowledge that this Tad is the same boy, for I never saw him before."

Both of the men lapsed into the attitude of laborious pondering. Now and then each looked at the other, as if to descry some intimation of the mutual effect.

Harshaw, with another bold effort to possess the situation, yawned widely and stretched his muscles.

"Oh — oh — oh — oh!" he exclaimed on a steadily descending scale. "Well, gentlemen," his features once more at rest, his voice normal, "I should be glad to continue our conversation to-morrow" — he waved his hand bluffly — "or next week. I ain't used to huntin', — that is, huntin' deer, — and I'm in and about knocked up. If you've got anything to say to me, say it now, or keep it till to-morrow."

The two looked doubtfully at each other.

"Mr. Harshaw," said Marvin, "we-uns air feared to let you-uns go."

"Go to sleep?" asked Harshaw jocosely.

Jeb grinned, weakly, however, and Marvin continued : —

"Ter go 'way at all."

"Well," said Harshaw, easily, with another demonstration of somnolence, "I'll stay just as long as you like; you're a clever lot of fellows, and I'll be contented enough, I'll be bound. Your sitting up all night is the only fault I've got to find with you."

They apparently submitted this answer from one to the other, and each silently canvassed it.

"Ye know too much," said "hongry Jeb."

"I'll know more if I stay. I'll find out whether you *are* moonshining now, sure enough, and where the still is."

"That's jes' what I hev been tellin' ye!" cried Mrs. Marvin's shrill voice from the ladder.

"Shet up, M'ria!" exclaimed Marvin, before "hongry Jeb" could interpose his pacifying "Shet up, Sam."

"Waal," resumed Marvin, in angry perturbation, "it's mighty ill-convenient, yer nosin' us out this way, up hyar, an' many a man fixed like me an' Jeb would fling ye off'n a bluff, ez ef ye hed fell thar, an' turn yer mare loose."

Once more Harshaw's rich, round laughter jarred the room.

"I'm in earnest," said Marvin, sternly. "That's what most men would do."

"Oh no, they wouldn't," said Harshaw, cavalierly.

"Why wouldn't they?" demanded Marvin, his curiosity aroused by this strange indifference.

"Because these fellows I was hunting with will be sure to find this place, and *they* would know I wouldn't go fall off a bluff of my own accord, after such a good

supper as I had here, and such a good bed. They
would n't know I was n't allowed to sleep in it, though,
on account of a long-jawed couple like you two."

He looked the picture of unconcern, — as if he had
not really credited their words.

"They could n't track ye hyar," argued Jeb; "ground
too dry in the evening fur yer critter's huffs to make
enny mark."

"Bless your bones!" cried Harshaw, contemptuously,
"I broke a path nigh a yard wide in the brush, and I
blazed every oak-tree I met with my hunting-knife, —
look and see how hacked it is, — and I cut my name on
the first beech I came across. Think I was going to
get lost in this wilderness without leaving any way for
my friends to find me? They know pretty well where
they left me. As soon as it's light enough they 'll be on
my track."

He lied seldom, but with startling effect. The verisimilitude of his invention, which had flashed upon him
at the last moment, carried conviction. The other two
men looked at each other in consternation.

This they thought was the secret of his ease of mind.
This was the reason that he was willing to abide with
them as long as they listed. These mysterious friends,
these lurking hunters, might materialize at any moment
when day should fairly dawn. The moonshiners asked
with eager curiosity the names of the party. Marvin
knew none of them, for it was a new region to him, and
his vocation restricted his social opportunities. He had
sprung up from the bed, and stood holding his ragged
beard with one hand, and gazing with perplexed eyes at
the recumbent lawyer. The frightful deed that he and
his confederates had contemplated, that had seemed their
only safe recourse, — to fling the intruder over a precipice, and to leave his mare grazing near, as if in his
search he had fallen, — had a predestined discovery
through the craft of the man who had marked the devious trail of his footsteps to their door. The moonshiner trembled, as he stood so near this pitfall into
which he had almost stumbled.

There had been a stir on the ladder; clumsy feet descended the rickety rungs. The movements below continued; there sounded the harsh scraping of a shovel on the rude stones of the hearth, and presently the newly kindled flames were crackling up the chimney; the flickering tallow dip was not so bright that the lines of light in the crevices of the flooring might not indicate how the room below was suddenly illumined. A smell of frying bacon presently pervaded the midnight.

"By Gosh!" cried Marvin, rousing himself from his brown study with a quick start, "air M'ria demented, ter set out a-cookin' o' breakfus' in the middle o' the night?"

He turned himself suddenly about, and started down the ladder. "Hongry Jeb," looking after him with a keen anxiety, rose abruptly, took the candle, and, holding it above his lean, cadaverous face, vanished by slow degrees through the trap-door, feeling with his feet for each round of the ladder before he trusted his weight upon it. Harshaw lifted himself upon his elbow, watching the gradual disappearance. His face was pink once more; the flesh that had seemed ten minutes since to hang flabbily upon it was firm and full; his opaque blue eyes were bright; the last feeble, ineffective rays of the vanishing candle showed his strong white teeth between his parted red lips, and his triumphant red tongue thrust out derisively.

Then he fell back on his pillow and tried to sleep. He felt, however, the pressure of the excitement; his pulses, his nerves, could not so readily accord with his calm mental conclusions, his logical inference of safety. The tension upon his alert senses was unrelaxed. The stir below-stairs made its incisive impression now, when he hardly cared to hear, as before, when he had strained every faculty to listen. He knew that it was Mrs. Marvin who had first devised the solution of the difficulty; she had already set about its execution while she advocated the measure, and insisted and argued with the men, who were disposed to canvass alternatives, and doubt, and wait. Often her shrill voice broke from the bated undertone in which they sought to conduct the conference, or she whispered huskily, with vibrant distinctness, hardly less intelligible.

"Ye an' Jeb take him," she urged. " Let the t'others go an' hide round 'bout the still. When the hunters git hyar they'll find me an' Mose an' the chillen, an' I'll tell 'em my old man be gone with Mr. Harshaw, a-guidin' him down the mounting. They'll never know ez thar be enny moonshinin' a-goin' on hyar-abouts, — nuthin' ter show fur it."

She clashed her pans and pots and kettles, in the energy of her discourse, and Harshaw lost the muttered objection.

" Ef ye don't," she persisted, in her sibilant whisper, — " ef ye kill him, fling him off'n the bluff or sech, — they'll find the body, sure ! "

A chill ran through the listener as he bent his ear.

" The buzzards or the wolves will fust, an' them men'll track him ter our door, an' track *ye* ter the spot."

The rain pelted on the roof; the flames roared up the chimney ; the frying meat sputtered and sizzled, and the coffee dissipated a beguiling promissory odor. One of the men — the lawyer thought it was " hongry Jeb " — suggested in a dolorous whisper that they could depend in no degree on Harshaw's promise of secrecy. No man regarded an enforced pledge as sacred.

" Them's all *old* offenses, ennyhows," argued the woman. " But this hyar, what ye men air a-layin' off ter do " —

" ' Ye *men* ' *!* " sneered her husband. " *Ye* war the bouncin'est one o' the whole lay-out fur doin' of it."

" But, Lord A'mighty," she protested, " who'd ever hev thunk o' sech a smart thing ez markin' his trail ter the very door ? He mus' be the devil. Smart enough, ennyways ! "

She clashed her pots and pans once more, and moved about heavily across the floor.

"I ain't misdoubtin' but what he *air* a big man whar he hails from, an' they sets store by him, an' they 'd be mighty apt ter stir round powerful arter him ef he was los'. An' this would be a new offense,—sure ter git fund out. An' Lord knows, we-uns hev been runned mighty nigh ter the jumpin'-off place from the face o' the yearth, an' I want ter be let ter set down, an' ketch my breath, an' see Philetus grow an' git hearty, an' let me hev a chance ter die in peace."

Once more Jeb's rumbling voice rose along the stairway.

"Shet up, Jeb!" she cried. "Ye hev jes' been a-settin' thar all the night a-shakin' yer head, an' a-lowin' ye wisht he hed done suthin' mean ter ye, so ez in gittin' rid o' him yer feelins would n't be hurt. Now yer feelins air safe, an' ye ain't got no mo' thankfulness 'n that thar cross-eyed, mangy hound fur the loan o' a pipe."

The mystery of cerebration; the strange, unmeasured force which works in uncomprehended methods to unforeseen results; the subtle process now formulating, and now erasing, an idea, like the characters of a palimpsest, was never so potently present to Harshaw as in contemplating the inspiration, the lucky thought, that had given him back to life, to hope, to sheer identity. He took himself to task, knowing that the obvious, the natural, the simple suggestion had lain all the evening in his mind, waiting the effective moment. He reproached himself that he should have suffered the agony of fright which he had endured. "I might have known," he argued within himself, in his bluff vanity, "that *I* 'd come out all right."

He fell asleep, presently, and when he was roused he rose with so genuine a reluctance that the last lurking doubt which Marvin and "hongry Jeb" had entertained vanished, as he went yawning down the ladder.

"I hate ter hev ter turn ye out'n my house 'fore day," Marvin remarked, "but ye know I 'm hunted like a b'ar, or suthin' wild, an' I can't be expected ter show manners like folks. Me an' Jeb air a-goin' ter take ye pretty fur off, so ez ye kin never find yer way back, an' by daylight ye'll be set in yer road. I'm hopin' yer friends won't git hyar; ef they does, I don't want 'em ter kem in, an' ef they hain't got no reason ter stop I reckon they'll go on. I'm powerful sorry ye kem along."

"Though ye be toler'ble good com'p'ny, an' we-uns ain't got nuthin' agin you-uns," remarked "hongry Jeb," politely.

"'Kase," continued Marvin, in a sing-song fashion, as he sat down at his table, on which the corn-dodgers and bacon smoked, "'kase we-uns air hunted an' driv by the law, — ez 'lows we sha'n't still our own corn ef we air a mind ter, — we hev been afeard ye'd tell 'bout'n we-uns an' whar we air hid."

"What for?" demanded Harshaw, with an incidental manner. He too was seated at the board; one elbow was on it, and he passed his hand over his eyes and yawned as he spoke. "So as to be dead sure to get beat like hell the next time I run for anything? An informer is mighty unpopular, no matter what he has got to tell. And make the biggest kind of hole in my law practice?"

"That's a fac'," said Jeb, impressed with the logic of this proposition.

"The favor of Cherokee and Kildeer counties is the breath of my political life, and you don't catch me a-fooling with it by letting my jaw wag too slack," continued Harshaw.

Philetus, the only member of the family that had gone to bed, slumbered peacefully in a small heap under the party-colored quilts. The dancing firelight revealed his yellow head, and again it was undistinguishable in the brown shadow. The pullet and Mose sat on a bench at one side of the fire, and the moonshiners tilted their chairs back on the hind legs, and watched the bright and leaping flames, which were particularly clear, the fire being rekindled upon a warm hearth and in a chimney already full of hot air. The occasional yawning of the group gave the only indication of the hour. The sharp-faced woman sat in her chair, with folded arms, and ever and anon gazing at her guest, who had so strangely commended himself. His clever ruse to insure being followed by his friends had induced infi..ite admiration of his acumen.

"I reckon ef ye wanted ter go ter Congress or sech, thar would n't be nuthin' ter hender," she said slowly, contemplating him.

She was a simple woman, and he a wise man. He flushed with pleasure to hear his cherished thought in another's words. He bore himself more jauntily at the very suggestion. He toyed with his knife and fork as he protested.

"There's a mighty long road to travel 'twixt me and Congress."

"Waal, you-uns kin make it, I'll be bound," she said.

And he believed her.

As he rose from the table, at the conclusion of the meal, he took out his purse.

"Nare cent," said Marvin hastily. "We-uns hev been obligated by yer comp'ny, an' air powerful pleased ter part in peace."

Harshaw insisted, however, on leaving his knife for Philetus, and expressed regret that one of the blades was broken.

"He can't cut hisself with that un, nohow," said the anxious mother, in graciously accepting it.

Harshaw divined that she might have valued it more if all the blades had been in like plight. She placed it carefully on the high mantelpiece, where, it was safe to say, Philetus would not for some years be able to attain it.

Harshaw never forgot that ride. As the light flickered out from the door into the black midnight, vaguely crossed with slanting lines of rain, to the rail-fence where his mare stood, saddled, the pistols in the holster, he experienced an added sense of confidence in his own methods and capacities, and an intense elation that so serious an adventure had terminated with so little injury.

When he was in the saddle he looked back at the little house, crouching in the infinite gloom of the night and the vast forests that overhung it, with no fierce recollection of his trepidation, of his deadly and imminent peril. In conducting himself with due regard for the representations he had made, his mental attitude had in some sort adapted itself to his manner, and he felt as unconcerned, as easy, as friendly, as he looked. He hallooed back a genial adieu to the household standing in the doorway, in the flare of the fire. Philetus, roused by the noise to the sense of passing events, appeared in the midst, rubbing his eyes with both hands. The group gave the guest godspeed, the dogs wagged their tails. As Harshaw rode out of the inclosure, the vista of the room seemed some brilliant yellow shaft sunk in the dense darkness. And then he could see nothing: the rain fell in the midst of the black night; he felt it on his hands, his face, his neck; he turned up the collar of his coat; he heard the hoofs of his mare splashing in the puddles, and he marveled how the beast could see or follow Jeb, who, mounted on the smaller of Marvin's two mules, led the way, while Marvin himself brought up the rear. He could only trust to the superior vision of the animal, and adjust himself to the motion which indicated the character of the ground they traversed: now through tangles and amongst rocks; now coming almost to a halt, as the mare stepped over the fallen bole of a tree; now a sudden jump, clearing unseen obstructions; now down hill, now up; now through the rushing floods of a mountain torrent. Harshaw's buoyant mood maintained itself; his bluff voice sounded in the midst of the dreary rainfall, and his resonant, gurgling laugh over and again rang along the dark, wintry fastnesses. His geniality was communicated to the other men, and the conversation carried on at long range was animated and amicable.

"I wonder what's become of those scamps I was

hunting with," he remarked. "I just know that shed of pine branches they fixed has leaked on 'em this night. I'll bet they're wallowin' in mud." He experienced a certain satisfaction in the thought. They had not been so badly scared as he, but at all events the camp hunters could not be happy under these circumstances.

How vast, how vast was the wilderness! Unseen, it gave an impression of infinite space. The wind clashed the bare boughs above his head. The pines wailed and groaned aloud. The commotion of the elements, the many subordinate, undetermined sounds, the weird, tumultuous voices of the forest, rising often to a terrible climax, had a mysterious, overpowering effect. It was a relief to detect a familiar note in the turmoil, even if it were the howl of a wolf, or the distant crash of a riven tree. How his mare plunged and floundered! — her head and neck now high before him, till he almost fell back upon her haunches, and now diving down so low that he had much ado to keep from slipping over the pommel.

"Well, Marvin," said Harshaw, once more on level ground, "if you and Jeb will come down to my farm and visit me, I'll promise you one thing, — I won't turn you out of the house at midnight in a downpour like this — ha! ha! ha! Confound you, old lady," — to the mare, as she stumbled, — "stand up, can't you?"

"You-uns ought n't ter set us down that-a-way," said Marvin, grieved at the reflection on his hospitality.

"Lord A'mighty!" exclaimed "hongry Jeb," — his tones from out of the darkness were vaguely yearning, — "talkin' ter me 'bout ever kemin' ter see ennybody at thar farm! Ye mought ez well ax that thar wolf ez we-uns hearn a-hollerin' yander, 'Jes' kem an' set awhile, Mister Wolf, an' eat supper at my farm.' I would n't dare no mo' ter show my muzzle in the settle-*mints* 'n he would his'n. The 'law 'lows both o' us air pests an' cumberers o' the groun', an' thar's a price on his head ez well ez mine. The law 'lows we air both murderers."

There was a pause, while the thud of the horses' hoofs was barely heard on the dank, soft mould. Then the voice of "hongry Jeb" seemed to detach itself from kindred dreary voices of the rain and the winds and the woods, and become articulate.

"That's edzac'ly whar it hurts my feelins. The wolf air enough mo' like the revenuers, a-seekin' who they may devour. I oughter played the sheep, I reckon, an' gin 'em my blood stiddier lead; but I'm human, — I'm human," insistently. "An' when a feller with a pistol draws a bead on me, I jes' naterally whips up my rifle an' bangs too. An' he war a pore shot an' I war a good un, an' he got the wust o' it."

The horses surged through the ford of an invisible torrent, stumbling among the rolling bowlders and struggling out on the other bank, and then they could hear again the monotonous falling of the multitudinous raindrops; the dreary wind took up its refrain, and the melancholy voice of Jeb began anew.

"'T would hev been self-defense, ef I hed n't been engaged in a unlawful act, preferrin' ter squeege the juice out'n my apples, an' bile an' sell it, 'n ter let 'em rot on the groun'. I war a fool. I 'lowed the apples war mine. Me an' my dad an' my gran'dad hed owned the orchard an' the lan' sence the Injun went. But 't war n't my apples, — b'long ter the governmint. I ain't never shot at no man ez did n't shoot at me fust. But 't ain't self-defense fur me. I 'm got ter play sheep."

The woful tenor of this discourse seemed to anger Marvin suddenly.

"Waal, I wish ye war slartered *now!*" he broke out. "I 'd jes' ez lief listen ter that thar wolf conversin' by the hour. What ails ye, Jeb, ter git set a-goin' so all-fired lonesome an' doleful?"

"Lord, nuthin'," said Jeb amenably, from the van of the procession. "I ain't lonesome nor doleful, nuther. When Mr. Harshaw 'lowed suthin' 'bout my kemin' ter see him on his farm, it jes' reminded me sorter ez when I war young, afore my diff'unce with the governmint, I used ter be a powerful lively boy, an' knowed plenty o' folks, an' went about mightily, — never lived like I does now. I war sorter o' a vagrantin' boy, — used ter consort with boys in the valley, an' they'd kem up ter the cove an' bide an' go huntin', an' I'd go down ter thar farms; an' that's how it kem I knowed whar ye live on Ow*el* Creek. Powerful good land some of it air, — mellow, rich sile; some cherty hillsides, though. None o' them boys hev turned out like me. Why, I used ter know Jeemes Gwinnan ez well ez the road ter mill, an' Jim's a jedge a-gracin' the bench, an' I'm — a wolf!"

Harshaw experienced a sudden quickening of interest. "You knew Gwinnan?"

"Lord, yes; ez well ez the bark knows the tree. Jeemes war a fine shot, an' he liked huntin' fust-rate. He hedn't his health very well, an' his mother, bein' a widder-woman, war more 'n naterally foolish 'bout'n him, an' war always lookin' fur him ter die. So she'd keep him out'n doors ez well ez she could. But he'd kerry his book along, an' read, 'thout he war a-huntin'. So she let him kem whenst he war jes' a boy, an' go huntin' in the mountings along o' the men growed. An' it done him good. He war ez fine a shot ez I ever see."

A wonderful thing was happening in the woods, — the familiar miracle of dawn. The vast forests were slowly asserting dim outlines of bole and branch, lodgment for the mist which clothed them in light and fleecy illusions of foliage. A gray revelation of light, rather the sheer values of distinctness than a realized medium, was unfolding before the eye. The serried slants of rain fell at wider intervals, and the equestrian form of Jeb became visible, — lank, lean, soaked with rain, his old white hat shedding the water from its brim in rivulets upon his straight and straggling hair. As he jogged along on the little mule, whose long ears seemed alternately to whisk off the shades of night, he seemed a forlornly inadequate individual to have had a "diff'unce with the governmint."

"Jim's what reminded me of how I war fixed in life,'

he went on, more cheerfully. "An' this hyar whole trip air what reminded me o' Jim. I guided him — mus' hev been fourteen year ago, or mo' — through jes' sech a rainy night ez this, an' through these hyar very woods — naw, sir! more towards the peak o' Thunderhead."

"I dunno ez ye hev got enny call ter be so durned pertic'lar 'bout the percise spot," said Marvin, significantly.

"That's a fac'," said Jeb, good-naturedly. "I guided him through the mountings an' over the line inter the old North State."

"What in hell did he want to go there for, in the rain and the dead of the night?" asked Harshaw. His breath was quick; he felt that he panted on the brink of a discovery. Now plunge!

"'Kase, stranger, he war obleeged ter, sorter like you-uns," said Jeb enigmatically.

He looked back over his shoulder, with perhaps some stirring doubt, some vague suspicion, at the man who followed; but Harshaw, now lifting a hand to thrust a branch from across the path, now adjusting the bridle about the mare's head, seemed so careless, so casual, in his curiosity that Jeb was reassured as to the innocuousness of his gossip, and went on.

"Ye see, them fellers he consorted with — huntin', an' a-pitchin' o' quates, an' a-foot-racin', an' sech — war mostly powerful servigrus, gamesome folks; an' some o' 'em war gin ter toler'ble wild ways, an' Jeemes — his mother never keered much what he done, so ez he'd quit stickin' so all-fired constant ter his law-books, 'kase he war a-studyin' law by that time in old Squair Dinks's law-office in Colbury — he war 'bout twenty-two year old — he war mixed up in a deal o' them goin's-on. An' from one little thing an' another he hed some ill-will started agin him wunst in a while. Him an' Eph Saunders hed a fallin'-out wunst. Eph war a tremenjious strong man, an' he kep' flingin' words at Jeemes. Sence Jeemes hed tuk ter studyin' o' law an' sech, an' 'peared right hearty, he tuk up with town ways powerful, an' went ter meet'n a-Sunday nights, escortin' the gals, an' dressed hisself like a plumb peacock. An' whenst Eph 'tended circus in Colbury he met up with Jeemes, who hed a lot o' his gal cousins along. An' Eph war drunk, an' Jim gin him a push aside, an' Eph, he fell on the groun'. Waal, sir, it like ter killed Eph, — ter be knocked down by a man o' Jeemes's weight! Jim could n't hev done it ef Eph hed n't been drunk. Eph jes' mourned like Samson arter his hair war cut off. Ye'd hev 'lowed he war *de*-sgraced fur life! An', like Samson, he war n't a-goin' ter bide stopped off an' done fur. He kep' a-sendin' all sorts o' words ter Jeemes; an' ez Jeemes never wanted no fuss with Eph, he kep' out'n his way for a while. An' Eph, he 'lowed ez Jim war afeard an' a-hidin'. Waal, sir, that hustled up Jeemes's feelins mightily. He jes' wanted ter keep out'n his mother's hearin', though; she war a powerful chicken-hearted, floppy kind o' woman, — skeered at everything. Then Jeemes, he sent Eph word ez he war n't a-goin' ter be beat inter a jelly fur nuthin' by a man twict his size; but he war a-kemin' up ter settle him with his rifle. An' Eph, he sent word he'd meet him at the big Sulphur Spring, thar on that spur o' the mounting nigh Gran'dad's Creek. Ef Jeemes so much ez dared ter cross the foot-bredge over Gran'dad's Creek, an' set his foot on the t'other side, Eph swore he'd shoot him dead. An' Eph, he sent word ter come Chewsday an hour by sun, an' bring his friends ter see fair play."

"Laws-a-massy!" exclaimed Marvin, in the fervor of reminiscence, "I kin jes' see that thar spot, — that thar old foot-bredge in the woods, an' the water high enough ter lap the under side o' the log; 't war hewn a-top, an' made toler'ble level footin'. An' me an' Jeb dodgin' in the laurel, fur fear Eph would shoot 'fore Jeemes crost."

"Jeemes seemed toler'ble long a-crossin'," Jeb resumed, — "I 'member that; an' he stopped at the furder eend, an' lifted his rifle ter his shoulder ter be ready ter shoot. An' thar stood Eph, a-sightin' him keerful ez he kem" —

"You were both there?" said Harshaw, hastily.

"Lord, yes," said Jeb. "Jeemes hed stayed at my dad's house the night afore. An' he never brung none o' his town friends, — afeard o' word gittin' ter his mother. So me an' Sam, — Sam, he lived nigh me, — we-uns went along."

"Did he kill Eph?" demanded Harshaw, the query swift with the momentum of the wish.

"Waal, not edzac'ly," drawled Jeb. "That's whar the funny part kem in. Eph, he knowed ef Jeemes shot fust he war a dead man, — mighty few sech shots ez Jeemes, — but he war n't a-goin' ter murder him by shootin' him afore he put his foot on the groun' an' tuk up the dare. So he waited, an' Jeemes stopped short right at the aidge o' the bredge."

"Lord, I 'members how he looked!" cried Marvin. "He had tuk off his coat an' vest, though we-uns hed tole him that thar b'iled shirt o' his'n war a good mark for Eph, ez looked jes' the color o' the clay bank a-hint him, in them brown jeans clothes. Jim's straw hat war drawn down over his eyes; he war jes' about the build o' his ramrod, — slimmest, stringiest boy!— ez delikit-lookin' ez a gal. One thing Eph called him, ez riled him wuss 'n all, war 'Miss Polly.'"

"He hev widened out mightily sence then, though he ain't got no fat ter spare yit," put in Jeb.

"An' then, suddint," resumed Marvin, "he jes' stepped his foot right on the groun'. In that very minute Eph's gun flashed. An' I seen Jeemes standin' thar, still sightin'. An' then Eph, he drapped his gun, an' held his hands afore his face, an' yelled out, 'Shoot, ef ye air a-goin' ter shoot! I ain't a-goin' ter stan' hyar no longer.' An' Jeemes, he looked ez scornful " —

"I never seen a boy's looks with sech a cuttin' aidge ter 'em," interpolated Jeb.

"An' Jeemes, he say, 'I ain't a-wastin' powder ter-day. I never 'lowed ez skunks war game.' An' he drapped his gun."

"Yes sir!" exclaimed Jeb, "he jes' hed that much

grit, — ter stan' up ez a shootin' mark fur Eph Saunders, an' prove he war n't afeard o' nothin'. He did sir!"

"Why, look here, my good friends!" cried the lawyer. "That was a duel. It was a cool, premeditated affair. They met by previous appointment, and fought with deadly weapons and with witnesses. It was a duel."

"Mebbe so," said Jeb, indifferently and uncomprehendingly. "I call it clean grit."

"Waal," went on Marvin, "I run across the bredge lookin' fur Eph's bullet. I said, 'Whar 'd it go?' An' by that time Eph an' them low down Kitwin boys war slinkin' off. An' sez Jeemes, 'Don't let 'em know it. I don't want my mother ter hear 'bout it. She air fibble an' gittin' old.' An' thar I seen the breast o' his shirt war slow a-spottin' with blood. Waal, sir, that 's how kem me an' Jeb an' him rid over the mountings inter North Car'lina, whar he hed some kinsfolks livin' 'mongst the hills."

"Ye see," — Jeb again took up his testimony, — "he did n't want the news ter git ter his mother afore he got well, 'kase he war delikit, an' she war always a-lookin' fur him ter die; an' Eph never knowed Jim war shot, an' could n't kerry the tale down ter Colbury. Waal, we-uns war all young an' toler'ble bouncin' fools, I tell ye, an' we sorter got light on that fac' whenst we-uns sot out ter ride with a man with a gun-shot wound — I furgits 'zac'ly whar the doctor say the bullet went in — miles an' miles through the mountings; an' the dark kem on an' the rain kem down, an' Jeemes got out'n his head. An' this ride with you-uns air what reminded me o' it."

"*I* ain't out of my head!" cried Harshaw, with covert meaning. "You bet your immortal soul on that!"

"Naw," — Jeb admitted the discrepancy, — "but the rain, an' the ride, an' the mountings, an' the darksomeness."

"Lord! a body would n't hev b'lieved how Jeemes's pride war hurt ter be called afeard!" exclaimed Marvin. "I 'low he 'd hev let Eph chop him up in minch meat ter prove he war n't. He air prouder of hisself 'n enny man I ever see. Thar's whar his soul is — in his pride."

"I 'm glad ter hear it," said Harshaw, so definitely referring to an occult interpretation of his own that the old white hat, bobbing along in front of him, turned slowly, and he saw the lank, cadaverous face below it, outlined with its limp wisps of black hair against the nebulous vapors. So strong an expression of surprise did Jeb's features wear that Harshaw hastily added, "A man that ain't got any pride ain't worth anything."

"Ef he hev got ennything ter be proud of," stipulated melancholy Jeb.

The day had fully dawned; the rain, the mists, the looming forests, had acquired a dull verity in the stead of the vague, illusory shadows they had been. Nevertheless, the muddy banks of the creek down which the mare slided, her legs rigid as iron; the obstructions of the ford, — rocks, fallen limbs of trees, floating or entangled in intricacies of overhanging bushes, — were all rendered more difficult, for Harshaw mechanically controlled the reins instead of trusting to the mare's instinct; as he sawed on the bit, while she threw back her head, foaming at the mouth, he brought her to her knees in the midst of the stream. The water surged up about the great boots which he wore drawn over his trousers to the knee, and the mare regained her footing with snorting difficulty. There were no expletives, and Jeb looked back in renewed surprise.

"Ye mus' be studyin' powerful hard, stranger," he commented, "not ter hev seen that thar bowlder."

"Yer beastis war a-goin' ter take slanchwise across the ruver whar thar war n't nuthin' ter hender, till ye in an' about pulled the jaw off'n her," Marvin said, as Harshaw pushed through the swollen flood and up the opposite bank. His flushed face was grave; his eyes were intent; he rode along silently. He was indeed thinking.

He was thinking that if what they had told him were true — and how could he doubt it? — Gwinnan in taking the official oath had committed perjury; he was disqualified for the judicial office, and liable to impeachment. Harshaw was vaguely repeating to himself and trying to remember the phraseology of the anti-dueling oath exacted of every office-holder in the State of Tennessee, — an oath that he had not directly or indirectly given or accepted a challenge since the adoption of the Constitution of 1835.

Under what pretext, what secret reservation or evasion, had Gwinnan been able to evade this solemn declaration? Or had he adopted the simple expedient of swallowing it whole? Harshaw wondered, remembering all the acerbities of Gwinnan's canvass and election, that the old story had not before come to light. But it was a section of frequent feuds and bloody collisions, the subject was trite and unsuggestive, and the details of an old fight might seem to promise no novel developments. How odd that he, of all men, should stumble on it, in view of its most signal significance!

Auxiliary facts pressed upon his attention. Nothing that could be now urged against an official was so prejudicial as the crime of dueling. The episode of Kinsard's boyish demonstration attested the temper of the public. With much difficulty had his friends shielded him by its ambiguity; and indeed only because it was a meaningless folly, without intention or result, had it proved innocuous. Even Kinsard, fire-eater as he was, had been forced to accept their interpretations of its harmless intent, and to subside under the frown of public displeasure. The more lenient members of the House had had cause to regret their clemency, the disapproval of their constituents being expressed in no measured manner by the local journals. But no ambiguity was here; this was the accomplished fact, this the clue that long he had sought. Even if the House should decline to act in the matter, Gwinnan could be removed by judicial proceedings. He would think it out at his leisure. How lucky, how lucky was this ride!

The rain had ceased at last. They were among the minor ridges that lie about the base of the Great Smoky. They had ridden many a mile out of their way, — Harshaw could not say in what direction, — so that he might not easily retrace his steps. The mists still hung about them when they turned from the almost imperceptible path, which Jeb had followed with some keen instinct or memory, into a road, — a rough wagon track. Bushes were growing in its midst, bowlders lay here and there; its chief claim to identification as a highway being its occasional mud-puddles, of appalling depth and magnitude, and its red clay mire, fetlock deep at least.

Harshaw roused himself suddenly, as the two moonshiners intimated their intention of parting company with him.

"Thar's yer way, stranger," said Marvin, pausing on the rise and pointing down the road. It was visible only a few rods in the mist, dreary and deserted, with deep ditches, heavily washed by the rain, on either hand; it might seem to lead to no fair spaces, no favored destination where one might hope to be. But Harshaw drew up his mare, and gazed along it with kindling eyes. His felt hat drooped in picturesque curves about his dense yellow hair, soaked like his beard, to a darker hue. His closely buttoned coat had a military suggestion. His heavy figure was imposing on horseback. He flushed with sudden elation. Alack! he saw more trooping down that prosaic dirt road than the mist, hastily scurrying; than the progress of the wind in the swaying of the stunted cedars, clinging to the gashed and gully-washed embankments; than the last trickling stragglers of the storm.

He did not notice, or he did not care, that the two men had remarked his silence, his evident absorption. He glanced cursorily at them, as they sat regarding him, — one on the little lank mule, his partner on the big lean one, both drenched, and forlorn, and poverty-stricken, and humble of aspect. The politician's mare, perhaps recognizing the road down into Kildeer County, where she had spent the first frisky years of her toilsome pilgrimage, showed a new spirit, and caracoled as Harshaw rode up to the two men to offer his hand.

"Farewell, stranger," they said; and in the old-fashioned phrase of the primitive Plain People, "Farewell," he replied.

They stood looking after him, hardly understanding what they lacked, what they had expected, as the mare, with a mincing, youthful freshness, cantered a little way along the grassy margin of the road, above the rivulets in the ditches, surging twelve or fourteen feet below.

Presently Harshaw paused, yet unobscured by the mist which had gathered about him, and glanced over his shoulder, — not to thank them for such aid and comfort as they had given him.

"Gentlemen," he said, a little ill at ease because of the restive mare, "I must thank you for the story you told me. You don't know how much good it did me. A pretty little story, with a pretty little hero. A very *pretty* little story, indeed."

He bent his roseate, dimpled smile upon them, and waved his hand satirically; with a bound the mare disappeared in the mist, leaving the grave, saturnine mountaineers staring after him, and listening to the measured hoof-beat of his invisible progress till it died in the distance.

Then they looked at each other.

"Sam," said Jeb, when they had turned again into their fastnesses, where they could ride only in single file, "I dunno ef we-uns done right las' night. This worl' would be healthier ef that man war out'n it."

"I ain't misdoubtin' that none," replied Marvin. "'Peared ter me powerful comical, the way he took off down the road, an' I ain't able ter study out yit what he meant. My gran'mam always 'lowed ez them ez talks in riddles larnt thar speech o' the devil, him bein' the deceivin' one. But 't warn't healthy fur we-uns ter kill him, even ef we could hev agreed ter do it. I reckon them hunters *would* hev tracked him. An' I don't b'lieve he war no spy nor sech."

"Nor me nuther," said "hongry Jeb," well enough satisfied with the termination of the adventure, "though I ain't likin' him now ez well ez I done a-fust."

They liked him still less, and all their old suspicions returned with redoubled force, upon reaching home, when the afternoon was well advanced. For no hunters had yet appeared, and the lurking moonshiners, becoming surprised because of this, had tracked Harshaw's way to the house by the broken brush, the hairs from the mane and tail of the mare, a bit of his coat clutched off by the briers, the plain prints of the mare's hoofs along a sandy stretch protected from the rain by the beetling ledges of a crag. There were many oak-trees along this path, — not one blazed by a hunting-knife. They understood at last his clever lie. And Marvin upbraided M'ria: —

"Thar air more constancy in the ways o' the wind, an' mo' chance o' countin' on 'em, 'n that thar woman. Fust he mus' be dragged out straight an' kilt, — flunged off'n the bluff, — else we-uns would all go ter jail, an' Philetus be lef' ter starve 'mongst the painters, ez would n't keep him comp'ny, but would eat him up. Then when the man limbered his jaw an' sot out ter lyin', she gits so all-fired skeered, she hed breakfus' cooked for we-uns ter journey 'fore I could sati'fy my mind 'bout nuthin'. Ef the truth war knowed, we'd all be safer ef M'ria were flunged over the bluff."

And Maria, staring at the line of oak-trees, all undesecrated by the knife, could not gainsay it.

She could only wring her hands, and rock herself to and fro, and revolve her troublous fears, and grow yet more wan and gaunt with her prescient woes for them all — and for Philetus.

XXV.

ON the second day of February, the ground-hog, true to his traditions, emerged from his hole, and looked about him cautiously for his shadow. Fortunately, it was not in attendance. And by this token the spring was early, and all the chill rains, and late frosts, and unpropitious winds, and concomitant calamities, that might have ensued had he found his ill-omened shadow awaiting him, were escaped. It was not long afterward that small protuberances appeared on every twig and wand and branch, although the trees had not budded save in these promissory intimations. The sap was stirring. The dead world was quickened again. That beautiful symbolism of the miracle of resurrection was daily presented in the re-awakening, in the rising anew of the spring. So pensively gladsome it was, so gently approaching, with such soft and subtle languors! The sky was blue; the clouds how light, how closely akin to the fleecy mists! Sheep-bells were tinkling—for what! the pastures were already green! And here and there a peach-tree beside a rail-fence burst forth in a cloud of blossoms so exquisitely petaled, so delicately roseate, that only some fine ethereal vagary of the sunset might rival the tint. Sometimes among the still leafless mountains these pink graces of color would appear, betokening the peach orchard of some hidden little hut, its existence only thus attested. The Scolacutta River was affluent with the spring floods: a wild, errant stream this, with many a wanton freak, with a weakness for carrying off its neighbor's rails; for snatching huge slices of land from the banks; for breaking off trees and bushes, and whirling them helplessly down its current, tossing and teetering in a frantic, unwilling dance. Many a joke had it played before and since the disaster to old Griff's mill. The sunbeams might seem the strings of a harp; whenever touched by a wing they were quivering and thrilling with songs. Slow wreathing blue smoke curled in fields here and there where the fires of rubbish blazed; sometimes a stump would burn sullenly all night and char slowly, and with a puff of wind burst anew into flames. The soft lustres of the Pleiades and the fiery Aldebaran were resplendent in the heavens, and the moon was the paschal moon. A vernal thrill had blessed the wild cherry, and it gave out its glad incense. For miles and miles the exquisite fragrance from its vast growths on the mountain-side pervaded the air. And presently the mountain-side wore the tender verdure of budding leaves, and even the gloomy pines were tipped with new tufts of vivid green, unlike their sombre hue; and here and there crags flaunted a bourgeoning vine, and the wild ivy crept on the ground where the wood violet bloomed. All day the ploughs turned the furrow, and the air echoed with the calls "gee, haw" to the slow oxen. .

And Mrs. Purvine was greatly distraught in the effort to remember exactly where she had stowed away certain bags of seed necessary, in view of their best interests, to be sown in the light of the moon.

Her sun-bonnet was all awry, her face wrinkled and anxious with the cares of the spring-tide " gyarden spot," her gestures laborious and weary, as she sat on her porch, the lap of her ample apron filled with small calico bags, each of which seemed to have a constitutional defect in its draw-string; for when found closed it would not open, and if by chance open it would not close. There was a sort of shelf in lieu of balustrade against the posts of the porch, and on this were placed two or three pieces of old crockery, — providentially broken into shapes that the ingenious could utilize, — in which seeds were immersed in water, that they might swell in the night, and thus enter the ground prepared to swiftly germinate. One of these broken dishes stood on the floor at her feet, and a graceless young rooster, that had the air of loafing about the steps, approached by unperceived degrees, picked up several of the seed, and was quenching his thirst, when spied by Mrs. Purvine, who was viciously pulling the strings of a recalcitrant bag.

"In the name o' Moses!" she adjured him so solemnly that the rooster stopped and looked at her expectantly. "I'm in an' about minded ter cut them dish-rag-gourd seed out'n yer craw, ye great, big, ten-toed sinner, you! Ye need n't turn yer head up 'twixt every sup, — so thankful ter the Lord fur water. Ye 'll find mo' water in the pot 'n that. A-swallerin' them few dish-rag-gourd seed ez nimble an' onconsarned, an' me jes' a-chasin' an' a-racin' an' wore ter the bone ter find some mo'! Ye 'd better leave 'em be."

The rooster, hardly comprehending the words, was about to again sample the delicacy, when aunt Dely, stamping to startle him, inadvertently overturned the dish and the seed on the floor. The fowl scuttled off, looking askance at the ruin, and the water dripped through the cracks of the puncheon floor.

So absorbed had she been that she had not observed an approach, and Alethea was at the foot of the steps when she lifted her eyes.

"Hyar I be, aunt Dely," said the girl, noticing Mrs. Purvine's occupation with a surprise that seemed hardly warranted, and speaking in a breathless, eager way. "Air you-uns feelin' enny better?"

For once in her life the crafty Mrs. Purvine was embarrassed; to conceal her confusion, she engaged in a strenuous struggle with one of the bags of seed.

"I feel toler'ble well," she said at last, gruffly.

"Waal!" exclaimed Alethea, in amazement. "From the word Ben Doaks brung ter Wild-Cat Hollow, ez he war drivin' up some steers ter the bald o' the mounting, we-uns 'lowed ez ye hed been tuk awful sick, an' war like ter die."

"I sent ye that word," said Mrs. Purvine with admirable effrontery. "I knowed thar war n't no other way ter git ye down hyar. When hev ye hed the perliteness ter fetch them bones o' yourn hyar afore?" She looked over her spectacles with angry reproach at the girl.

"Waal, aunt Dely," said Alethea in her dulcet, mollifying drawl, sitting down on the step as she talked, "ye know I hev hed ter do so much o' the ploughin' an' sech, a-puttin' in o' our craps. We-uns hev got sech a lot o' folks up ter our house. An' I dunno when Jacob Jessup hev done less work 'n he hev this spring."

"Thought ye be always 'lowin' ye ain't layin' off ter do his work," said the elder tartly.

"Waal," rejoined Alethea wearily, "I don't 'pear ter hev the grit ter hold out an' quar'l over it, like I used ter do. I reckon my sperit 's a-gittin' bruk; but I don't mind workin' off in the field, 'thout no jawin', whar I kin keep comp'ny with my thoughts."

"I would n't want ter keep comp'ny with 'em," said aunt Dely cavalierly. "I 'll be bound they air heavier ter foller 'n the plough. Mighty solemn, low-sperited thoughts fur a spry young gal like you-uns! Ef yer head could be turned inside out, thar ain't nobody ez would n't 'low it mus' outside be gray. They 'd say, ' In the name o' Moses! old ez this inside, an' yaller outside! 'T ain't natur'!'"

The girl had taken off her bonnet. Her beauty was undimmed, despite a pensive pallor on her delicate cheek. She fanned herself with her sun-bonnet, and the heavy, undulating folds of her lustrous yellow hair stirred softly. "I 'm powerful glad ter find ye hevin' yer health same ez common," she said.

"I 'm s'prised ter hear ye say so," declared Mrs. Purvine, tart from her renewed conflicts with the bag. "I ain't sick, bless the Lord, but I wanted ye ter kem down hyar an' bide with me, an' I knowed I could n't tole ye out'n that thar Eden, ez ye call Wild-Cat Hollow, 'thout purtendin' ter be nigh dead. So I jes' held my han' ter my side an' tied up my head, an' hollered ter Ben Doaks ez he went by. He looked mighty sorry fur me!"

A faint smile flickered across her broad face. "I hed laid off ter go ter bed afore you-uns kem, though. I will say fur ye ez ye travel toler'ble fas'. Yes, sir!" she went on, after a momentary pause. "I live in a ongrateful worl'. I hev ter gin out I'm dyin' ter git my own niece ter kem ter see me. An' thar's that thar Jerry Price, ez I hev raised from a ill-convenient infant ez won't do nuthin' I say, nor marry nobody I picks out fur him. I'll be boun' he would n't hev no say-so 'bout'n it ef his aunt Melindy Jane hed hed the raisin' of him. An' Bluff ez good ez 'lowed this mornin' ez he'd hook me ef I did n't quit foolin' in his bucket o' bran, — 'kase I 'lowed ez mebbe the saaft-soap gourd war drapped in it, bein' ez I could n't find it nowhar, an' I war afear'd 't would n't agree with the critter's insides. An' thar's that rooster," — he was now out among the weeds, — "he war a aig ez got by accident inter a tur-r-key's nest, an' when he war hatched she would n't hev him; an' ez I hed no hen ez war kerryin' o' chickens his size, *I* hed ter care fur him. I useter git up in my bare feet in the middle o' a winter night ter kiver up that thar rooster in a bat o' cotton, fur he war easy ter git cold, an' he could holler ez loud ez a baby. An' arter all, he kem hyar an' eat up 'bout haffen my dish-rag-gourd seed! I dunno what in Moses' name is kem o' the other bags. Never mind!" — she shook her head as she addressed the jaunty and unprescient fowl, — "I'll git up the heart ter kill ye some day; an' ef I can't eat ye, bein' so well acquainted with ye, I'll be boun' Jerry kin."

Alethea, apprised how precious the seeds were, began to gather them up as she sat on the step.

"Listen ter Jerry, now!" exclaimed Mrs. Purvine, with whom the world had evidently gone much amiss to-day. "Need n't tell me he don't hurt Bluff's feelins, callin' him names whilst ploughin', an' yellin' at him like a plumb catamount. Ef Bluff hed n't treated me like he done this mornin', I'd go thar an' make Jerry shet up."

Now and then the ox and the man at the plough-tail came into view at the end of the field that sloped down to the road. One of aunt Dely's boys was dropping corn in the furrow, and the other followed with a hoe and covered the grain in. Alethea watched them with the interest of a practical farmer.

Aunt Dely, too, looked up, repeating the old formula: —

> "One fur the cut-worm an' one fur the crow,
> Two fur the blackbird an' one fur ter grow."

Jerry, glancing toward the house, called out a salutation to Alethea, and then at long range entered upon a colloquy with Mrs. Purvine touching the lack of seed.

"Whar 's that thar t'other bag o' seed-corn?" he demanded.

"Waal, I ain't got none!" cried out Mrs. Purvine peremptorily. "I mus' hev made a mistake, and fedded that thar bag o' special an' percise fine seed-corn ter the chickens, — I wish they war every one fried. I disremember now what I done, an' what I done it fur. Ye jes' gear up Bluff in the wagin an' go ter mill, an' see ef ye can't git some thar."

"Laws-a-massy!" objected Jerry, "'t ain't no use ter make Bluff go. I kin git thar an' back quicker an' easier 'thout him 'n with him."

"Ye do ez ye air bid," said Mrs. Purvine; and while Jerry stared she presently explained, as she sawed away on the draw-strings of a bag, "I want ye ter take Lethe along ter the post-office, ter see ef thar 's enny letter fur me."

Now, Mrs. Purvine had never written nor received a letter in her life; in fact, would not have understood the functions of a post-office, had it not been for her husband's incumbency some years ago. Nevertheless, in common with half the country-side, whenever she thought of it she gravely demanded if there were a missive for her, and was gravely answered in the negative, and went her way well content.

Both young people understood her ruse well enough, — to throw them together, in the hope that propinquity might do a little match-making. Since Mink's long sentence of imprisonment had been pronounced upon him, she felt that there was no longer fear of rivalry from that quarter, as the Supreme Court would hardly reverse so plain and just a judgment. And now, she thought, is Jerry's golden opportunity. However, she elaborately justified the expedition upon the basis of convenience.

"Ye *could* fetch the letter an' the corn too," she observed, in a cogitating manner; "but then, goin' ter mill, ye'd be apt ter git meal sprinkled onto it. I reckon I'd better send Lethe too. Ye kin leave her at the post-office till ye go ter mill."

This verisimilitude imposed even upon Alethea.

"Who air ye expectin' a letter from, aunt Dely?" said the girl.

Mrs. Purvine was equal to the occasion.

"I 'lowed," she said, with swift inspiration, "ez some o' them folks ez we-uns bided with down thar in Shaftesville mought take up a notion ter write ter us."

Alethea thought this not unlikely, and set out with Jerry with some interest, fully prepared to preserve the precious letter from any contact with meal.

Mrs. Purvine, her ill-humor evaporating in the successful exploiting of her little plan, gazed after them with a benignant smile illuminating her features, as they creaked off in the slow little ox-cart, its wheels now leaning outward and now bending inward, as the loose linchpin or some obstruction in the road might impel. She noted, however, that the old slouch hat and the brown sun-bonnet, with its coy tress of golden hair showing beneath its curtain, were seldom turned toward each other, and there was evidently little disposition for conversation between the two young people.

"Bluff hev got mos' o' the brains in that thar comp'ny," she said to herself with indignation because of their mutual indifference. "But Lethe Ann Sayles air mighty diffe'nt from some wimmin, ef she kin hold her jaw fur twenty year, an' keep that thar dead-an'-gin-out look on her face fur Mink Lorey. He can't git back 'fore then. An' Jerry's got ez good a chance ez Ben

Doaks. But it's mighty hard on a pore old woman like me, ez hed trouble enough marryin' herself off thirty year ago, a-runnin' away an' sech, ter gin herself ter studyin' 'bout sech foolishness in her old age ez love-makin', an' onsettlin' her mind, 'kase they hain't got enough sense ter do thar courtin' 'thout help."

But this unique grievance was so inadequate that Mrs. Purvine gave up the effort to eke out thereby her ill-humor, and gazed about with placid complacence at the spring landscape, tossing all the bags of seed together into a splint basket, to be sorted at some more propitious day.

In Bluff's slow progress along the red clay road, the gradual unfolding of the scene, the vernal peace, the benedictory sunshine, had their benignant effect on Alethea. Absorbed as she had been, in descending the mountain, by her anxiety for the specious aunt Dely's illness, she had not noted until now how far the spring was advanced in the sheltered depths of the cove, how loath to climb to the sterile fastnesses of Wild-Cat Hollow.

"The season 'pears ter be toler'ble back'ard in the hollow, jedgin' by the cove," she remarked, her eyes resting wistfully upon the tender verdure on the margin of the river. The sun was warm, for it was not long past noon, and Bluff stopped to drink in the midst of the ford. The translucent brown water above the bowlders, all distinct in its clear depths, washed about the miry wheels, and lapped with soft sighs against the rocky banks; great silvery circles elastically expanded on its surface about the ox's muzzle, distorting somewhat the image of his head and his big, insistent, sullen eyes and long horns, as he drank. Whenever the sunbeams struck the current a bevy of tiny insects might be seen, skittering about over the water; and hark! a frog was croaking on a rotten log in the dank shadow of the laurel. From the fields beyond the call of the quail was sweet and clear. The ranges encompassing the cove on every hand seemed doubly beautiful, doubly dear, with the tender promise of summer upon them, with the freshened delights of soft airs pervading them, with the predominant sense of the liberated joys of nature in the bourgeonings and the blooms, in the swift rushing of torrents, in the whirl of wings. The wooded lines of those summits close at hand were drawn in fine detail against the sky, save where the great balds towered, — symmetrical, ponderous, bare domes; further mountains showed purple and blue, and among them was a lowering gray portent that might have seemed a storm-cloud, save to those who knew the strange, cumulose outline of Thunderhead.

Everywhere birds were building. A couple of jays were carrying straws from a heap in a corner of a fence; they rose with a great whirl of blue and white feathers, as Bluff, his horns nodding, approached them. A dove was cooing in a clump of dog-wood trees, whitely blooming by the road. There was a great commotion of wings in the air from a lofty martin-house in a wayside dooryard, as the plucky denizens chased a hawk round and round and out of sight.

"Thought that thar war the way ter the post-office at Squair Bates's, Jerry," Alethea observed, pointing down one of those picturesque winding roads, so common to the region, threading the forests, its tawny red convolutions flecked with shadow and sheen, showing in long, fascinating vistas, and luring one to follow.

"Yes, sir," said Jerry, "but I hev got ter take ye ter the post-office at Locust Levels. Ain't ye hearn aunt Dely 'low that? An' I hev got ter leave ye thar whilst I go ter the grist-mill nigh by, off the road a piece."

Alethea flushed with a dull annoyance, recognizing the device that the long drive might be still longer. She nevertheless made no comment. They were each too dutiful to vary the plan of the journey, although aunt Dely might have considered this only obedience in the letter, and not in the spirit, as neither again spoke for a mile or more.

"This be Kildeer County," said Jerry, at last, breaking the long silence. "We-uns crossed the line back thar 'bout haffen hour ago."

Alethea's pensive enjoyment of the gentle influences of the scene was marred. To be sure, aunt Dely had an unequivocal right to send, if she liked, to the post-office at Locust Levels, a hamlet of Kildeer County, rather than to the one nearer, in her own county; but it was a patent subterfuge that she should expect to receive letters here from their friends in Shaftesville. It was Alethea's excellent common sense that had preserved her from the folly of the continual anticipation of a letter, so common among ignorant people, who, with no acquaintances elsewhere, beset the post-offices with their demands. She had never asked for a letter for herself, and there had begun to be revealed to her the fact that it was not a post-office which could produce an epistle for Mrs. Purvine; she needed a correspondent.

"Ef ye 'low ye'll feel like a fool axin' fur that thar letter, Lethe," said the acute Jerry, divining her thoughts, "I'll do it. I never mind feelin' like a fool, — thar's a heap o' 'em in this worl'. An' whenever I acts like one, I remembers I'm in powerful good company. An' that's why I don't try ter be no smarter 'n I am."

But Alethea said that she would ask for the letter, as aunt Dely had directed. When she alighted from the wagon at Locust Levels, Jerry and Bluff drove off at a whisking pace, which indicated that both might feel relieved.

At the post-office the wood-pile was in front of the house, and therefore the approach was over chips, splinters, and shreds of bark, which gave out a pungent fragrance. It was a low little gray cabin, partly of log and partly of plank, and with a blossoming company of peach-trees about it. They hung over the fence, and all the steep bank down to the road was covered with their pink petals shed in the wind. Some golden candlesticks and "butter-and-eggs" were blooming inside the rickety little palings, and a girl stood upon the porch beside a spinning-wheel.

Alethea noted the unrecognizing stare bent upon her. She opened the gate with difficulty, and went up on the shaded porch. The girl had stopped spinning, but was still gazing at her. A yellow dog, who had been asleep on the floor, his muzzle on his fore-paws, also scanned her curiously, not stirring his head, only lifting his eyes. When she faltered her inquiry for a letter for Mrs. Purvine, the dog got up as briskly as if he were the postmaster.

"Fur who?" demanded a masculine voice, as a man with a plough-line in his hand stepped around the corner, lured by the sound of the colloquy.

"Mis' Purvine," repeated Alethea.

He looked at her with a touch of indignation. He would never get through his spring ploughing at this rate. He strode into the house, however, to investigate. "I never hearn o' her in all my life," he said tartly.

And Alethea began to have a realization how very wide this world is.

The walls of the room bore many flaming graces of advertisement, pasted over the logs. They were of more fantastic device and a newer fashion than Mrs. Purvine's relics of her husband's postmastership. There were two neat beds in the room, a very clean floor, and a woman in the chimney-corner, smoking her pipe, who nodded with grave courtesy to Alethea.

The postmaster inserted a key in the lock of a table-drawer, and there, by some perversity, it stuck; it would neither come out nor go further in, nor turn in either direction. The dog had entered, too, as he always did, with a business-like air, and was standing beneath the table, slowly wagging his tail and lolling out his tongue; what strange ideas did he connect with the distribution of the mail? His position involved some danger, as his master struggled and pulled at the drawer, and jerked the table about. Finally, one of its legs came in contact with the foot of the dog, who had the worst of it. As his shrieks filled the room, the perspiring man turned to Alethea.

"I know thar ain't no letter fur no Mis' Purvine," he declared. "Thar air jes fower letters in this hyar dad-burned drawer, an' they be fur Judge Gwinnan. Ye see I can't open it."

The mail seemed indeed in safe-keeping. His daughter, who had been peering down the road, suddenly spoke:—

"Ye'll hev ter open it. Fur thar be Jedge Gwinnan now, a-ridin' up on that thar roan colt o' his'n, what he hev jes' bruk."

A little play with the key, and the drawer abruptly opened.

There was, indeed, no letter for Mrs. Purvine, and snatching up the four for Judge Gwinnan, with some newspapers, the postmaster ran hastily out, hailing the rider as he drew rein at the corner of the orchard fence.

Alethea hesitated for a moment at the gate, gazing at the equestrian figure that had paused under the soft pink glamours of the orchard. She had heard of his belated plea for Mink Lorey. He evidently bore no grudge for his injuries. Suddenly there flashed into her mind a word that she might say for that graceless and forlorn wight, — a word which, perhaps, might not be taken amiss; and if it should do no good, it could at least work no harm. It was an abrupt resolution. She stood in eager impatience, yet loath to interrupt him.

Gwinnan read his letters, one by one, while the postmaster went back to the plough, where the gray mare dozed in the furrow.

As Gwinnan gathered up the reins, looking absently ahead, the girl waiting by the roadside signed to him to stop. He did not see her. Somehow Alethea could not speak. She sprang forward with a hoarse cry, as he was about to pass like a flash, and caught his bridle. The young horse swerved, instead of trampling upon her, but dragging her with him.

"Take care!" cried out Gwinnan sharply. He drew up his horse with an effort, and looked down at her in amazement as she still clung to the bridle.

The next moment he recognized her.

XXVI.

UNDER the strong pull on the curb, the young horse stood quivering in every limb beneath the blossoming peach boughs that overhung the grassy margin of the road. There seemed a reflection of their delicate roseate tints in Alethea's upturned face, as with one hand she still grasped the bridle. Her old brown bonnet, falling back, showed her golden hair in its dusky tunnel. The straight blooming wands of the volunteer peach sprouts, that had sprung up outside the zigzag barriers of the rail fence, clustered about the folds of her homespun dress, as she stood in their midst.

All at once she was trembling violently. Her luminous brown eyes suddenly faltered. In her every consideration she herself was always so secondary — not with a sedulous effort of subordination, but yielding with a fine and generous instinct to the interest of others — that until this moment she had had no self-consciousness in regard to the jealousy which had resulted in Gwinnan's injuries. For this he had been struck down and brought near to death. Some sense of a reciprocal consciousness, an overwhelming deprecation of Mink's folly in fancying him a rival, a vague wonderment as to the effect of the idea upon Gwinnan, seized upon her for the first time now in his presence, as if she had had no leisure hitherto to think of these things. She could not speak. She could not meet his serious, intent, expectant eye.

"Did you have something to say to me?" he asked, taking the initiative.

It was the same tone that had given her sympathetic encouragement in the court-room, charged with a personal interest, a grave solicitude, all unlike the superficial, unmeaning courtesy of the lawyers. She spoke impetuously now as then, and with instant reliance upon him.

"I hearn, jedge," she cried, looking up radiantly at him, "ez how ye hev gin out ez ye never wanted Reuben Lorey ter be prosecuted fur tryin' ter kill ye, an' axed fur him ter be let off, an'_I 'lowed ye hold no gredge agin him. 'Pears ter me like ye war powerful good 'bout'n it."

"But he was prosecuted," the judge said quickly, fancying that she was under a delusion.

"I know!" she cried, with a poignant accent. "I know! I hearn it all."

She thought of his justification, his fancied provocation, and once more timidity beset her. How could she have found courage to speak in his behalf to Gwinnan? The judge himself was embarrassed; she knew it by the way he turned the reins in his hands. She noted details which usually, when her faculties were not so abnormally alert, would not have arrested her attention: the sleek coat of the handsome young horse, which now and then shook his head as if in disdain of her grasp; the superfine accoutrements of saddle and bridle; the smooth hands that held the reins; the severely straight lineaments, shadowed by the brim of the hat; and the searching, intent gray eyes, which saw, she felt, her inmost thought.

The postmaster, ploughing, came ever and anon down to the fence, pausing there to turn, and sometimes to thrust with his foot the clinging mould from the share. Occasionally he glanced at the incongruous couple, but as if the colloquy between them were a very normal incident, and with that courteous lack of curiosity and speculation characteristic of the region. All the fowls of the place followed in the furrow, clucking with gustatory satisfaction; now and then, with a gluttonous outcry, they darted to certain clods upturned by the plough, and the pantomime indicated much mortality among those poor troglodytes, the worms of the earth.

"You wanted to speak to me about him," said Gwinnan, with, it seemed to her, wonderful divination.

"Ye know, jedge," she said, more calmly, instantly reassured whenever he spoke, "they hev fund out ez 't war n't him ez bust down the mill. A boy seen it done, an' he war feared ter tell afore. I reckon that war what set Reuben off so awful onruly, — knowin' he never done it, nor drownded Tad nuther, — an' the 'torney-gin'al makin' folks 'low I seen a harnt."

"I dare say," remarked Gwinnan, dryly.

"An' I 'lowed," she continued, looking at him with beautiful, beseeching eyes " ez 't won't do him much good ef he does git off at his nex' trial, 'kase then he 'll be bound ter be in the prison arterward, ennyhow, fur twenty years. An' I 'lowed I 'd ax ye. seein' ez ye don't hold no gredge agin him, — I wonder at ye, too! — ef ye can't do nuthin' ez kin git him out now."

The wind waved the peach boughs above their heads, and the pink petals were set a-drifting down the currents of the air. Among the blossoms bees were booming, and on a budding spray a blue and crested jay was jauntily pluming its wings. Gold flakes of sunshine shifted obliquely through the rosy, inflorescent bower delicately imposed upon the blue sky. In its fine azure cirrus clouds were vaguely limned. On the opposite side of the road was the bluff end of a ridge, presenting a high escarpment of grim splintered rocks; among the niches ferns grew and vines trailed downward; there came from them a dank, refreshing odor, for moisture continuously trickled from them, and a hidden spring in a cleft by the wayside asserted its presence, — its tinkling distinctly heard in the pause that ensued.

He looked meditatively at the jagged heights. Then suddenly he turned his eyes upon her.

She was only a simple mountain girl, but it seemed to him that never since the first spring bloomed had woman worn so noble and appealing a face, so fine and delicate a personality. The crude dialect, familiar enough to him accustomed to the region, significant of ignorance, of poverty, of hopeless isolation from civilization, of uncouth manners, was in her all that speech might be, a medium for her ideas; the coarseness of her dress could hardly impinge upon the impression of her grace, — it was merely a garb. Her embarrassment had ceased. She looked straight at him; the unconscious dignity of her manner, the calmness of her grave eyes, the fading flush in her cheek, betokened that she had made her appeal to his generosity and that she had faith in it.

He was not a man who gave promises lightly. He was still silent. Again he looked up the road, with an absorbed and knitted brow. He tipped his hat further forward over his face; he shifted the reins uncertainly in his hands; the horse impatiently shook his head and struck the ground with his forefoot.

"It would be the worst thing I could do — for you," Gwinnan said at last, surprised himself at the tone he was taking.

She made no rejoinder; her face did not change; she only looked expectantly at him.

"You ought not to marry a man like that," he continued. "You are too good for him; and that is not saying much for you either."

"Oh," she cried, renewing her hold upon the bridle, and looking up with a face that coerced credence, "'t ain't fur myself I want him free! It air jes' fur him. He 'peared ter set mo' store by another gal than me. I ain't thinkin' ez we-uns would marry then. Like ez not he 'd go straight ter Elviry Crosby."

Another man might have experienced an amusement, a sort of self-ridicule, that he should remember the names of the infinitely insignificant, uncouth and humble actors in the little drama played in the court-room. But to Gwinnan people were people wherever he found them, and he had more respect for their principles than for their clothes. He recollected without effort the mention of Elvira in the testimony.

Nevertheless, with the many-sided view of the lawyer, he rejoined, oblivious of the suggestion conveyed, "I think not. It was on your account he attacked me."

Her face crimsoned, but with that fine instinct of hers

she steadfastly met his gaze, intimating that she placed no foolish interpretation upon his words or actions. She answered quietly enough, " Reuben air sometimes gin ter reckless notions. I reckon he noticed ez ye tuk up fur me whenst them lawyers war so besettin'. He war n't used ter sech ez that in Wild-Cat Hollow. Folks ginerally air sot agin me. Though I ain't treated mean, noways," she added, hastily, lest she might decry her relatives. " Only nobody thinks like me."

A forlorn isolation she suggested, — away up in the Great Smoky Mountains, thinking her unshared thoughts.

There was an increased attention in his face as he demanded, "Think differently about what?"

He had an imperative eye, an insistent voice. It did not occur to her that his interest was strange. And indeed he was not a man to be questioned.

She paused for a moment, her eyes full of a dreamy retrospection. She was not looking at him, but at the boughs of pink blossoms above his horse's head, and then she absently glanced at a black butterfly, bespangled with orange and blue, flying across the road to the ferns about the spring. As the fluttering wings disappeared she seemed to start from her reverie.

" Jedge," she said, in a piteous deprecation, "things seem right ter me, an' other folks thinks 'em wrong. An' I feel obleeged ter do what I 'low air right, an' it all turns out wrong. An' then I 'm besides myself with blame ! I reckon ye would n't b'lieve it, but it 's all my fault 'bout'n this trouble o' Reuben Lorey's. Ef it hed n't been fur me, he would n't hev gone down ter Shaftesville ter gin up all he hed ter old man Griff — like I tole him ter do ez soon ez I hed hearn 'bout bustin' the mill down. I tole him ter do it, an' he done it. An' look, — look ! "
She lifted her hand as if she drew a veil from the disastrous sequences. Her voice choked, her eyes were full of tears. " An' then I told that thar moonshiner ez I would n't promise ter keep his secret, an' they runned away fur fear o' me, 'kase Tad went thar arter he got out o' the ruver. I seen Sam Marvin arterward, an' he

'lowed ter me they s'posed he war a spy, an' beat him, an' — an' — I dunno *what* else they done ter him. None o' that would hev happened ef I hed promised ter hold my tongue. But it did n't 'pear right ter me."

"Then you were right not to promise," he said, reassuringly. "No one can do more than what seems right; that is," — it behooves a man of his profession to modify and qualify, — "within the limits of the law."

She looked up at him a little wonderingly. Her latent faculties for speculation were timorously developing in the first realization of intelligent sympathy that had ever fallen to her lot. How strange that such as he — and somehow she subtly appreciated in him that unification of mental force, education, civilization, natural endowment, and moral training, of the existence of which she was otherwise unconscious — should tolerate her doctrine; nay, should revere and accept it as a creed!

"A heap o' harm an' wrong hev kem of it," she said, submitting the logic of Wild-Cat Hollow.

"That is not our lookout. The moral law is to do what seems right, no matter what happens."

A vague smile broke upon his face; his eyes were illumined with a new light; he seemed suddenly young and very gentle.

"You need never be afraid of doing any harm; you may rely on it, you know what is right."

He was laughing at himself a moment later, — to gravely discuss these elementary ethics with a weighty sense. And yet he was glad to reassure her.

"Oh, jedge!" she cried, overcome with a sense of relief, with her happy reliance on his superior knowledge, — was not he the judge? — "that ain't what folks tell me. They 'low I be like that thar harnt o' a herder on Thunderhead; ef I can't kill ye, I jes' withers yer time an' spiles yer prospects. Oh!" — she struggled for self-control, — "I hev studied on that sayin' till it 'peared 't would kill me."

"Whoever told you that was very cruel, and I dare

say very worthless," said Gwinnan sharply. He was prompted by a vicarious resentment; he was picturing to himself some harsh-faced mountain neighbor as he asked sternly, " Who said it ? "

She saw the indignation in his countenance and suddenly feared that she was near to wrecking her lover's interest with the powerful man whom she sought to enlist.

" I — I can't tell," she faltered.

He waived the matter. " All right," he said, hastily. His face had hardened ; he was laughing a little, cynically. Who it was he knew right well. He had known right well, too, and many months ago, that she was infatuated with this young fellow, — how dashing, how spirited the scapegrace looked in his sudden recollection ! — and only now he began to definitely resent it. He glanced down at her with reprehensive, reproachful eyes. He was but a man, for all that he sat upon the bench and knew the law.

Alethea noted the subtle change in his face. It bewildered and confused her, but the surprise of it was as naught to the amazement that overpowered her to discover that the sky was reddening, the sun was sinking low to the purple Chilhowee, all the intervenient levels were suffused with a golden haze, and down the tawny, winding road she discerned a moving speck, which she divined might be Jerry Price and Bluff coming for her from the mill. Her rigorous conscience took her to task that, beguiled by a word of sympathy, of comprehension, she should have let the forlorn interests of her captive lover wait while she listened.

" Oh, jedge," she exclaimed, clinging to the bridle, — and it seemed he heard for the first time the voice of supplication, — " I know ye ain't one ez medjures a gredge an' pays it back. An' I 'lowed I 'd ax ye ter do suthin' fur him. He air a onruly boy, I know, but he never meant ter do sech — no harm — leastwise he — He war harried by things turnin' out so ez he could n't git jestice. An' leastwise, jedge " —

Poor Alethea was unskilled in argument, and even Harshaw had been fain to let Mink's moral worth pass without emblazonment.

"Oh, jedge," she cried, " ef ye could do suthin' fur him, 't would be sech a favor ter him, — all his life 's gone in that sentence, — an' — an' ter me."

He slowly shook his head.

"Not to you. It surprises me that you, who know so well what is right and good, should care for a man like that. He has only two alternations: he is either mischievous or malicious."

She was once more helplessly feeling aloof from all the world; for here his sympathy ended.

"It is a folly, and that is very wrong. You have mind enough, if you would exert it, to be sensible, to be anything you like."

And because he thought, with all the rest, that she was too good for the man she loved, he would not help? Ah, what joys of liberty, what griefs of long laborious years, what daily humiliation of that sturdy pride, what inexorable tortures to break that elastic spirit, — for break at last it must, — had Mink's half-hearted affection cost him! Her face had grown pale suddenly; the ebbing of her hope, that had rushed in upon her in a strong, tumultuous tide, was like the ebbing of life. Her eyes filled with tears, and her despair looked through them at him.

He had known much of the finalities of life. He dealt in conclusions. Volition, circumstance, character, might all make vital play in the varied causes that brought the event under his jurisdiction, but he wielded the determining influence and affixed the result. All human emotions had been unveiled to him: he could finely distinguish and separate into its constituent elements hate, misery, despair, fear, rage, envy; he even must needs seek to analyze the incomprehensible black heart of the murderer. He was a man of ample learning, of high ambitions, of excellent nerve, untouched by any morbid influence. He had pronounced the death sentence without a tremor. He was deliberate, cautious, reserved.

And yet because her cheek paled, because her eyes looked at him with the reproach of a dumb creature cruelly slain, because she said no word, he was pierced with pity for her. He was definitely aware now of his own generosity when he promised aught for her lover. He was amazed at himself, — amazed at the pang that it gave him when he said, —

"But I 'll try, — I 'll see what can be done. I shall be in Nashville soon, and I 'll talk to the governor, and make a strong effort to get a pardon. Not at once, you understand, but after a little time."

He gathered up the reins; the long horns of Bluff, approaching very near, were affronting the tender sensibilities of the roan colt, who snorted and stamped at the sight of them, and seemed likely to bolt. Alethea had, perforce, moved back among the pink blossoms by the wayside; from amidst them she looked up at Gwinnan with a rapture of gratitude, of admiration, of benediction, for which she had no words. She felt that she did not need them, for he understood so well, he understood so strangely, her most secret thought. He nodded to her and to the staring Jerry, who sat in the ox-cart. And then the restive roan bounded away into the golden spring sunshine, his glossy coat and flying mane distinct against the delicate green of the wayside, far, far up the road; and presently he was but a dwindling atom, and anon lost to view.

XXVII.

The spectacular effects of the newly built railroad through Cherokee County are of ceaseless interest to the denizens of the little log-cabins that lie at wide intervals upon the route, along which, indeed, for many miles, the only trace of civilization and progress is the occasional swift apparition of the locomotive, and the long parallel rails glistening in the sun. The dwellers in a certain hut near the river might be considered to afford typical manifestations. The children appear behind the rickety fence, or perhaps perched on the giddy eminence of the topmost rail, and salute the engine with the dumb show of much shouting and sometimes of derision. An old man hastily hobbles to the door; a woman busy in hanging out clothes in the sun on the althea bushes desists, to stare; the round-eyed baby on the doorstep becomes motionless in amaze; the gazing dogs wag approving tails; the farmer, leaning on his plough-handles, watches it till it is but a speck in the distance; a cow in the pasture breaks into a shambling run and turns her head to look back in affright; and near the woods-lot is a panic-stricken filly, plunging, and kicking, and snorting. And however often the sight of it may be vouchsafed, always the great splendid burnished motor, with its clouds of white steam, its thunderous gait, its servitors standing upon the platforms, and all its trains of loaded coaches, from which human faces look forth, to be curiously scanned, is thus greeted. But at night a mystery hangs about it. The reverberations of its footsteps may sound in the deepest dreams. Where is the darkness so dense, when is the storm so wild, that it cannot make its way as it lists? It seems then to these simple folks like some development of abnormal force, as it rends the gloom with its white glare, as it skims the denser medium of the earth like a meteor through the sky, — or some strange serpent with a glittering eye, drawing swiftly its sparkling lengths along. The rocks clamor with the wild clangors it has taught them, and the tumultuous, exultant shrieks of its whistle pierce the night. And for a time after it is gone the rails shiver with the thought of it, and the hills cry out again and again with fear.

It might appear that in the river lurks some danger for this bold marauder; always it slackens its speed and bates its voice when it approaches the bridge, and gives to the current a thousand glittering gauds of reflection. If the hour is not too late, the wayside family gather at the door to watch the train cross. When it reaches the other side, and speeds away with a loud cry of triumph and a renewed redundancy of motion, the old man turns, with an air of disappointment and a wag of the head and a muttered insistence: "Can't do that thar fool trick *every* time." He had opposed the theory of railroads, and had looked for a judgment to descend; in especial he had watched the building of the bridge in a spirit of indignation, prophesying that there would be a "big drownding" there one day, and had even lavished his advice upon the engineer in charge of the work, who, nevertheless, did not desist. Always he was convinced that that gossamer web, that union of strength and lightness, would give way sometime under the weight, and one spring night, as he hobbled to the door as usual to look at the flying and fiery dragon, no longer mythical, the catastrophe seemed imminent.

There was a variety of passengers in the smoking-car. The commercial traveler, returning with the swallow, was taking his way once more to the places that knew him. Conference had been held in a neighboring town, and the reverend gentlemen, homeward bound, were secular of aspect, genial and jolly, enveloped in clouds of tobacco smoke of their own making. The deputy-sheriff of Cherokee County was on board, and in his charge was Mink Lorey, on his way to stand his new trial in Shaftesville, handcuffed with Pete Owens, of the same county, who had had the misfortune to lose his temper on a small provocation, and to kill his brother. They and the guards were also a merry party. The deputy was undisguisedly glad to see Mink again, and rehearsed for his benefit the news from the town, and the rumors from the coves, and the vague echoes from the mountains, as he sat facing his prisoner, his elbows on his knees, fanning himself with his hat, now and then tousling his rough hair with one hand as he laughed, as if to add this dishevelment to the contortions and grotesqueness of his hilarity.

Mink listened with the wistful attention of one for whom all these things are forever past. This world of redundant interest was to be his world no more. Already it wore only the tender glamours of memory. The brown shadows and yellow lights from the lamps were shifting and shoaling, as the train jogged and lurched continually. The fluctuating gleams showed that his face was a trifle thin, perhaps; the expression of his vivid brown eyes had changed; they were desperate and hardened, but quickly glancing and even brighter and larger than before. His white wool hat was thrust on the back of his head as he leaned against the red velvet cushion, and his auburn hair, longer than ever, curled down upon the collar of his brown jeans coat. Now and then, when the deputy waxed facetious, Mink laughed aloud in sympathy.

The moon was a-journeying, too, with all the train of stars. Always through the open window one could find a serene transition from the interior, with its gaudy colors, its lounging masculine figures, its wreathing tobacco smoke, and the suffusion of yellow light and alternating brown shadow. The sky was pure and blue; the young mountaineer marked the weather-signs; the wind was astir, — a breeze other than that caused by the motion of the train; he saw the trees on the hillsides

waving in the sweet spontaneity of the air ; he noted the
shadow of the great locomotive swiftly traversing the
wheat-fields, with its piles of smoke scurrying behind it,
and seeming not less material. He leaned toward the
window, and called to the deputy to mark how forward
the crops were. And then he fell back with a white
despair on his face, for the train was thundering through
a forest, and the interfulgent sheen and shadow amongst
the great trees had caught the woodland creature's eye.
The sylvan fragrance came to him for a moment. The
fair, lonely vista lured him. How long, how long it had
been since he had trodden such wilds! Rocks towered
in the midst, and he was glad when they closed about
the way, and the reverberating clamors of the cut drowned
the groan that burst from him. And then they grew
fainter, and here were the levels once more, and suddenly — the Tennessee River! How should he fail to
know its splendid breadth and muscle, its majestic sinuosity as it curved! He leaned once more toward the
window, catching at the sill; the man with whose hand
his own was manacled complained of the strain. He
dropped his hand, and once more looked out as the train,
at a bated and circumspect pace, drew its slow length upon
the bridge. Most of the passengers were looking out,
too, under the fascination that the water of a landscape
always exerts upon travelers. The moon hung above the
broad vista of the dark, lustrous stream, flinging upon
its surface some gigantic magical corolla, softly refulgent,
to float on the water like a great white lily. The dense
forests, with a deeper gloom of shadow at their roots,
stood solemn and silent on either hand. The glare of
the head-light fell distorted on the ripples, and the lanterns of the brakemen evoked twinkling reflections below.
The dank vernal odors from the banks came in on the
breeze, and the wheels rolled slowly, and yet more slowly;
they were just beginning to accelerate their speed when
one of the passengers, glancing within to comment to a
friend, saw the lithe young prisoner rise suddenly and
liberate his hand with a violent jerk, while his companion

in shackles with a hoarse cry, clutched frantically at him. The guard turned with a start, as the young mountaineer, with an indescribably swift and elastic bound, sprang through the window and caught the timbers of the bridge. A violent jerk, a bell's sharp jangle, and an abrupt shiver ran through all the length of the train. Then the reflection of the glare of the head-light and the lesser gleaming points in the river were motionless. The train was at a stand-still in the middle of the bridge. A wild clamor arose from many voices; the brakemen on the platforms flashed their lanterns back and forth; a heavy body sprang into the swift waters with a great splash, and the sharp crack of a pistol echoed from the dark woods on either bank.

The startled passengers were treated to a fine display of conflicting authorities as they poured out on the platform of the smoking-car, where it seemed that the conductor of the train was laboring under the delusion that he could arrest the deputy-sheriff of Cherokee County.

"You had no right to pull the bell-cord and stop my train,—and stop it on the bridge!" he exclaimed.

"I'm bound ter ketch my prisoner!" cried the deputy-sheriff, wildly. "He was handcuffed with this one, and he slipped his paw out somehow, an' lept through the window, an' perched thar on that timber o' the bredge; an' I knowed he war expectin' the train ter go right on, an' I pulled the rope ter stop it. I'd hev hed him,—I'd hev hed him, ef the durned Mink hed n't tuk ter the water! Lemme go! Lemme go!"

But the train was in motion again, slowly crossing the bridge, and the officer could only rush to a window and look wildly over the waters, illumined by the head-light and the glimmer of the moon, and fire at devious black floating objects that showed resemblance to the head of a swimming man struggling for his life. Several of the passengers derived great sport from this unique target-shooting, and the quiet was invaded with cries of excitement mingled with the reiterations of the pistol pealing over the water. There! a fair shot! the object sinks,—

only a floating rail, for it is distinct as it rises once
more to the surface; and again the balls make havoc
only among the ripples. The quarry eludes, — eludes
strangely. He must have had great practice in diving,
or, as one hopeful soul cries out, he must be at the
bottom of the river.

Its current was placid enough when the train was
safely on the other side at a stand-still, and the people
from the little log-cabin below climbed the embankment
to hear the cause of the unprecedented stoppage. The
bridge did not break on this occasion, but the old man is
very sure they cannot do this "fool trick" again.

Although the train waited for a time while the banks
of the river were patrolled, it was gone clanging on its
way long before the rocks had ceased to echo the tramp
of excited horsemen and their hoarse cries, as they beat
the bushes in the neighboring woods, for the whole country-side was roused. The opinion that the reckless young
mountaineer had, in leaping into the river, struck against
some floating log, and had been killed by the concussion,
or had gone to the bottom among the bowlders with a
fatal force, gained ground as the day gradually dawned
and no trace of him was detected.

By degrees the search degenerated into the idler phases
of morbid curiosity. Many people visited the spot,
ostensibly to join in the effort, who stared at the bridge
and speculated on its height, and strolled up and down
the banks, wondering futilely. Even when the sunset
was reddening the river; when the evening star was
tangled in the boughs of a white pine on the bank; when
the sound of lowing kine was mellow on the air; when
the bridge doffed its massive aspect, and became illusory,
a shadow not more material than its shadow in the current below, — footing for the moonbeams, lodgment for
the dew, a perch for a belated bird, familiar of the mist,
— vague figures still lingered about the water-side, and
raucous voices grated on the evening air. But at last
the darkness slipped down; the train came and went;
silence fell upon the river, save for its own meditative,

iterative voice, the croaking of frogs, and the exquisite melody of the mocking-bird, as he sang in the slant of the moonbeams glistening through fringes of the pines. A wind rose and died away. The night was inexpressibly solitary. Far off a dog howled. The constellations imperceptibly tended westward. And presently, in the dark loneliness of the dead hour, something, — an otter, a musk-rat, a mink? — some stealthy wild thing, stirred itself at the water's edge, beneath a broad ledge of the jagged, beetling rocks along the bank, under the current, on the gravelly shallows. It made much commotion; the water receded in widening circles far out toward the middle of the river, — a scramble, a stroke or two, and it rose to its full height, and waded to the shore; for it was the battered image of a man. He wore no hat; his long locks hung in straight wisps down upon his shoulders. He glanced about him continually with fearful eyes, as he hobbled stiffly up the bank. Once he sat down on the roots of a tree in the shadow, and essayed to draw off the great boots, heavy with water, and hampering his every motion. But the leather, so long steeped, had swelled, and he could not divest himself of them.

"Mought lose 'em, ennyhow, ef I war ter take 'em off," he said, sturdily adapting his optimism to the cumbrous impediments. And so he limped on. He shivered in every limb. Over and again his breath seemed to fail him. More than once his head whirled, and he leaned against a tree to steady himself. The air was chill, but although the wind blew he was not sorry; it would the earlier dry his garments.

"An' I reckon I hev done cotch all the rheumatiz I kin hold, ennyways, a-layin' thar under the aidge o' the ruver, half kivered with water fur a night an' a day."

When the woods began to give way to fields he hung back, feeling desolate and affrighted. How could he barter these sheltering shadows, this nullifying darkness, for those wide, exposed spaces of the pasture? Its dewy slope, with here and there an outcropping rock, but never a bush nor a tree, lay under the slanting light of the moon. The mountains, however, he knew were in that direction; and presently he took courage to climb the fence, and with his hobbling shadow at his side, — from which he sometimes shrunk with sudden fear, glancing over his shoulder askance, — skulked across the grassy expanse, now in the melancholy sheen, and now in the vague shade of a drifting cloud. There were sheep huddled and white, at one side of the slope, all asleep, save one, that held its head up and looked at him with a contemplative eye as he passed. A dog seemed their only guardian. He did not bark, but came down toward the stranger with a sinister growl. Mink had no fear of dogs, and somehow they trusted him. The shepherd sniffed in surprise at his heels, bounded up to lick his hand, followed with a wagging tail till he climbed the fence, and regretfully saw him take his way down the road. For his courage was renewed by its own achievements. He was bold enough presently to invade a garden where potatoes had lately been planted, and he dug up the sliced fragments, each carefully cut that it might contain two or more "eyes." He found, too, some turnips, and was greatly refreshed and strengthened by his surreptitious meal. As he rose from the garden border and turned away among the currant bushes, he was confronted suddenly by the figure of a man. He sprang back, his heart plunging. He thought for a moment that he was discovered. And yet — it stood so strangely still. Only a suit of clothes stuffed with straw, and surmounted by an ancient and battered hat.

Mink gazed gravely at the scarecrow, that had surpassed its evident destiny in frightening that larger fowl, a jail-bird.

It might seem that with the weight of his heavy cares, the anguish of his forlorn plight, the dispiriting influence of his imprisonment, the jeopardy of his tortured freedom, his doubtful future, — exhausted, chilled, sore, — he would find scant amusement or relish in the grotesque image. One might wonder at the zest with which he applied himself, with convulsive, feeble efforts, to uproot the pole that sustained it. He conveyed it across the garden, — daring the dogs, — and placed the scarecrow where it might seem to peer into the front window of the house. He stood looking at it with intense satisfaction for a moment, — so like a man it was! He could forecast how the women of the household would cry aloud with terror when they should see it, how the mystified men would stare and swear. He did not laugh; the feat in some other method satisfied his sense of the ludicrous. It did not occur to him as a futile waste of his time and strength, — of both he presently stood in sore need. For the day was breaking when he still trudged between the zigzag lines of farm fences, along a road that bore evidences of much travel, in a country which he did not know, of which the only familiar objects were the dying moon and the slowly developing outline of the Great Smoky Mountains, far away.

"I 'll git ter Shaftesville in time ter stan' my trial, ef I don't mind, 'fore the dep'ty does," he said to himself in a panic.

Nowhere were forests visible promising shelter. Here and there a limited woods-lot lined the road; more often fields of corn, barely showing tender sprouts above the ground, or stretches of winter wheat or millet, or pastures. He was in the midst of a scene of exclusive agricultural significance, when the startling sound of wagon wheels broke upon the air, and the figure of a man driving a pair of strong mules rose gradually from over the brow of the hill.

Mink's clothes were already dry; his hair curled freshly once more, but he was painfully conscious of the lack of his hat, and he knew that the teamster's eyes rested upon him in surprise. The man drew up his mules at once. But the wily fugitive hailed him first.

"Howdy," Mink remarked, advancing sturdily, putting one foot on the hub of the front wheel and his hand on the off mule's back, and looking up with his bold, bright eyes at the driver. "Do you-uns hail from nighabouts?"

"Down yander at Peters' Cross-Roads," responded the stranger promptly.

"I ax kase I 'lowed mebbe ye hed hearn some word o' that thar prisoner ez got away from the sher'ff o' Cher'kee County, — Reuben Lorey."

"*Mink* Lorey, I hearn his name war," corrected the teamster.

"Waal," — Mink's careless glance wandered aimlessly up and down the sunny road, — "he oughter be named Mink, ef he ain't; mean enough."

"Ye 're 'quainted with him, I reckon," said the teamster, still looking at his hatless head.

"Mighty well! He hev gin me a heap o' trouble. I dunno but I 'd nigh ez soon he 'd be in the bottom o' the Tennessee Ruver ez not. We-uns hail from the same valley, — Hazel Valley."

"What ye doin' 'thout no hat?" demanded the saturnine, perplexed, and vaguely suspicious man.

"Lost it in the ruver. Been fishin'. I hev been visitin' some folks in the flatwoods ez I be mighty well 'quainted with. I 'm goin' ter git me another hat at the store."

There was a pause.

"'They 'low that thar man war drownded," said the teamster, discursively.

"Waal," said Mink, drawlingly, "I 'lowed I 'd ax, so ez when I git ter Hazel Valley I mought tell his folks a straight tale."

The teamster's wonderment, being satisfied as to the bare head of the young fellow, he was eager to proceed on his journey. Certainly all imaginable suspicions must have been allayed by the pertinacity with which Mink hung upon the wheel, and talked about the rheumatism he feared he had caught a-fishing, and declared he had found no sport in it.

Finally, with apparent reluctance, he took his foot from off the hub, and the teamster was glad to go creaking along on his journey.

Although the danger was so successfully thwarted, the

strain upon his ingenuity, his nerves, and his presence of mind had told heavily upon Mink's reserve force of strength and courage. When at last he reached the deep woods he was more dead than alive, as he flung himself down in the hollow of a poplar-tree, struck long ago by lightning, — its great length fallen, its branches burned, only its gigantic stump standing to boast the proportions this chief of the savage wilds had borne. The young mountaineer doubted, as he fell asleep, if he would ever wake. But exhaustion did not prevail. Over and again, with a nervous start, consciousness would seize upon him, and he would be himself long enough to contrast his forlorn plight with the feignings of his dream, and so sink again into troubled slumber. And yet it was with a deep satisfaction that he gazed out at intervals upon the lonely crowded sylvan limits. The underbrush closed about him; the great trees upreared their heads against the sky, showing only a glimpse of the blue or a flake of the burnished vernal sunshine. How restful the sight, how reassuring the sound of the wind in the leaves! A squirrel frisked by, sleek and dapper, with a brilliant, unaffrighted eye and a long curling tail. The familiar creature seemed like a friend. "Howdy, mister," observed Mink. "Ye air one citizen ez I ain't afeard on."

But the squirrel came no more, although ever and anon Mink lifted himself to look out. He noted the moss, green and gray, on the bark of a rotting log; he started to hear the woodpecker tapping; he listened for a time to a crested red-bird's song, but its iteration was somnolent in its effects, and when Mink next opened his eyes darkness enveloped the world. He could hardly say whom he might be; he did not know where he was. The oppression of his familiar cell in the Glaston jail filled his consciousness until, as he groped about him, he felt the rotting sides of the old tree and realized that he was free.

"I mus' be a-travelin'," he said to himself.

Free, but with so burning a pain in every limb that he

could hardly stand upon his feet; and what was this new
misfortune? His forlorn boots were bursting into fragments. As he staggered into the moonshine he sat down,
and putting one foot on his knee examined the sole in
rueful contemplation.

"Now don't that thar beat kingdom come! Them
boots war mighty nigh new when I went ter jail, an' I
never stood on 'em none thar sca'cely. Mus' hev been
the soakin' they got. I ain't useter goin' bar'foot lately,
an' how 'll I travel thirty mile this-a-way?"

It was at a slow gait that he hobbled along; now and
then he stumbled, and would have fallen but for his
hasty clutch at a bush or a tree. His feet were pierced
by flints through the crevices of his boots, and he was
presently aware that he was marking his steps with his
blood. He made scant progress, although he struggled
strenuously, and it was long before day when he was
fain to lie down in a rift in a great bank of rocks, and
recruit his wasted energies with sleep. "I hope I ain't
a-goin' ter die in sech a hole ez this," he said, "ez ef I
war a sure-enough mink. But Laws a-massy, what be I,
ef I ain't a mink?"

He laughed sarcastically as he turned himself over.
He had evolved some harsh theories of worldly inequalities. If he had knocked Jerry Price or Ben Doaks
senseless with a bit of iron, he argued, he would have
hardly been in jeopardy of arrest; the affair would perchance have been chronicled by the gossips as "a right
smart fight." But he must forfeit twenty years of his
life for assaulting a man of Gwinnan's quality. And he
had some bitter reflections to divert his mind, with the
functions of a counter-irritant, from his aching bones,
his bleeding feet, his overpowering sense of fatigue.

It was the next night — for he again lay hidden all
day — that he at last passed through the gap of the
mountain and entered Eskaqua Cove. His spirits had
risen at the sight of the familiar things, — the foam on
the river dancing in the light of the moon, the dense
solemn forests, the great looming, frowning rocks. He

hardly cared how steep the hillsides were, how his sore feet burned and ached, how heavily he dragged his weight. He could have cried aloud with joy when he beheld the little foot-bridge which he knew so well, albeit he could scarcely stagger over the narrow log; the low little house on the bank where Mrs. Purvine lived. It was dark and silent under the silver moon, for the hour was late, reckoning by rural habits, — about ten o'clock, he guessed. He hesitated for a moment when he was in the road beside the fence. He thought he might shorten the way by crossing the corn-field, for the road made a bend below. He had climbed the fence and was well out in the midst of the sprouting grain, when suddenly he started back. There was a shadow coming to meet him. He could not flee. He could not hope to escape observation. And yet, when he looked again, the dim figure was curiously busy, and was not yet aware of his presence. It was the figure of a woman, and he presently recognized Mrs. Purvine. Her head was evidently much wrapped up against the night air, and her sun-bonnet was fain to perch in a peaked attitude, in order to surmount the integuments below; it was drawn down over her face, and by other means than the sight of her countenance he identified her. It might seem an uncanny hour for industry, but Mink could well divine that Mrs. Purvine had experienced belated pangs of conscience concerning sundry rows of snap-beans, left defenseless, save for her good wishes, against the frost. She was engaged in covering them, — detaching a long board from a pile beside the fence, and placing it with a large stone beneath either end above the tender vegetable. Her shadow was doing its share, although it gave vent to none of the pantings and puffings and sighs with which the flesh protested, as it were, against the labor. It jogged along beside her on the brown ground in dumpy guise, and stooped down, and rose up, and set its arms akimbo to complacently observe the effect of the board, and even wore a sun-bonnet at the same impossible angle. It started off with corresponding alacrity to the pile to fetch another board for another row, and was very busy as it stooped down to adjust a stone beneath. It even sprang back and threw up both arms in sudden affright, when Mrs. Purvine exclaimed aloud. For a deft hand had lifted the other end of the board, and as she glanced around she saw a man kneeling on the mould and placing the stone so that the delicate snapbeans might be sheltered.

"In the name o' Moses!" faltered Mrs. Purvine between her chattering teeth, as she rose to her feet, "air that thar Mink Lorey — or — or " — she remembered how far away, how safe in jail, she had thought him — "or his harnt?"

Mink turned his pallid face toward her. She saw the lustrous gleam of his dark eyes.

He hesitated for a moment. Then, he could not resist. "I died 'bout two weeks ago," he drawled circumstantially.

Mrs. Purvine stood as one petrified for a moment. Then credulity revolted.

"Naw, Mink Lorey!" she said sternly. "Naw, sir! Ye ain't singed nowhar. Ef ye war dead, ye 'd never hev got back onscorched." She shook her enveloped head reprehensively at him.

Regret had seized upon him. The fleeting privilege of frightening Mrs. Purvine scarcely compensated for the risks he felt he ran in revealing himself.

He stood silent and grave enough as she set her arms akimbo and gazed speculatively at him.

"How d' ye git out'n jail?" she demanded.

"Through thar onlockin' the door," said Mink.

Mrs. Purvine knitted her puzzled brows.

"War they willin' fur ye ter leave?" she asked, seeking to fathom the mystery.

"Waal, Mis' Purvine," equivocated the fugitive, jauntily, "I ain't never fund nobody, nowhar, right up an' down *willin*' fur me to leave 'em. They hed ter let me go, though."

"Waal, sir!" exclaimed Mrs. Purvine, with the accent of disappointment. "I never b'lieved ez Jedge Gwinnan war in earnest whenst he promised Lethe Sayles ter git ye pardoned. Whenst she kem back rej'icin' over it so, I 'lowed the jedge war jes' laffin' at her."

The man, staring at her with unnaturally large and brilliant eyes, recoiled suddenly, and his shadow seemed to revolt from her words. "Jedge Gwinnan! pardon!" he cried, contemptuously, his voice rising shrilly into the quiet night. "He got me no pardon! I'd hev none off'n him, damn him! I'd bide in the prison twenty year, forty year, — I'd rot thar, — afore I'd take enny faviors out'n *his* hand! Lord! let me lay my grip on that man one more time, an' hell an' all the devils can't pull me off!"

His strength failed to support his excitement. He staggered to the pile of boards and leaned against them, panting. Mrs. Purvine noted how white his face was, how exhausted his attitude.

"Ye 'pear sorter peaked," she remarked, prosaically, "an' ye walk toler'ble cripple."

"Yes," observed Mink, with his wonted manner, "it 'peared ter me a toler'ble good joke ter jump off the middle o' the bredge inter the Tennessee Ruver. But it turned out same ez mos' o' my jokes, — makes me laugh on the wrong side o' my mouth."

Mrs. Purvine began to understand. Her lower jaw dropped. "Whar hev ye hed ennything ter eat?" she demanded, with bated breath.

"Waal," said Mink, argumentatively, "eatin' 's a powerful expensive business; we-uns would all save a heap ef we 'd quit eatin'."

Mrs. Purvine received this in pondering silence. Then she broke forth suddenly : —

"Ye air a outdacious, sassy, scandalous mink, an' I hev 'lowed ez much fur many a year, but I never looked ter see the time when ye 'd kem an' prop yerse'f up in my gyarden-spot, an' look me in the eye, an' call me stingy. How war I ter know ye war n't ez full ez a tick, ye impident half-liver? I kin see ez ye ain't fat in nowise, but how kin I tell by the creases in a man's face what he hed fur dinner?"

"Laws-a-massy, Mis' Purvine!" exclaimed Mink, truly contrite for the untoward interpretation which his words seemed to bear. "I never meant sech ez that. Ef it hed been enny ways nigh cookin' time, I'd hev kem right in, — ef I hed n't been afraid ye'd tell on me, — an' axed ye fur a snack. Ain't I eat hyar time an' agin along o' Jerry Price? I hev hed a heap o' meals from you-uns, — more 'n ye know 'bout, fur I hev treated yer watermillion patch ez ef it hed been my own."

If Mrs. Purvine was placated, she did not at once manifest the fact. "What d'ye know 'bout cookin' time, or cookin', ye slack-twisted, lazy, senseless critter? Jes' kerry yer bones right inter that thar door, fur eat ye hev got ter. In Moses's name!" she ejaculated piteously, "the boy kin sca'cely walk."

But Mink hesitated. "I don't wanter see Jerry," he said. "I dunno what Jerry mought think 'bout'n it all."

"Jerry's dead asleep, an' so air all the boys," declared the industrious Mrs. Purvine. "Ye reckon ye air goin' ter find ennybody up this time o' night 'ceptin' a hard-workin' old woman like me? I can't be no surer o' ye 'n I be a'ready. Go 'long in, 'fore I set Bose on ye."

He was sorry for himself, — to gauge the joy, the comfort, that the very sight of the humble and familiar room afforded him. The fire had been covered with ashes, but Mrs. Purvine promptly pulled out the coals and piled on the pine knots, and the white flare showed the low-ceiled apartment, the walls covered with the old advertisements; the puncheon floor; the many strings of pepper and hanks of yarn hanging from the beams, and the quilting-frame clinging to them like a huge bat; the two high beds; the glister of the ostentatious mirror; the prideful clock, silent on the shelf. As the interior became brilliantly illuminated, Mink looked suspiciously at the glass in the windows; he experienced a relief to note that the batten shutters were closed.

"I did n't want nobody ter git a glimge o' me," he said, "'kase I dunno but what they mought try ter hold ye 'sponsible fur feedin' me, cornsiderin' I be a runaway." "They ain't never ter goin' ter find out ez ye hev been hyar now," said Mrs. Purvine.

"They mought ax ye," suggested Mink.

"Waal, lies air healthy." Mrs. Purvine accommodated her singular ethics to many emergencies. "Churchyards air toler'ble full, but thar ain't nobody thar ez died from tellin' lies. Not but what I'm a perfessin' member," she qualified, with a qualm of conscience, "an' hev renounced deceit in gineral; but ef ennybody kems hyar inquirin' roun' 'bout my business, — what I done with this little mite o' meat, an' that biscuit, an' the t'other pot o' coffee, — I answer the foolish accordin' ter his folly, like the Bible tells me, an' send him reji'cin' on his way."

Mink, his every fear relieved, thought it a snug haven after the storms that he had weathered, as he sat in Mrs. Purvine's own rocking-chair, and felt the grateful warmth of the blaze. He had hardly hoped ever again to know the simple domestic comforts of the chimney-corner. The coffee put new life into him, and after he had eaten the hot ash cake and bacon, broiled on the coals, he took, at her insistence, another cup, and drank it as she sat opposite him near the hearth. In this last potation she joined him, having poured her coffee into a gourd, to save the trouble, as she explained, of washing another cup and saucer.

"How do Lethe keep her health?" he asked.

"Fust-rate," said Mrs. Purvine. Her tone had changed. She looked at him speculatively from under the brim of her sun-bonnet, which she wore much of the time in the house. "She air peart an' lively ez ever."

His lip curled slightly. He was sarcastic and critical concerning Alethea's mental attitude, — the reaction, perhaps, of much rebuke and criticism received at her hands.

"I reckon she ain't missed me none, then?" he hazarded.

"Waal, she never seen much o' you-uns las' summer, bein' ez ye war constant in keepin' company with Elviry then; though she's missed ye cornsider'ble. Ye need n't never 'low the gals will furgit ye, Mink," she added graciously. " The las' time Lethe seen Jedge Gwinnan she war a-beggin' him fur ye, — an' he promised, too. Lethe's pretty enough ter make a man do mos' ennything, — leastwise these hyar town folks think so."

The color had sprung into Mink's face. He stood up for a moment, searching for Jerry's tobacco on the mantelpiece. He lighted his pipe by a coal which he scooped up with the bowl, and as he put the stem between his lips he looked hard at Mrs. Purvine's placid face, as she drank her coffee from the gourd, and meditatively swung her foot; the right knee was crossed over the left; the other foot was planted squarely upon the floor; a narrow section of a stout gray stocking was visible above a leather shoe, laced incongruously with a white cotton cord, the kitten having carried off its leather string, and Mrs. Purvine continually "disremembering," to more properly supply its place.

"Ben Doaks, — air he still thinkin' 'bout marryin' Lethe?" demanded Mink between a series of puffs.

"Ef he air, he air barkin' up the wrong tree, I kin tell ye!" exclaimed Mrs. Purvine, angrily. "Lethe Sayles air goin' ter marry a town man, — leastwise that's what all the kentry air sayin'. He 'lows she be plumb beautiful! An' I always did think so, though she air my own niece," as if this ought to be an obstacle. "I names no names," — which would have been difficult, under the circumstances, — "but he air a town man, an' hev got a high place, an' air well off. Some folks don't keer nuthin' 'bout money, but I ain't one of 'em. An' he air o' good folks. — fust-rate stock; an' I sets store on fambly, too."

Mink was leaning forward, with his elbows on his knees; his eyes burned upon her face; his pipe-stem was quivering in his gaunt hand.

"Whar did she meet up with him?"

"Down in Shaftesville, when she went ter testify fur

you-uns," said Mrs. Purvine. Then, with her sudden felicity of inspiration. "He seen her fust in the court-room, an' he war smitten at sight."

She could not accurately define the impression she was making. But she grew a little frightened as she watched the keen, clear-cut face, changing unconsciously, responsive to her intimations; his wild dark eyes, in no sort tamed or dimmed, dwelt steadily on the white vistas of the fire; his fine red hair was tossed back, curling on his collar. As she looked at him, constrained to note how handsome he was, she wished very heartily, poor woman, that that mythical fortunate suitor had added to the charming qualities with which she had endowed him the simple essential, existence.

Mink burst suddenly into a satiric laugh, startling to hear. Mrs. Purvine turned upon him, the gourd trembling in her hand.

"Ye ain't got no manners, Mink Lorey," she said, trying to resume her note of superficial severity. "What be ye a-laffin' at?"

"Jes' at thoughts," he said enigmatically; "thoughts!"

"Thoughts 'bout me, I'll be bound," said Mrs. Purvine aggressively.

"Naw; jes' 'bout Lethe an' that thar town man." He whirled from the fire, and walked up and down the floor with his hands in his pockets.

"Waal, don't ye say no mo' 'bout'n him," said Mrs. Purvine, desirous of contemplating him no longer, "an' don't ye ax me who he be — fur I won't tell ye!"

"Thar ain't no need ter ax ye; I *know*."

Mrs. Purvine pondered on this for a moment. She forgot it in her effort to persuade the young fellow to accept the hospitalities of the spare bedroom, of which she was so proud. "Ye kin jest stay in thar all night, Mink, an' all ter-morrer. Ye won't wake up fur no breakfus' arter the tramp ye hev hed, an' a long sleep 'll ease yer bones. An' ter-morrer night, 'bout ten o'clock, arter all the chill'n hev gone ter sleep I'll gin ye a good meal, an' ye kin set out, heartened up an' strong. I'd rather

Jerry an' the boys did n't know 'bout yer bein' hyar, 'kase I dunno what the law does ter folks ez holps them ez be runnin' from jestice — or injestice; 'bout the same thing, ez fur ez I kin make out. An' I don't want them ter git inter trouble."

"Mebbe the sher'ff 'll kem arter you-uns," Mink warned her.

"Waal, I 'll tell him I ain't got no time to waste, an' ter take himself off the way he kem;" and Mrs. Purvine dismissed the imaginary officer with a lofty sniff.

It seemed to Mrs. Purvine, the next day, that many immediate requisites were stowed away temporarily in the bedroom. She was continually on the alert to prevent Jerry or the boys from invading it. "Keep out 'n that thar bedroom. I ain't keerin' ef ye *ain't* got no symblin' seed. I ain't goin' ter let ye s'arch *thar*. I hev got all my fine quilts what I pieced myself — 'ceptin' with a leetle help from Lethe Sayles — a-hangin' up thar ter air. Hang 'em up in the sun, ye say? Who d 'ye reckon wants ter fade them gay colors out?"

When at last Jerry desisted in deference to this new strange whim, one of the boys was beset with anxiety to get his shoes which he had set away there.

"That's the way the shoe-leather goes, — walkin' on it," said aunt Dely reasonably. "Naw, sir! save them soles, an' go bar'foot. The weather's warm now."

The youngest, the most pertinacious and hard to resist, was tumultuous to get a certain "whang o' leather" which Bluff needed to complete his gear, in order to continue ploughing.

"I ain't a-keerin' ef one o' Bluff's horns war lef' in thar, an' he could n't wink without it. I ain't goin' ter hev them quilts disturbed."

She presently became drowsy, because of her long vigil of the preceding night, and placed her chair before the door that no one might enter without rousing her, and thus, a solemn sentinel, she alternately knitted and nodded away the afternoon.

It was a great relief to her when the house was still,

the family all asleep, and the fugitive's meal prepared. She had taken special pains with it, albeit she went about it yawningly, and had filled a tin pail with provisions that he might carry with him.

She waited ten minutes or so after all was ready. She listened as she knelt on the hearth. There was no sound from within but the stertorous breathing of the sleepers in the roof-room. From without only the murmur of the river, the croaking of a frog, the stir of the wind came in at the open back door, through which she could see the white moonshine, lying in lonely splendor upon the dark, prosaic expanse of the newly ploughed fields. She rose and closed it, that the fugitive might not be revealed to the casual eye of any nocturnal fisherman, striking through her domain on his way to the river bank. Then she went to the bedroom door.

As she tapped on it, the door moved under the pressure, and she saw that it was unbuttoned on the inside. "That thar keerless boy ought ter hev buttoned this door!" she exclaimed. "The sher'ff could hev gone right in and nabbed him whilst he war asleep. Ye Mink! *Mink!*"

There was no answer.

"Waal, sir! I never seen the beat." Then in imperative crescendo, "*Ye Mink!*"

She pushed the door open, presently. The moonlight slanted through the porch and into the little bedroom, revealing the bed, empty, the room deserted save for Mrs. Purvine's rows of dresses hanging by the neck, and the piles of quilts on a shelf, rising in imposing proportions to attest her industry and a little help from Lethe Sayles.

He had fled, — when, why? She could not say; she could not imagine. She stood staring, with a vacillating expression on her face. She was ready for an outburst of futile anger, could she construe it as one of his minkish tricks; he might even now be far away, laughing to picture how she would look when she would stand at the open door and find the room empty. Her face reddened at the thought. But perhaps, she argued, more generously, he had taken some alarm, and fled for safety.

Mrs. Purvine had had no experience in keeping secrets, and her colloquial habits were such as did not tend to cultivate the gift. More than once, the next day, as she pondered on the mysterious disappearance of Mink, she would drop her hands and exclaim in meditative wonderment, "Waal! waal! waal! This worl'! This worl'! an' a few mo' ekal ter it."

It went hard with her to resist the curious questionings that this demonstration was calculated to excite. But when asked what she was talking about she would only reply in enigmatical phrase, "Laros to ketch meddlers!" and shake her head unutterably. Nevertheless, when it became evident that her household had exhausted all their limited wiles to elicit the mystery of which she seemed suddenly and incomprehensibly possessed, and had reluctantly desisted, her resolution grew weaker instead of stronger, and she was bereft of a piquant interest in their queries and guesses. She began herself to play around the dangerous subject; her remarks seemed to excite no suspicion and no surprise, and thus she was astonished in her turn.

"I wonder, Jerry," she said, as he and she, their pipes freshly lighted after supper, strolled about the "gyarden-spot" to note how the truck was thriving, Bose and a comrade or two at their heels, — "I wonder how high that thar new bredge be over the Tennessee Ruver?"

"Never medjured it," returned Jerry, his eyes twinkling as they met her serious gaze.

"Ye g' 'long!" exclaimed Mrs. Purvine tartly. She was addressing only the unfilial spirit that prompted his reply, for she had no intention of dismissing the audience, as she resumed at once in her usual tone. "Waal, from all ye hev hearn, would n't ye 'low ez ennybody jumpin' off'n it war 'bleeged ter break thar neck?" she argued.

"I'd hev thunk so," admitted Jerry, "but it seems not."

She looked sharply at him from over her spectacles as she canvassed his reply. It must have been accident. How could he know aught of Mink? She was for a moment so impressed with a sense of danger here that she took refuge in silence.

"Them peas 'll hev ter be stuck afore long," Jerry remarked presently, complacent in their growth.

But the simple pleasures of a garden were too insipid to enchain the interest of the sophisticated Mrs. Purvine; her mind reverted to her burning secret and the many speculations to which it gave rise. She hardly noted the red sky, stretching so far above the purple mountains; the river, with reflections of gold and pink amidst its silver glinting. In the south Procyon, star of ill-omen, swung in the faint blue spaces. A whip-poor-will sang. Darkness impended.

Once more she skirted the forbidden topic.

"Waal, I would n't advise nobody ter try it." She was alluding not to the industrial necessity of sticking the peas, but to jumping off the bridge.

"Naw, sir," Jerry assented quietly. "'Bout some things Mink 'pears ter hev the devil's own luck, though ginerally they run agin him. I reckon nobody but Mink could hev lept from that bredge an' swum out'n the ruver 'thout gittin' cotched."

Mrs. Purvine trembled from head to foot. As she turned her face toward him the light of the evening struck upon her glittering spectacles in the depths of her sun-bonnet, and it seemed a fiery and penetrating gaze she bent on her adopted son.

"In the name o' Moses, Jerry Price!" she solemnly adjured him. "How did you-uns know ennything 'bout Mink Lorey?"

"Same way ye did," said Jerry, in the accents of surprise.

Mrs. Purvine sat down abruptly on the pile of boards beside the fence.

Jerry, astonished at her evident agitation, proceeded:

"Yer mem'ry air failin' surely, ef ye hev furgot ez

the dep'ty sher'ff tole us 'bout'n it yestiddy, — rid his critter right up thar ter the side o' the fence, an' I lef' Bluff whar I war a-ploughin' an' went down an' talked ter him."

"What war I a-doin' of?" demanded Mrs. Purvine, feebly.

"Ye war settin' knittin' right in front o' the bedroom door, — ter keep we-uns from raidin' in on them quilts ez ye war airin' in the bedroom whar thar ain't no air."

Mrs. Purvine breathed more freely. She had a vague memory of hearing a man hallooing at the fence, and of seeing Jerry running to meet him; the rest was lost in the deep slumber which she called "dozin' off," as she sat sentinel in front of the door.

"I mus' hev been noddin'," she said, trembling again at the idea that the sheriff and the prisoner had been at such close quarters. "I never hearn none o' it."

"Waal," explained Jerry, "he hed traced Mink up somewhar nighabouts. An' he war mighty keen ter ketch him. He 'lowed Mink war a turrible fool ter hev runned off, kase they hed n't lef' Glaston more 'n two hours 'fore Mink's pardon kem. Jedge Gwinnan hed gone an' beset the gov'nor, an' tole him 't war a plumb mistake, an' Mink war n't no reg'lar jail-bird, nor hardened critter, nor nuthin' but a simple country boy. An' he 'd hed a reg'lar martyrdom o' injestice, an' sech. An' the 'sault war jes' a boy's hittin' a feller ez he 'lowed war gittin' the better o' him. 'T war n't 'count o' the trial. He war jes' jealous. Jedge Gwinnan 'lowed ez the fight war mighty onfair, kase Mink war chained an' he war n't. An' he would n't hev let him be prosecuted ef he could hev knowed it in time ter hev holped it. An' ez Mink's case hed been affirmed by the S'preme Court the gov'nor pardoned him. Skeggs 'lowed folks say the gov'nor war right down glad ter do it, kase he hev hed ter be toler'ble hard on some folks lately ez applied fur pardons; an' he war glad Mink's case kem along, kase he did n't want ter git onpop'lar, an' ter 'pear set agin mercy ez a constancy."

"Waal! waal!" exclaimed Mrs. Purvine, divided between surprise and an effort to gauge the effect of this intelligence on the prisoner listening in the little room.

"Skeggs 'lowed 't war mighty mean in Mink ter hide out an' leave him ter ketch all the consequences, — he air 'sponsible fur the 'scape, — kase they don't want Mink fur nuthin' now but that thar leetle case 'bout'n the mill, an' everybody knows Tad ain't dead, an' Mink never bust down the mill nohow. Mr. Harshaw 'lows he seen Tad when he war huntin' up in the mountings. An' Lethe, she seen him. An' Skeggs air honin' an' moanin' 'bout'n it, an' 'lows Mink mought kem an' be tried, ef he hed the feelins o' a man stiddier a mink."

Mrs. Purvine rose slowly, and bent her meditative steps toward the door, wondering all the more why Mink should have disappeared so mysteriously, cognizant as he must have been of how his dangers had lessened, whither he had gone, with what purpose.

"Aunt Dely," said Jerry, suddenly, following her slowly, "how did ye know ennything 'bout Mink, ef ye never hearn Skeggs tell it?"

"Jerry Price," said Mrs. Purvine, sternly, "ef ye hed been raised by yer aunt Melindy Jane, I.'ll be bound ye'd hev larned better 'n ter ax fool questions with every breath ye draw."

XXVIII.

HARSHAW considered a knowledge of human nature as essential a tool of his trade as the Tennessee Reports, and the common human attributes, so far as he had discerned them, were definitely abstracted and tabulated in his mind, — for he was systematic mentally.

Nevertheless, he was profoundly ignorant of these traits as manifested in his own personality. Had another member of the legislature risen in his place one day, when the spring was just beginning to open, stating that he desired to make a motion based on public rumor, to which he considered the attention of the House should be directed, Harshaw could not have failed to note the ring of triumph in the voice, the predatory gleam in the eye, the restive eagerness of address, the swift fluency of excited words. He would not have been slow to deny to the demonstration those motives so insistently arrogated, — public justice, patriotism, sense of duty.

His manner had riveted the attention of the House, which was more than usually quiet. It had that sombre, undecorative aspect common to assemblages exclusively of men. The effect of uniformity of attire was, however, annulled in a measure by the varying expressions in countenance, in age, in attitude. The metropolitan representatives had a more dapper appearance than the members from the outlying districts, who were distinguished by a solid and serious mien that promised an intolerance of flippancy in matters of religion, and morals, and manners.

Here and there was a face individual enough to arrest attention. Kinsard's head, with its high, earnest brow, its roving, melancholy black eyes, its sharp, characteristic features, stood out from the rest in strong relief, canceling the heads about it to a nebulous suggestion of humanity. He lounged in one of the most negligent of his dislocated postures. He had a smile of bitter contempt on his face, which bore no relation to his attitude of indifference, and expressed an energy of anger which he was at a loss how best to wreak. More than once he looked away from Harshaw, as if to divert his thoughts, to allay his irritation, by the contemplation of the scene without.

The windows stood open to the bland spring air. The languid, quiescent sunshine loitered along the great white stone porticoes, looking in often, a smiling, sheeny presence, upon the grave deliberations within. The river glistened in lustrous curves between high banks fringed with green as far as the eye could reach. The roofs of the city below were almost smokeless, — only here and there a wreathing hazy curl. The old forts on the hills wore all the dismantled and sunken aspect of desuetude, and gathered into the scars of war the blossoms of peace and the nestlings, and garnered the songs and the smiles of spring to make the waste places merry.

Hardly a sound entered at the window, — only the droning of a portly bee which, arrayed in a splendid buff jerkin and a black belt, came swiftly in and went again in a slant of sunshine. Harshaw's voice, echoing from the stone walls, seemed doubly weighty and impressive and resonant.

The House had already received an intimation of what he was about to say, and although his animosity to Gwinnan impugned his credibility and relaxed the surprise which had been occasioned, his bold overt allusions to his antagonism, his sturdy, undaunted address, had their effect. He said he must impinge upon the indulgence of the House for some personal explanation. Had he consulted his own inclinations he would have let the matter pass. It had come to his knowledge with no solicitation, no suspicion, by accident, or — with a reverent intonation — providentially, he might better say. But (suspended effect) he was sworn (with a wag of the head) to serve the interests of the people of Tennessee, and (he thumped the desk) right zealously would he discharge that precious and supreme trust! The duty of laying this matter before the representatives of the people was the more distasteful to him because he was personally in antagonism to Judge Gwinnan, whose title to the judicial office it controverted and whose integrity it assailed. He did not seek to disguise the truth ; he wished it to be understood — and let the fact have what weight it might — that he would be glad to see Judge Gwinnan removed from the office which it was charged he had profaned. Apart from all else, he had practiced in Gwinnan's circuit; he had experienced his tyranny; he had seen a jury snatched from their deliberations and clapped into jail for some petty ignorant infringement of the deep reverence which Judge Gwinnan exacted for his presence. No! — and the walls rang with the strong, robust tones, — he would esteem Judge Gwinnan's removal a source of great gratulation and a furtherance of justice. But he would be glad, for his own private considerations, if the circumstances upon which the motion would presently be made could have come to the ear of some other member; he appreciated that there was (sneering and smiling) a lack of grace, of seemliness, in the emanation of the proposition from him, an avowed personal enemy ; moreover, he might expose himself to suspicions of his motive.

"Right for once!" cried the unruly Kinsard, striking in suddenly.

The gavel sounded, and the interruption subsided.

Harshaw's opaque blue eyes turned mechanically in the direction of the voice, but with a preoccupied air of seeing nothing he went on, holding the lapels of his coat, as he stood squarely beside his desk.

He could have evaded ; he could have delegated the duty to another member, — have made the facts known, have had the witnesses canvassed, have set the machinery in motion, without himself appearing at all. "But. Mr. Speaker," with an arrogant port, "it is not my habit to beat about the bush. I may be maligned by my foes, I may be misinterpreted by my friends, I may be misjudged even by my constituents, but it is my principle to come forth openly, and let my personal feeling weigh for whatever it may be worth."

He paused for a moment, stroking his yellow beard with an excited gesture, his flushed face grave, his eyes intent, absorbed ; his whole presence instinct with determination, a hazardous tenacity, a ponderous force. Then dropping his voice to the artificial dead-level elocutionary intonation, he proceeded to make a formal motion that a committee be appointed to investigate and report upon the accusations brought against Judge Gwinnan, charging him with having fought a duel, thus being disqualified for office ; and with perjury in taking the official oath.

There was an interval of absolute silence when he had resumed his seat. Significant glances were interchanged. It seemed that the motion would be lost, until a little bland, cat-like fellow arose to say in a falsetto voice, " Mr. Speaker, I second the motion."

Kinsard turned his indolent anatomy about and looked with a scathing eye at the little man, as, flushed and flustered, he took his seat. There was no possible propriety in the charge of collusion ; the two members had all the liberties of consultation and coöperation. Then why, he argued within himself, should Forsey look like a cat stealing cream? Bestirring his recollection, he recalled in him a certain willingness to think ill of Judge Gwinnan when previously threatened by Harshaw ; and still dredging for a motive, he remembered, though it happened some years ago, that Gwinnan, sitting as special judge, had blocked the game of a big public contract swindle, in which Forsey had had a large money interest.

Forsey had not the nerve of Harshaw, who was looking about him in reddening displeasure and frowning prognostication of the baffling of his vengeance. If he had indeed no backing but the irresolute Mr. Forsey, the measure would be defeated by a most triumphant majority. The prospect roused all his belligerent spirit, and he held up his head with a snort of defiant welcome, like a war-horse smelling the battle from afar, when, the question being stated from the chair, a member rose to say that he doubted the jurisdiction of the House.

" If this matter be reported correctly as I have heard it during the last two or three days, — to my very great surprise, — if Judge Gwinnan be disqualified by reason of having before his incumbency fought a duel, then he never was a judge except *de facto*. As I understand it, only an officer *de jure* can be impeached for crimes committed in office."

Forsey wanted to know if perjury in taking the official oath were not a crime committed in office.

Another member asked whether it was the commission of the crime itself which disqualified, or the conviction of the crime.

The gavel sounded, and the member who had the floor persisted.

" I take it that the House cannot prefer articles of impeachment against a private citizen who has unlawfully usurped an office. If he is removed at all, it should be by proceedings in the chancery court in the nature of a *quo warranto*."

Mr. Kinsard rose, half leaning against his desk with a swaying negligence of posture, to call attention to the fact that anything in the nature of *quo warranto* would n't begin to do. To have a little one-horse chancellor way up yonder in the seclusion of the mountains dump Judge Gwinnan out of his office would not serve the purpose. Could any man imagine that that proceeding, known merely to the members of the bar and the few intelligent citizens of that benighted district who took note of such matters, would satisfy such an animosity as the member from the floaterial district of Cherokee and Kildeer had avowed, with a cheek which might be contemplated only in astounded admiration? Would the infliction of that limited degradation glut the member's ravening greed for revenge for his personal grudges? No! the member wished to disgrace Judge Gwinnan with all the publicity that even the attempt to impeach would entail — he designed that it should be canvassed throughout the length and breadth of the State. It should resound through the clarion columns of every newspaper. Every State in the Union should know that the Senate of Tennessee had organized as a court of impeachment, and the name of Gwinnan should be the synonym of contumely. Upon his word, he could hardly take in the vastness of the effrontery that emboldened the member to acknowledge, to proclaim to this House, his gross, his sordid personal motives, in attacking one of the most able, most respected, most diligent, most upright, of the State judiciary. He appealed to the higher feeling of the House. He begged that they would not be driven like so many sheep into an investigation which was in its very inception an insult, an outrage, and a scandal.

A member demanded from his seat if it were not an obligation imperatively imposed upon the House to inquire into such a rumor, for the purpose of ascertaining and eliciting the truth or falsehood it promulgated. Since such a rumor was abroad, it behooved Judge Gwinnan's friends to advocate an investigation, for it was his only hope of vindication if he were maligned.

Harshaw, leaning forward, both arms on his desk, attentively listening, pursed up his red lips meditatively and nodded with abstracted affirmation, as if pondering the position. He gave no outward expression of gratulation, but he was quick to mark the accession of recruits to his ranks. He could command a stalwart and callous fortitude. He could receive without wincing, without anger, without shame, Kinsard's jeers and thrusts, for the sake of the aroused antagonism which seemed the natural sequence of the young man's insistent arguments.

"It specially becomes the House," continued the member, "to countenance no leniency in regard to dueling and all that pertains to it, after the will of the people has been so unequivocally expressed in regard to the matter of the challenge, or what was so construed, upon this floor."

The member was rebuked here for infringement of parliamentary usage in upbraiding, as it were, the previous actions of the House and interrupting the member who had the floor.

Kinsard, restive under the interpolation, seized the opportunity to resume. "There is no pretense of justification for adopting formal resolutions to asperse the oath of an honorable man, least of all at the instigation of his avowed personal enemy. The story we have heard is at its worst merely a country boy's 'taking up a dare.' I will venture to say that there is not a man within the sound of my voice who has not had similar affrays,— has not in the days of his youth 'taken up a dare,' has not fought by appointment."

"Will the member explain what he means by a duel?" demanded Harshaw. He did not turn his big yellow head; he only cast his opaque blue eyes at Kinsard, and once more looked down at his hands clasped on his desk.

For a moment Kinsard, taken unaware, was checked.

"Perhaps the member had best begin at the beginning, and define a challenge," suggested a satiric voice from the rear.

There was a sharp call to order from the chair, and Kinsard, rallying himself, went tumultuously on.

"I am not a dictionary," he proclaimed angrily. "I am not here to enlighten your ignorance."

Harshaw, elated by the allusion to the old question of the challenge, intimating anew a flocking to his standard, interrupted cleverly: "I have a dictionary right here,— a law dictionary." He read aloud, "Dueling is the fighting of two persons, one against another, at an appointed time and place, on a precedent quarrel."

Kinsard vociferously claimed the floor, although it had become very evident to the House that the interest he advocated fared hardly less severely at the hands of its friend than its foe. In debate he was no match for the wily Harshaw,— his natural endowments, his enthusiasms, his finer emotions, succumbing to a practiced logic, and a militant habit, and an instinctive discernment of the vulnerable point.

"It is impossible to seriously maintain that a fight

between a couple of country boys is a duel," he vehemently insisted. "Everybody knows that the common acceptation of the idea of a duel is a combat between men — men of station" (Harshaw leaned forward with an air of mock attention, placing his hand ostentatiously behind his ear) — "on some question of honor, fighting under the control and direction of their seconds, at a specified number of paces, and with pistols" —

"Enactment provides that they shall be silver-mounted, hair-trigger?" sneered Harshaw.

Once more there was a call to order. But Kinsard, badgered, turned at bay.

"I heard Judge Gwinnan tell you once that unless you kept out of his way he would beat you with a stick, like a dog. How you do tempt the cur's deserts!"

Harshaw rose hastily to his feet. He stood for a moment, his head lowered, his eyes flaming from under his knitted brows; he looked like the champion mad bull of an arena, about to charge. Suddenly he turned, and without a word resumed his seat. There was a storm of applause from every quarter of the House. A dozen voices were crying that the offensive words should be taken down; the clerk hastily obeyed; they were read aloud, and the speaker called upon Kinsard to deny them or retract.

Kinsard could have said with all the fervor of truth that he was sorry indeed, but it was in an inapplicable sense. He saw, with a sinking of the heart, the havoc he was making in another's fate, — the moral murder that hung upon his hands. He looked about with despair at the faces around him: they had been friendly, partisan, when he began to speak against the motion; now they were reluctant, alienated, antagonistic. It were better for Gwinnan had he had no friend but his own repute. The impetuous young fellow felt that he had done the worst that was possible. He would not now eat his words. He looked at Harshaw with an indignant divination of his motives, when that gentleman, begging the indulgence of the House, moved that the matter be dropped. He was not here to maintain personal consequence. He was willing — nay, eager — to waive any individual considerations which hindered the deliberations of the House and the course of justice. If the member were so ungenerous as to decline to apologize for words spoken in heat, confirming them in cool malice, he himself was able to overlook them, the more as his character was, he trusted, too favorably known to be injured by these reflections.

He sat down in the midst of a clamor from a number of eager occupants of the floor, — one of whom the speaker presently recognized, — protesting against the unparliamentary nature of the proposal. The objectionable words were again read, and the speaker called upon Kinsard to apologize or to deny them.

Perhaps Kinsard alone appreciated in this edifying demonstration Harshaw's policy. He could not be tempted to run counter. He would not slack his pursuit of Gwinnan for another trail, however alluring. He had higher game in view than the stripling's insults could furnish. And he had made himself an example of marvelous tolerance, forbearance, and dignity.

Kinsard, lowering and pierced with all the barbed realization of futility and defeat, adopted his words, refused to retract or apologize, and, being commanded by the speaker to withdraw, took up his hat, and, with a scornful, indifferent manner that angered every member as if charged with a personal relation, strode out of the room.

Harshaw had followed his motions with narrowing eyelids. His attention had relaxed with momentary exultation at this result. He was smiling a little in his beard, and he glanced in a debonair preoccupation out of the window near his seat. The sky was red, for the sun was going down. He noted the flush with a casual eye, unprescient how it should be with him when the day, fading now and dropping its dulling petals on every side, should whitely bloom again. Then he reverted with zest to the proceedings within.

Kinsard walked slowly along the portico to the flight of steps. A belt of clouds, their edges glinting with gold, obscured the scarlet disk of the sun, but from their lower verge a great glory of yellow light gushed down, each of the multitudinous rays distinct, giving a fibrous effect, upon the blue hills of the horizon, upon the city in the foreground. Here and there they struck upon a spire or a tin roof that responded with a glister fiercely white. The intervals showed soft shadows of restful tints, the tops of the budding trees, the silver-gray shingles of an old house, and here and there an open space where the renewed blue-grass grew apace. It wore a dark richness all adown the slopes of the Capitol hill. Somehow as he noted it there was borne upon him for the moment a subtle intimation of the serenity of that life of Nature close to our artificial existence, — mysterious, inevitable, quiescent. The contrast gave a sharpened sense of the turmoils of his heart, the weariness of his spirit, the rasping jars of his petty cares. He paused on the sidewalk and looked about him. Then he produced a cigar, and took his way down into the city.

He did not fear the sentence of the House. He was resolute in the position he had taken, but he carried throughout the evening an imperative sense of abeyance. He noticed with a secret scorn the clumsy efforts of his legislative friends to sound his state of mind, when they came down from the Capitol; he divined their fear of a collision, their anxiety that the asperities with Harshaw should be allowed to quietly drop. They sought to have him observe that they considered he had the best of it, and that an apology now from him would mean merely a desire to promote public interest. Only the age of another adviser — his father's friend as well as his own — restrained him from openly ridiculing the deep satisfaction which this mentor evidently derived from the fact that the young man's mind would be occupied with lighter themes during the evening, and he might forget the rancors of the debate. His thoughts, however, were incongruous enough with the scene of a fashionable wedding, where he officiated as an usher, and he paced the aisles of the church with as mechanical a notice of his surroundings as a somnambulist. His attention hardly pretermitted its hold upon the subject that had absorbed him, and when again at liberty he went at once to his room at the hotel, with a view of changing his dress to attend the night session of the House.

It was the slightest matter that attracted his notice. He had lighted the gas, and as he glanced into a drawer of the bureau some trivial difference from the usual arrangement of his effects caught his eye. He stood for a moment in motionless surprise. Perhaps it was accident, perhaps his alert divination, but he slipped his hand beneath the pile of garments and touched a wooden case of pistols. He flushed slightly, and for a moment he was ashamed. He had doubted if it were still there. He had thought that perhaps his cautious friends might have robbed him, pending the time when he was in anger, of the means to do more than war with words. He had taken instant fire at the idea of an interference with his liberty. It was the smouldering embers of this thought that actuated him rather than any serious expectation, but suddenly he turned back to the bureau and lifted the case. He opened it slowly. It was empty. He gazed at the vacant space, his eyes flashing, his cheek flushing. The pistols had been abstracted and the case left that his attention might not by its absence be directed to the weapons. He could easily divine all of his friends' arguments. He would not notice the disappearance of the pistols, they must doubtless have said, unless he wanted them. He would not want them unless he were intent upon some fatal folly. He could not supply himself anew, for all the shops were closed, and by to-morrow he would be in a cooler frame of mind.

His indignation was natural enough. He took heed, too, of contingencies of which his anxious friends, accustomed to him always in the character of assailant, lost sight. "I should be helpless," he said, "if that man should attack me. I should be incapable of self-defense."

Suddenly he caught up a light spring overcoat, threw it over his arm, and left the room. As he went down the staircase into the rotunda of the hotel, he seemed the embodiment of handsome, gay, fortunate youth. His cheek was flushed; his eyes were very brilliant. He paced up and down the floor for a moment in front of the counter, for strangers were registering their names and the clerks were busy. The fountain tossed up its spray, and the tinkling drops fell into the basin; around it plants were blooming. Somebody journeying from the South had presented the hotel with a little alligator, that splashed about in the water and was a source of diversion to the out-comers and in-goers, many of whom paused to rouse it up with their canes and punch the head of the infant saurian. Kinsard walked presently to the desk.

"I want to borrow a pistol," he said to the clerk, to whom he was well known.

The official, fancying that the guest contemplated a journey or a long nocturnal drive into the country, and that the request was a matter merely of precaution, turned with alacrity, took a pistol out of a drawer, and laid it on the counter. He was looking for the cartridges, when an acquaintance of Kinsard's demanded casually, "What do you want a gun for?"

Kinsard lifted his brilliant, reckless eyes. "To shoot Bob Harshaw," he declared.

The clerk turned hastily from his search and made a motion to clutch the pistol.

Kinsard's grasp had closed upon the handle.

"Man alive!" he cried angrily, "do you think I would use it except for self-defense?"

He hastily thrust it into his pistol-pocket and went out into the night.

It was moonless and very dark, despite the myriads of scintillating stars. The Capitol was visible only as suggested in the irradiations of its great, flaring, yellow windows and the lights without on either side of the long flight of steps. As Kinsard ascended he noticed on the broad portico a group of men, separating at the moment, three of them going within and one approaching the steps.

He could not fail to recognize Harshaw's bluff manner, his portly figure, his long, yellow beard, and his brisk, light step; and as the younger man walked along the portico, Harshaw's eyes, glancing out sharply from under the brim of his slouch hat, identified him. There was no one by to note how they should meet; the significance of the encounter might have rejoiced the lovers of sensation. Kinsard was about to pass without salutation, but Harshaw, whirling half round on his light heel, paused, and with a bantering smile on his dimpled pink face showing in the gaslight above their heads, "Great news!" he exclaimed. "They've appointed a committee to investigate 'the jedge'!"

Kinsard experienced a sharp pang of dismay for Gwinnan's sake.

"And I suppose you are satisfied now," he said, bitterly.

"Oh, no, my dear little sir. I am not half satisfied!" cried Harshaw, with his liquid rotund laugh. His foreshortened shadow swayed on the blocks of white limestone as if it could scarcely contain itself for laughter.

He had lost the poise which he had endured so much to maintain that day. He was intoxicated with his triumph; and indeed he could afford to indulge it, for he felt that there was nothing now at stake.

"And that is the reason," continued Harshaw, "that I feel I owe you an obligation which I must not let pass without acknowledgment. In your able and cogent speech this afternoon you did more to effect Judge Gwinnan's impeachment than, unaided, I could possibly have compassed. Let me beg you to accept my thanks —ha! ha! ha!"

Deeply wounded by this thrust, and conscious of the injury he had done Gwinnan's interests, Kinsard turned upon him, but not without dignity.

"Mr. Harshaw," he said, "if I believed you to be sincere in this matter, if I thought you were not ingeniously perverting the facts and the law, I should most willingly coöperate with you. But I know your motives to be a rancorous jealousy and an insatiable spite. And if I have not done anything to nullify them, it is not because I am without the will."

He looked at his interlocutor from head to foot, as if he found a source of surprise in his very embodiment.

"I cannot imagine how a soul so petty should be so corpulently lodged. It might appropriately animate some tiny writhing worm that, showing venom, could be crushed by a foot."

"Look here, youngster," said Harshaw, sneering and showing his strong white teeth, his eyes gleaming under the brim of his hat, "I know you mean you'd take my life if you could defy the consequence. But you'd better mind how you go to extremes in Gwinnan's service. I have a contempt for you, but a pity, too. I know you are only his miserable tool, his abject creature."

Kinsard sprang forward with the suddenness of a tiger. A stinging thrill ran through Harshaw's face before he could realize that with an open palm he had been struck upon the cheek.

It was the impulse of the moment, — he never could afterward explain it to his will, he never could justify it to his policy; he was shocked with an extreme surprise when the keen, abrupt tone of a pistol rang upon the chill night air, and he became conscious that he was shaking a smoking weapon in his right hand, jarred in some manner by the discharge. The young man had flung himself upon him; he saw as in a dream Kinsard take one convulsive step backward and fall from the verge of the great portico to the stones below. There was a moment of intense silence. Harshaw looked wildly to the doors, the windows, expecting the issuance of startled men, roused from their deliberations. It was strange; if the pistol-shot had been heard, it had doubtless been accounted some violation of the law prohibiting target-practicing within the corporate limits. Hardly a minute had elapsed when Harshaw ran down the long flight to where the man lay, half in the shadow and half in the light, at the foot of the stone wall.

"Are you hurt?" he cried in an agonized voice, as he bent over the motionless figure. "Are you dead — already?"

He took one of the listless white hands, — very listless it was, and chill.

As he moved the submissive figure he felt the pistol in the pocket; he drew it forth, glad at least that the man was armed. As he turned it in his hands he saw in despair that it was unloaded. What theory of self-defense could this bear? The next moment his quick eye noted that the bore and make were the same as his own weapon's. He slipped in a cartridge, two, three, and replaced it in Kinsard's pocket. Then he rose to his feet to summon help. He turned as he was about to ascend the steps, and looked back fearfully over his shoulder.

The sudden remembrance of his vision smote him. He gazed upon the scene as if he had before beheld it. The man lay there at the foot of great rocks, motionless and with an averted face.

He had braced himself as well as he might to endure the shock of public reprehension, surprise, repulsion, reacting on his own nerves, sensitive to every variation of popular opinion, when he should go to his associates, his weapon in his hand, the report of his own foul deed upon his lips. And yet, strong as he was, he faltered, he tottered, he fell almost fainting against the door at which he entered. He had a vague idea of the startled faces turned toward him, the expectant stillness, the sound of his hoarse, disconnected words in an appalled staccato, the sudden rush, the wild clamor. He hardly recognized the two men who disengaged themselves from the turmoil and came to him, — the best friends he had in the world, he might be sure now. He was only aware of what he had said and how well he had said it, when he was supported between them to a carriage, and was driving with them and with the officer who had been summoned at his request, to the magistrate's house. His friends were talking together in respectful undertones of this " unfortunate affair," and arranging the details, — a little complicated because of the late hour, — that there might be naught more unseemly than giving speedy bail. Neither intruded on his reserve. The officer was silent, unofficial, respectfully null, effaced. The stars were bright in the dark sky. The horses' hoofs flashed fire.

The magistrate, roused to the fact that justice may not sleep when wrongs are to be righted, made the necessary inquiries in so grave and courteous a tone that it seemed he recognized that the occasional killing of a gentleman may be lamentable to the deceased and inconvenient to the surviving, but was nothing to unduly stretch the limits of his elastic impartiality and abeyance of harsh opinion. He promptly accepted the proffered bail, and Harshaw's friends left him only at his bedroom door, where they shook hands gravely and kindly with him, and in response to some muttered thanks declared they proposed to see him through.

He found beneath the door the cards and notes of other friends who, hearing some wild rumor of the trouble, had called to proffer services. His lips curled triumphantly as he scanned them one by one. They represented the estimation in which he was held. They intimated a reliance on his good faith and motive in any deed.

" But I tell you, Mr. Harshaw," he said ceremoniously to himself, " 't would have been mighty different if 't was n't for your own smartness ! " For he could hardly thank his craft enough for the timely expedient of slipping the cartridges into Kinsard's empty pistol.

He slept badly in the earlier part of the night, but toward day he fell into a deep and dreamless slumber, and woke refreshed. It was later than usual, and he was solitary at breakfast save for the company of strangers. The corridors were well-nigh deserted when he came out with his unfolded newspaper in his hand, — he would not look at it

earlier. Most of the members who sojourned at the same
hotel had gone to the Capitol. The reading-rooms were
quite empty, but for the presence of the sunlight in glittering white blocks upon the carpet. He had lighted a cigar
and flung himself into a chair, nerving himself to read the
accounts of the shooting and the comments, when suddenly
one of his bondsmen came into the room with so precipitate
a manner, so perturbed a face, that the trouble so cleverly
manipulated assumed anew an indefinitely threatening aspect. He felt his muscles tighten, his pulses quicken as
he asked hastily, "What's up?"

He could not mistake the nature of the look the man
bent on him; it made him tingle from head to foot.
And yet his errand was the last offices of friendship.

"You're too quick on the trigger in more ways than
one, Harshaw," he said. "Kinsard was not hit."

If Harshaw's conscience had suffered one pang, this announcement might have weighed more with him than all
that was to come. The extreme surprise told only on
his nerves: his heart thumped heavily; his breath was
short, his face flushed; he looked at his interlocutor with
eyes that seemed lidless in their intentness.

"Kinsard was not shot. He lost his balance and was
stunned by the fall. They have been working with him
all night long, but the doctor says he'll pull through now."
The man faltered a little. It was hard to look into another
man's eyes and say this. "He revived once before you
left. He saw you in the gaslight load his pistol with your
cartridges. And then he fainted again. I thought I'd
tell you. The whole town's talking."

It was admirably managed,— Harshaw's long, amazed
stare, the slow rising from the chair, the rotund resonant
laughter filling the room. It renewed his friend's faith in
him.

"Lie, eh?" he asked anxiously.

"Go away!" Harshaw bluffly waved him off. "I'm
done with you. Coming to *Me* with a cock-and-bull story
like this,— the visions a stunned man saw between his
faints!"

As he took his way boldly down into the rotunda amongst the crowds of men assembled there, the effect of his presence, his manner, his bluff hilarious voice as he canvassed the story, did much to annul its credibility, in fact might have destroyed it but for the recollection of the clerk's declaration — silently pondered — that the pistol loaned was new, had never been discharged ; that the box of cartridges was unopened in his possession ; that Kinsard went straight from him to the Capitol ; that the shooting occurred within fifteen minutes.

The subtle perception of this mental reservation had no influence on Harshaw's capable swagger and burly ridicule, but as he noted it he was saying again and again to himself, "You're a mighty smart man, Bob Harshaw. You're just a little mite *too* smart. There's no mistake this time. It is you who are dead — politically as dead as Hector."

No action was taken in the matter by the legislature, for it bristled with unprecedented difficulties. The session was drawing to a close, and Harshaw's term ceased with it. His usefulness ceased previously. Whatever measures he had advocated were tainted with suspicion and encountered disfavor. Bereft of the influences of his enmity toward Judge Gwinnan, the committee appointed to investigate the charges against him deliberated, and dawdled, and finally reported adversely to the resolution to prefer articles of impeachment. Their doubt of the jurisdiction of the legislature was said to be the determining cause of their action. It was a perplexed and a troublous question. And thus they washed their hands of it.

It had been in this cause that Harshaw had flung himself away, and it was in this result that he experienced the extremest rigors of defeat. It added to the helpless chagrin with which he watched his future, coming on so fast that already its coarsened grotesque features were wearing the immediate aspect of the present. A fine contrast he was, to be sure, to the man whose seat on the bench he had sought to shake, still serenely immovable, while he, the loiterer about the tavern at Shaftesville, beginning to drink heavily now, although his habits had been temperate, telling idle stories to the other loiterers with the zestful skill acquired as a politician, useless now, must needs watch all the interests that he had spent his life to conserve dwindle by degrees, till, case after case withdrawn from him, he should become a mere hanger-on in those courts in which he had aspired to preside.

And then there came to him news for which he felt he had no commensurate capacity for astonishment. Gwinnan, aggrieved by the indecision of the legislature, was clamoring for a vindication. It was nominally at the relation of a third party that the attorney-general brought a suit in the chancery court to test his title to office; and in the interval before the trial Mr. Harshaw had a great deal to say about judicial whitewashing, and speculated much concerning the probable result of the case, and pondered deeply on Gwinnan's motives in encountering its hazards.

Sometimes he was half minded to accredit their probity, and then, ambitious of all that may serve to lift, he fell envious again, and railed at his harsh penalty, that, being not all base, one crafty deed — sequence of how many crafty thoughts! — should determine his future and affix his life sentence.

XXIX.

It seemed to Mink Lorey, trudging on toward the mountains, as if they had been suddenly caught up in the clouds. The horizon had fallen from their invisible summits to the levels of the cove, and where the flat stretches of the perspective met the nullities of the enveloping vapors the scene had all the prosaic, denuded desolation of prairie distances. Yearning for the sight of the blue peaks, he felt as if it were in rebuke, in alienation, that they had hidden their faces from him, had drawn the tissues of the air about them and veiled their heads. As the day unfolded hour by hour, as the distance lessened mile by mile, he sought if perchance in a rent of the mist he might not glimpse some dome, the familiar of his early life, unchanged through all the vicissitudes that time had wrought for him. Once he was not sure if it were mountain or cloud outlined in individual symmetry amongst the indeterminate, shapeless masses of vapor. Then the haze thickened, and he lost the semblance, whether of earth or air.

It was before dawn that he had escaped from the haven he had found, and Mrs. Purvine, throughout the day, keeping watch over these snug quarters, guarded an empty nest. After the first deep, dreamless slumber of exhaustion he had silently slipped out, taking his way toward the Great Smoky, the thought of Alethea heavier than all his calamities. He knew naught of the report of his pardon; he hardly cared now what might betide him. He would see her and tax her with her fickle heart, and then he would flee whither he might. Sometimes, as he toiled along, he would raise his arm with a frantic gesture, and again and again his lips moved unconsciously as he forecast in sibilant mutters the words that he would say.

There was little danger at this early hour of meeting any traveler along the deserted road, but he hardly felt safe until he reached the base of the Great Smoky, and was amongst the dense laurel of those mighty forests, still veiled with the mists and effaced from the day. He turned back often, despite the numbing clutch of despair in his heart and the turbulence of his rage, hoping that he might see again Chilhowee with the sunshine on it; with the circuit of birds in the adjacent domains of the sky; with detached flakes of mist, like stole-clad figures, in airy processional pacing the summit to elusive evanescences; with its colors of bronze-green, and anon purple, and, stretching far away, more finely, softly azure than the heaven it touched. Alas, no,— this he might remember. And yet he had chance rencontres with old familiars. A torrent, gray-green, glassy, whitely foaming, darted out from the vapors suddenly, and was suddenly withdrawn into the blank spaces. And was he akin to the balsam firs; could he have met brethren with more joy? Even when they towered undistinguishably above him, they whispered to him a word now and then, and filled the air with the cordial, inspiriting sense of their presence. And what was this? He stood still to listen, staring into the white vagueness of the invisible woods. A fitful, metallic tinkling. Was he so high up the great steeps that already he could distinguish the bells of the herds, or was this a stray? He heard a hoof struck upon the ground presently, the sound of munching teeth, and suddenly a horse's head was thrust forward amongst the mists, showing a black mane and wide brilliant eyes and the arch of a claybank neck.

"Thar ye be, Grasshopper! At it agin, air ye?" Mink called out, with the rancorous formula of an old reproach.

It was a horse that he knew, and knew well,— one of the charges of the herders during the previous summer. — a wild young creature, with a proclivity for breaking bounds and straying. The animal pricked up his ears at the sound of his name, and his eyes met Mink's with seeming recognition. The young mountaineer reflected

that it was he who had usually salted the animals. With
a hope of bettering his plight he held out his hand.
"Cobe! Cobe!" he called seductively. The horse
looked dubiously at him, as he stood, one hand thrust in
his leather belt, his white hat — an old one belonging to
Jerry Price, which Mrs. Purvine had loaned him —
perched on the back of his head, his red hair limp with
the moisture of the damp day. The creature approached
gingerly, snuffing at the empty hand. He moved back
abruptly, detecting the deception; but Mink had caught
him by the halter which he wore, and sprung upon his
back.

"Gimme a lift up the mounting, Grasshopper," suggested Mink placidly.

The stray reared and plunged and kicked, striving to
unhorse the rider, who, although without saddle or
bridle, contrived to maintain his seat, but could neither
govern nor guide the animal, that at last bolted off
through the woods, running as rapidly as the nature of
the ground would permit. On he went, invading the
mists; piercing the invisibilities of the wilderness; up
hill and down; among bowlders and gigantic trees,
dimly looming; fording streams and standing pools and
morasses; pausing to kick and rear and plunge anew,
and away once more. Mink waited calmly till the stray
should exhaust his energies. This proved longer than
he had anticipated. But after several delusive intimations of abating speed the horse fell into a canter, then
into a trot, and as Mink pulled on the halter the comity
with his rider was renewed once more, and he lent himself to guidance. Looking about him, the young mountaineer could hardly say where he had been carried.
Once as the mist shifted he saw through the limbs of
stunted trees a great peak, a mile away perhaps, appearing and disappearing elusively among the rifts. He began to understand that he was on the summit of the
ridge in the interval between two great uprising domes.
Often he must needs lie flat on the horse's back, lest the
low boughs of the ancient dwarfed trees sweep him to

the ground; as it was, they played cruel havoc with his old jeans coat, and once snatched his hat away. He drew up with difficulty, and as he clapped it on his head he heard again, in the momentary silence of his horse's hoofs, the tinkling of bells other than the one which the nomadic Grasshopper wore at his neck. He rode toward the sound. It led him into a limited open space where the trees, struck and burned by the lightnings, had fallen charred upon the earth; two or three cows were pausing to crop in the lush grass, despite the crack of a whip and the call of a herder. Mink recognized the voice of his old comrade, Doaks.

The mounted figure of the fugitive loomed, half discerned, gigantic in the mist, as Ben Doaks stood and stared. The horse, restive, freakish, rose upon his hind feet. pawing the air. The young mountaineer, half doubting the policy of revealing himself, his prudent fears returning, hesitated, then leaned forward and waved his hand. He did not speak, for Doaks suddenly, with a wild shrill cry of terror, turned and fled.

Mink sat his horse motionless, staring in amazement. An angry flush rose to the roots of his hair.

" Ben's 'feared ter hev enny dealin's with law-breakers an' sech," he sneered. "'Feared the law mought take arter him."

He rode along for a few moments, pondering his jeopardy and the long imprisonment to which he was sentenced. If this demonstration were any indication of the feeling against him, he would be taken again here amongst the herders, or at his home in Hazel Valley, or in Wild-Cat Hollow.

" I ought n't ter go ter see Lethe," he said to himself. "I ought jes' ter hustle over inter North Carliny, whar they dunno me, an' git in with some o' them folks ez lives lonesome, the herders, or them Injuns at Quallatown, till the sher'ff gits tired o' huntin' fur me. Nobody 'lows but what I'm dead 'cept Mis' Purvine, an' she ain't a-goin' ter tell on me. I dunno 'bout Lethe; mebbe she'll 'low 't ain't right, 'specially sence she air so powerful pleased with the jedge. I'll git cotched sure ef I keep a-roamin' 'round hyar like a painter, or that thar harnt o' a herder ez rides on Thunderhead."

With the words there flashed upon him a new interpretation of Ben Doaks's sudden flight. He recollected the significance of an equestrian figure here, strangely silent, looming in the mist. As he looked about him, catching vague glimpses of the neighboring peaks, he recognized the slopes of Thunderhead.

"Ben mus' hev been over ter s'arch fur strays, an' I reckon ye air one of 'em, Grasshopper," he said.

His lips were curving, and his eyes brightening beneath the brim of the old wool hat. His prudent resolves vanished. He leaned forward and deftly divested the horse of the bell. He tossed his head gayly as he struck his heels against the flanks of the animal with an admonition to get up.

"Ef I don't ride up thar an' skeer them herders on Thunderhead inter fits, I'm the harnt Ben takes me fur, that's all."

That misty morning was long remembered on Thunderhead. To the herders, busy with their simple, leisurely, bucolic avocation on the great elevated pastures, as aloof from the world, as withdrawn from mundane influence, as if they herded on lunar mountains, there appeared, veiled with the mist and vague with a speedy gait, the traditional phantom horseman: more distinct than they could have imagined, more personally addressing its presence to the spectators, silently waving its hand, and once leaning forward and clutching at the empty air, as if it would fain reach them, and once assuming an aggressive aspect and leveling an unseen weapon.

The cattle had not all arrived at their summer pastures from the coves and the "flat woods." To-day young Bylor, whose father was a farmer on the slopes below, had driven up a "bunch" of cows, and while he was standing quite alone at some distance from the cabin, engaged in readjusting a brass tag which had been lost from the horn of one of the animals, he heard the sound of an approach, and glanced about him in the fleecy white nullity that had taken the place of the erased world. He did not recognize in the dim figure of the horseman the terrible ghostly herder, the steed rearing and plunging, the erect figure looming gigantic, merging with no distinct outlines into the enveloping uncertainty of the mist. He stood stolidly gazing for a moment; then he hailed it.

"Howdy, stranger!" he cried.

The figure paused; the horse fell upon his haunches and pawed the air with his forefeet, while the rider leaned forward, beckoning slowly as Bylor approached. What monition induced him to pause he could hardly have said. The significance of the insistently beckoning apparition flashed upon him in the moment. He turned precipitately, stumbling over the roots of a tree and falling prone upon the ground; then recovering himself, he ran at full speed through the blinding fog toward the cabin. He swore afterward that he heard behind him the tramp of a horse's hoofs and a voice laughing mockingly.

At the herders' cabin he found Ben Doaks and his partner from Piomingo Bald, pallid and shaken, among the other herders who had gathered there, all panic-stricken, and each arguing to shift to his partner the responsibility of the care of the cattle, that he might leave the weird, haunted summits, and find rest and peace and reassuring human comradeship in the prosaic depths of the cove.

"From what I hev hearn tell 'bout that thar herder," said Doaks, with his facile credulity, "none o' we-uns air a-goin' ter hev sense enough ter keer fur cattle 'n' nuthin' else fur a year an' a day. Leastwise that hev been the 'speriunce o' other folks ez hev viewed the harnt."

He laid on another stick of wood, for the day was chill, and the great fire crackled and sparkled, and the red and yellow flames darted up the rude and tremulous chimney, and gave the one bright element of illuminated color to the dark interior. The bearded men grouped about the fire were seated one upon a keg of salt, three on a log, and Ben Doaks had dropped on a saddle flung down upon the hearth. The door was closed; once it came unbuttoned, and every face turned quickly to scan the shivering mists, pallid and cold and opaque, crowding to the entrance, to be shut out summarily into the vast vagueness of the outer world.

"I dunno ez I feel ennywise lackin'," observed another, after a long introspective pause. He rubbed his hand meditatively over his beard. "I never 'lowed ez I war special gifted, but I ain't a spang fool yit."

"I reckon we hain't hed time ter 'speriunce it," said Doaks, as he settled himself to wait for the dreaded doom, a little astonished, subacutely, to be conscious of no diminution of mental power.

"I seen him so close!" cried Bylor. "I wish ter goodness I hed shot at him!"

"Bullet would jes' hev gone through him," said Doaks, "'thout interruptin' him none."

"Waal," rejoined Bylor, "I hev hearn some folks 'low ef ye shoots at a harnt they don't like it, an' sorter makes tharse'fs sca'ce arter that. I dunno what ailed him ter take arter me. I never herded with him on Thunderhead. I ain't no herder, an' never war. I hate powerful ter go down inter the cove ter drivel fur a year an' a day. I never done no work sca'cely las' year, through feelin' sorter keerless 'bout'n it. An' ef I hed drempt bout'n' this hyar harnt a-takin' arter me I'd hev put in my work then."

"Waal, ye can't git the time back," said Ben Doaks; and many an idler before and since Bylor has learned this melancholy truth.

He sat silent for a time, ruefully pondering upon his blasted industrial prospects. Then he broke forth fretfully once more: —

"I war fool enough ter go so close. I seen the very hat he wore," — his tones were full of a despairing regret, — "a big white hat sot onto the back o' his head."

"That war jes' Josh Nixon," said the elder of the herders, gravely shaking his head. "That war the very kind o' hat he wore, an' sct the same."

Three of the five hats in the room were of that exact description; in fact, it was a fashion common enough in the region for Jerry Price to have two alike, and the old one which Mrs. Purvine had lent the fugitive was hardly distinguishable from Mink's own, floating down the Tennessee River.

It did not shadow a face altogether appreciative of his own pranks, as Mink drew it down over his brow and rode away in the mist, when convinced that the herders were likely to come out no more for the present.

"I can't take no sure enough enjyemint in nuthin'," he complained. "I feel so badgered an' hunted."

He looked about him doubtfully. A few strides of his horse and he would be across the state line, and safer than for many a day. He stood drearily contemplating the vacancy of the clouds above the Carolina side, as unresponsive to the imagination as his future, which in vain he sought to forecast. He suddenly wheeled.

"I'm bound ter see Lethe, though! I'm bound ter tell her I hev fund her out. She'll know what I think o' her afore I 'm done."

He pressed the horse, broken now to a steady gait, into the elusive ways of the herders' trail through the weird, stunted woods along the ridge to the great Piomingo Bald; thence into a path that led down into Wild-Cat Hollow. He noted its well-worn and smooth curves.

"Ben Doaks hev made a reg'lar turnpike, a-travelin' ter see Lethe Sayles," he said, with some half scornful pity that would not bestir itself to be jealous.

He made a wide detour of the little house, nestling in the great cleft of the mountain, occasionally becoming dimly visible as the mist shook out its gauzy folds in long pervasive shivers, and anon obliterated as it dropped its denser curtain. Over the valley it was torn into fringes, a slant of sunlight gilding it, the blue of the sky showing through.

One of the sudden precipitous ascents from the deep depression of the hollow was distinctly imposed against the horizon. There were great rocks, with herbs and grasses growing in niches, on either side of a narrow gorge. Two splintered cliffs amongst them were like a rude and gigantic gateway giving access to the higher verdant slopes of the mountain. His eyes, turning mechanically toward the opening vista, were arrested by the sight of Alethea high up the gorge, standing in the clifty gateway. Her sun-bonnet, still tied under her chin, had fallen on her shoulders; her yellow hair was like the golden sunlight denied to the dreary heights; her familiar brown homespun dress was distinct against the tender green of the slope; a basket of herbs was on her arm. Now and then she moved a step and plucked a sprig from a niche, and again she would pause looking down upon the valley, where the white glister of the mist united with the suffusion of yellow sunshine beyond in a gauzy, splendid sheen that now and then parted to reveal the purple mountains, the blue sky, the silver river, the fields as radiantly green as the meadows of the blest. His heart beat with emotions he hardly comprehended, as he noted her luminous, grave, undimmed eyes, her fair, delicately tinted face.

He dismounted and hitched the horse by the halter to a tree. She did not see him; she heard nothing; she silently looked about her, and plucked the herb she sought. He took his way softly up the gorge among the fallen fragments of rock; he was standing still in the great rift that simulated a gateway when she turned slowly, and her eyes, widening with fear, with surprise, with rapture, fell upon him.

His heart could but thrill at her loud, wild cry of joy. He had meant to upbraid her. She was sobbing on his shoulder, and he held her in his arms.

The mists flickered and faded about them; the sunshine slanted down through the clouds. The wind lifted its wings, for they heard the flutter of the breeze, and beside some hidden nest amongst the gray old rocks a mocking-bird was suddenly singing—singing!

"Ye war pardoned! I know it!" she cried. "I know it!"

He had for once a thought for her,—a vain regret to annul her joy. When had Alethea looked thus?—the radiant spirit of love, the triumphant delight of the spring.

He delayed replying. He stooped to gather up the herbs that had fallen on the ground; for the old hound that followed her had smelt the basket, and was thrusting his intrusive muzzle among them.

"What be ye a-doin' of, Lethe?" asked Mink, restoring them, and setting the basket up on a bowlder.

To detail the simple domestic errand relaxed the tense agitation of their meeting, and it was a relief to him to listen.

"A-getherin' wild sallet fur dinner," she drawled, her happy smiles and tears together in her eyes. "Our turnip patch never done nuthin', sca'cely, an' ez we-uns ain't got no turnip-greens I 'lowed I 'd gether a mess o' wild sallet. The chillen hone so fur suthin' green."

There was no quivering sense of deprivation in her voice; the hardships of poverty would wear to-day the guise of triumphant expedient.

"I hev got about enough," she said, smiling up at him. "Ye kem on ter the house an' I 'll gin ye a soon dinner. Ye mus' be tired an' hongry with yer travels. They 'll all make ye welcome."

He hesitated. In the supreme happiness of the moment, his face had in a measure lost the lines that anxiety and suffering had drawn. But now, as he stood doubtful of what he should say, she noted his changed expression.

"Reuben," she cried, in tender commiseration, laying her hand on his arm, "what makes ye look like that? What hev happened ter you-uns?"

"Waal," said Mink, leaning against the wall of rock behind him, " right smart o' different things, — fust an' last."

The simple heart's-ease in being near her again, — he had not realized how dear he held it, — in hearing her voice, full of solicitude for him, in the renewing of his unconscious reliance upon her love, had begun to give way to the antagonism inevitable between them, with their widely opposing views of life and duty, their uncongenial characters and aims.

He laughed satirically. " Ye talk 'bout pardon! I hain't got no pardon. I 'low ye wimmin-folks hev got no feelin' nor pride nuther. I would n't hev no pardon off'n Gwinnan. I would n't take a favior from him, — not ter save him from hell, nor me nuther. But I hev got no pardon."

"Ye air foolin' me, Reuben, ain't ye?" she exclaimed, hopefully.

He shook his head.

She gazed gravely at him. " How 'd ye git away?"

" Bruk an' run."

She stood still; her heart sank; her eyes filled with tears. " Oh," she cried, with all the despair of a relinquished hope, " I could n't but b'lieve yestiddy, when Jacob Jessup kep' a-lookin' so secret an' m'licious, ez thar war good news cz he would n't lemme hear, — more 'n he told 'bout what Jedge Gwinnan said when he rid up ter the cabin, whilst we war all away ter the churchhouse ter the revival. An' I b'lieved 't war ez you-uns war pardoned. I hev drempt of it! I hev prayed fur it! I 'd hev died fur it!"

" Look hyar, Lethe Sayles!" he exclaimed, tense and erect again. "That thar ain't a true word ez ye air a-tellin' me, — ez that thar man hev kem ter Wild-Cat Hollow!" His eyes blazed upon her.

She was deprecating and downcast. Her intuition warned her that it behooved her to be careful. She was too deliberate. He broke out vehemently:

" He hev! An' 't war ter see you-uns."

"I know 't war, Reuben, but" —

"I swear ter Heaven," he cried, lifting his clenched right hand, "ez the Lord never afore built sech a fool ez me!" His self-pity and self-contempt were pathetic. "Ain't I jes' now been down yander ter Mis' Purvine's, an' hear her tell how that man — oh, curse him, curse him! — air nigh dead in love with ye, an' ye hed promised ter marry him!"

"No, Reuben, no! 'T ain't true. It air jes' one o' aunt Dely's notions."

"An' I kem hyar fit in mind ter kill ye dead," he went on. "An' the minit I see ye I furgit it all, an' ye twist me round yer finger the same ez ef I war a bit o' spun truck! G' way, Lethe!" — his voice broke; "don't ye tech me." He moved away, that she might not lay her remonstrant hand on his shoulder. "I wait on yer word like a child. Ye got me inter all this trouble through heedin' yer wisdom ez turned out folly fur me. The foolishness o' them ez air bereft air wise ter me! Ye done it!"

He struck his hands despairingly together as he thought of his forlorn past. Perhaps he was the happier that his reflective moods were so rare.

"I know, Reuben, — I know I did. But I never meant it. I jes' wanted ye ter do what war right."

"Yes, but I hev got ter abide by the consequences o' what *ye* think air right, — don't ye know it?" he demanded.

"Ef I could hev suffered fur it, stiddier you-uns," she declared, in tears, "I 'd hev gone ter jail happy — happy."

His manner changed suddenly. He was at once shocked and displeased. "What air ye talkin 'bout, Lethe?" he said, in stern rebuke. "Don't ye know thar ain't no 'spectable wimmin in jail?"

This had not occurred to her. She only sighed, and looked away at the shifting mist over the sunlit valley at the heavier masses of cloud dropping down upon the mountain above. A great eagle, near enough to show the gallant spread of his broad wings, swept from their midst, poised in the sunlight high above the cove, and swooped to the slopes below. Mink's gaze followed the bird, his easily diverted interest quickening. Alethea strove to take advantage of the moment. " I jes' want ter tell ye, Reuben " — she began.

" I don't want ye ter tell me nuthin'! " he cried, fixing on her his brown fiery eyes, with a bright red spark in their pupils. " Ye make a fool out'n me. Ye don't let me hev no mind o' my own. I reckon it air 'kase I be in love with ye, — an' nobody else. All the t'other gals war in love with me."

There was none of his jaunty self-sufficiency as he said this, — only a dreary recognition of the fact.

" Ye hev cut me out'n a heap, Lethe; enny one o' 'em would hev been mighty willin' ter put up with me an' my ways. They never harried me none, ez ef I could n't do nuthin' right. I reckon I 'd hev been happy an' peaceable married ter enny o' them."

" I know, Reuben, an' that 's the reason I wanter tell ye " — She paused, expecting to be interrupted. But he was looking at her coolly and calmly, waiting and listening. He was saying to himself that he might safely hear; it was best that he should know. He would be on his guard. He would not blindly fall again under her influence. He felt with secret elation, stern and savage, the handle of a pistol in his pocket. He had thought it no harm to borrow Jerry Price's for the purpose of resisting arrest, finding it on the shelf in the spare room at Mrs. Purvine's, the less because it was he who had given it to his friend, with his wonted free-handedness, — but indeed he had won it lightly, shooting for it at a match.

He stood with one hand on his hip, the other laid against the rock. His head was a little thrown back, his hair tossing slightly in the · renewing breeze ; he looked at her with dissent and doubt in every line of his face.

" Ye see, he kem hyar ter ax me 'bout Sam Marvin. Ye know I tole on the trial 'bout him moonshinin'."

Mink nodded. The thought of those terrible alternations of hope and despair and remorse was very bitter to him still.

"An' he 'lowed I knowed whar Marvin be now."

"What's he want along o' Marvin?" demanded Mink, surprised.

"He wanted Marvin, but mostly Jeb Peake, ter testify fur him, 'kase he 'lows thar air goin' ter be some sort'n trial agin him. Mr. Harshaw got it up, Jacob Jessup said. Jacob 'lowed the jedge war powerful outed ter find out ez Jeb war s'pected o' hevin' kilt a man, 'kase he war feared nare one o' 'em could be tolled out ter testify fur him. An' Jacob tole him ez Marvin hed quit this mounting, but he hed hearn ez down on one o' them ridges nigh Thunderhead thar war a strange man ez war a-moonshinin', — Jacob's mighty apt ter know sech ez that, — an' he hed tuk old man Craig's house, what he hed lef' ter go ter North Car'liny ter live with his son. An' from the account Jacob hearn o' these folks he would n't be s'prised none ef them war Sam an' Jeb. An' the jedge knowed the house an' whar it be. An' he jes' lit out ter ride over thar an' see. He went yestiddy evenin', an' he air kemin' back hyar ter-day. 'Kase he tole Jacob ef he could n't toll Sam or Jeb ter testify thar 'd be no witnesses but his enemies. He 'lowed he 'd stay all night at Bylor's house, though Jake tole him ter be mighty keerful how he talked about Sam an' Jeb thar, fur old man Bylor air runnin' fur office, — sher'ff, or constable, or jestice, or suthin', — an' would n't ax no better 'n ter git a chance ter harry law-breakers. An' the jedge 'lowed ez things hed come ter a pretty pass with him, an' rid off."

She looked up at Mink gravely, earnestly. She had sat down on one of the rocks beside the basket; her hand toyed with a sprig of the herbs within; her dense golden hair, heavily undulating, was all the brighter for the contrast with the dark green vine that draped the gray rocks behind and above her, the delicate coloring of her face the finer, the tint of the saffron kerchief, knotted beneath her chin, the more intense. Her brown gown lay in straight, simple folds about her lithe figure; the gaunt old hound sat down at her feet and leaned his head on her knee.

Mink had not always been definitely aware of her beauty, — it was not of the type which most appeals to the rural admirer; but its subtle, unrealized fascinations had swayed him unconsciously. Now he looked at her critically, speculatively, striving to behold her as she appeared to Gwinnan, to adjust his estimate to Mrs. Purvine's report of the florid judicial compliments. He cared naught for the rumor of the impending trial. He felt no gratulation that Harshaw had been able to compass the jeopardy, if not the disgrace, of the man he hated. He gazed at her with sedulous attention, to see her with Gwinnan's eyes.

"Lethe," he said, suddenly, — he had dropped down upon the ground near her feet, and leaned back against the rock, — "did Jedge Gwinnan say ennything ter you-uns 'bout me?"

She was in a tremor instantly.

He did not seem to notice. He was affecting to offer the dog a morsel in a deceptive bit of stone, and as the creature, with a dubiously wrinkling and sniffing nose, would attempt to take it he would snatch it away. "Did he?" he persisted, looking up at her from under the brim of the old white hat.

"Whenst I talked ter him an' begged him ter git ye a pardon or suthin'," she said. She was not without the tact to avail herself of discreet ellipses; but she forecast with dread that with these he would not be content.

"What did he say?" He was suffering the hound to lick the stone in baffled reproach, and turn away disdainful. Mink's lip was curling with fierce sarcasm as he reiterated, "What did he say?"

"I could n't ondertake ter remember all he said, Reuben. 'T war down yander at the post-office at Locust Levels. Me an' Jerry Price rid thar in the wagin ter see ef thar war enny letter fur Mis' Purvine."

"I'll be bound I kin tell ye suthin' *ye* said!" exclaimed Mink. "Ye tole him ez he war powerful good ter hold no gredge agin me."

She turned her despairing eyes upon him. He could read the truth in their clear depths.

"An' he tole ye ez ye war too good ter marry me."

There was no need to answer.

"An' ye b'lieved him!"

"Oh, Reuben, ye know better 'n that!" she exclaimed, reassured to speak freely. "He jes' talked 'bout'n ye like my step-mother, an' aunt Dely, an' Jake Jessup's wife; none o' them air gamesome, an' they don't set store on gamesome ways. 'T war jes' sech talk ez theirn."

He listened, his chin in his hand, his elbow on the rock. She should not delude him again; he would not succumb to her influence. He felt the handle of the pistol in his pocket. There was affirmation in its very touch.

"Gamesome ain't what *he* said. He 'lowed I war m'licious."

Once more he glanced up to read the truth in her eyes.

He slowly pulled himself to his feet. He stood for a moment, erect and jaunty, his hand thrust in his leather belt, his eyes bright and confident, his hair tossing back as he moved his head.

"Ye tole him how good he war," his merciless divinations went on.

She cowered beneath his serene and casual glance.

"Ye don't deny it, an' yit ye expec' me ter not b'lieve what the whole kentry air a-sayin', — ez ye hev promised ter marry him an' hev gin me the go-by."

He turned abruptly away. "Reuben," she cried, "air ye goin' agin, when ye hev jes' kem back?" She laid her importunate hands upon his arm. His resolution was strong now; he could afford to be lenient and to humor her.

"'Bleeged ter, Lethe," he said softly, looking down

upon her with the calmness of finality. She did not loose her hold. "Ef ye keep me a-foolin' hyar longer 'n I oughter stay, I mought git cotched agin," he warned her — "fur twenty year! Jake Jessup would ez soon arrest me ez not."

She relaxed her grasp, looking fearfully about her in the mist and at the summit of the great rocks. She followed him, the old hound by her side, down to the spot where the horse still stood hitched.

"But ye'll kem back agin, Reuben?" she said, her heart-break in her voice, her eyes full of tears.

"Laws-a-massy, yes; times an' times. I kin whistle plumb like a mocking-bird, an' whenever ye hear one a-singin' the same chune three times ye kem out 'mongst the rocks an' ye'll find me."

Once more he held her at arm's length and looked searchingly at her tearful face. Suddenly he mounted his horse and rode away.

XXX.

HE did not maintain this sedulous semblance of calmness as he galloped the wild young horse along the mountain slopes in the mist. His eyes burned; his teeth were fiercely set; sometimes he lifted his right hand and shook it clenched as if he held his vengeance within his grasp and would not lightly let it go. Over and again he cried aloud a curse upon the man he hated, and then he would fall to muttering his grudges, all unforgotten, all registered indelibly in his mind despite its facile laxity, despite its fickle traits. He reviewed the events since the morning that Alethea had stood by the judge's desk, and he laid down his pen to gaze, to the afternoon when, amongst the blossoms and the sunshine and the birds, they had talked together, and she had asked a futile thing, doubtless to beguile the hour, and he had warned her solemnly.

"I ain't goin' ter North Car'liny, an' leave 'em hyar tergether," he declared vehemently. "I'll meet up with him somewhar this side o' the Craig house. I'll dare him ter fight, an' ef he don't kill me I'll kill him, an' kiss the hand that does the deed!"

The mists shivered to listen; the rocks repeated the threat, and again in hesitant dread, and still once more a word in an awed and tremulous staccato. On and on he went,—never abating speed, flying over the broken ground; deaf to the sound of horn and hounds borne fitfully from the slopes below on some hardly perceptible current of the air, and again dying to the dumbness of the shrouded woods; blind to the burly apparition of a bear trotting out of the clouds and in again, although the horse reared and pawed the air; callous to the keen chill of the torrent, swollen out of its banks with the spring rains till it surged about his limbs as he forded through. Over and again the mountain water-courses intercepted his path, but only once his attention was attracted to his surroundings, and this was because there seemed here a check upon his progress, and he must needs take heed of his way. The stream known as Gran'dad's creek showed in the thickening mist a turbulent volume, a swollen breadth, covering rocks and brush and gullies, and washing the boles of trees far from its normal channel; he hardly knew where he might safely take the ford. Now the water elusively glimmered, swift, foaming, full of enormous bowlders, and with trees standing in its midst; and as he went down to the verge in a cleft of the rock the vapors closed again, and it seemed to recede into invisibility. The horse had become restive. He resisted and snorted, and finally deliberately faced about, as he was recklessly urged to enter the stream. He was forced again to the margin, when suddenly Mink thought he was dreaming. The fluctuating vapors parted once more, and in the rifts he saw on the opposite bank the man he sought. He stood in numb surprise; a strange overwhelming sense of hatred possessed him with the image thus palpably presented; he quivered with a recollection of all his wrongs. This was no dream. It was Gwinnan returning from the moonshiners' house. He rose from his stirrups and waved his hand with a smile. Mink heard his ringing halloo. Then Gwinnan pressed his roan colt down to the margin of the water and took the ford.

"Saved us wettin' our feet agin, Grasshopper," Mink observed. He was very distinct as he sat on the bareback stray; his feet dangling without stirrups, his big wool hat, his flaunting auburn hair, his keen, clear-cut face, all definitely painted on the opaque white background of the mist; a bole was barely outlined here and there behind him, or a towering crag, as if there were other elements of the picture merely sketched in. More than once Gwinnan lifted his grave eyes toward him. But when the mist came between them, surging in a great cloudy volume, Mink drew the pistol from his pocket.

"Ye don't kerry straight. I 'member yer tricks. I reckon he hev got a six-shooter, but I'll resk ye, ennyhows. I'll wait till he kems across an' then dare him to fight."

As he waited it might have seemed that he was the only human creature in the world, so desolately vacant were the barren mists, so unresponsive to the sense of the landscape that they hid, so null, so silent, save for the river, forever flowing on like life, resistless as eternity. The interval was long to his impatience, — so long that, alarmed at last lest his revenge be snatched from him by some mischance, at this supreme moment when it had seemed the fierce joy he had craved was vouchsafed, he hastily rode along the clifty bank above the tumultuous current. Once more the mist lifted. Suddenly he saw the roan colt, his full eyes starting from his head, his scream almost human in its frantic terror, pawing the cliffs, to the base of which the encroaching waters had risen; finding no footing, no shallows, only the forbidding inaccessibilities of the rocks. The saddle was vacant. The rider had been swept away by the wanton vagaries of the current.

The young mountaineer stared stolidly and uncomprehendingly for a moment. In a sort of daze he dismounted from his horse. He hardly realized what had happened, until, as he climbed deftly down among the splintered crags, lithe, agile, sure-footed as a deer, he saw clinging to a bramble growing from a fissure, and supported on a ledge of the rock, the unconscious figure familiar to his dream of vengeance. It was forestalled! The wild freak of the mountain torrent had given him his heart's desire, and yet his hands were clean. The wolves, the wild dogs, and the vultures would not leave the man to creep away were there yet life left in him.

And there was life. He noted the convulsive fluttering of breath, the trembling clutch of the fingers; for the nerves remembered the saving boughs that the senses had forgotten.

As Mink stood looking down he suddenly lifted his head with a quick start, as if a word had been spoken to him from out the silence. Why this gratuity of pity, this surging fellow-feeling, this clamorous instinct to aid? Was a hand held out to him in his hour of need? Nay, he might have known rescue and release, his future might now be fair and free, but for the device of this man who had bestirred himself to thwart the friendly mob. Was not his hope attained, his prayer? Here was a sublimated revenge. His enemy would die at his feet, and yet his hands were clean.

And at this moment he was muttering, " I 'll be bound ef he hed a leetle wild-cat whiskey now 't would save his life ez respons'ble ez ef 't war ez legal ez the taxed corn-juice."

He stood thinking for a moment. There was Marvin's still at the Craig house, as Alethea had said, two miles away; the man would be dead of exhaustion before help could come thence. But not a quarter of a mile below, on one of the divergent ridges of Thunderhead, was Bylor's home. Mink started with affright. The old man was a candidate for office. The certainty of arrest awaited him there, whatever his mission. It was a decision swift as an impulse. It meant twenty years' imprisonment at hard labor, and he realized it as he sprang upon the bare back of his horse.

" I reckon I kin make a break an' run, or tunnel out, or suthin'," he said, with his preposterous hopefulness; "leastwise, I can't leave him thar ter die that-a-way, half drownded and harried ter death by wolves an' painters an' buzzards. Ef the darned critter," he cried out, in a renewal of despair, " would hev jes' stood up an' been shot like healthy folks! "

Mink never reached his destination.

It was not held to be a strange nor an unjustifiable action that young Bylor was led to do. He said afterward that that day, as he made his way home in the midst of the clouds that begirt the mountain, he was affrighted to behold again, evolved from their expressionless monotony, the equestrian figure of the mystic herder that rides on Thunderhead. His nerves were shaken, for before that morning he had seen the "harnt," and at close quarters. He noted the wildly beckoning hand vague in the mist; he heard, or thought he heard, a shrill, insistent hail; he quickened his pace, pursued by the thunderous hoofs of the spectral steed, riding him down, as he feared. He faced about in desperate terror and fired his rifle.

Then he knew what he had done, for the rider lurched from the horse and fell, and the animal dashed past him, running at full speed. It was Mink Lorey whom he found upon the ground, — strong enough only to gasp out his errand; and though Bylor rose instantly to obey his behest and go to succor Gwinnan, Mink was dead before he left.

No great loss, the country-side said, and indeed it was suspected for a time that Gwinnan's straits had resulted from Mink's wanton mischief. When the facts became known, one or two reflective souls — recognizing in his deed that universal vital element of better possibilities astir within him insistently militant, enlisting every sterling trait common to humanity — were moved to say that he was not all mink.

No one in the mountains, however, fully appreciated the impulse that had controlled him except Alethea. To her it served as a sacred apotheosis, and she adored his memory for what he might have been, and forgot what he was. Often, when the spring bloomed, or the summer was flushing with the wild roses and the roseate dawns and the red sunset-tides, she hearkened to the mocking-bird's singing, thrice — thrice the mystic strain, and she was wont to go and search for her lover at their tryst among the crags. And when she would come back, her face so full of peace, her eyes softly luminous, her drawling formula, "Jest been talkin' with Reuben 'mongst the rocks," pervaded with tranquil joy, her step-mother and Mrs. Jessup would whisper apart and look askance upon her, and start at any sudden jar or sound, as if it were instinct with her spectre lover's freakish presence.

And so, patient drudge though she was, they listened to Mrs. Purvine's eager insistence to have her bide in the cove ; and although she went to live with this cheery soul, it was with tears and sighs and sadness to leave the clifty gorges that he haunted.

But she found the mocking-bird singing there, thrice, thrice the mystic strain, amongst the rocky banks of the Scolacutta River. And so she smiled again.

Except for this delusion she gave little indication of the unsettling of her mind. She was placidly happy with her aunt, though the two women were much alone, for Jerry Price presently married Sophy Griff. He became the sole dependence of the miller and his grandchildren, but a measure of Mrs. Purvine's jaunty prosperity seemed to follow him. Old Griff's little log cabin took on a more pretentious guise, and there was a slipshod thrift within. Jerry lifted the millstones and rebuilt the mill, and the whir began anew as if it had never left off ; and the old miller sat without the door, and listened, and grew garrulous and cheerful and dusty with meal and flour, and brightened into some faint reflection of his old imperative self. Tad never reappeared from the moonshiners' lair, and they still successfully elude the law.

The failure to secure their testimony proved no disaster to Gwinnan, as the chancellor held that a duel is a matter of deliberate and formal arrangement between men who recognize both the nature of the proceeding and the law infringed.

Nevertheless, Gwinnan was not satisfied. He had never regarded the matter as a duel ; he had forgotten even the circumstances. Once brought forcibly to his mind, he dissented from the decision of the case, which he had watched more as if from the bench than from the bar. He resigned when reinstated.

The relinquishment of his ambition was very bitter to him. He had infused into it much of the essence of his identity ; it had amply promised the end for which he had rejoiced to labor ; it had borne a lofty and isolated existence. And yet, as he brooded on his despoiled life, his trained mind, applied to moral discernment, could but perceive at length that it had been sheerly a technical excellence toward which he had bent his energies, a selfish end he had held in view. Without a high ennobling purpose, without a dominate hope to dispense benefit, his unsanctified ambition had only lured with a wish to rise, and despite the heights to which it had attained it had been held to earth by its own inherent weight.

Works of Fiction.

PUBLISHED BY

HOUGHTON, MIFFLIN AND COMPANY,

4 PARK ST., BOSTON; 11 E. 17TH ST., NEW YORK.

Thomas Bailey Aldrich.
Story of a Bad Boy. Illustrated. 12mo $1.50
Marjorie Daw and Other People. 12mo 1.50
The Same. Riverside Aldine Series. 16mo . . . 1.00
Prudence Palfrey. 12mo 1.50
The Queen of Sheba. 12mo 1.50
The Stillwater Tragedy. 12mo 1.50

Hans Christian Andersen.
Complete Works. In ten uniform volumes, crown 8vo. A new and cheap Edition, in attractive binding.
The Improvisatore; or, Life in Italy 1.00
The Two Baronesses 1.00
O. T.; or, Life in Denmark 1.00
Only a Fiddler 1.00
In Spain and Portugal 1.00
A Poet's Bazaar 1.00
Pictures of Travel 1.00
The Story of my Life. With portrait 1.00
Wonder Stories told for Children. Illustrated . . . 1.00
Stories and Tales. Illustrated 1.00
    The set 10.00

William Henry Bishop.
Detmold: A Romance. "Little Classic" style. 18mo 1.25
The House of a Merchant Prince. 12mo 1.50
Choy Susan, and other Stories. 16mo 1.25

Björnstjerne Björnson.
Works. *American Edition*, sanctioned by the author, and translated by Professor R. B. Anderson, of the University of Wisconsin.
Synnöve Solbakken 1.00
The Bridal March, and Other Stories 1.00

Works of Fiction Published by

Captain Mansana, and Other Stories $1.00
Complete Works, seven volumes in three. 12mo.
The set 4.50

Alice Cary.
Pictures of Country Life. 12mo 1.50

John Esten Cooke.
My Lady Pokahontas. 16mo 1.25

James Fenimore Cooper.
Complete Works. New *Household Edition*, in attractive binding. With Introductions to many of the volumes by Susan Fenimore Cooper, and Illustrations. In thirty-two volumes, 16mo.

Precaution.	The Prairie.
The Spy.	Wept of Wish-ton-Wish.
The Pioneers.	The Water Witch.
The Pilot.	The Bravo.
Lionel Lincoln.	The Heidenmauer.
Last of the Mohicans.	The Headsman.
Red Rover.	The Monikins.
Homeward Bound.	Miles Wallingford.
Home as Found.	The Red Skins.
The Pathfinder.	The Chainbearer.
Mercedes of Castile.	Satanstoe.
The Deerslayer.	The Crater.
The Two Admirals.	Jack Tier.
Wing and Wing.	The Sea Lions.
Wyandotté.	Oak Openings.
Afloat and Ashore.	The Ways of the Hour.

(*Each volume sold separately.*)
Each volume 1.00
The set 32.00
New Fireside Edition. With forty-five original Illustrations. In sixteen volumes, 12mo. The set . . . 20.00
(*Sold only in sets.*)

Sea Tales. New *Household Edition*, containing Introductions by Susan Fenimore Cooper. Illustrated.
First Series. Including —
The Pilot.   The Red Rover.
The Water Witch.   The Two Admirals.
Wing and Wing.
Second Series. Including —
The Sea Lions.   Afloat and Ashore.

Jack Tier.   Miles Wallingford.
The Crater.
  Each set, 5 vols. 16mo $5.00
Leather-Stocking Tales. New *Household Edition*, containing Introductions by Susan Fenimore Cooper. Illustrated. In five volumes, 16mo.
The Deerslayer.   The Pioneers.
The Pathfinder.   The Prairie.
Last of the Mohicans.
  The set 5.00
Cooper Stories; being Narratives of Adventure selected from his Works. With Illustrations by F. O. C. Darley. In three volumes, 16mo, each 1.00

Charles Egbert Craddock.
In the Tennessee Mountains. 16mo 1.25
The Prophet of the Great Smoky Mountains. 16mo . 1.25
Down the Ravine. Illustrated. 16mo 1.00
In the Clouds. 16mo 1.25

Thomas Frederick Crane.
Italian Popular Tales. Translated from the Italian. With Introduction and a Bibliography. 8vo . . . 2.50

F. Marion Crawford.
To Leeward. 16mo 1.25
A Roman Singer. 16mo 1.25
An American Politician. 16mo 1.25

Maria S. Cummins.
The Lamplighter. 12mo 1.50
El Fureidîs. 12mo 1.50
Mabel Vaughan. 12mo 1.50

Parke Danforth.
Not in the Prospectus. In "Riverside Paper Series." 16mo, paper covers 50

Daniel De Foe.
Robinson Crusoe. Illustrated. 16mo 1.00

P. Deming.
Adirondack Stories. "Little Classic" style. 18mo . .75
Tompkins and other Folks. "Little Classic" style. 18mo 1.00

Thomas De Quincey.
Romances and Extravaganzas. 12mo 1.50
Narrative and Miscellaneous Papers. 12mo . . . 1.50

Works of Fiction Published by

Charles Dickens.
Complete Works. *Illustrated Library Edition.* With Introductions by E. P. Whipple. Containing Illustrations by Cruikshank, Phiz, Seymour, Leech, Maclise, and others, on steel, to which are added designs of Darley and Gilbert, in all over 550. In twenty-nine volumes, 12mo.

The Pickwick Papers, 2 vols. Dombey and Son, 2 vols.
Nicholas Nickleby, 2 vols. Pictures from Italy, and American Notes.
Oliver Twist.
Old Curiosity Shop, and Reprinted Pieces, 2 vols. Bleak House, 2 vols.
Little Dorrit, 2 vols.
Barnaby Rudge, and Hard Times, 2 vols. David Copperfield, 2 vols.
A Tale of Two Cities.
Martin Chuzzlewit, 2 vols. Great Expectations.
Our Mutual Friend, 2 vols. Edwin Drood, Master Humphrey's Clock, and Other Pieces.
Uncommercial Traveller.
A Child's History of England, and Other Pieces. Sketches by Boz.
Christmas Books.

Each volume $1.50
The set. With Dickens Dictionary. 30 vols. . 45.00
Christmas Carol. Illustrated. 8vo, full gilt 2.50
The Same. 32mo 75
Christmas Books. Illustrated. 12mo 2.00

Charlotte Dunning.
A Step Aside. 16mo 1.25

Edgar Fawcett.
A Hopeless Case. "Little Classic" style. 18mo . 1.25
A Gentleman of Leisure. "Little Classic" style. 18mo 1.00
An Ambitious Woman. 12mo 1.50

Fénelon.
Adventures of Telemachus. 12mo 2.25

Mrs. James A. Field.
High-Lights. 16mo 1.25

Harford Flemming.
A Carpet Knight. 16mo 1.25

Baron de la Motte Fouqué.
Undine, Sintram and his Companions, etc. 32mo . . .75
Undine and other Tales. Illustrated. 16mo . . . 1.00

Johann Wolfgang von Goethe.
Wilhelm Meister. Translated by Thomas Carlyle.
Portrait of Goethe. In two volumes. 12mo . . . $3.00
The Tale and Favorite Poems. 32mo 75

Oliver Goldsmith.
Vicar of Wakefield. *Handy-Volume Edition.* 32mo,
gilt top 1.00
The Same. " Riverside Classics." Illustrated. 16mo 1.00

Jeanie T. Gould (Mrs. Lincoln).
Marjorie's Quest. Illustrated. 12mo 1.50

Thomas Chandler Haliburton.
The Clockmaker ; or, The Sayings and Doings of
Samuel Slick of Slickville. Illustrated. 16mo . 1.00

A. S. Hardy.
But Yet a Woman. 16mo 1.25
The Wind of Destiny. 16mo 1.25

Miriam Coles Harris.
Rutledge.   A Perfect Adonis.
The Sutherlands.   Missy.
Frank Warrington.   Happy-Go-Lucky.
St. Philips.   Phœbe.
Richard Vandermarck.
Each volume, 16mo 1.25
Louie's Last Term at St. Mary's. 16mo 1.00

Bret Harte.
The Luck of Roaring Camp, and Other Sketches. 16mo 1.50
The Luck of Roaring Camp, and Other Stories.
Riverside Aldine Series. 16mo 1.00
Mrs. Skaggs's Husbands, and Other Sketches. 16mo 1.50
Tales of the Argonauts, and Other Stories. 16mo . 1.50
Thankful Blossom. " Little Classic " style. 18mo . 1.25
Two Men of Sandy Bar. A Play. 18mo 1.00
The Story of a Mine. 18mo 1.00
Drift from Two Shores. 18mo 1.25
Twins of Table Mountain, etc. 18mo 1.25
Works. Rearranged, with an Introduction and a
Portrait. In five volumes, crown 8vo.
Poetical Works, and the drama, " Two Men of Sandy
Bar," with an Introduction and Portrait.
The Luck of Roaring Camp, and Other Stories.
Tales of the Argonauts and Eastern Sketches.

Works of Fiction Published by

Gabriel Conroy.
Stories and Condensed Novels.
  Each volume $2.00
  The set 10.00
 Flip, and Found at Blazing Star. 18mo 1.00
 In the Carquinez Woods. 18mo 1.00
 On the Frontier. "Little Classic" style. 18mo . . 1.00
 By Shore and Sedge. "Little Classic style." 18mo 1.00
 Maruja. A Novel. "Little Classic" style. 18mo . 1 00
 Snow-Bound at Eagle's. "Little Classic" style. 18mo 1.00
 The Queen of the Pirate Isle. A Story for Children.
  Colored Illustrations by Kate Greenaway. 4to . 1.50

Wilhelm Hauff.
 Arabian Days Entertainments. Illustrated. 12mo . 1.50

Nathaniel Hawthorne.
 Works. *New Riverside Edition.* With an original etching in each volume, and a new Portrait. With bibliographical notes by George P. Lathrop. Complete in twelve volumes, crown 8vo.
 Twice-Told Tales.
 Mosses from an Old Manse.
 The House of the Seven Gables, and The Snow-Image.
 The Wonder-Book, Tanglewood Tales, and Grandfather's Chair.
 The Scarlet Letter, and The Blithedale Romance.
 The Marble Faun.
 Our Old Home, and English Note-Books. 2 vols.
 American Note-Books.
 French and Italian Note-Books.
 The Dolliver Romance, Fanshawe, Septimius Felton, and, in an Appendix, the Ancestral Footstep.
 Tales, Sketches, and Other Papers. With Biographical Sketch by G. P. Lathrop, and Indexes.
  Each volume 2.00
  The set 24.00
 New "*Little Classic*" *Edition.* Each volume contains Vignette Illustration. In twenty-five volumes, 18mo.
  Each volume 1.00
  The set 25.00
 New *Wayside Edition.* With Portrait, twenty-three etchings, and Notes by George P. Lathrop. In twenty-four volumes, 12mo, gilt top 36.00
 New *Fireside Edition.* In six volumes, 12mo . . . 10.00
 A Wonder-Book for Girls and Boys. *Holiday Edition.* With Illustrations by F. S. Church. 4to . . 2.50

Houghton, Mifflin and Company. 7

Twice-Told Tales. *School Edition.* 18mo $1.00
The Scarlet Letter. *Holiday Edition.* Illustrated by
  Mary Hallock Foote. 8vo, full gilt 3.00
Popular Edition. 12mo 1.00
True Stories from History and Biography. 12mo . 1.25
The Wonder-Book. 12mo 1.25
Tanglewood Tales. 12mo 1.25
The Snow-Image. Illustrated in colors. Small 4to . .75
Grandfather's Chair. *Popular Edition.* 16mo, paper
  covers 15
Tales of the White Hills, and Legends of New Eng-
  land. 32mo 75
Legends of Province House, and A Virtuoso's Col-
  lection. 32mo 75
True Stories from New England History. 16mo,
  boards 45

Oliver Wendell Holmes.

Elsie Venner. A Romance of Destiny. Crown 8vo. 2.00
The Guardian Angel. Crown 8vo 2.00
The Story of Iris. 32mo 75
My Hunt after the Captain. 32mo 40
A Mortal Antipathy. Crown 8vo 1.50

Augustus Hoppin.

Recollections of Anton House. Illustrated. Small
  4to 1.25
A Fashionable Sufferer. Illustrated. 12mo . . . 1.50
Two Compton Boys. Illustrated. Small 4to . . . 1.50

Blanche Willis Howard.

One Summer. A Novel. *Holiday Edition.* 12mo . 1.50
New *Popular Edition.* Illustrated by Hoppin. 12mo 1.25

William Dean Howells.

Their Wedding Journey. Illustrated. 12mo . . . 1.50
The Same. Illustrated. Paper covers. 16mo . . .50
The Same. "Little Classic" style. 18mo 1.25
A Chance Acquaintance. Illustrated. 12mo . . . 1.50
The Same. Illustrated. Paper covers. 16mo . . .50
The Same. "Little Classic" style. 18mo 1.25
A Foregone Conclusion. 12mo 1.50
The Lady of the Aroostook. 12mo 1.50
The Undiscovered Country. 12mo 1.50
Suburban Sketches. 12mo 1.50
A Day's Pleasure, etc. 32mo 75

Works of Fiction Published by

Thomas Hughes.
Tom Brown's School-Days at Rugby. *Illustrated Edition.* 16mo $1.00
Tom Brown at Oxford. 16mo 1.25

Henry James, Jr.
A Passionate Pilgrim, and Other Tales. 12mo . . 2.00
Roderick Hudson. 12mo 2.00
The American. 12mo 2.00
Watch and Ward. "Little Classic" style. 18mo . 1.25
The Europeans. 12mo 1.50
Confidence. 12mo 1.50
The Portrait of a Lady. 12mo 2.00

Anna Jameson.
Studies and Stories. New Edition. 16mo, gilt top . 1.25
Diary of an Ennuyée. New Edition. 16mo, gilt top . 1.25

Douglas Jerrold.
Mrs. Caudle's Curtain Lectures. Illustrated. 16mo . 1.00

Sarah Orne Jewett.
Deephaven. 16mo 1.25
Old Friends and New. 18mo 1.25
Country By-Ways. 18mo 1.25
The Mate of the Daylight. 18mo 1.25
A Country Doctor. 16mo 1.25
A Marsh Island. 16mo 1.25
A White Heron and Other Stories. 18mo 1.25

Rossiter Johnson.
"Little Classics." Each in one volume. 18mo.

I. Exile.
II. Intellect.
III. Tragedy.
IV. Life.
V. Laughter.
VI. Love.
VII. Romance.
VIII. Mystery.
IX. Comedy.
X. Childhood.
XI. Heroism.
XII. Fortune.
XIII. Narrative Poems.
XIV. Lyrical Poems.
XV. Minor Poems.
XVI. Nature.
XVII. Humanity.
XVIII. Authors.

Each volume 1.00
The set 18.00
The Same. In nine volumes, square 16mo . . . 13.50
(*Sold only in sets.*)

Charles and Mary Lamb.
Tales from Shakespeare. 18mo 1.00

The Same. Illustrated. 16mo $1.00
The Same. *Handy-Volume Edition.* 32mo, gilt top . 1.00

Harriet and Sophia Lee.
Canterbury Tales. In three volumes. The set, 16mo 3.75

Henry Wadsworth Longfellow.
Hyperion. A Romance. 16mo 1.50
Popular Edition. 16mo 40
Popular Edition. Paper covers, 16mo 15
Outre-Mer. 16mo 1.50
Popular Edition. 16mo 40
Popular Edition. Paper covers, 16mo 15
Kavanagh. 16mo 1.50

Flora Haines Loughead.
The Man who was Guilty. 16mo, paper covers . . .50

Married for Fun.
By an Anonymous Author. 16mo, paper covers . . .50

S. Weir Mitchell.
In War Time. 16mo 1.25
Roland Blake. 16mo 1.25

Elizabeth Stuart Phelps.
The Gates Ajar. 16mo 1.50
Beyond the Gates. 16mo 1.25
Men, Women, and Ghosts. 16mo 1.50
Hedged In. 16mo 1.50
The Silent Partner. 16mo 1.50
The Story of Avis. 16mo 1.50
Sealed Orders, and Other Stories. 16mo 1.50
Friends : A Duet. 16mo 1.25
Doctor Zay. 16mo 1.25
An Old Maid's Paradise. 16mo, paper covers 50
Burglars in Paradise. 16mo, paper covers 50
Madonna of the Tubs. Illustrated. 12mo. 1.50

Marian C. L. Reeves and Emily Read.
Pilot Fortune. 16mo 1.25

Riverside Paper Series.
1. But Yet a Woman. By A. S. Hardy.
2. Missy. By Miriam Coles Harris.
3. The Stillwater Tragedy. By T. B. Aldrich.
4. Elsie Venner. By O. W. Holmes.
5. An Earnest Trifler. By Mary A. Sprague.
6. The Lamplighter. By Maria S. Cummins.
7. Their Wedding Journey. By W. D. Howells.

8. Married for Fun. Anonymous.
9. An Old Maid's Paradise. By Miss E. S. Phelps.
10. The House of a Merchant Prince. By W. H. Bishop.
11. An Ambitious Woman. By Edgar Fawcett.
12. Marjorie's Quest. By Jeanie T. Gould.
13. Hammersmith. By Mark Sibley-Severance.
14. Burglars in Paradise. By Elizabeth Stuart Phelps.
15. A Perfect Adonis. By Miriam Coles Harris.
16. Stories and Romances. By H. E. Scudder.
17. Leslie Goldthwaite. By Mrs. A. D. T. Whitney.
18. The Man who was Guilty. By Flora Haines Loughead.
19. The Guardian Angel. By O. W. Holmes.
20. The Cruise of the Alabama. By P. D. Haywood.
21. Prudence Palfrey. By T. B. Aldrich.
22. Pilot Fortune. By Marian C. L. Reeves and Emily Read.
23. Not in the Prospectus. By Parke Danforth.
24. Choy Susan, and Other Stories. By W. H. Bishop.
25. Sam Lawson's Fireside Stories. By Harriet Beecher Stowe.
26. A Chance Acquaintance. By W. D. Howells.
Each volume, 16mo, paper covers $0.50

Riverside Pocket Series.

1. Deephaven. By Sarah Orne Jewett.
2. Exile. ("Little Classics.")
3. Adirondack Stories. By P. Deming.
4. A Gentleman of Leisure. By Edgar Fawcett.
5. Snow-Image, and other Twice-Told Tales. By N. Hawthorne.
6. Watch and Ward. By Henry James.
7. In the Wilderness. By C. D. Warner.
8. Study of Hawthorne. By G. P. Lathrop.
9. Detmold. By W. H. Bishop.
10. Story of a Mine. By Bret Harte.
Each volume, 16mo, cloth 50

Joseph Xavier Boniface Saintine.

Picciola. Illustrated. 16mo 1.00

Jacques Henri Bernardin de Saint-Pierre.

Paul and Virginia. Illustrated. 16mo 1.00
The Same, together with Undine, and Sintram. 32mo .75

Sir Walter Scott.

The Waverley Novels. *Illustrated Library Edition.* Illustrated with 100 engravings by Darley, Dielman, Fredericks, Low, Share, Sheppard. With glossary and a full index of characters. In 25 volumes, 12mo.

Waverley.	The Antiquary.
Guy Mannering.	Rob Roy.
Old Mortality.	St. Ronan's Well.
Black Dwarf, and Legend of Montrose.	Redgauntlet.
	The Betrothed, and The Highland Widow.
Heart of Mid-Lothian.	
Bride of Lammermoor.	The Talisman, and Other Tales.
Ivanhoe	
The Monastery.	Woodstock.
The Abbot.	The Fair Maid of Perth.
Kenilworth.	Anne of Geierstein.
The Pirate.	Count Robert of Paris.
The Fortunes of Nigel.	The Surgeon's Daughter, and Castle Dangerous.
Peveril of the Peak.	
Quentin Durward.	

Each volume $1.00
The set 25.00

Tales of a Grandfather. *Illustrated Library Edition.* With six steel plates. In three volumes, 12mo . . 4.50
Ivanhoe. *Popular Edition.* 12mo 1.00

Horace E. Scudder.

The Dwellers in Five-Sisters' Court. 16mo 1.25
Stories and Romances. 16mo 1.25

Mark Sibley Severance.

Hammersmith: His Harvard Days. 12mo 1.50

J. E. Smith.

Oakridge: An Old-Time Story of Maine. 12mo . . 2.00

Mary A. Sprague.

An Earnest Trifler. 16mo 1.25

William W. Story.

Fiammetta. 16mo 1.25

Works of Fiction.

Harriet Beecher Stowe.
Agnes of Sorrento. 12mo $1.50
The Pearl of Orr's Island. 12mo 1.50
Uncle Tom's Cabin. *Illustrated Edition.* 12mo . . 2.00
The Minister's Wooing. 12mo 1.50
The Mayflower, and Other Sketches. 12mo . . . 1.50
Dred. New Edition, from new plates. 12mo . . . 1.50
Oldtown Folks. 12mo 1.50
Sam Lawson's Fireside Stories. 12mo 1.50
My Wife and I. Illustrated. 12mo 1.50
We and Our Neighbors. Illustrated. 12mo . . . 1.50
Poganuc People. Illustrated. 12mo 1.50
    The above eleven volumes, in box 16.00
Uncle Tom's Cabin. *Holiday Edition.* With Introduction, and Bibliography by George Bullen, of the British Museum. Over 100 Illustrations. 12mo . 3.00
The Same. *Popular Edition.* 12mo 1.00

Gen. Lew Wallace.
The Fair God; or, The Last of the 'Tzins. 12mo . 1.50

Henry Watterson.
Oddities in Southern Life. Illustrated. 16mo . . . 1.50

Richard Grant White.
The Fate of Mansfield Humphreys, with the Episode of Mr. Washington Adams in England. 16mo . 1.25

Adeline D. T. Whitney.
Faith Gartney's Girlhood. Illustrated. 12mo . . . 1.50
Hitherto: A Story of Yesterdays. 12mo 1.50
Patience Strong's Outings. 12mo 1.50
The Gayworthys. 12mo 1.50
Leslie Goldthwaite. Illustrated. 12mo 1.50
We Girls: A Home Story. Illustrated. 12mo . . 1.50
Real Folks. Illustrated. 12mo 1.50
The Other Girls. Illustrated. 12mo 1.50
Sights and Insights. 2 vols. 12mo 3.00
Odd, or Even? 12mo 1.50
Boys at Chequasset. Illustrated. 12mo 1.50
Bonnyborough. 12mo 1.50
Home-Spun Yarns. Short Stories 1.50

Lillie Chace Wyman.
Poverty Grass. 16mo 1.25

www.ingramcontent.com/pod-product-compliance
Lightning Source LLC
Chambersburg PA
CBHW022106300426
44117CB00007B/609